SERIOUS FUN

Serious Fun

A History of Spectator Sports in the USSR

ROBERT EDELMAN

New York   Oxford
OXFORD UNIVERSITY PRESS   1993

Oxford University Press

Oxford   New York   Toronto
Delhi   Bombay   Calcutta   Madras   Karachi
Kuala Lumpur   Singapore   Hong Kong   Tokyo
Nairobi   Dar es Salaam   Cape Town
Melbourne   Auckland   Madrid

and associated companies in
Berlin   Ibadan

Copyright © 1993 by Robert Edelman

Published by Oxford University Press, Inc.,
200 Madison Avenue, New York, New York 10016

Library of Congress Cataloging-in-Publication Data
Edelman, Robert, 1945–
Serious fun : a history of spectator sports in the USSR /
Robert Edelman.
p. cm.   Includes bibliographical references and index.
ISBN 0-19-507948-5
1. Sports—Soviet Union—History.   2. Sports and state—Soviet
Union.   I. Title.
GV623.E27   1993
796'.0947—dc20   92-23762

9 8 7 6 5 4 3 2 1

Printed in the United States of America
on acid-free paper

For Victoria

moia pobeda

Preface

The Western understanding of Soviet sports was formed overwhelmingly through the prism of international competition. Once the USSR joined the global community of sports after World War II, it enjoyed enormous success, dominating the most visible international event, the Olympic Games, with a continuing parade of red-shirted medal-winners. Over the course of nearly four decades, Soviet sportsmen and sportswomen became international heroes. Global televising of the Olympics made the gymnasts Olga Korbut and Nelli Kim, the weightlifters Iurii Vlasov and Vasilii Alekseev, the jumpers Valerii Brumel' and Sergei Bubka household names everywhere. These victories were explained in the West as the final product of a "Soviet sports machine" that churned out state-sponsored professional athletes, who, competing under the fig-leaf of official amateurism, received lavish support and used scientific training methods to achieve victory after victory. The goal of this "system," familiar to anyone who paid attention to international sports, was to win prestige for the USSR and demonstrate the superiority of the Communist way of life. This was the view from the outside.

This image of "totalitarian" sports, the view from the outside, was so strong that it survived even into the post–Cold War era. As late as the summer of 1991 the *Washington Post* could still report, "To many outsiders, the Soviet sports machine inspires awe. These are the grim superhumans who win almost everything at the Olympics."[1] At much the same time, the *Los Angeles Times'* Pulitzer Prize winner Jim Murray would write: "Athletic supremacy was politically important to countries that called themselves, 'Democratic Peoples' Republic.' They not only weren't very democratic, they weren't very amateur. The athlete was as much a creation of the state as the statue of Stalin in the park."[2] Rather than deny most of these claims, the Soviets suggested that their best athletes were merely the tip of a vast pyramid based on participant sports for the masses, practiced in modern facilities provided by the state in order to generate healthier, more productive workers and fitter defenders of the Fatherland. The Soviet Union, they claimed, was "the greatest sporting nation on earth." This, too, was the view from the outside.

As both James Riordan and Henry Morton have shown in their seminal works on Soviet sports, the popular Western image of monolithic success obscured significant problems and contradictions; but it is not my purpose in this work to focus either on Olympic sports or on the system that produced so many winners. Nor will I be examining the organization of mass sports and exercise, what the Soviets have called physical culture. These subjects have also been well covered by others.

Instead, my approach to Soviet sports will be informed by the issues and debates surrounding the politics of popular culture. Therefore, I will not be concerned with all sports but rather with the specifically modern phenomenon of mass spectator sports. The production of world-class, high-performance athletes has been extensively documented, but we know far less about the Soviet public's consumption of the sports spectacles in which those athletes competed. Accordingly, my emphasis will be on domestic rather than international matters, and I will focus on the sports Soviet citizens actually chose to watch, as opposed to the sports the government tried to promote.

For many years it was a common belief of Westerners that Soviet success across the full range of Olympic sports reflected domestic interest in the numerous so-called minor sports. Most of the medals were awarded in such sports, few of which enjoyed great popularity in the West. If the Soviets were good at wrestling and kayaking, Westerners assumed, following the implications of the market model, that the success was the result of the popularity of those sports in the USSR. We now know that the Soviets excelled at these sports precisely because the government pursued a conscious policy of supporting them. A medal in luge was as much of a medal as one in basketball, and the goal of the state was to win the most medals. Soviet citizens, however, were as indifferent to these sports as most people. Rowing, archery, and fencing did have their publics, but they never generated interest comparable to that aroused by the leading professional sports in capitalist countries. If one examines the attendance figures, it becomes clear that the range of mass spectator sports in the USSR was every bit as narrow as elsewhere in the world.

To qualify as a spectator sport in the modern world, a game must regularly attract significant numbers of ticket-buying fans to enclosed arenas, and larger numbers of viewers to their television sets. Given this definition, we quickly learn that the number of such sports in the USSR was extremely limited. Only soccer (football), men's basketball, and ice hockey fit this definition, and significantly, all three are sports played and watched by men. Women's sports, actively supported by the government as political window-dressing, had little public following among women or men. No sport, not track and field, swimming, wrestling, or even boxing ever came close to attracting the vast numbers of spectators soccer did. Although attendance fell off in the 1980s, ice hockey enjoyed significant support starting in the late 1940s. Men's basketball, always a distant third to the big two, was also capable of filling large arenas. Accordingly, my emphasis will be on soccer, hockey, and men's basketball. Nevertheless, I will have occasion to mention track and field, volleyball, boxing, and other sports on the Olympic program, and I will also examine some of the rituals surrounding sports, especially the bizarre and elaborate festivals seen during the annual "Days of Physical Culture," when tens of thousands of sportsmen and sportswomen paraded through Red Square before the Communist Party leadership.

This emphasis on spectator sports, therefore, puts the Olympics in the background of this study. My primary concern will be with the "consumption" rather than the production of sports events. The system that generated the athletes who won so many Olympic victories was part of that production process, but most of the sports on the Olympic program did not have a mass audience in the USSR. Nevertheless, an approach that stresses the audience for sports does not permit the scholar to ignore entirely the process of production. One can, after all, consume only what is produced. Changes in the process of production of sports events and sports heroes necessarily affected the character of the spectacles made available to the public, but my first concern here will be with the audiences not its organizers.

In following this approach, one soon comes to realize the basic incongruence between the goals of the state's sports system and the interests of Soviet fans. For the government, the aim of high-performance (or elite) sports was to inspire citizens to exercise and therefore become better workers and soldiers. Elite athletes were to be heroic role-models for their fellow citizens, who would learn lessons of discipline, orderliness, honesty, fitness, patriotism, and respect for authority. In this sense, spectator sports' organizers sought to gain public consent for the dominance of the state by advertising its norms and goals. Olympic victories and international successes were supposed to enhance the power of the dominant authorities in the USSR, but Soviet fans did not watch sports spectacles with official values in mind. Big-time sports for the public were, instead, a source of play and entertainment. This basic difference undermined the state's aims. As Victoria de Grazia demonstrated in her study of mass leisure in fascist Italy, even powerful authoritarian governments could not universally impose their tastes and preferences: "The fascist intervention in leisure-time activities was most successful, as might be expected, when the social needs of the participants corresponded to the interests of local elites, the aspirations of the *organized* to the aims of the *organizers*"[3] (italics added). As we shall see, the aspirations and interests of the organizers and those of the organized clashed repeatedly throughout the course of Soviet history.

This fundamental dissonance places the relationship between politics and popular culture at the center of my concerns. While spectator sports differ from other forms of Soviet popular culture in significant ways, I will focus on the political impact of this particular form of popular culture. For decades the Soviets shared the Western political left's antipathy for big-time, capitalist professional sports. They also shared the belief that spectator sports was but one of the many entertainment industries that filled workers' heads with useless thoughts and diluted their interest in politics. Most socialist politicians and intellectuals subscribed to the idea that Western spectator sports supported capitalism's dominance, and until very recently, no Soviet student of Western sports doubted the truth of this view.

Sports, however, were a particularly visible part of Soviet life, and sports spectacles were a compelling element of Soviet popular culture. Thus, it would seem a contradiction that the Soviets should have supported the same practices they long criticized in the West. We then may ask if those practices had the same results in the USSR as the left thought they had under capitalism; i.e., the support of established authority. For this reason, my introductory chapter traces the historical evolution of socialist thinking on popular culture in general and on spectator sports in particular. This task is the necessary prelude to asking the question of whether spectator sports did or did not enhance popular acceptance of the Communist Party's authority.

My object in this work is to determine if there can even be such a thing as socialist spectator sports. Perhaps the very idea is an oxymoron, one best expressed by the title of this book (on the streets of America's cities and on its television screens, it is, of course, no oxymoron at all). The notion that moments of pleasure and play ("fun") might be planned with more utilitarian or didactic goals in mind ("serious") seems absurd or at least dubious, but in no small measure the concept of planned "spontaneity" or "serious fun" has been the historic task of mass culture in the USSR. If all forms of human activity in Soviet society had to be purposeful, what, then, happened to play? In this light, the matter of fun becomes very serious.

The contradiction between "serious" and "fun" also suggests several different ways to read this work. For those interested in "fun," I commend the descriptive chapters Two through Seven. Students of the social and cultural history of the Soviet Union will want to pay particular attention to Chapters Two, Three, and Four, which trace the development of spectator sports from the 1917 revolution up to the death of Stalin in 1953. Chapters Five and Six look at the years Soviet sports emerged on the world scene (1953 to 1985). Here, I will not discuss material already covered so well by James Riordan. Instead, I will discuss only the aspects of this period that pertain to the themes raised in the earlier chapters. In Chapter Seven, I cover the changes that took place during the now-concluded period of perestroika.

In the third and last section of Chapter One, "Marxism, Sports, and Popular Culture—Theoretical Debates and Approaches," I attempt to link Soviet spectator sports to larger issues about politics and popular culture. Here I lay out the particular methodological approach I will be using throughout my study. This portion of the text is intended primarily for specialists in the histories of sports, popular culture, and the USSR. General readers may want to read only the first two sections of Chapter one: "Professional Sports and the Left" and "Meanings of Spectator Sports East and West," while skipping or skimming the final section.

This book is the by-product of many research trips to the Soviet Union, beginning in 1965. While in the USSR, I was studying matters of prerevolutionary Russian history. It would be less than truthful to describe these stays as pleasure cruises, and in order to maintain my spirits, I tried to do some of the things that have given me pleasure and comfort while at home. Watching, reading about, talking about, and even playing sports became a large part of my Soviet leisure time. This book is informed by the personal experience of more than twenty-five years as a Soviet sports spectator, but a memoir of that experience would not be enough. In a work of this sort, it has also been necessary to move through uncharted territory. One must spend a great deal of time systematically exploring particular sources merely to establish the basic facts and chronology. Accordingly, I make no claim here to have exhausted this subject, and subsequent students of Soviet sports will find there are many fruitful areas for future research.

The Soviets have produced a vast literature on sports and physical culture that cannot be read in a single lifetime, but most of these works have little relevance to the subject of spectator sports.[4] Athletes' memoirs and biographies of stars, a large part of the available literature, say little about those who watched. Instead, it has been necessary to base this work on a close perusal of the press, in particular, the national sports daily *Sovetskii sport,* published since 1924. As historical sources, newspapers in any country have their strengths and weaknesses, and the state-controlled press of the USSR would seem an especially dubious place to learn "the truth." Furthermore, sports in every nation have always been fertile ground for rumor and gossip that never reach print.

Sovetskii sport, however, was something of an exception in the less-than-independent world of Soviet journalism. The core of this newspaper was always the straightforward description of games. This relatively unadorned approach to journalism gave *Sovetskii sport* a greater reputation for honesty and professionalism than the rest of the press enjoyed. Its criticisms of sports authorities, coaches, and players created a type of discourse that in significant ways resembled Western sports-writing. Western sports journalists have liked to describe themselves as the voice of the fan, asking the same questions of athletes and coaches as the average spectator, had she or he had the same access. More than other newspapers, *Sovetskii sport* was able to play such a role.

While it would be absurd to say that *Sovetskii sport* did not suffer from the faults common to Soviet journalism, its subject and its professionalism made it one of the USSR's most popular and respected newspapers long before the coming of glasnost. Coaches, players, and organizers regularly used *Sovetskii sport* as a forum for their views, and such writers and poets as Evgenii Evtushenko, Iurii Trifonov, and Robert Rozhdestvenskii, as well as the satirtists Ilf and Petrov, discussed their visions of sports on its pages. Unlike many other Soviet newspapers, *Sovetskii sport* did not always speak with a single voice.

Although most Soviet newspapers, both national and local, did not have regular sports sections, neither did they ignore sports entirely. Accordingly, I have consulted several other periodicals as a necessary corrective to the sports press which, despite its considerable candor, was always controlled by whatever form of the State Sports Committee existed at any given moment. In addition, the memoirs of coaches and players have been combed for those few mentions of the sports audience. These works have been supplemented by annuals and instructional manuals. I have also interviewed several older fans, sports journalists, and managers. These conversations were useful (if not always accurate). Finally, it has been possible since 1985 to receive Soviet television in the West, and the systematic viewing of the daily diet of the Soviet sports fan has afforded even more insight into the changes of recent years.

Only a small portion of the abundant secondary material on Soviet sports directly discusses the practices of spectator sports. Nevertheless, these sources (the press and television) may be seen as findings in themselves. The experience of being a sports spectator involves far more than simply watching games in stadiums. People read about sports, watch them on television, and discuss them among themselves. In this sense, the process of research allows the scholar to replicate the experience of having been a Soviet sports fan in some previous era, and the relative freedom of the sports press makes this exercise worthwhile from the historian's point of view. To read the description of an upcoming (but long-completed) game creates genuine anticipation, and the turning of the page that yields the result can give equally genuine pleasure or sadness. If this process entails certain obvious analytical difficulties, it also explains why the study of Soviet spectator sports can, in fact, be serious fun.

This book began life as a conference paper, and I wish to thank Harry Scheiber, as well as Michael Holquist and Katerina Clark, for inviting me to the conferences at which it was presented. Much of the early research was conducted at the facilities for receiving Soviet television available at Columbia University's Harriman Institute, and I thank Jonathan Sanders for letting me use this resource and thinking up the idea in the first place. At the Rand Institute, Clayton Griffin and Ted Karazek were vital helpers in using Soviet television. Paul Lowenberg of the Associated Press gave me a chance to work as a sportswriter, and without that experience, this book would have been far poorer. I am especially grateful to Rex Lardner of Turner Broadcasting and Stan Kasten of the Atlanta Hawks for taking me to the Soviet Union with them in 1988 for the Hawks' historic tour. Special thanks to Bill Needle for keeping at least some of us on the trip sane. Kim Bohuny, then of TBS, now of the National Basketball Association, was a constant source of information and help, as was Sara Gordon of the Goodwill Games. Harley Frankel, then of the Portland Trail Blazers, now of the Los Angeles Clippers, afforded me a special opportunity to learn of the back alleys of international sports. Alexander Volkov, Sarunas Marciulionis, Gundars Vetra, Sergei Bazarevich, and Igor Miglinieks gave me the athlete's perspective.

I owe an enormous debt to the Soviet Union's leading basketball writer, Vladimir Titorenko, then of *Sovetskii sport,* now of the independent daily *Sportekspress.* Through his intervention I was able to use the library at *Sovetskii sport* and obtain press credentials that allowed me to attend any sports event. While working in the newspaper's offices I was treated kindly by many of its staff members. My *zemliak,* (''homeboy'') Leonid Trakhtenberg, took me by the hand and guided me through the intricacies of the soccer and hockey worlds. Vladimir Kuchmi, Elena Vaitsekovskaia, Lev Rossoshchik, Vladimir Geskin, and Evgenii Malkov were only too willing to share their experience and wisdom with me. They, too, have all now gone over to *Sportekspress.* The retired, but still highly active, Arkadii Galinskii proved a font of knowledge and insight about the history of Soviet sports. Gennadii Gasparian and his parents provided a true home for me in Moscow, without which I could never have supported the furious pace of my research stay. Sergei Guskov was good enough to invite me to Moscow's famous Institute of Physical Culture and arrange for the use of its library.

My greatest intellectual debt is to John Hoberman, the true pioneer in the study of sport and political ideology. He has been a constant guide throughout this project, and his readings of several drafts have been enormously helpful. Ron Suny provided his usual support and encouragement. By giving me a chance to share my earliest thoughts on this subject with his colleagues, he helped me realize that it was possible to write a book about this topic. He, too, has read several drafts and imparted much wisdom. Jim Riordan, to whom all students of Soviet sports owe an enormous debt, has been a tremendously generous correspondent and manuscript reader. John Bushnell read several versions of the draft and gave it his own special street-wise Moscow insight. David Nasaw, Willie Forbath, Judy Coffin, Jon Wiener, Marc Poster, Steve Ross, Kevin Thomas, Albion Urdank, and Jerry Palmer have helped me formulate many of my ideas about popular culture. Larry Herzog was good enough to check that my discussions of soccer were technically correct. Valerii Lutskevich, formerly of the Spartak sports society, proved a highly valuable research assistant and very knowledgeable informant. Sergei Zamashchikov and Al Senn shared their knowledge of the Soviet sports scene with me. My colleagues in the joint University of California doctoral seminar on Soviet history—Hans Rogger, John Hatch, Lynn Mally, and Arch Getty—have enriched my knowledge of the now completed Soviet period of history and have read and commented on the manuscript; as did Viktor Bortnevskii of St. Petersburg. Lennart Bourin of ABC News helped me obtain footage of the 1972 Olympic Basketball final.

I am particularly thankful to Wayne Wilson of the Paul Ziffren Sports Resource Center in Los Angeles. His enormous professionalism helped me track down things I could not find and find things I did not even know existed. Neal Victor of ''Sportsbooks'' gave much useful advice as well. The funding for my research trip to the Soviet Union was partially provided by the research fund of the Academic Senate of the University of California, San Diego. I am especially grateful to Walter Lippincott of Princeton University Press for encouraging me to write a book on this subject. My greatest debt is to my closest companion and friend, Victoria Yablonsky. This was my first venture into the field of what today is called ''cultural studies.'' To have someone at my side with deep experience in this field proved decisive for the realization of the project. Often I could not find the words, and she found them. In reading various drafts, she knew me well enough to know when the voice I was using was truly my own and when it was not, and she did not shrink from telling me when it was not. Frieda helped, too, but I am not sure quite how.

R. E.

Los Angeles
October 1992

Contents

SERIOUS FUN

1

Socialism and
Spectator Sports

In 1946 the world-renowned Soviet composer Dmitri Shostakovich wrote a letter to the national sports daily, *Sovetskii sport*. A rabid and knowledgeable soccer fan, but hardly a defender of Communist law and order, Shostakovich expressed his outrage that crowds in Soviet stadiums were rowdy and ill-behaved: "I look at kids who so much wish to see a sports event, but they are pushed, cursed, and shoved. My son, Maxim, also loves sport, but I rarely let him go to the stadium. Children are pushed around, not only at the entrances but in the stands."[1]

For more than two decades before this date, sports events in the USSR had been organized with the official goal of instilling discipline, order, and culture in the masses. Well-trained and obedient athletes were supposed to serve as examples for those who watched. Instead, as Shostakovich revealed and everyone already knew, spectators at Soviet sports events were as unruly as their capitalist counterparts. As often as not, Soviet stadiums were scenes of bedlam rather than decorum. From the famous Odessa riot of 1926 right up to the final season of Soviet soccer in 1991, disorderly fans and players were a constant part of the sporting scene. Quite clearly, Soviet spectators never really succeeded in making the connection, sought by the state, between watching sports and behaving "properly."

It must be said that the theories of politically organized socialism and the practices of modern spectator sports were also not closely linked when both emerged, more or less simultaneously, during the late nineteenth century.[2] Each phenomenon was a product of industrialization and urbanization, but they were rarely mentioned in the same breath. If socialists and other progressives even considered the matter, they did so with the

3

view that sports, especially spectator sports, undermined prospects for social change and revolution. Surely the Bolshevik Party that made the revolution of 1917 numbered few, if any, hard-core sports fans among its members.

Although there were many opinions on the left, most socialists before World War I felt that modern capitalist professional sports, along with the many other forms of the newly emerging mass culture industries, depoliticized workers and diverted them from the class struggle. Spectator sports, like jazz, movies, music halls, and amusement parks, were thought to anesthetize the proletariat by providing a set of irrational concerns divorced from the world of politics. While this point of view was often primitively stated, it did contain a kernel of truth that provided a basis for later more sophisticated theorizing. As a result, much of the left maintained a critical view, not only of capitalist spectator sports, but of other forms of mass culture throughout the twentieth century, a view that was long shared by official Soviet students of the West.[3]

During these same years, however, large numbers of Soviet citizens regularly attended games and competitions among highly skilled, professional athletes. Spectator sports were widely practiced and enjoyed in the Soviet Union. At the same time, most of those competitions were organized by a state that, at various times, described itself as Marxist-Leninist, socialist, or Communist. Accordingly, one might well ask—given the left's historical antipathy to Western professional sports, what role did spectator sports play in Soviet history?

In the summer of 1937, seventy thousand "lovers of football" filled Moscow's Dinamo Stadium on three separate occasions to watch the city's leading clubs take on a visiting team of Basque all-stars representing the soon-to-be-overthrown Republican government of Spain. Were these spectators much the same ignorant, soccer-crazed louts that peopled the stands of capitalist arenas, or were they enlightened Soviet citizens taking part in a unqiuely socialist sporting "holiday"? What, if anything, made Soviet spectator sports different from the capitalist variety?

At the outset, it can be said that there was one important difference. Those who produced Soviet sports events brought decidedly noncapitalist values to their task. Anticommercialism and formal amateurism deeply influenced the evolution of sports in the USSR. Athletes were not to be commodities, nor were sports to be a source of profit for those who controlled the presentation of events. As far as the outside world was concerned, professional sports were not supposed to exist in the USSR. This most-official of views was clearly stated in the English-language introduction to a 1939 photo album on Soviet sports holidays:

The country knows and honors its champions. . .but all these champions are not professional sportsmen. They are workers in factory or office, they are Red Army men, collective farmers or students who devote their leisure hours to sports. Professional sports is unknown in the U.S.S.R. The Soviet sportsman has no need to exchange the seconds and centimeters of his records for coins; he has no need to "make money" out of his football or boxing glove.[4]

These ideas were taken seriously by the organizers who provided Soviet audiences with sporting entertainments. The same, however, cannot be said of the organized—the fans who watched the games and the athletes who performed.

Spectator sports have always implied the existence of non-participant masses observing the deeds of a skilled and trained few. The structure of watching sports necessarily undermined the concern of much of the socialist movement for social and economic equality. Such practices squarely raised the question of professionalism. If those who watched would pay for the privilege, should not those who were watched be compensated for their skills and efforts? Among the practitioners of elite sports—athletes, coaches, and club officials—the answer, from the earliest days of Soviet power, was affirmative. Stars were sought out, compensated, and rewarded in a wide variety of ways. During the late 1930s the Politburo would formally allow the Spartak soccer team to pay its players a "stipend" above and beyond their wages as "instructors" for the parent sport society; nor were such measures exceptional.

Yet these practices troubled many socialists because they raised the possibility of creating a sporting elite, divorced from the laboring classes. That discomfort took the form of an official ideological preference for the purity of amateurism, albeit an amateurism very different from the kind that emerged in England during the second half of the nineteenth century. The left had always considered the Victorian attitude toward sports to be motivated by an aristocratic desire to keep the working classes out of the fun and games. If sports were not a way of earning a living, then they could be seriously pursued only by those who did not need to work. Accordingly, the early Bolsheviks wanted no part of the Olympic movement's elitist version of amateurism. In the 'twenties and the 'thirties, they boycotted the Games and organized their own workers' sports pageants.

After World War II, however, the Soviets eventually came to accept the formal eligibility standards of the Olympics, a step taken only in order to participate in the Games. In 1947, anticipating entry into the Olympic movement, the government formally outlawed financial rewards for top Soviet athletes, a step that, in effect, admitted the prior existence of professionalism—professionalism that had not been much of a secret. The Soviet press had always recounted tales of shady recruiting and quasi-legal payments. The paying of stars did not, in turn, mean that sports teams and sports events were run as profit-making businesses. While the athletes were professional, it did not necessarily follow that all of Soviet sport was run on the same commercial basis as professional sports in the West.

The Soviets' embrace of the Olympic Code in 1952 meant that they accepted the then-prevailing world standards of amateurism. They did not, however, stop subsidizing their athletes. Instead, it was simply no longer possible to talk or write publicly about such payments. Accordingly, the Soviets' later turn to open professionalism during the period of perestroika did not signify the final acceptance of some long-denied truth about human nature and sports. Since they had failed to beat the West, it may have appeared they were joining it, but the concepts of Western professionalism and Soviet amateurism had changed over the course of seventy years. The differences became blurred.

Seen in this light, the issue of amateurism versus professionalism is much less important than has been previously thought. Since most elite athletes, everywhere in the world, have been subsidized in some way, the more important questions were: Who controlled sports, bureaucrats or businessmen? and what was the purpose, profits or propaganda? Accordingly, the "shamateurism" of the years between 1952 and 1988 can best be understood as a long but exceptional episode in the larger history of Soviet sports. Those involved in the day-to-day work of the sports world always understood that top-flight athletes had to be supported materially and allowed to practice their craft. They received that support, even if the various sport clubs and societies that paid the athletes were not run as enterprises in the capitalist sense.

Aside from the not-inconsiderable hypocrisy of calling their athletes amateurs, Soviet sports authorities did sincerely share at least one ideal of Baron Pierre de Coubertin, founder of the modern Olympic Games. Healthy participation was deemed by both the Soviets and the modern Olympians to be preferable to slothful watching. Accordingly, spectator sports in the USSR were considered useful from the state's point of view primarily because they could inspire participation. Soviet sports critics felt that passive watching of spectacles produced by a small number of professionals was degenerate and dehumanizing to athlete and audience alike. Therefore, watching sports in the USSR was not supposed to be an end in itself, a pleasurable way of passing time. Rather, its clearly didactic goal was to improve the health and efficiency of the nation by demonstrating the benefits of exercise, while instilling values of honesty, obedience, discipline, culture, sexual equality, and selflessness. This project would not, however, succeed. Soviet citizens instead saw spectator sports as an opportunity for pleasure and fun, an arena of unabashedly male bonding, a chance to exhibit the joking cynicism and irony of all sports fans, and a place to idolize heroes of their own, rather than the state's, choosing.

Professional Sports and the Left

The leadership of the electorally successful socialist parties of Europe paid only limited attention to sports during the late nineteenth and early twentieth centuries. Most socialist newspapers commented little on the growth of professional spectator sports in Western Europe, ignoring the very activities that had captured the passions of a considerable portion of their putative base of support. When the socialist press turned its attention to these matters, it did so in the most critical of tones. In 1904 the organ of the British Independent Labour Party praised football (soccer) as a form of physical exercise:

> ... but when it comes to sports syndicated, trustified, and professionalized, that is a different thing: when it comes to troupes of trained athletes performing for hire before excited spectators, whose only exercise is the exercise of lung power, that is not sports, nor exercise, nor recreation—it is a spectacle and a debasing spectacle at that; and when it comes to absorbing from year's end to year's end, the minds of the great mass of the workers, rendering them incapable of understanding their own needs and rights...then it becomes a menace to all democratic and social progress....We are in danger of producing a race of workers who can only obey their masters and think football.[5]

Four years later, a writer in the Newcastle-on-Tyne *Northern Democrat* blamed not only the industry that produced the spectacles but the workers who watched them:

> I do not suggest there is anything wrong with football, but there does seem to be something wrong with the majority of people who habitually attend football matches and fill their heads with things that don't matter.... Difficult though the task may be to push football out of heads and push Socialism in, the task must be undertaken, for just as surely as football doesn't matter, Socialism matters a very great deal.[6]

Like all major social theories of its era, socialism did not anticipate the explosion of sports activity that occurred after mid-century.[7] During those years, the burgeoning laboring classes, through political and trade union struggles, gained a measure of free time from arduous and continuous factory labor. The proletariat used this increased leisure in a wide variety of ways; among others, to play and watch sports. Socialist leaders, however, preferred that the workers use the new opportunities either to improve themselves intellectually or to engage in political activity. When workers took time to relax, socialists hoped that their pursuits would be rational and healthy, and a number of socialists sought to promote sporting and other cultural activities for the masses in the belief that they could teach valuable lessons of solidarity and comradeship. This view, however, would be a minority position, and the various party leaderships remained largely indifferent to the new trends that were entertaining so many workers.[8]

After World War I, the left—and Marxists in particular—came to appreciate more fully the deleterious impact spectator sports had on the working class. The father of Soviet socialist realism, the writer Maxim Gorky, condemned the enormous expansion of sports spectacles during the 1920s. This trend, he argued, had nothing to do with sport's nobler qualities. Instead, sport had become part of what he called the corruption and pandering of capitalism's entertainment and pleasure industries.[9] At the same time, the far subtler thinkers who were part of interwar Germany's famed Frankfurt School, most notably Theodor Adorno, Max Horkheimer, and Herbert Marcuse, began developing an extended critique of mass culture, stressing its appeal to the more irrational instincts of society. Spectator sports, jazz, and other amusements were seen as harmful compensations for capitalism's distortions of the human spirit.[10]

The intellectuality and rationality of the Marxist tradition made it difficult for many socialists to make sense of sports' more irrational elements. Because Marxism was a theory of history that placed labor and production at the center of its analysis, it was poorly equipped to comprehend the worlds of play and leisure. Its leaders were able to distinguish between sports' "healthy biological and psychological core" and its potentially harmful "social historical form."[11] When confronted with workers playing or watching soccer on Saturdays, however, most socialist politicians still expressed the preference that the masses spend their free time in the classroom or on the picket line. The result was discomfort not only with sports, but with other popular amusements and entertainments.

If Marxists centered their analyses on work, then it is hardly surprising that they had difficulty making sense of the world of play. By contrast, conservative intellectuals proved more comfortable with the study of leisure. The Dutch historian Johan Huizinga focused on the many varieties of play in his famous work *Homo Ludens*. By no means synonymous with sports, play was, for Huizinga, fundamentally irrational, something that resisted analysis. Animals, he pointed out, play, and surely did so well before people did: "Since the reality of play extends beyond the sphere of human life, it cannot have its foundations in any rational nexus, because this would limit it to mankind."[12]

Huizinga sought to portray the play impulse as a timeless element of nature through which humans, as distinct from animals, created culture. He did not consider modern professional sports to be an element of play, though. For him, the organized leagues that were first established in Britain in the late nineteenth century were something "apart from the culture creating process."[13] Coubertin, also a conservative, had similar reservations about spectator and professional sports. Embracing the aristocratic amateurism of contemporary England, Coubertin feared the popular disorders that spectator sports had so often engendered.[14] Ortega y Gasset, who also thought sports to be a source of nobility and creativity, was equally contemptuous of the masses of soccer fans who simply watched.[15]

The conservative early–twentieth-century German philosopher Max Scheler, in seeking to justify social hierarchies, developed one particular idea that eventually became a cornerstone of subsequent conservative social theory, and, oddly enough, of Soviet sports theory as well. Scheler argued that the superior members of society must serve as guides to the less-endowed. Those at the bottom of society, he argued, should look to its higher ranks for inspiration.[16] Implicit in this vision was the concept of the role model, an idea that today has become one of the clichés of the sports world. During the 1930s, this conservative concept was embraced by Stalinist sports theorists, who placed the inspirational function of the elite athlete at the center of their vision of spectator sports.

Seen in this light, many Soviet ideas about sports turn out to be exceptions to the left's widely shared aversion to spectator sports as a potentially retrograde form of popular amusement. One approach (ultimately not followed) was advanced by Leon Trotsky. Writing in 1923, Trotsky accepted the legitimacy, reasonableness, and probable persistence of a broad range of forms of mass entertainment that others on the left had condemned as corrupt. In an essay entitled "Vodka, the Church, and the Cinema," Trotsky wrote about film. His words, however, could as easily have applied to the phenomenon of spectator sports, which was only weakly developed in Russia both before and immediately after the revolution of 1917: "The character of a child is revealed and formed in its play. The character of an adult is clearly manifested in his play and amusements. But in forming the character of a whole class . . . like the proletariat, amusement and play ought to occupy a prominent position. . . . The longing for amusement, distraction, sight-seeing and laughter is the most legitimate desire of human nature."[17] Unfortunately, Trotsky never was able to expand on the possible forms socialist amusements might assume in a postrevolutionary society. That task fell to his political opponents.

In the context of Marxist sport theory, Stalinist sport doctrine can also be seen as exceptional. Beginning with the 1930s, the Soviets developed competitive, high-performance sports that were to be used for the now-familiar political purposes of glorifying the state, enhancing the efficiency of production, and improving the condition of the military. In those competitions there were winners and losers. All were not equal, and as Stalinist society evolved, competence and talent came to be rewarded. As early as 1931, Stalin had condemned leveling social policies and claimed the very idea of equality was a "petty-bourgeois" distortion. In following these cues, the leaders of Soviet sports demonstrated an acceptance of the same kinds of social hierarchies that would soon emerge in many other spheres of Soviet society.

This shift, which emerged after the mid-1930s, represented a break with earlier leftist ideals of equality and anticompetitiveness. Not all those in the revolutionary movement had shared the goal of a broad-based egalitarianism, but a considerable portion of the socialist movement did have a commitment to leveling policies.[18] During the 1920s there were in the USSR many adherents of a variety of experimental, even utopian, approaches to sports that eschewed and criticized competition.[19] But the debate about the proper Communist approach to sports was resolved (at least for those at the top) as early as 1925, when the Party's Central Committee passed a resolution urging the development of a high-performance athletic elite.[20] Successful athletes were to play the same role that enthusiasm-generating Stalinist "shock" (high-tempo) workers and Stakhanovite labor heroes later came to play. It was their job to inspire the less able or energetic to greater efforts. The new attitude was best summed up by the ubiquitous factory wall poster of the period: "Every shock worker a sportsman; every sportsman a shock worker."[21]

The sports world's ready acceptance of the state's use of the tool of the role model, with all its conservative political implications, tells us much about the conformist nature of sporting life in general. Athletes and coaches were more accepting of political order and external discipline than artists and intellectuals. At the same time, stars have always been a fundamental element of spectator sports, and the state clearly felt a need to create its own stars. Therefore, it is not surprising that the anti-egalitarian shift in sports took place five or six years ahead of the abandonment of similar leveling policies in most other spheres of social, cultural, and economic endeavor.

Despite the involvement of the state, Stalinism's use of athletes and athletics differed sharply from that of the contemporary fascist regimes of Italy and Germany. The Communist and fascist approaches to sports are by no means subsumable under some broader "totalitarian" category. Sports in the USSR were to be organized bureaucratically and rationally with the concrete goal of supporting the efficiency of production.[22] Fascism, by contrast, embraced a wide range of irrational appeals, and its approach to sports similarly stressed the joy, ecstasy, aggressiveness, and (for them) virility of athletic competition. In contrast to the comparative asceticism of Stalinism, fascists were fully in tune with the erotic appeal of sports. Mussolini, who often stripped to the waist in public, sought to make a cult of his own and other male bodies, while Germans were similarly concerned with describing the minutest details of the perfect Aryan form.[23] Mass sporting spectacles in

Germany and Italy became familiar tools used to glorify the leaders who attended these events. The 1936 Berlin Olympics are usually considered the most notorious case of such a politicized sporting extravaganza.[24] By contrast, Stalin never spoke at the huge annual Physical Culture Day parades that were held annually in Red Square.

In emphasizing the "virile forcefulness" of sport, fascists stressed the spontaneity and action of athletic activity. They celebrated what they saw as man's (their emphasis) natural aggressiveness.[25] This rejection of reason ran counter to official Soviet ideology, which sought to create a planned society, ruled by consciousness and deliberation. Spontaneity, as is well known, had played little theoretical role in the development of the Leninist tradition.[26] While historical reality turned out to be quite different from the prescriptions of that ideology, this theoretical difficulty with the uncertainties in all athletic contests led fascist critics to describe Marxism, even in its Stalinist version, as fundamentally anti-sport.

It must be said that there is some truth to this last argument. Spontaneity is an irreducible element of any sporting competition, and as a result, sports played a surprisingly problematic role in Soviet historical development. The authorities may have used sports for political ends, but the sporting world proved ill suited to be a precise instrument of the Party and the state. Sports could never be fully controlled. While they were far from independent of political concerns, sports also enjoyed a great degree of autonomy. The Soviet government may have used spectator sports in highly pedantic ways to enhance its power, but because of sports' inherent uncertainties, this particular form of popular culture also offered a variety of possibilities for individuals and groups to avoid and deflect that power as well.

Meanings of Spectator Sports—East and West

Any discussion of Soviet spectator sports must be preceded by at least some examination of the roles it has played in capitalist societies. I have already described the simply stated socialist argument that spectator sports were "bread and circuses" for the oppressed. The need to give the masses a "safe" set of entertainments was seen by many on the left as the very reason for the existence of spectator sports. The success or failure of that project was, in the view of John Hargreaves, determined by "the extent to which dominant classes and groups are able to use [sport] to impose their views and interests on others, and the extent to which subordinate classes and groups are able to resist and overcome those attempts."[27] Soviet critics of Western sports admitted the attraction of watching highly trained athletes perform difficult physical feats, but they considered this "healthy" aspect of spectator sports to be corrupted by the commercial pressures of the market.

They shared the view that spectator sports under capitalism played a diversionary and therefore conservative political role.[28] In 1963 the Olympic weight-lifting champion, Iurii Vlasov, later a critic of Soviet sports practices, wrote an article in *Izvestia*. In it, he attacked those who argued that professional sports could be seen as detached from politics and, therefore, were incapable of serving the interests of dominant classes:

> All sorts of negative phenomena appear in professional sport. Having been torn from its basic purpose of demonstrating the poetry of strength and beauty, this kind of sports becomes a demonstration of the animal character of man, his simian nature. It is not simply a matter of two or three hundred who are killed in the professional arena. It is a matter of the negative effect of these spectacles on the public. The unstated but clear meaning of the slogan "to live outside politics" is the attempt . . . to divert the people from any kind of attempt at political consciousness.[29]

Other observers, Western as well as Soviet, non-Marxist as well as Marxist, have argued that spectator sports, regardless of the social system, can, for better or worse, generate social cohesion.[30] If those societies were capitalist, then spectator sports generated support for capitalist values and political parties.[31] In Communist societies, spectator sports were supposed to win support for Communist values and for the Communist Party. As the American sociologist Janet Lever has suggested, sports can help complex, modern societies cohere, by building "people's consciousness of togetherness." In her study of Brazilian soccer, she examined the ways "large-scale sports presents an alternative mechanism for using primordial loyalties to build political unity and allegiance to the modern, civil state."[32] In a recently modernized, far-flung, multinational state like the Soviet Union, sports had the potential to perform just such a function, and the leading pre-glasnost Soviet philosopher of sports, N. I. Ponomarev, often stressed the integrative role played by sporting spectacles, especially the multinational, multisport *Spartakiads*.[33] Regardless of the social system, spectator sports can be viewed as an element of socialization and cohesion, blurring people's perceptions of otherwise divisive class and ethnic distinctions and creating a unity that may be illusory but that has significant political consequences.

Spectator sports have also been seen as a harmless way of releasing potentially dangerous pent-up aggression. The athlete acts out the anger, rage, and frustration the fan experiences as part of a mundane daily existence. In this sense, spectator sports have played the role of safety valve, a vicarious experience through which members of the public seek to compensate for the inadequacies and hurts of their own lives. This theme was echoed during the 1960s by sports critics of the New Left, and even the highly orthodox Ponomarev suggested that Soviet sports spectacles provided a stimulating contrast with the necessary repetitiveness of the labor process in the USSR.[34]

The transplanted British sociologist Norbert Elias offered a far more sophisticated version of this approach. For him, sports contests replicated the excitement of battles, but did so in the context of rules that limited the violence that accompanied real battles: "spectators at a football match may savour the mimetic excitement of the battle swaying to and fro on the playing field, knowing that no harm will come to the players or to themselves."[35] Elias, who saw sports as part of the civilizing process, argued that the excitement of watching such contests could be "liberating" and have a "cathartic effect," which could "counterbalance the stress tensions of . . . non-leisure life."[36] A humanist who abhorred violence, Elias approved of spectator sports precisely because they afforded a comparatively peaceful way of providing excitement and release.

If spectator sports performed any or all of these functions in capitalist countries—admittedly an unresolved issue—then what role did they play over the course of Soviet history? The two approaches alluded to in the title of this work represent two different ways of looking at this question. The first, here labeled "serious," stresses the activities of the state and the Party, the set of sports practices that can fairly be described as Stalinist. The other, here labeled "fun," focuses on sports as a form of entertainment and pleasure-seeking. This emphasis looks at the variety of ways different social and cultural groups responded to and made use of spectator sports over the course of Soviet history. It would be misleading, however, to draw a simple distinction between the state's attempt to ascribe certain meanings to sports and the entertainment-seeking public's desire to avoid those meanings. Those who sought "fun" in spectator sports were not simply engaged in a search for the apolitical in an overpoliticized society. In looking for entertainment, Soviet citizens were doing more than simply avoiding the messages of the state. They were also making choices about which entertainments they accepted and which they rejected. By doing this, they could, in limited but important ways, impose their own meanings and derive their own lessons from sports and from other forms of popular culture as well.

In keeping with this emphasis, I will be focusing, not simply on the state, but also on a tenuous, yet far from invisible, civil society. Recently, many social historians of the USSR have argued that such a civil society existed throughout Soviet history. Some of them have claimed that these elements escaped the attention of both specialists and the general public. Moshe Lewin has defined such a civil society as "the aggregate of networks and institutions that either exist or act independently of the state or are unofficial organizations capable of developing their own, spontaneous views on national or local issues and then impressing those views on their members, on small groups, and finally the authorities."[37] As I have noted, an approach that focuses on society requires an examination of the audiences for spectator sports, but in contrast to the situation in the West, the reactions of the Soviet sports audience were often unrecorded, diverse, and confusing. In recent years, however, this imbalance has changed, as Western students of the Soviet Union have shifted their attention from high politics and ideology to social and cultural history.

More than in any other form of popular culture, the audiences for spectator sports have not simply watched but have also played visible roles in the spectacles. Furthermore, those roles can be studied through a variety of different, previously untapped sources. Aside from a very few exceptional moments, Soviet citizens were not required to attend sporting events. They were able to make choices from the menu offered them by the state, and Soviet media regularly reported the attendance levels at these events. Therefore, we know which sports were watched and which were not, which teams were loved and which were not, which heroes were worshipped and which were not. The raw statistics on attendance allow the observer to determine, with great accuracy, the true preferences of the Soviet sports audience, and it is possible then to draw a number of conclusions about popular attitudes, based on this raw data.

What I have called the Stalinist or "serious" approach to sports emerged in the 1930s. Its basic structures continued to exist well into the postwar period, long after the surrounding society had ceased to be Stalinist.[38] Sports in the USSR were seen, by both Soviet and Western observers, as a bastion of authority and order, a view summarized as early as 1939 by the sportswriter and soccer star Andrei Starostin. "The government considers it its duty to widen the popularity of sports and thereby to improve the health of the people and harden them physically for labor and defence."[39]

While this emphasis explained much of the state's approach to sports, it was never entirely relevant to the practices of watching them.[40] Spectator sports were supposed to play an instrumental role as part of a rationally and bureaucratically organized sports system, with the athlete-heroes paid and supported by the state.[41] To see Soviet sports simply as a Stalinist product is to ignore two facts, however. The state was not always consistent in the uses it made of sports, and Soviet citizens did not uncritically accept the sporting spectacles and messages placed before them by the offical agencies.

If one sees spectator sports as Stalinist—as serving the interests of the state and expressing the messages of official ideology, as "serious"—then one can present a picture that is consistent, even rational. If, on the other hand, one focuses on society and its consumption of spectator sports, the picture becomes much more complicated. In the West, watching professional sports may have contributed to the authority of politically dominant groups, but it is by no means clear that the watching of professional sports in the Soviet Union generated similar consent for the authority of the Party and the government. If anything, there were ways that Soviet spectator sports fostered forms of behavior that can be called destabilizing, even counter-hegemonic.

As we shall see, the aspirations, aims, and preferences of the organizers of sports often clashed with the desires, wishes, and tastes of those who were to be organized. The nature of spectator sports posed difficult problems for the Party and the state. No form of sport, participant or spectator, can be practiced without sufficient leisure, and free time was far from abundant throughout much of Soviet history. Aside from orthodox Marxism's theoretical difficulty in comprehending the Western concept of leisure, the tasks of modernization, war, recovery, and finally perestroika, simply never afforded Soviet citizens the kind of free time necessary for spectator sports to become the large-scale activity it became in the West. When Soviet citizens did actually experience relative increases in leisure time (the late 1930s and the early 1960s), spectator sports did, in fact, grow as well.[42] Not surprisingly, those spurts also corresponded to similar growth in the number of city dwellers, the primary audience.[43]

Soviet sports scholars continually referred to the popular "consumption" of sports spectacles, and one can properly call these activities part of the sphere of consumption.[44] Yet Soviet economic planners always placed production, not consumption, at the center of their concerns. Heavy industry historically dominated the economic priorities of the state. Under Khrushchev and Brezhnev this emphasis was modified but not fundamentally changed. Historically, the state afforded only limited resources to the sphere of consumption and consumer goods. Therefore, consumer-oriented activities, like spectator sports played a highly ambiguous role in a nation that historically gave its first priority to heavy industry and producer goods. In this sense, the state sports system, with its emphasis on success in the Olympics, can be seen as a correlate of the huge steel mills, dams, and turbine factories long favored under Communism, while spectator sports can be viewed as yet another element of the long-neglected consumer sector. The dams and factories may have contributed to the growth of an industrial giant, but, as we now know, it was a giant that did little to meet the personal needs of most citizens.

Throughout Soviet history, the processes of consumption reminded citizens of the inadequacies of a system that produced things people did not want and, as often as not, failed to produce what they did want. In this way, the daily tasks of providing for oneself or one's family distanced the populace from the state. Consumption became a series of acts through which Soviet citizens struggled in various and often subtle ways to impose their desires on the authorities. The minuscule daily dramas of consumption were far less visible than the overt and highly public activities of the state's agencies. Yet the actions of ordinary Soviet citizens did not go unregistered. The gross number of an attendance figure is, in fact, composed of thousands of individual decisions—to go or not to go. These choices constitute a form of resistance that is elusive precisely because it escapes the control and purview of formal political structures.

Michel de Certeau described the ways "ordinary" citizens have used consumption to resist and deflect the power of dominant orders in precapitalist and capitalist societies. But his words pertain perhaps even more to the case of Communist societies:

> To a rationalized, expansionist and at the same time centralized, clamorous, and spectacular production corresponds *another* production called "consumption." The latter is devious, it is dispersed, but it insinuates itself everywhwere, silently and almost invisibly, because it does not manifest itself through its own products, but rather through its *ways of using* the products imposed by a dominant economic order.... Pushed to their ideal limits, these procedures and ruses of consumers compose the network of an antidiscipline.... The tactics of consumption, the ingenious ways in which the weak make use of the strong, thus lend a political dimension to everyday practices [italics in original].[45]

In a nation where so many of those "procedures" and "ruses" were parts of vast black and gray markets, there could be no escaping the political dimension of consumption.

The irreducible spontaneity of spectator sports also posed numerous other difficulties for the state. The sports world was a place in which talent could be rewarded, regardless of the political views of the athlete, and pleasure could be experienced, regardless of the political allegiance of the fan. At the same time, the descriptions of sporting activity were comparatively free and uncensored. As in the West, sports enjoyed considerable autonomy from the structures of society, even if they were also far from fully independent.

The production of sports spectacles also put the state in the always-suspect and often-corrupt entertainment business, presenting high quality products that at certain times contrasted sharply with the drabness of other officially sanctioned forms of mass culture.[46] Finally, the organization of sporting events had the potentially dangerous effect of bringing large numbers of people together in enclosed spaces to engage in activities that aroused their passions in ways that could be uncontrollable and therefore undesirable. Often these emotions were tied to nationalist concerns, and disturbances did occur, sometimes with deadly consequences. Shostakovich was far from the only observer to note the potential for chaos and bedlam when Soviet fans gathered to root for their favorites. The soccer riot, so common throughout much of the world, was always part of the Soviet sports scene.

It is important, therefore, to remember that high-performance sports were not something simply foisted on an unwilling public by a coercive and manipulative government for a variety of purposes. Soviet citizens did wish to watch sports spectacles, but they consumed them in very different, far more playful ways than the state had in mind. When the quality and excitement of these events were deemed insufficient, Soviet sports fans refused to attend.[47] Their indifference was always noted in the press, and the power of their boredom often forced authorities to make changes. If soccer became too defensive, measures were taken to increase scoring and bring fans back to the stands. If competition became too one-sided in hockey, it was necessary to change rules on player transfers to add intrigue to the domestic season. The Soviet sports audience was far from passive, and in various ways it was able to influence and form the character of the events placed before it.

Spectator sports in the Soviet Union were not simply a vehicle for the state's moralistic enforcement of values that assured obedience and acceptance. Rather, the terrain was always contested. For the state, spectator sports exhibited both "healthy" and "dangerous" elements. The government sought to control the aspects it found undesirable, but it was not always able to do so.[48] Scholarly approaches that stress the role of the state emphasize the manner in which sports were used to control the masses. A different approach, however, which emphasizes society's responses, can show us the ways spectator sports and other forms of popular, as opposed to mass, culture may actually have undermined the authority of state and Party. This undermining did not take on revolutionary or even overtly oppositional forms. It would be going too far to suggest that sporting festivals and spectacles consistently offered the population the controlled possibilities for cultural and social inversion ("the world turned upside down") associated with Mikhail Bakhtin's oft-invoked concept of the carnivalesque. Yet spectator sports did encourage behavior that discomfited a conformity-seeking state, creating possibilities for what Peter Stallybrass and Allon White have called a "politics of transgression."[49] That political dimension, while subtle, was nevertheless very real.

Marxism, Sports, and Popular Culture—
Theoretical Debates and Approaches

As I have noted, orthodox Communism's difficulty with popular culture, leisure, play, and sports owed much to the fact that the particular version of Marxism practiced in the Soviet Union put work and production at the center of its theory of history. As a result, play and consumption became problematic. Throughout the first half of the twentieth century, the Marxist tradition, inside and outside the USSR, was relatively unified in its attitudes toward capitalist spectator sports and other forms of mass culture. During the 1960s, however, fundamental differences emerged between Soviet and Western Marxists, as leftist thinkers living in capitalist countries attempted to incorporate play and leisure into their theories of social change.

Traditional Marxists had considered sports to be a relatively healthy form of human activity. They had always argued that the surrounding social context determined the extent to which sports were either pure or corrupt. This view was contested by thinkers of the New Left, who criticized not only spectator sports but all athletic activity when it involved competition.[50] Neo-Marxist writers in America, France, and Germany instead idealized play, which they argued was subverted by modern high-performance sports.[51] Olympic victories required inhuman discipline and self-denial. The sexual sublimation demanded by these activities was seen as repressive. Both participant and spectator sports, these critics argued, provided outlets for worker aggression that could otherwise have been channeled into political activity. These arguments were not new. In their preference for the freedom of unfettered play, however, New Left sports theorists like Jean-Marie Brohm and Gerhard Vinnai were, ironically, much closer to the spirit of Huizinga's conservative position than to the more ascetic Marxist tradition.[52] Accordingly, Neo-Marxists condemned sports in Eastern Europe, with its utilitarian concerns for labor, productivity, and warfare. They criticized established pro-Soviet Communist parties that still embraced competitive sports and applauded the sporting triumphs of the USSR and other Communist nations.

This critique of sports, and spectator sports in particular, was but one element of Neo-Marxist thinking on the political impact of mass culture. This approach drew heavily on the thinkers of the Frankfurt School, many of whom had emigrated to the United States on the eve of the Second World War. As attuned to Freud as they were to Marx, these writers were highly sensitive to the psychological dynamics and subconscious drives aroused by all forms of sports activity. Scarred by the triumph of fascism, Adorno, Horkheimer, Marcuse, and others sought to find an explanation for the defeat of the left in Germany and elsewhere in Europe. They advanced a sophisticated and complex version of the diversion theory that made mass culture a leading villain and spectator sports, in particular, one of the more significant culprits. Adorno was the most vocal opponent of these debased forms of amusement. Focusing on jazz, he claimed the products of the industries of mass culture reduced their consumers to states of "masochistic passivity."[53] This disdain for the very activities so many workers had come to enjoy led later critics to condemn Adorno and his colleagues for an elitism that had damaging political consequences. The Frankfurt School's contempt for mass culture derived not from the fact that such culture was democratic but precisely from the fact that it was not.[54] The industries that generated the products of mass culture were in no way controlled by the people. Nevertheless, the Frankfurt School shared the asceticism and intellectualism of the rest of the Marxist tradition. In reaction to fascism's cult of the body, these writers came to reject activities that placed primary importance on anything but the mind. For those who had lived through the interwar period in Germany, the Nazi glorification of physical aggressiveness was tied too closely to militarism for its victims ever to be fully comfortable with any expression of the sports mentality.

With the political eclipse of the New Left in the mid-1970s, Marxists and other leftist intellectuals came to change their attitudes about sports and popular culture. The views of Neo-Marxists and the Frankfurt School no longer were seen as all-embracing, despite the fact that they continued to explain much about the political ideology of spectator sports. As an explanation for the left's failures in the 1930s and the 1960s, Neo-Marxism had its attractions, but this approach also led to a political pessimism others were not so willing to accept. To admit the power of the capitalist industries of pleasure and entertainment was to accept likely political defeat. The descendants of the Frankfurt School were repelled by the fact that much of the working class, even many leftist intellectuals, had come to enjoy the pleasures of spectator sports, but they knew that the elitism of this rejection of mass culture in all its forms could only lead to estrangement from the masses. To criticize capitalist sports may have made sense intellectually, but to attack all sports and popular culture as repressive was an act of political suicide.

Beginning with the 1970s, others on the left sought to incorporate both sports and a new understanding of popular culture into their analyses of social change. Such sports theorists as Rob Beamish and Richard Gruneau felt it was no longer politically possible simply to dismiss these phenomena as contemptible. Instead, they argued that sports' "unregulated, boundary-straining, spontaneous component" was potentially liberating and progressive.[55] John Hargreaves suggested that sports could be seen as a utopia in which the promises held out but denied by capitalism could be realized in microcosm. Hargreaves did not claim that sports could be a model for a properly functioning capitalism. Rather, athletic contests could indicate ways of transcending the limitations of the social system they might be a part of.[56] While these theories had echoes of the conservative cult of play for its own sake, these writers were arguing that the left should not cede the most attractive, even joyful, elements of sports to the political right.

In the late 1970s and early 1980s, sports also became a subject of study for more traditional Marxist historians. They were part of a larger cohort of social historians who came to examine, not only sports but other practices of play and leisure as well. Such scholars as Robert Wheeler and Eric Hobsbawm reaffirmed the relationship between the rise of professional spectator sports and the maturation of industrial capitalism in the late nineteenth century.[57] Their analysis accepted the connection between a specific phase of capitalist development and the emergence of professional sports, but avoided seeing spectator sports as part of a conscious, diversionary conspiracy hatched by the forces of order. Wheeler and Hobsbawm sought instead to put sports in historical context and demonstrate the ways the mode of production influenced the practices of athletic competition. Capitalist sports were shown to differ from pre-capitalist sports. Wheeler, in discussing the European workers' sports movements of the 1920s and 1930s, sought to extend this analysis by suggesting ways socialist sports could differ from capitalist sports.

Other scholars studied the varying practices of leisure in specific historical contexts. In his work on nineteenth-century French painting, T. J. Clark examined the recreational patterns and modes of play of the Parisian bourgeoisie. In doing so, he demonstrated the necessity of seeing leisure, not as an autonomous realm of undifferentiated pleasure, but as highly varied experiences practiced in different ways by different classes at different moments of history.[58] To say that a social group engaged in a particular practice—be it sports, movies, or music—merely as a form of entertainment was to ignore the larger question of precisely what it was that made such practices entertaining. Along much the same lines, Chris Waters examined pre-1914 arguments among British socialists about popular culture and found that working-class leisure practices were also contested terrain over which leftist politicians competed with capitalist entrepreneurs for the hearts and minds of the working class.[59] Studies of the early American film industry by Steven J. Ross have similarly demonstrated a multiplicity of struggles among radical politicians, labor organizers, workers, studio heads, and distributors, the results of which were by no means preordained.[60]

Stuart Hall and others at Birmingham University's Centre for Contemporary Studies offered a variety of theories about popular culture that provided similar alternatives to earlier New Left thinking. Hall opposed the Frankfurt School's implicit suggestion that the public uncritically accepted the messages of popular culture placed before it. He rejected this approach as "deeply unsocialist."[61] Rather, different groups and individuals manifested a variety of responses. For Hall, popular culture has been the terrain on which a contest between dominant and subordinate classes takes place: "Popular culture is neither the popular traditions of resistance to these processes [of social transformation] nor is it the forms which are superimposed on or over them. It is the ground on which the transformations are worked."[62] In this sense, "popular culture" can be distinguished from "mass culture," which comprises the products generated by the industries in these fields. "Mass culture," then, can be seen as one of the constituents of popular culture, but it is not, by itself, popular culture.

Hall suggested three broad categories of response to mass culture. In what is called a "dominant" response, the messages of these products are fully accepted by the public that consumes them. In a "negotiated" response, certain elements of the message may be disputed, but the overall system is still accepted. Finally, there is the possibility of an "oppositional" response, in which the public rejects not only the messages but the system that produces them.[63]

As applied to sports by Hargreaves, this approach suggests there are many popular responses to the sports spectacle. The result is less a direct diversion than a fragmentation and disorganization of various subordinate social groups. This process, in turn, facilitates what has widely come to be called the political and cultural hegemony of dominant classes, who no longer require the tools of direct control, ruling instead by consent.[64] In this sense, hegemony becomes, as Raymond Williams has suggested, not a formal system, ideology, or conscious conspiracy, but "a whole body of practices and expectations, over the whole of living. . . ."[65]

Other thinkers have reached similar conclusions. In analyzing sports under capitalism, the French sociologist Pierre Bourdieu stressed the idea of popular resistance in a way that can also make sense of the Soviet situation: "the social definition of sports is an object of struggles. . . . the field of sporting practices is the site of struggles in which what is at stake . . . is the monopolistic capacity to impose the legitimate definition . . . and . . . function of sporting activity.[66]

This view may overstate the struggle as it applies to the Soviet Union. Nevertheless, Bourdieu suggests that society is able either to reject the products placed before it or to transform the meanings of those products in ways their creators never intended.

The Soviet audience was clearly in no position to control the production of spectator sports, but society's varied responses to sports spectacles permitted it to modify the nature, practices, and meanings of sports. Of all the forms of popular culture to appear in the USSR, sports proved particularly problematic as a tool for accomplishing the ends of the government. As has been noted, sports is relatively autonomous and cannot be completely controlled. It may support the power of dominant elites, but it does so in a less than fully efficient manner. Hargreaves's characterization of the capitalist state's use of sports may also be relevant to the Soviet experience: "the attempt to subject sports to a capitalist pattern of rationalization and to program sport in the 'national interest' exists in tension with the nature of sport as an autonomous sphere of expression."[67] Similarly, Williams noted the capacity of televised sports to retain a fundamental core of purity, despite attempts to control, organize, and impose meaning on it.

There's always the sport. Or so people say, more and more often, as they become sadder about what is happening to the rest of television . . . But there is some truth in it. The Grand National, the Cup Final, the rugby internationals, the athletics meetings: only a few programmes, of other kinds, have this openness, clarity, and excitement.[68]

In adapting these ideas to the Soviet situation, I do not wish to imply that Soviet sports can be seen simply as an autonomous sphere in what was an otherwise politicized society. Rather, the nature of spectator sports makes them a highly imperfect tool for advancing the desires of any state. Thus, for all the attractiveness of the analyses offered by Hall, Bourdieu, Williams, and Hargreaves, they cannot be applied to the Soviet case without recognizing four particular difficulties.

The *first* difficulty is the composition and character in Soviet society of what might be the "dominant" classes. Basile Kerblay has argued, "Far from being classless and free of conflicts, Soviet society is stratified into many different social groups, with distinctive lifestyles and levels of consumption, culture, political power, and status."[69] It is not entirely clear if those Soviet elites, who lived lives of privilege, can be seen as a unified ruling class. Many educated and privileged citizens were among the supporters of change and reform. Others were actively opposed to the state. Nevertheless, Vera Dunham has described a social compact (in her words, the "Big Deal") between the state and a comfortable and relatively privileged Soviet middle class consisting of so many "Soviet Babbits and organization men as well as white-collar mid-culture men and women."[70] These groups dominated Soviet society from the mid-1930s, benefiting from the reinforcing of official ideology, and there are some scholars who have gone so far as to argue that these elements, the state and Party's leading cadres (the *nomenklatura*), did come to assume many of the characteristics and attributes of an acutal "ruling class" in the Marxist sense of the term.[71]

The rituals and practices associated with spectator sports can then be adjudged either to support or to undermine the authority of the privileged elites whose interests were served by the preservation of order and stability. Christel Lane, in discussing the role of ritual in the USSR, described the way this process worked: "Since the middle thirties . . . cultural revolution, or more properly cultural management, has become a substitute for social revolution and has assumed a conservative character. Consequently it has achieved a position of great importance in the arsenal of means to exert social control employed by political elites."[72] Sporting rituals do not always perform this function with precision, but it is in this sense that I will be describing the possible conservative potential of Soviet spectator sports.

A *second* difficulty concerns the social composition of the masses, the "consumers" of Soviet spectator sports. The character of these groups is equally difficult to specify. Here the problems are less of definition than of method. The field of Soviet sociology only began to revive in the late 1980s after a long dormancy. In the 1920s a rich series of time-budget studies was produced concerning popular attitudes toward such matters as leisure and free time, but this research did not consistently focus on groups other than those called "industrial workers." Distinctions among professionals, white-collar workers, and industrial laborers were introduced by some researchers, but the few time-budget studies that raised class distinctions did not always differentiate clearly among various types of leisure activities.[73] In particular, no distinction was ever made between participant sports and spectator sports. Given Hargreaves's emphasis on the differing responses of various social groups, it is difficult to pinpoint the ways spectator sports may have divided the multilayered Soviet masses, allowing for the continuing hegemony of dominant social groups.

A *third* difficulty is posed by the relative inattention of Soviet scholars to sports spectating. There is no direct equivalent for the term "spectator sports." One confronts the word *bolshoi* (big) used to describe "big-time" sports, but this usage refers to all elite sports, including those that attract few fans. The word *zrelishche* ("spectacle") is often used in connection with the description of sporting events. Games that are interesting and compelling may be described as *zrelishchnyi.* One rarely, if ever, came across the most direct translation, *zrelishchnyi sport,* however. The concept of the "sports spectacle" was discussed by a very few Soviet specialists, but these scholars and publicists did not employ any of the categories and terms used by the Birmingham School, the Frankfurt School, or any other Western Marxists.

Fourthly, one should note the differing goals of the mass-culture industries in capitalist and noncapitalist societies. Capitalist mass culture tailored its messages to win an audience, while Soviet mass culture tailored its messages to teach its audience. The products of mass culture in the USSR were not supposed to make profits for their creators. Tickets to musical, theatrical, and sporting events were always highly affordable. Books, movies, and records were similarly cheap. Buying the products of mass culture was always less of a problem than obtaining them when they were particularly desirable. Nevertheless, this contrast, while useful, does tend to overstate the differences. Many products of Soviet mass culture were intended solely to entertain audiences. Mindless film melodramas and musicals were produced in significant numbers. Much of pop music, even before rock 'n' roll, was empty and even silly. The circus always received lavish state support, despite its thoroughly apolitical character, and more novels were written about "boy meets girl" than about "boy meets tractor." Conversely, it would be naïve to argue that capitalist entertainments have been lacking in overt or covert advocacy of the values of dominant classes, even if their only conscious aim was to give the audience pleasure.

Despite these caveats, the ideas of Hall, Hargreaves, Bourdieu, Williams, deCerteau, and others (including the Frankfurt School) can help us make sense of the role of spectator sports in the USSR. These approaches, however, require the study, not only of the products of mass culture, but of its audience as well. Until the 1992 publication of Richard Stites' masterful survey of Russian popular culture in the twentieth century, most previous studies of Soviet popular culture focused on more readily available texts. It is far more difficult to learn how those texts were received. The consumers of Soviet spectator sports did not uncritically accept the political-ideological messages the state and Party sought to ascribe to sports. Rather, as one element of popular culture, sports proved to be an arena of ongoing contention. Accordingly, Hall's suggestion of multiple responses to mass culture allows us to study the reaction of the Soviet sporting audience to officially produced sports events. In this analysis, society is not simply the passive object of an all-powerful state.[74] Instead, state and society in the USSR interacted dynamically, each affecting and modifying the other.

The paradigm of a powerful state and a passive society will be familiar to students of Russian and Soviet history. Until relatively recently, this conceptual approach was the established orthodoxy for the scholarly study of Russia and the USSR. This emphasis on the great continuity of a strong, centralized state, dating from Ivan the Terrible in the sixteenth century through Stalin and beyond, caused much of the literature on Russia and the USSR to emphasize high politics and elite culture to the exclusion of the rest of society, which was seen as atomized and helpless. The paradigm was also largely consistent with the totalitarian model, long popular among Sovietologists, which stressed the omnipresence of the state and the centrally causal role of ideology. This emphasis distorted the study of the USSR in a number of ways well described by Stephen Cohen:

> More was obscured than revealed. Historical analysis came down to the thesis of an inevitable "unbroken continuity" throughout Soviet history, thereby largely excluding the stuff of real history—conflicting traditions, alternatives, turning points, and multiple causalities. Political analysis fixated on a regime imposing its "inner totalitarian logic" on an impotent, victimized society, thereby excluding the stuff of real politics—the interaction of governmental, historical, social, cultural, and economic factors; the conflict of classes, institutions, groups, generations, and personalities.[75]

In sports, the totalitarian approach led to an emphasis on the Olympic "sports machine" to the near exclusion of other manifestations of sporting activity. Speaking even more broadly, the idea of a dynamic and dominating Russian or Soviet state retarded the study, even denied the existence, of popular culture in the USSR.

Yet this bias may have been as much methodological as it was theoretical. Officially produced texts have always been easier to find and study than the less visible responses of the audience. It is now possible, though, to examine Soviet spectator sports from the inside, as they were experienced by fans, athletes, journalists, and officials. It is no longer necessary to be satisfied with the view from the outside, the picture the government made available for external consumption. One must ask of the Soviet experience the same questions that have been asked about professional sports in the West. What was the political and ideological role of spectator sports? Did they support the state or undermine it? Were they a cog in a totalitarian machine, turning out fit workers and soldiers, or a form of popular recreation and entertainment that subverted official efforts to produce obedient and satisfied citizens?

In the wake of Communism's collapse, it has become necessary to describe the system's internal contradictions and weaknesses as well as its strengths. The Party's attempt to use mass culture to crystallize its own representation of the popular will faced enormous obstacles. The regressive, spontaneous, and playful character of all popular culture, not just spectator sports, undermined its effectiveness as a tool of control. The humor and irony of the fans in the stands always clashed with the sober and heroic official image of the sportsman or sportswoman. Spectator sports audiences did not share the seriousness of the state's intentions. Instead, the citizens of the USSR saw this form of popular culture as an arena in which they could have fun, crack a silly joke, or scream loudly as they rooted for heroes of their own choosing.

2

The Search
for a Mode

When the Bolshevik Revolution took place in 1917, the matter of culture in all its forms—high and low; popular and elite—was opened to broad debate. Over the course of the next decade, a galaxy of groups and individuals contended with each other for ascendancy and support. Many in society as well as in the revolutionary movement felt the slate had been wiped clean, and the struggle for a new form of postrevolutionary culture, were it proletarian, Soviet, or universal, could now be engaged. Others contended that the cultural heritage of the past should not be rejected but used as the basis for subsequent development. In the context of these larger arguments, there were those who sought to answer this question as it pertained to sports. What role, if any, would sport and physical culture play in the new society?

Most Bolsheviks and their cultural fellow-travelers had harbored grave doubts about sports. Many felt that pre-revolutionary sports had always demonstrated strong ties to Tsarist militarism and to the political right. Some Bolsheviks, Lenin in particular, understood the benefits of exercise and healthy participation, but there were few sports fanatics among the men and women who made the October Revolution. As such, if the place of noncompetitive physical culture was uncertain after the revolution, it is safe to say that spectator sport, with its previous history of corruption and diversion, figured little in the political and cultural debates among postrevolutionary thinkers concerning the proper place of sports in postrevolutionary society.

From the time of the 1917 revolution up to the mid-1930s, soccer and the few other sports that had won an audience searched for a mode of organization that would advance the goals of the Party and the state, while providing a rapidly changing population with sports and entertainment. Much

26

of this activity and discussion went on outside the purview of the intellectuals who were debating the proper role of physical culture and sports in the new society. These processes were confused and halting. Various schools of thought competed for control of Soviet sport in the first postrevolutionary decade, and they did so under the most difficult of conditions. Facilities were primitive, and athletes and fans did not take easily to the discipline that was required to make sports orderly and successful. When a high-performance, competitive sport system finally did emerge in the 1930s, it arose as a response to a rich and often confusing prehistory that requires examination.

Watching Games Before the Revolution

Tsarist Russia lagged behind the industrialized West in many areas, and spectator sport was no exception. Wherever it has appeared, this particular form of popular culture has been largely an urban phenomenon. The gathering of large numbers of people in closed arenas could occur far more readily in cities than in the countryside, but the Russian Empire was overwhelmingly rural. The vast majority of the population, the peasantry, had little time or energy either to watch or to participate in sports. Backbreaking labor in warm months left little leisure except for drinking and fighting. The freezing cold of winter confined most peasants to their homes, although some rural dwellers did ski and skate. Peasants hunted and fished as well, but these activities had more to do with survival than with sports. Nevertheless, peasants did create a number of games over the centuries. *Gorodki* (a form of bowling with sticks) and *lapta* (a bat and ball game not unlike baseball) were two of the most popular pastimes, while various football-like games were played in the northwest near Tver and Pskov. These activities took place on special occasions, often as part of carnivals or festivals. Peasants did not train for them, nor were they organized in the modern sense of the term. While peasants might watch their neighbors engaging in various contests, access to the sites of these events was not usually restricted, nor was admission charged.

Despite the vastness of the empire's rural sector, more than a fifth of the population had come to live in towns by the time of the 1917 Revolution. The industries of entertainment that had been growing so swiftly in the cities of the West were comparatively weakly developed in Russia, though. Many urban dwellers were literate, and a mass circulation press did arise to meet their needs.[1] Additionally, music halls, circuses, and cinemas could also be found in Russian cities, but they did not exist in great numbers.[2] Compared to their English or French counterparts, Russian workers had much less free time, and a considerable portion of their disposable incomes was sent back to relatives in the countryside.

After decades of struggle, Western workers had won more leisure time. By comparison, the Russian proletariat was still young, and its movement less developed. The typical twelve-to fourteen-hour work day left little opportunity for variegated recreation, and it was hardly accidental that the eight-hour day quickly became a widespread demand among the Russian proletariat. In 1901, a textile worker named F. P. Pavlov described the limits on workers' leisure:

> So if you do not see genuine merriment among the holiday factory crowd, it is because the conditions of everyday life place a mass of obstacles and inconveniences in the path of reading, and physical exercises and sports have not become part of the custom, and aesthetic entertainment in the form of concerts, exhibitions, theater, and museums, such as open their doors to workers in Germany, England, and other Western European countries, are inaccessible to our Russian workers.... Where, then can the worker go? And how can he spend his rare day off?[3]

Organized sporting events that sought to attract large audiences were very few and were largely patronized by members of the propertied classes. A wide range of sports was practiced in Russia before the revolution, but the social base of this activity was relatively narrow. As was common throughout Europe, sports were organized by clubs, supported by dues-paying members who considered themselves to be amateurs. Because most of this activity was urban, members of Russia's burgeoning bourgeoisie were the main patrons and practitioners of sports.[4] Their openness to Western cultural practices made them particularly eager to engage in activities that elsewhere had become associated with progress, energy, and industry.

Because early Russian sports were dominated by the propertied and educated, the laboring masses found obstacles to their participation. Membership fees in the sport clubs were usually beyond the reach of working men and women, and all sports groups, like any organization in Tsarist Russia, had to be formally chartered by the Ministry of the Interior. Imperial bureaucrats feared that laborers would use sports to mask gatherings that in fact had revolutionary purposes, and until 1914, they repeatedly rejected attempts by workers to establish their own sport clubs.

A wide range of sports familiar in the West began to filter into Russia after the peasant emancipation of 1861. Many of these games were introduced by foreigners, especially Britons living in the capital, St. Petersburg. Yacht and rowing clubs were formed in 1868, along with gymnastic circles. In 1881, speed skating was formally organized. Two years later, cycling made its appearance. This sport proved successful as both a participant and a spectator activity, often attracting large crowds to professional races.[5] Track and field was introduced in 1888, while horse-racing and other forms of equestrian sports had a long and rich domestic tradition. Weightlifting and wrestling were also popular, as a result of their ties to the circus. While workers and peasants had long practiced a highly popular version of semi-organized brawling, it was not until 1897 that boxing, with its modern rules, was first seen in Russia. That same year witnessed the first organized soccer matches.[6]

As early as the 1860s, British sailors in the Black Sea port of Odessa had played soccer, and the British are generally given the credit for popularizing the game in Petersburg at the turn of the century.[7] Some accounts describe spontaneously organized games in such places as Kharkov, Kiev, and Moscow throughout the last decades of the nineteenth century, and at the height of Stalinism (1948), two Russian writers living in Georgia even went so far as to argue that the British did not invent soccer. Football, they claimed, had its roots in the Georgian game *Lelo,* and also in the Russian *Shalyga,* which had been played in the northern provinces of Tver and Novgorod.[8]

Nevertheless, the first organized modern match in Russia is thought to have been played in the capital by the KLS (*Kruzhok liubitel'i sporta,* "The Sport Lovers' Circle") in 1897. Soccer grew quickly in popularity, and a city league was formed in 1901. Its best known teams were called *Sport, Merkur, Unitas,* and *Kolomiagi.* This activity was strictly amateur, and most of the first players were foreigners, particularly British engineers, foremen, and managers working for Russian firms.[9] Foreigners dominated and controlled the organization of soccer in these early years, but by 1908, clubs composed entirely of Russians were able to challenge them. Subsequently, tensions between Russian and foreign teams became intense and often bitter, leading many foreigners to form their own leagues.

Soccer caught on in Moscow soon after it appeared in the capital. There, too, it was practiced by private, officially chartered clubs, including *Union,* OLLS (*Obshchestvo liubitel'i lyzhnogo sporta,* "The Society of Lovers of Skiing"), and SKL (*Sokolniki klub lyzhnikov,* "The Sokolniki Ski Club"), based in Sokolniki Park in the northeast sector of Moscow.[10] These last two clubs would evolve after the revolution into two of the Soviet Union's most important sports societies. OLLS would go through several permutations until 1928, when it became the Central House of the Red Army (TsDKA). SKL similarly passed through several stages until it appeared in 1935 as the Spartak Society.[11]

The Russian prerevolutionary industrialist Morozov built the finest soccer field in Russia on the site of his Orekho-Zuevo factory, and his English general manager, Harry Charnock, introduced the game to the plant's workers as early as 1894. While workers were given an opportunity to play soccer at the new "stadium," Morozov also fielded a highly talented team, called *Groza Moskvy,* composed largely of English engineers and managers whom he advertised for in the British press. A league was formed in Odessa, another big center of British influence, in 1911. Kiev followed suit the same year, and Kharkov and the Donbass formed leagues in 1913. During 1911, an All-Russian Football Union was formed in preparation for the 1912 Olympics at Stockholm. This new group also provided an organizational umbrella for the increasing number of games between select teams from the major cities. Petersburg and Moscow began an annual series of matches starting in 1907. These games, dominated by Petersburg, continued through war, revolution, and civil war well into the Soviet period.[12]

The soccer teams of this era were almost entirely amateur, and games between clubs attracted crowds that by Western European standards were still quite small.[13] James Riordan reports that a 1908 game between *Sport* and *Victoria* drew what was then a record gate of two thousand. "Stadiums" consisted of a few hastily erected wooden stands. Adequate, grass-covered fields were few. Goals with nets were almost as rare. Hardly any of the places where soccer was played had permanent seating, and even fewer had fences and barriers restricting access to ticket-buying customers.

A 1911 game between Petersburg and Kiev in Kiev was typical of this level of organization. The Petersburg team was met at the train station by their hosts, who provided dinner and breakfast the next day. The game had aroused unusual interest, and before the opening whistle, the largest soccer crowd in Kiev's history, three thousand, surrounded the city's best field. This playing space, provided by the Gelferikh factory, had the unusual amenities of dressing rooms, showers, and stands for the spectators. During the warm-up, these fans, none of whom had bought a ticket, surged around the players, and only the referee's whistle, signifying the beginning of the contest, succeeded in clearing the field for the game, won by Kiev 3–0. Another three thousand fans paid the unusually high sum of fifty kopecks for tickets to see an international match in 1913 between Russia and Sweden in one of Moscow's best stadiums, owned by the Sokol'niki Sport Club. In 1910, a visiting Czech team, Corinthians, had attracted sellout crowds of four thousand spectators to each of three games in the capital, one of which was actually won by the Petersburg selects. The next year, the famed English professional club Bolton Wanderers played three games in Petersburg before similar audiences.[14]

Compared to England's, this level of attendance was minuscule, and the involvement of the working classes was equally small. Alongside the amateur clubs of the wealthy, however, a tradition of spontaneous worker soccer also emerged. These teams were called "wild" (*dikii*) or "outlaw" and, because of their proletarian composition, were unchartered by the state. These teams played with inadequate balls and boots on any space available. In many cases these "fields" were the courtyards (*dvory*) of apartment houses, and to this day the term for "sand-lot" soccer is *dvorovyi futbol*. The proverbial vacant lot was another common site for this spontaneously organized and free-flowing proletarian football, which provided an outlet that the formal and amateur groups could not.[15] There were, however, times when the *dikii* teams were able to rent the fields of the established clubs, and by 1914, many worker teams were finally able to receive legal charters.

Members of the stronger worker teams would at times be invited by officially sanctioned clubs to fill out their rosters, and several factory owners, following the example of Morozov, sought to provide recreation for their employees. A textile plant in Petersburg, along with the famous Putilov armaments factory, even went as far as to invite workers, who were not employed in their enterprises to play for these "factory" teams. Here was the first seed of professionalism, but the workers' poverty soon ran into the contradictions of amateurism. When the textile plant's team was to play a 1912 match in Moscow, the players were required to pay their own transport. Train tickets were beyond the means of the workers who then refused to play. The matter came before the governing body of the Petersburg league, which ruled in favor of the team organizers. The workers then quit the team, which soon went out of existence.[16]

Despite the growth of interest in soccer, the development of the game in Russia lagged far behind the rest of Europe. The Russian national team was annihilated by officially amateur squads at the 1912 Olympics, and most international contests resulted in victories for foreign opponents. There was no professional league organized on the Western model. By contemporary European standards, crowds were small and stadiums even smaller. Moreover, the involvement of the working class in soccer was limited to unorganized participation, not passionate spectatorship. Additionally, the associated industries that fanned interest in spectator sports were weakly developed before 1917. The sporting press was in its infancy, and most daily newspapers had limited coverage of soccer. Such elite dailies as the liberal *Rech'* and the conservative *Novoe Vremia* gave only two or three inches each day to horse-racing; nor were sports extensively covered in the penny press. There was a weekly, called *Russkii sport,* which covered the sporting activities of the propertied and educated while proletarian soccer was described, more haphazardly, in a publication called "To Sport" (*K sportu*).[17] In the socialist press, one never found the sort of denunciation of soccer engaged in by the British left. In fact, leftist newspapers gave little, if any, mention to soccer and other sports at all. Spectator sport as a diversion from class struggle was an extremely limited part of the life of the Russian working class, and one may speculate that its absence had something to do with the special revolutionary militance of Russian workers compared to their Western comrades.

Along with soccer, ice hockey attracted considerable interest before the revolution. Russians did not play the game that was invented in Canada. Instead, they practiced a version of hockey popular throughout the Nordic countries. Sometimes called "bandy," this game resembled field hockey on ice. The playing surface was almost the size of a soccer field. Eleven players skated after a small ball with rounded sticks. Six-inch boards surrounded the field, keeping the ball in play. There was only one small artifical rink in pre-revolutionary Petersburg, and it was reserved for figure-skating. Therefore, Russian hockey could only be played outdoors when the weather was cold enough for the ice to form. The weather was not a problem for the players, who were active and could keep warm. Stationary spectators, though, often had to brave severe conditions in order to take in a game. This fact alone limited the sport's ability to attract large numbers of fans. Nevertheless, the Russian version of ice hockey did succeed in finding an audience before the revolution.

Soviet histories of hockey make passing reference to versions of bandy played in numerous locations in the last decades of the nineteenth century. Most often it was played on the tennis courts and ponds of noble estates. Organized hockey played by Russians appeared roughly at the same time and place as soccer. English and some German residents played the game in Petersburg in an organized fashion in 1897, and by 1901, regularly scheduled games were taking place in the capital among teams representing many of the same clubs that had fielded soccer teams.[18] Quite a few of these matches were held on the estate of the enormously wealthy Usupov family, where crowds of relatives and friends rarely exceeded two hundred.

By 1905, organized hockey had spread to Moscow and Tver, and by 1910, clubs and city select teams were journeying to meet opponents in other towns. These games could attract as many as one or two thousand spectators willing to brave the cold.[19] Soccer and tennis players looking for exercise in the winter comprised the majority of players, but, unlike soccer, the comparative expense of equipment and the difficulty of finding available playing surfaces meant that few laborers were able to take part in ice hockey. Despite its popularity, ice hockey's social base remained limited, and it could scarely be called a spectator sport in the modern sense of the term.

While sporting activity was far from undeveloped before 1917, the watching of sport had not taken on a mass character. The vast majority of the population—the peasantry—did not live in cities, the historic locus of spectator sport. Nor had workers who lived in urban areas attained the leisure time that would allow them to pursue the playing and watching of sports in large numbers. Other industries of mass culture had made their appearance by the turn of the century, but they, too, were still in their infancy when the

Bolshevik Revolution created a new terrain for the production and consumption of popular culture.

New Society and Old Ways of Watching

The period of the Civil War (1918–1921) permanently marked the role of sports and physical culture in the USSR. During those difficult years, with the survival of the first socialist state at stake, exercise and fitness became essential elements in the preparation of the new Red Army. In May 1918, a new organization was set up to supply the army with fit defenders of the revolution. Virtually all sports organizations came under the aegis of this new organization, which became the central organization for universal military training (*Vseobshchee voennoe obuchenie* or *Vsevobuch*).[20] As James Riordan has demonstrated, this close relationship between military preparedness and physical culture became one of the distinctive characteristics of all sporting activity throughout subsequent Soviet history.

This concern for the production of healthy and strong soldiers affected the practices of spectator sport. The end of the Civil War in 1921 did not take the security forces out of the sports business. Many of the earliest teams that attracted sizable crowds were supported by sport societies associated with the army and the police. The first so-called Voluntary Sport Society was founded by the Ministry of Interior in 1923. Called *Dinamo* it fielded teams in numerous sports in a large number of cities.[21] In addition, the clubs of the Red Army also supported a wide variety of sporting activities. Both the police and the army were interested in training high-performance athletes for public competitions that would be watched by the masses. In the 1920s, however, this elitist and competitive tendency had to contend for influence with other groups who held quite different views about the proper role of sports in a socialist society.

Under the relative freedom that prevailed during the years of the New Economic Policy (1921–1928), several tendencies struggled to define a properly postrevolutionary culture for the masses. These debates and disputes covered all modes of cultural expression, from film and literature, to education and family practices. In the field of sports, the military's concern for producing competitive elite athletes was challenged by those who were highly critical of the prerevolutionary traditions Soviet sports had first tried to build on. One such postrevolutionary faction called the "Hygienists," rejected all competitive sports, contrasting sports with healthy exercise and physical culture. Such games as soccer, boxing, and weight-lifting were deemed injurious to mental and physical health. The Hygienists instead favored participation over watching sports, calling for an end to grandstands and spectators.[22] They were quite influential in the first half of the decade and actually succeeded in limiting the number of public competitive events that might attract sports fans to stadiums.

The Proletarian Culture Movement, or *Proletkult,* which rejected all prior culture as bourgeois, sought to advocate a specifically class approach to all areas of culture, including sports. The practices of the prerevolutionary period had to be abandoned, and an entirely new culture, practiced by and for the working class, was to take its place.[23] This concern led them to criticize any form of competitive sport derived from bourgeois society. They preferred instead what they called "production gymnastics, excursions, and pageants." At times they invented specifically proletarian games, two of which were "Rescue from the Imperialists" and "Smuggling Revolutionary Literature across the Frontier." These and other Proletkult pastimes were participatory activities. No Proletkult member dreamed of creating a "National League of Literature Smuggling" for either fun or profit. For both the Proletkult and the Hygienists spectator sport was anathema.[24]

In many areas of cultural activity, these experimental and utopian approaches survived well into the early thirties before their eventual eradication under Stalin. But, in the sphere of sports and physical culture, these debates were formally settled by a resolution of the Central Committee of the Communist Party as early as July 13, 1925. Rejecting the utopian and experimental tendencies, the leadership decided in favor of a high-performance, competitive approach that could inspire proper values and instil respect for authority.[25] Yet this shift at the top did not lead to the immediate abandonment of non-competitive sports. In the context of NEP culture, such a decision by the Party did not mean that all practitioners in a particular field had to accept Moscow's dictates. Nevertheless, while many experimental approaches to physical culture continued to be practiced into the late 'twenties, those who organized them were swimming against the current.

The peculiarities of sports do much to explain why radical approaches were abandoned far more quickly than in other spheres of culture. Order, discipline, and the winning of victories had historically been far more important in the world of sport than in the arts, and even the prewar leftist sports tradition had not entirely rejected these values. Therefore, one would expect that sport and physical culture would not be particularly fertile terrain for cultural experimentation. Instead, the production of an athletic elite to inspire the masses quickly became a central element of subsequent Soviet practice. After 1925, the Party considered competition to be healthy, and the watching of athletic contests was no longer deemed unsocialist. Thus the elite, competitive Soviet sports system that we have come to know emerged earlier than did Stalinist practices in other spheres of mass culture.

The creation of a visible sports elite required the privileging of successful athletes; raising, in turn, the matter of professionalism. Many of the earliest Soviet stars were supported either by the security organs or by the army, continuing the close relationship between high-performance sports and military preparedness. This relationship would be made even more explicit during the war scare of 1927. At that time, a flood of rumors swept Moscow in the wake of England's suspension of diplomatic recognition. Consistent with this mood, Soviet sports periodicals immediately announced a campaign for the "militarization" of physical culture.[26] *Krasnyi sport* proclaimed: "At the present moment our broad and concrete task is to introduce a series of military elements into physical culture. Each physical culture circle and physical culturalist, even if not in the Red Army, must make broad use of sport for the defense of the country and for the armed class struggle."[27] The weekly magazine *Fizkultura i sport* stressed the special importance of track and field, swimming, and motor racing. These sports, it was argued, were particularly useful for preparing warriors for the class struggle. More competition was required to raise the fighting level of athletes and soldiers, and even as non-dogmatic a figure as Anatoli Lunacharsky, the first head of the Commissariat of Enlightenment, argued that workers must train for "the coming struggle with the bourgeoisie."[28]

Once the sports system was fully established by the mid-'thirties, the idea of competition took on international implications. It was possible to demonstrate the nation's preparedness by setting records that surpassed those of athletes in the bourgeois world. Yet this task could not be performed by the masses or even by physically fit soldiers. It required the creation of a highly trained sports elite. In 1935, Alexander Kosarev, head of the Komsomol, the Party's youth organization, would announce, "Soviet athletes must not only improve All-Union records but beat world records as well. In the Soviet physical movement, 1935 must be the year of the world record."[29] These calls were repeated throughout the press, and soon some outstanding results were achieved, particularly in weight-lifting.[30] Beginning with the middle of the decade, the demand for world records became a constant theme that was never abandoned. In accepting his gold medal as a member of the 1938 championship soccer team, Andrei Starostin, the captain of Moscow Spartak, told thirty-five thousand fans: "We understand that the task before Soviet physical culture is to educate a healthy young generation and help it raise its chest in defense of our homeland by equalling and surpassing Western European, bourgeois records."[31] These calls gave rise to the phenomenon of *rekordsmenstvo*, ("record-seeking") but not all in the Party and government were pleased by this trend. Nevertheless, a hierarchy was created in the sports world that mirrored similar developments in society. Athletes were now the same kinds of heroes as model workers. The politically conservative socializing tool of the role model was employed extensively, as the sports world soon became entwined with the much-celebrated Stakhanovite movement for increased labor productivity that began in the middle 'thirties.[32]

One universal element of spectator sport has been the creation of individual stars, and the Soviet press, regular as well as sporting, participated in the manufacture of idols and heroes. Individuals were raised above the masses. The leading figures of Soviet sports were described as worthy of emulation, and they became recognizable figures. A 1935 *Izvestia* report on a soccer tournament noted that fans already knew the faces of the leading players (at this time they did not wear numbers) and expected good performances from these stars.[33]

Stakhanovite labor heroes were treated like para-athletes. The qualities that made an individual worker a labor hero were thought to be similar to those exhibited by great sportsmen. *Krasnyi sport* described the case of Peter Tikhomirov, a twenty-one-year-old Stakhanovite at the Kuibishev Electrical Works: "Last year Tikhomirov was required to take part in the local cross-country race, sponsored by [the newspaper] *Komsomolskaia pravda.* Unexpectedly for him and for his comrades Tikhomirov came in first. The physical strength, speed of movement, and visual acuity that he showed in his work-place [*tsekh*] proved useful in sport."[34] Stakhanovites were urged to take up sports, and leading athletes were sent to factories and mines to organize competitions, establishing a close relationship between labor productivity and sporting success.[35] "Prepared for Labor and Defense" (*Gotov k trudu i oborone*) was the inscription on the medals received by those citizens who passed the nationwide system of fitness tests first established in 1931.

Better workers and fitter soldiers were the desired products of sports activity, while high-performance athletes were to play the same role as Stakhanovite labor heroes. As models for emulation, they were supposed to inspire their comrades. Yet, as Lewis Siegelbaum has shown, Stakhanovism had a particularly peculiar place, not only in the politics of Soviet production, but also in the international socialist movement's own traditions and theories about organizing the industrial process. During the 'thirties, the Party leadership came to move away from the egalitarian and leveling social policies of the first Five-Year Plan (1928–1931), coming instead to accept the necessity for some sort of hierarchy in society. Many old professional elites were accommodated and given a variety of privileges. Thus, while the creation of an elitist sport system, with its emphasis on competition and record-setting, may have been exceptional in the context of some earlier socialist thinking on sport, it was fully consistent with the evolution of the Soviet social and political systems during the 1930s.

The Early Rituals of Stalinist Sport

For athletes, coaches, officials, journalists, and serious fans, sport is a daily process of games, training, discussion, and evaluation. All the same, there have been exceptional moments in Soviet history when the Party chose to organize sporting festivals and rituals in order to crystallize the meaning it sought to attach to physical culture. It is important to remember that these occasions were not necessarily sports events. Rather, they were political events that used sports as their subject. While they may have been sporting spectacles, they did not constitute spectator sports in the sense of the term I have been using here. Nevertheless, as the apotheosis of a statist approach to sport, they merit attention. The massive displays and pageants that gave Soviet sport its Orwellian or totalitarian image were the wrapping rather than the package, but they were the moments at which the state most overtly intervened in the sporting process to impose meaning on that process.

It would, of course, be absurd to suggest that sports, outside of these rituals, were an oasis of apoliticism, even if there is a sharp distinction to be drawn between sports as practiced by those who knew and loved them and sports as portrayed in the government's occasional holidays, rituals, and festivals. In the 1920s and 1930s, the most important sports pageants were the multisport, Olympic-style Spartakiads and the annual Physical Culture Days, with their elaborate parades through Red Square in the presence of the Party leadership. While these events may not tell us all we would like to know about our primary concern—the public's consumption of sport—they are very revealing about the values and lessons the state and Party sought to attach to sports.

The Spartakiad—After the revolution, the young Bolshevik government chose not to participate in the quadrennial Olympic Games that had been revived in 1896. The Soviets objected to the aristocratic character of the movement's leadership, and they felt the Olympic code of amateurism inhibited proletarian participation. But, the model of the multisport festival had its attractions for demonstrating the virtues of physical culture and testing the level of athletic preparation. Given a different class character, the Olympic model of the multisport special competition, with its allusions to the supposedly timeless humane values of ancient Greece, could be used for the purposes of the Party and state.[36]

In 1913, the Social Democratic parties of Europe had established an international sports movement. It was revived at Lucerne in 1920. The Social Democrats held two hugely successful worker Olympics in Prague (1921) and Frankfurt (1925). To oppose their enemies in the revolutionary movement, the Communists set up their own Red Sport International in 1921. Thus the first Olympic-style sports festival in the USSR, the Spartakiad of August 1928, was a conscious Communist response to the "bourgeois" Olympics of that same year and to the so-called reformist games organized by the Social Democratic Sports International. In naming the event, the Communists were consciously challenging the Social Democrats, referring not simply to Spartacus, the rebellious slave of the ancient world, but also to the German Spartacist movement that had been crushed with Social Democratic participation in 1919.[37] The president of the All-Union Council of Physical Culture, V. Mikhailov, stressed this distinction:

> The reformist Lucerne Sports International helps the bourgeoisie with its policy of using sport to divert the workers from the revolutionary-class tasks of the proletariat. Everyone remembers how the English trade unionists, in the midst of the [1926] general strike sought to divert the workers with their "portentuous" resolution: "To call on workers to organize soccer games with the police on the days of the strike." The Red Sport International must use all means to strengthen its work in the struggle against using sport to divert the broad masses from the revolutionary tasks of the working class.[38]

A. Enukidze, the head of the Organizing Committee of the Spartakiad, drew the contrast with the Olympic Games:

> Our Spartakiad is sharply distinct from the bourgeois Olympics, now taking place in Amsterdam. At those games there is an attempt to achieve victories at any cost and establish new records. Defending "national honor" with specially prepared athletes is an end in itself. The Spartakiad has the task of demonstrating physical culture and sport as one form of preparing workers in the struggle for socialism.[39]

The Spartakiad also was to be distinguished from the Olympics by the inclusion of military events, folk dances, and noncompetitive pageants. In addition to a parade through Red Square, the games were opened with a water festival on the Moscow River and a mass "stroll" (gul'ian'e) of thirty thousand through the Lenin Hills. This last event replicated one of the most typical and long-standing of peasant leisure practices,[40] and some of the events in this part of the Spartakiad were indeed more reminiscent of a summer camp field day than a sober, utilitarian sporting event.

The core of the program, however, was the same as that of the Olympics. Such sports as track and field, swimming, wrestling, and cycling were seen as "cultured" or civilized pursuits in which the Party now sought to interest the workers. Yet the Spartakiad fell short of its goal of uniting the working class behind the goals of proletarian sports. Many of the groups that operated stadiums, including the Red Army, demanded such high rents that the Spartakiad had difficulty finding venues. Among the 7,125 athletes, judges, and doctors, only 28.7 per cent were members of the working class, and 0.4 per cent were peasants. The majority of those taking part did not work with their hands, including white-collar workers, or *sluzhashchye* (38.7 per cent) and students (16.4 per cent). For all the talk of the "militarization" of sports, only 8.8 per cent of the participants were from the army.[41]

The most telling fact of all was the comparative indifference of the working class to the so-called cultured sports that made up the bulk of the program. The only sport that drew large crowds was soccer. Track and field only rarely filled the 15,000-seat Tomsky Stadium during the days of competition, while the newly constructed Dinamo Stadium stuffed as many as 50,000 into its every crevice for a number of important soccer matches. The level of interest is even more impressive since the semi-finals and finals were held on weekdays during working hours.[42] Even preliminary games drew larger crowds than the most important events in other sports.

Although workers and soldiers received half-price discounts on tickets (50 to 75 kopecks for the general public), they did not exhibit great interest in any sport except soccer.[43] Thus, the Spartakiad revealed a fundamental dissonance between the Party's idea of a good sporting time (the multisport festival) and the proletariat's (soccer and little else). Multi-sport competitions would eventually prove especially attractive to the Party as a sporting vehicle, far more so than events that centered on a single sport. In competitions of that type, the dominant discourse—of fans, participants, and observers—was about the tactics, styles, and results of the particular game in question. By contrast, when so many games were played at once, the dominant discourse was not about the many sports, but about sport itself, about the coming together of athletes from different republics and nations in festivals of youth, dynamism, and optimism. Over the course of several decades, it would prove far easier for the state to ascribe a changing series of meanings, lessons, and signs to Spartakiads, and later, Olympiads, than to competitions in a single sport, in which the game itself was the thing.

One of the great attractions of the soccer tournament at the first Spartakiad was the chance to see foreign teams play Soviet squads representing the various republics and the cities of Leningrad and Moscow. Because of the USSR's diplomatic isolation, the Soviets had little opportunity to test themselves against clubs from the West. Soviet players were limited to engaging teams representing workers' sport groups. Only revolutionary Turkey was willing to send its national team to play the Soviet *sbornaia*. Thus, the public was willing to overlook the fact that the foreign teams that came to Moscow in 1928 were also composed of workers and not professionals. German and Austrian Communists were to send teams, but the interference of their governments forced them to stay at home. England, Finland, and Switzerland were represented, but the group that drew the most attention was from Uruguay. Composed of workers and a few journalists, this team was far from professional. The global reputation of Uruguayan soccer was so great at this time, however, that even an amateur team could arouse intense excitement in the Moscow fans.[44] Both *Krasnyi sport* and the weekly *Fizkultura i sport* had consistently devoted extensive coverage to foreign soccer, and the Uruguayans were no mystery to the Soviet sports audience.

In the first days of the tournament, 15,000 people saw the Uruguayans play the team of the Ukrainian Republic. The Ukrainians won 3–2 in a game filled with violent play. After two Uruguayan goals were disallowed by the Soviet referee, the Uruguayans lodged a formal protest. At first their claim was denied, but the next day the entire competition was reorganized. The previous games were declared to have been "friendlies," and the teams were now divided into two groups. All the foreigners, plus teams from the various republics, made up one group of twelve teams, while the Russian Republic (RSFSR) put twelve teams in another group. This plan guaranteed that at least one of the finalists would be a Russian team.[45] Such seeding techniques have been employed the world over in order to enhance the chances of the home team's making the final, and even at this early stage, the Soviets were not above this sort of gamesmanship and control. Uruguay would be eliminated in the semifinal, while Moscow defeated the Ukraine 1–0 in the final before 50,000 fans, the largest crowd yet to see soccer in the USSR.

There were other moments when the Spartakiad did not run like a well-oiled machine. Several days of the track competition had to be postponed due to lack of proper apparatus. Distribution and sale of tickets was marked by confusion.[46] Yet the model had clearly been put in place. The performances in most sports at the Spartakiad were far below world-class levels. Nevertheless, the goal of breaking verifiable records was established early. While the Spartakiad's organizers tried to stress the mass character of an event with more than seven thousand participants, they were also clear that competitions of this type were necessary to hone the skills of future Soviet champions.

The aims and practices of a high-performance sports system were in place as early as 1928. The Olympic movement may have been anathema because of the social composition of both its leaders and participants, but Soviet sports authorities were drawn to the kinds of sports comprised by the Olympic program and to the classical, broadly humanistic themes evoked by Olympiads. In the West, few of these games (boxing and soccer excepted) had been played or watched by workers, but by organizing multisport festivals, the leaders of Soviet sports sought to popularize these civilized activities among the masses. Olympic sports had been the pastimes of the educated in the bourgeois world, and the Soviets hoped that workers and peasants could be induced to take up such "cultured" activities.

The Spartakiad would become the model for bringing athletes from various sports together. The importance and excitement of these events were enhanced through elaborate rituals and ceremonies that had little to do with sport itself. In the 1930s, there would be trade-union Spartakiads, army Spartakiads, student Spartakiads, even collective-farm Spartakiads. While quite a few of these events were simply glorified field days, many others would yield increasingly impressive results. Some of the mass, noncompetitive events, including the mass *gul'ian'e,* would disappear, and the seriousness of purpose would become starker. Gradually these festivals took on the shape and style we associate with sport under Stalin. The frivolous experiments of the first Spartakiad withered away, to be replaced by more sober activities. When the Soviets finally entered the Olympic movement in 1952, they were not starting from scratch. Instead, they had long experience with the various sports on the Olympic program and were comfortable with the organizational forms and rituals common to Olympiads.[47]

Physical Culture Day—The first holiday devoted to sport and physical culture took place in 1923. Several poorly organized competitions were held at a small stadium in the park of the Agricultural Exhibition in the north of Moscow. A number of similar "holidays" were organized during the late 'twenties. By 1929, Dinamo Stadium was filled for a formal Physical Culture Day, which came to include a parade of physical culturalists, relay races, and a soccer game between teams from the Russian and Ukrainian republics. Finally, in 1931, it was decided to celebrate this holiday with a mass parade through Red Square in the presence of the entire Party leadership.[48]

The annual celebrations of this event took on all the trappings that are commonly associated with sports in the period of Stalinism. The mass gymnastic displays, bizarre and idiosyncratic floats, and omnipresent portraits of Stalin would become part of the folklore of Soviet sport, especially for foreign observors. At first glance, these parades recalled contemporaneous sports festivals in Germany and Italy, and, while significant differences did exist between fascist and Stalinist sports holidays, one can say, at the very least, that the Physical Culture parades did represent the closest thing to a "totalitarian" expression of Soviet sport and physical culture to emerge during the 1930s.

The Physical Culture Day Parade was not a sporting event, nor was it a spectator sport. It was a theatrically orchestrated political event that focused on physical culture first and competitive sport only secondarily. The Stalinist leadership used this event to ascribe a changing series of values and meanings to sports and fitness. While this most official expression of the Soviet sporting mentality is not at the center of my present concerns, it does require examination in order to demonstrate the ways that the concrete practices of spectator sports eventually came to differ from their ideal representation in these "holidays."

The Physical Culture Parade took place annually during the summer, with the date changing from year to year and the number of participants ranging from 75,000 to 125,000. The square itself was filled with spectators, including Stalin and the rest of the leadership, who viewed the three-to four-hour display from the Lenin mausoleum. While the parade was filled with portraits, slogans, and speeches lavishly praising "the greatest friend of Soviet physical culture," Stalin never spoke at these events. The parade was thoroughly rehearsed and scripted, with the order of march and the choice of floats, slogans, and exercises reflecting the particular priorities of the year. As a result, spontaneity, one of sport's irreducible elements, was all but eliminated. Instead, these well-organized rituals were designed to dramatize the excitement of physical culture by linking it to the enthusiasm of youth struggling to build socialism.

As Rosalinde Sartori has made clear, there was nothing about these and other Stalinist rituals of the late 'thirties (unlike earlier festivals) that embraced the "carnivalesque." Rather than depict the "world turned upside down," the weak dominating the strong if but for a day, the Physical Culture parades sought to justify the newly emerging hierarchies in Soviet society and gain public acceptance for the dominance of those who had risen to the top.[49] The event was so important that it could not be left in the hands of the sports authorities, nor could spontaneity threaten its intended effect. The theater director N. Okhlopkov, who directed these extravaganzas, remarked in *Izvestia:* "At these types of holidays, physical culture ceases to be purely academic. The theater comes to its aid—the director, the artist, the composer. They put on a monumental mass spectacle in close creative contact with masters of sport and physical culture."[50]

In the early 'thirties, the parades stressed the mass and egalitarian character of physical culture. Entrance to Red Square was not restricted. These more open practices would soon change, however. Later parades would be limited to those who had either achieved the rank of "master of sport" or who had demonstrated the required level of fitness to win one of the badges that certified them "Ready for Labor and Defense" (*GTO, gotov k trudu i oborone*). This shift occurred in 1937 at the behest of I. I. Kharchenko, the first president of the newly reorganized All-Union Committee for Physical Culture and Sport. By 1939, access to Red Square was limited to only those who had been issued tickets. Leading political figures, however, were admitted merely by showing their Party identification documents.[51] What had begun as a mass holiday with egalitarian overtones became instead another marker of Stalinist society's embrace of hierarchy.

In 1937, an attempt was made to introduce some small element of sporting spotaneity into the parade. Nikolai Starostin, one of four famous soccer playing brothers and the head of the recently organized Spartak sports society, proposed the playing of a soccer game in the square before the leadership atop the mausoleum. Starostin's team had quickly become the archrival and competitor of Moscow Dinamo supported by the police. The two teams were to play a half-hour match on a huge green carpet of 136 by 64 meters, which was sewn by members of the Spartak society during the evenings several weeks before the parade.[52] They stored the carpet in the GUM department store across the square from the mausoleum. The day before the parade, however, Starostin was approached by a representative of the police, who announced that a rug over the cobblestones of Red Square was too dangerous a surface to play on. Starostin protested that the surface was, in fact, softer than the grassless fields one often found in the southern republics. Nevertheless, Dinamo withdrew. Instead, Spartak's first team played its youth squad. Spontaneity had to go out the window, and seven goals were prearranged to maintain the interest of Stalin, who, it was feared, would become bored and cut the game short.[53] In subsequent years, the huge green carpet, with its oasis of the unexpected, became a regular highlight of the parade.

Descriptions of the parades sought to avoid making the annual display of well-proportioned, less-than-fully-clothed male and female bodies either an end in itself or an expression of an otherwise repressed eroticism. The press always rhapsodized over the physical beauty of the participants but never drew distinctions between what made women attractive as opposed to men. In 1939, *Izvestia* remarked, "the thousands of spectators were enthralled by the tanned, strong, and fit bodies of the athletes who marched before the mausoleum."[54] The human body, however, was not to be developed apart either from the mind or from the goals of the Party and the state:

> In the ceremonial march, young patriots, in the blinding light and play of colors and in a sea of movement and sound, demonstrate those qualities of freshness, youth, health, dexterity, and braveness that must be instilled in our young generation.... Soviet physical culturalists take part not only with their muscles but with their hearts and brains. This is why the beauty of this excellent spectacle does not block, but rather underlines its sense.[55]

The Stalinist ideal body was clearly not eroticized. In 1937, Evgenii Kricher described the male and female participants' figures as "beautiful machines." Somewhat contradictorily, he said their models were the warriors (obviously all male) of ancient Greece, who, Kricher claimed, not entirely correctly, were always well proportioned and never over-muscled. The body as a tool of industrialization even became part of the parade itself in 1940 when "a huge railroad bridge was formed on Red Square out of hundreds of tanned, graceful bodies."[56] Similar "sculptures" of human bodies became a feature of later parades.

The strongest theme of the parades, however, was the link between physical fitness and military preparedness. Each year, as war became increasingly likely, the relationship of physical culture to warfare became ever more explicit. *Izvestia* described the participants in the 1938 parade: "They are reminiscent of the soldiers of ancient epochs. Today, they will demonstrate their grace and skill before the leaders of the Party and the government. . . . This Stalinist generation is ready to stand as one in the ranks of the Red Army to deal a crushing blow to the enemy, wherever he may come from."[57] Another article in *Izvestia* described the appearance of students from the Stalin Institute of Physical Culture that same year: "If tomorrow there should be war.' This troubling theme is the basis of the participation of the physical culture students . . . who, in breathtaking and demonstrable form, show that the Red Army is the healthiest, most physically strong, and hardiest army in the world."[58]

Physical culture not only made the army strong, but, more important, physical culturalists made the best-prepared soldiers: "If tomorrow there should be war. . . . The students will throw off their sporting outfits and we will see what will be, if war breaks out tomorrow. There will no longer be gymnasts, footballers, and hockey players. In their place will be tankists, pilots, snipers, and sailors."[59] These sorts of statements hardly require interpretation. They make clear the Party's belief that sports and fitness were essential elements of national defense, and the rituals organized by the authorities were the most obvious demonstration of the link between sports and the military. Masters of sport and athletic heroes were to inspire their comrades to exercise for better health, efficiency, and preparedness. Yet these rituals were not the daily fare of the Soviet lover of sports. That diet would be composed primarily of a few team sports, of which soccer was by far the most popular.

Soccer—The Game of the Working Class

The history of Soviet soccer before the Second World War can be divided into two clear phases, before and after the organization of the league in 1936. It took nearly two decades for the Soviets finally to adopt the pattern that had been established throughout Europe. But soccer in the USSR throughout its entire history would continue to differ from the Western European experience in one fundamental way. The relatively mild winter in much of Europe allowed the soccer season to begin late in the summer and continue through the spring. In the Soviet Union, soccer was, of necessity, a summer game, and the fact that soccer revived in the spring gave it a special meaning and poignance for the average Soviet fan.

Much like American baseball, the beginning of the season was a sure sign of spring and renewal. The special harshness of the Russian winter made this pleasure all the more intense. Opening day of the soccer season was always a joyous "holiday" with ceremonies, marches, bands, and other games. Newspaper and memoir accounts of the first day of the soccer season are always filled with emotion, nostalgia, and an atypical romanticism. From the first days of Soviet power, soccer was number-one in the affections of sports fans.

From the Revolution to the Formation of the League—While the various contenders for cultural authority were debating the proper role of sports, the working classes of the major cities, even in the midst of the Civil War, began to play and watch soccer in increasingly large numbers. As early as October 14, 1918, the tradition of the Petrograd-Moscow game was revived. In the conditions of civil war, the Petrograd team could not send its best players to Moscow, and they lost this tenth renewal of the rivalry by the lopsided score of 9–1, a rare victory for the Muscovites.[60]

In the wake of the revolution, many of the prerevolutionary clubs were taken over by proletarian members, and with the end of the Civil War, other new organizations were formed as well. The prerevolutionary OLLS came under the control of the military's *Vsevobuch* organization. It was renamed OPPV (*Opytno-pokazatel'naia ploshchadka vsevobucha*), and in 1928, it would become the primary sport club of the Red Army. Moscow's *Union* would come under the sponsorship of the Moscow soviet. As mentioned above, one of the first acts of the newly formed Dinamo Society (1923) was the creation of a topflight soccer team, and in 1925, the Dinamo branch in Tblisi also formed its own team of "masters."[61] In 1922, the party committee in the Sokolniki region of Moscow had taken over two prerevolutionary clubs, the RGO (*Russkoe gimnastisticheskoe obshchestvo*) and the OFV (*Obshchestvo fizicheskogo vospitania*). The two groups were combined and renamed *Krasnaia Presnia*. The Komsomol was among the first sponsors of this new team which was led by the four soccer-playing Starostin brothers: Nikolai, Alexander, Andrei, and Petr. Nikolai Pashintsev, president of the Party's Krasnopresenskii Region Executive Committee, became the team's chief patron, and it followed him as he moved to other organizations. Thus the Starostins came under the wing of the Dukat tobacco factory when Pashintsev went to work at that firm. In 1926, the team switched its sponsorship to the food workers' union (the team was called *Pishchevik*). In 1931, Starostin's team came under the control of a wealthy group of self-financing (*khozraschetnyi*) retailing enterprises, called *Promkooperatisa,* but two years later they switched back to Dukat.

In 1934, at the urging of Alexander Kosarev, head of the Komsomol, the team came under the umbrella of a new sports society that was to be funded by *Promkooperatsia.* This multisport organization was to be called *Spartak.* Throughout the various phases of its existence, Spartak (as well as its earlier incarnations) had been the chief opponent of Dinamo for the leadership of Moscow soccer. After 1935, when the Spartak society was formally founded, the rivalry between these teams became even more spirited.[62] The Starostin brothers all assumed leading roles in what quickly became a powerful organization, and *Promkooperatsia*'s resources enabled Spartak to attract many top athletes in a number of the more visible sports. The new organization quickly won the sympathy of much of the Moscow public. Precisely because it was tied neither to the army nor to the police, and it soon was the most popular team in the capital.

Domestic soccer competition before 1936 took place on two levels. As many as a hundred or more clubs participated in city championships that stretched out over the entire summer season. National championships, however, were contested only by select, all-star teams from each city, the same approach that had been followed before 1917. Intercity games took place throughout the season, with the best two teams meeting in Moscow for a national final that always filled the largest stadium available. In keeping with the haphazard structure of the game, these championships did not take place every year. The first tournament was held in 1922, but it was not repeated until 1928, when it was part of the Spartakiad. The championship was then renewed in 1931, 1932, and finally in 1935.[63]

The various local club competitions quickly attracted a sizable audience. According to Mikhail Iakushin, a star for Dinamo in the 1930s and later a highly successful coach, matches of the leading teams had already become "great events" in the early 1920s: "From the earliest morning on weekends, a great 'tramway' movement began in Moscow, with players and fans travelling toward the numerous stadiums and fields of the capital. On the average, the leading teams attracted five to ten thousand spectators."[64] In 1924, *Krasnaia presnia* played a game against MSFK (*Moskovskii soiuz fizkultury*) that overflowed the 5,000-seat capacity of the former Zamoskvoretskii Stadium. Thirty extra trolleys had been added to handle the crowds, and all windows of the box office were opened hours before the game.[65] While gates of this size were not uncommon during the 1920s, only the most pivotal games between the strongest teams were able to attract this many paying spectators. Games between less-popular clubs rarely brought more than a few hundred customers into the stadium.

Konstantin Beskov, who would also become a successful player and coach, described the audience at these games: "The public was the simplest possible—working people. They were dressed very simply and pretty much the same, wearing Russian-style blouses and jackets, with their pants stuffed into the top of their boots."[66] During this period, the clubs had to be profitable under the semicapitalist conditions of the NEP, but by 1927, ticket prices had risen beyond the reach of the average worker, leading to a drop in attendance. The next year, the various trade union teams lowered their ticket prices "several times," down to fifteen and thirty kopecks a game.[67] This change was made in response to reports in *Krasnyi sport* that tickets had become too expensive for the "workers' pocket." Since workers made up "the mass of spectators who were most interested in football," the sport ran the risk of losing its mass base. The new prices did have the desired effect, and soon games between such Moscow favorites as Pishchevik and Dinamo were attracting as many as ten thousand fans. By the standards of contemporary Western Europe, audiences of this size were still quite small, but in comparison to pre-revolutionary Russia, it was clear that soccer had struck roots with the working class and was becoming a mass phenomenon.[68]

Intercity matches became fixtures on the calendar, as Moscow and Leningrad continued a rivalry that had begun in 1907. Before the revolution, Petrograd had regularly won. They would continue this success in the first half of the decade, but, predictably, Moscow came to dominate. Kharkov and Odessa also had strong teams, and any game with the visiting Moscow selects was a big attraction in the provinces. The Spartakiad added the element of republican all-star teams after 1928, and these confrontations, especially between the Russian and Ukrainian republics, proved hugely popular.[69]

Spectator sports are, of course, not possible on a mass basis without arenas and stadiums that can accommodate sizable crowds, but until the construction of Dinamo Stadium in 1928, soccer was played in relatively small venues. Originally Dinamo had 35,000 seats. Constructed in Petrovskii Park in the northwestern part of Moscow, it initially had a horseshoe configuration, with a bicycle track extending out the east end. During the Spartakiad, however, spectators would stand on the field as well as the running and bicycle tracks, allowing as many as 50,000 to take in the finals of the competition. In 1935, the track was removed and the arena enclosed, and in 1940, lights were added to permit night games. Today, Dinamo's official capacity is 55,000 seats, but over the years as many as ninety thousand fans have been stuffed into its every cranny for truly big events.[70]

The opening of Dinamo Stadium allowed soccer to become a mass spectacle on the scale it had achieved in other countries. During the 1930s, this arena was filled on numerous occasions, not only for soccer games but for a wide variety of other events, some of them more political than sporting. Until 1928, however, Soviet soccer was played in much smaller facilities, inhibiting its chances for greater popularity. The largest arena in Moscow before 1928 had been built in 1926 by the food workers' union. Originally called Pish-chevik, it had 15,000 seats around a running track. Renamed Tomsky Stadium for the Spartakiad, it still stands today, near Dinamo stadium, but is now called Young Pioneer Stadium. Before 1926, clubs had to play in the small stadiums, inherited from the various pre-revolutionary clubs. The largest of these, ZKS (*Zamoskvoretskii klub sporta*), had five thousand places on rickety wooden bleachers. Most fields were only partially covered with grass. Scoreboards and public address systems were nonexistent, while toilets and food concessions were minimal. Dressing rooms, when they existed at all, were primitive. In fact, for the players, the greatest achievement involved in the construction of Dinamo Stadium was not the huge number of places for fans. They were pleased, instead that, for the first time, a Soviet locker room had showers with hot water. By the middle of the 1930s, however, sizable stadiums (of more than 20,000 seats) had been constructed in Leningrad, Tblisi, Baku, Erevan, Odessa, Kharkov, Stalingrad, Kiev, and several other cities. This construction represented the first great wave of stadium-building. In all, 650 "stadiums" (capacity over 1,500 places) were built during the decade.[71] The larger arenas would eventually be the homes of the club teams that would join the league in 1936 and later.

From the very earliest days, Soviet players, coaches, and fans were enormously interested in the chances of their best teams against foreign clubs. The new Soviet republic believed that the principles of socialism, especially collectivism, could contribute to the development of a specifically Soviet style of play that could be as good as, or superior to, that of the bourgeois teams of the West. The USSR's diplomatic isolation, though, hindered the possibilities for topflight international competition in the period before 1936. The Soviets were not members of international sporting organizations. As a result, it proved difficult to arrange games. The only ready opponents were drawn from foreign workers' clubs. Even the Social Democratic Sport International refused to allow its representatives to play Soviet teams on a regular basis; but despite these roadblocks, a number of matches were arranged both on the club and on the national levels.

Any international game proved highly attractive to Soviet fans, regardless of the caliber of the opposition. Eventually it was the large crowds that came to these matches during the 1920s that created the demand for the construction of as large an arena as Dinamo Stadium. The first international meeting took place in September 1922, when a Finnish workers' team was defeated by two Moscow club teams and the Moscow selects. The next year, the selects of the RSFSR toured Sweden and Norway, where they played "bourgeois" amateur teams from the Swedish and Norwegian leagues, winning eleven games and tying three. The only opponent willing to meet Soviet teams on the national level, however, was Turkey, which sent its team in 1924 to play two games against the Moscow selects, one against Odessa, and a final match against the USSR national team. The Turks lost all four matches, but great numbers of spectators flocked to these games, filling the trams and making the collection of fares impossible. The Turks would return in 1931, 1933, 1934, and finally 1936; and in 1925 and 1932, the Soviets went to Turkey.[72]

Soviet specialists were quick to admit that these opponents were not among Europe's soccer powers. One-sided victories over German, Austrian, and French worker teams attracted large crowds, but these games were unsatisfactory as a strategy for improving the level of Soviet play.[73] After the 1927 season, *Krasnyi sport* complained that the performance of Soviet teams had actually gotten worse in the last year. The reason was the Soviets' isolation from the rest of the soccer world: "How can we explain this situation: the halt in development and the decline in class? We are stewing in our own juice. We have no one to study from, and no one teaches us the newest tactics and techniques. There are no games with the strongest of opponents who can enliven our play."[74]

The diet of games versus worker teams, plus the occasional match with Turkey or Norway, continued through the early 'thirties. After 1933, however, with the Nazi takeover in Germany, the quality of possible proletarian opponents improved, as the Comintern shifted from its disastrous policy of confrontation with Social Democratic parties to one of cooperation in the anti-fascist Popular Front. As a result, it became possible to play teams associated with the larger Lucerne Sport International. But even here, difficulties cropped up. In August 1934, the Moscow selects were to play in Basel against a mixed Swiss squad composed of what *Krasnyi sport* described as "seven class players from bourgeois teams and four from reformist workers' unions." But the Swiss government, not yet in the spirit of the Popular Front, refused to grant the Muscovites visas, and the match was then moved across the nearby border to the small French town of Saint-Louis where Nikolai Starostin and Mikhail Iakushin led their team to a 5–2 victory before 5,000.[75]

The breakthrough came a few months later, when the Moscow selects were invited for a tour by the workers' sports union of Czechoslovakia. Not only were they to play the usual proletarian teams, but a match was promised with one of two Prague professional teams, either *Sparta* or *Slavia*. At this time, Czech soccer was among the best in Europe. That spring, the Czechs had barely lost to Italy in the World Cup final played in Rome. After the Moscow team arrived in Prague and had beaten six trade-union teams by enormous scores, the Czech federation announced its refusal to allow the Prague teams to play the Soviets because the USSR was not a member of international soccer's ruling body, FIFA. Instead, a game was hurriedly arranged with the weaker *Zhidenitsa* team of Brno. On October 14, 1934, ten thousand fans jammed into the small local stadium to see the first game between a Soviet and a first division professional team. Moscow won 3–2.[76]

The next pivotal moment came less than a year later. In the late summer of 1935, the team of the Ukrainian Republic was invited to Paris to play the first-division team Red Star. Soviet teams had a large advantage in these friendly or pre-season exhibition games. While Western teams were just rounding into shape and looking ahead to their league seasons, their Soviet opponents were in midseason form and had trained for these highly exceptional moments in their schedules. Despite these advantages, no one expected the Ukrainians to win so convincingly (6–1). This was the moment Soviet soccer had waited for. A. Bukharov's description of the game in *Krasnyi sport* spared nothing:

> Victory, victory brilliant and incontrovertible.. . . In the thirty years of my sporting life I have lived through many of the difficult moments and hours that every athlete does, but the struggle between the Ukraine and Red Star was the maximum I have experienced in the emotional sense. . . . Appearing against one of the strongest Parisian bourgeois professional clubs, we established not only the success of Ukrainian football, but passed a test defining the level of Soviet football. . . . There they were, Red Star, the hope of the bourgeoisie. There they were, professionals of whom we had only heard until a few minutes ago. . . . The examination is over. Bourgeois Europe must take notice.[77]

In the wake of the Paris victory, a visit by a Prague select team of professionals in late September 1935 attracted enormous attention.[78] Forty thousand filled Lenin Stadium in Leningrad, and the game was sold out days in advance. Seventy-five thousand crammed into Dinamo Stadium for the match against Moscow, and the stadium in Kiev was similarly filled. The first two games were broadcast on radio, still a rarity, and matches were attended by the highest Party officials, who witnessed elaborate ceremonies before each game. The Czechs tied their games in Leningrad and Moscow and won in Kiev. As far as the Soviets were concerned, this was a satisfactory result. Their best city selects had played on even terms with a strong team from one of Europe's leading football nations. Highly sought-after self-respect had been won. The Soviets now had a sense of the possibility of ongoing and normal sporting relations with the outside world. *Krasnyi sport* reported after the Moscow match: "The teams played a tie. The fans left the stadium never ceasing to discuss the game. They leave so that they can return many more times and take in these international meetings; so that they can see how world records will be beaten *in our stadium*. They return to watch foreign sportsmen who much more often will be the guests of our hospitable republic and its capital''[79] (italics added).

The successes against Red Star and the Prague selects led to an invitation in December 1935 that would fundamentally change Soviet soccer. The Communist sporting union of France invited Spartak and Dinamo Moscow to tour against several worker teams in January 1936. To make the trip more attractive, a Moscow select team was also invited to play one of the leaders of the French league, Racing Club de France.[80] Recently purchased by the Parisian businessman Bernard Levy, Racing included players from many countries. It was considered equal to the better English teams and had just played a 2–2 tie with London's Arsenal. The Soviets were uncertain if they should accept the invitation. Their season had been over for two months, and most players were out of shape. It was also feared that the Soviet teams would have difficulty in handling what was then the newly fashionable attacking formation, the "W." Until this point, all Soviet teams had played in the more conventional style of five attackers in a line, and some Soviet coaches had gone as far as to dismiss the "W" as a "bourgeois" style.

Finally, it was decided that a combined team of Spartak and Dinamo players would represent Moscow in the match, set for New Year's Day, 1936. Sixty thousand filled the Parc des Princes to see the Moscow selects with Iakushin and Il'in from Dinamo and Alexander and Andrei Starostin from Spartak lose 2–1. Brother Nikolai noted in the press that under the circumstances this was a fully respectable result.[81] Nevertheless, the loss provoked a discussion at all levels of Soviet soccer that finally convinced its leaders they should follow the example of the Western professionals. A league now had to be formed.

The Problem of Professionalism Before the League's Formation—The creation of the league that spring would force Soviet players and coaches to organize their efforts in a more consistent and permanent manner. They were now to devote the bulk of their energies to sports, a change that meant less time for work and raised the issue of professionalism. While the extent of the league's demands on players' time was indeed new, many of the practices and customs of professional sports had been common in Soviet soccer well before 1936. As early as the 1920s, Soviet athletes were being paid, and this fact was generally known among the sporting public.

Competition for the best players had been keen throughout the NEP period. Under-the-table payments, no-show jobs, and better housing were just a few of the standard inducements employed by the leading clubs, and these matters were widely discussed in the press. While accounts of professionalism were nearly always critical, they were such a journalistic staple that there can be no doubt that the practices they condemned were widespread. The semicapitalist world of the NEP had its shady operators who found in soccer a ripe object for fun and profit. As Moshe Lewin has said, "NEP had its share of venality, crooked business deals, and ways to spend the profits, including night clubs, *cafés chansants,* gambling dens, and houses of prostitution."[82] Inevitably, as in the West, less-than-upright figures were drawn to so significant an object of public attention as soccer. While some of this activity slacked off during the First Five-Year Plan, it quickly resumed, even before the creation of the soccer league.

In any competitive situation, amateur or professional, teams seek to attract the best possible players within, and often outside of, the rules agreed upon by the competitors. Even if early Soviet soccer had been amateur, some player movement would have occurred, but in a fully amateur situation, one could expect most players to stay with their original clubs. Movement from group to group, not to mention city to city, signified that players put their individual welfare above that of the collective. This practice was seen by many critics as a sign of professionalism, a negative development. However, in the conditions of the NEP, gate receipts were still an important element of a team's survival. As everywhere else, excellence on the field meant success at the box office. Semicapitalism gave rise to semiprofessionalism.

The demand for good players appeared very quickly, and the ablest soon found their services in demand. They could shop themselves to the highest bidders. As early as 1926, *Krasnyi sport* lamented that this process had been going on for some time, and it stressed that the methods of attracting good players were primarily financial:

> These "well-known" players move about according to their own taste. Little by little, with the approach of the close of the transfer period, a small but substantial number of players appears, ready to sell themselves to whomever they want to, whenever they want. [They ask] only the highest price.... It is especially shameful that organizations that are not what they seem to be take part (of course not openly) in the financing of these "commerical" operations. These organizations are interested in setting up strong teams for their groups in the name of "hurrah patriotism" and with the aim of collecting thousands in gate receipts.[83]

Two years later, the weekly *Fizkultura i sport* lamented this same process and remarked that many players had played for a different team every year. The magazine also ran a large editorial cartoon that satirized the annual movement of players from team to team.[84]

At the heart of this process was the phenomenon that became known as *chempionstvo.* The members of many sports societies began to object that their organizations were devoting too much attention to attracting and supporting elite athletes. As a result, the physical education of the working masses was being neglected. This criticism was not directed simply at those athletes who, by virtue of their talents, happened to be successful: "The dispute is not simply about 'champions' but about those 'champions' who, having achieved something, bargain for themselves, seeking a comfortable place from the institution for whom they will appear. . . . It is necessary to struggle decisively against those organizations engaged in the 'buying and selling' of champions. . . ."[85]

The abandonment of the New Economic Policy did little to stem this phenomenon. The market for stars may have been less overtly financial with the coming of the first Five-Year Plans, but by the mid-'thirties, top athletes still found many suitors for their services. In 1933, the sports press was again complaining about this practice, and two years later, *Krasnyi sport* detailed an elaborate ring of "sports businessmen" who traded in players. Both the businessmen and the players received such sizable sums as three thousand rubles for these "transfers." By the end of 1935, the practice had become so widespread that the Central Committee of the Komsomol and the All-Union Council of Physical Culture (VSFK) published a resolution decrying player transfers.[86]

Rewards of this sort were not entirely unreasonable, since big-time soccer was in the process of becoming a full-time occupation. Nikolai Starostin has recalled that, in the early 'thirties, teams practiced three times a week and played games on Sunday. Players on city selects and national teams would be taken from their work for long periods of time, and the top teams would spend as much as a month preparing for the season in the south. Mikhail Iakushin recounts that he enrolled in an engineering institute in 1935 but soon found that soccer demanded so much time that he had to abandon his studies.[87]

The Conduct of Players and Fans—In the early years of Soviet soccer, matches were taken very seriously, and gentlemanly play was far from the norm. Player conduct on the field was often extremely rough and undisciplined, and the situation was made all the worse by the fact that skilled and experienced referees were few. As a result, fights and other forms of "hooliganism" were common. Perhaps the most famous incident of this sort took place in November 1926. The Moscow selects were invited for two games in Odessa against that city's first and second teams. In the first few minutes, it was clear that the Muscovites were far stronger than the second Odessa team, and, to compensate for their lack of talent, the Odessa players began to foul regularly. Soon one of the Moscow stars was seriously injured, leading to the disqualification of the guilty Odessa defender. In the second half, the Muscovites lost their patience and began to retaliate. Several Odessa attackers were brought down in their tracks by Moscow defenders, and eventually one

"SPRING TRANSFERS"

member of the Moscow team began to kick an Odessa player who was lying on the ground. This action provoked a riot, and the crowd invaded the field— from which they were cleared only with great difficulty, by mounted police-men. An investigation ultimately found the causes of the incident to be weak refereeing and (what would become a constant theme), "insufficient educational work" among the players.[88]

Fights, dirty play, and other transgressions were not just products of the supposedly lower moral standards of the NEP period. Unnecessary roughness was still common in the 'thirties. In one game during the 1935 Moscow city championship, a player was disqualified for kicking an opponent in the head. A year before, a game in Leningrad dissolved into a mass brawl and had to be abandoned. At a game in Simferopol, two "notorious hooligans," the Bolsenov brothers, began to beat up their opponents' goalie. When the referee intervened, the brothers punched the referee in the mouth. At other games in Simferopol, players showed up drunk and kicked opponents in the face.[89] In what would become a familiar theme, *Krasnyi sport* attributed these incidents to

> . . . the low cultural level of the players. During the game and after it they are to be found in the closed atmosphere of the sporting crowd. . . . No one is surprised by the corrupt, hooligan jargon of these players. It is considered a normal

part of our sport. . . . Sport is not only a pleasant way to pass time. It is a weapon of culture, a means of education, and a way to organize the cultured leisure time of the masses.[90]

Soccer, in particular, was not a sport of the intelligentsia. Those who played it were largely a rough-and-ready crowd who had not accepted the values of orderliness and discipline that the authorities sought to inculcate through sports. "Cultured" (*kul'turnyi*) sportsmen did not kick prostrate and injured opponents, nor did they punch referees in the mouth. Educational (*vospitatel'nyi*) work was required of team captains and leaders, but their efforts were miminal and ineffective.

The citizens who came to see these games also did not watch them with any special regard for official values. Very early, the public, especially the working class, adopted favorite teams and players, whom they rooted for with a passion and intensity not unlike that of their counterparts in capitalist countries. The vicarious and not always healthy pleasures of fanship were much the same as they were elsewhere in the world. For some workers, their identity as followers of a team became more important than their identity as proletarians, as the diseases of diversion and apoliticism emerged even within postrevolutionary society. Passive watching, as opposed to active participation, was, in official eyes, something to be feared. In 1927, *Krasnyi sport* described a hypothetical worker they called "Ivan Spiridonovich":

> What could be Ivan Spiridonovich's relationship to sport? . . . Does he run the hundred meters or pole vault? No, he is a soccer player. And not the kind of player who runs on the field in shorts. Quite the opposite, he is part of the public. . . . By his profession, Ivan Spiridonovich is a metal worker but in his true essence he is a food worker [*pishchevik*]. "The food workers, there's a soccer team," he says. And sure enough the food workers [*Pishchevik*] do have a team.[91]

Given its importance to workers, sport was supposed to play a role in raising the cultural level of the proletariat, and soccer's popularity among the working class made it especially important but potentially problematical. *Krasnyi sport* noted this fact in 1927: "Let's take a big factory center like Orekho-Zuevo or the workers' suburbs in Leningrad. We will see that sport, and football in particular plays a role of the first importance in the leisure time of the worker. At the last trade union congress it was noted that big games draw so many spectators that the mines in the Donbass are completely empty on the days of important matches."[92]

For this reason, it was especially unfortunate that the experience of watching a game was difficult and testing for the spectator. Not only were most stadiums less than comfortable, they were poorly run. Only one or two ticket windows might be open, and the same held true for entrances. On big game days, the box offices and entryways were the scenes of what *Krasnyi sport* called "real battles." In this crowded and disorderly atmosphere, any confrontation on the field or act of bad refereeing could have serious consequences for public order. Riots were by no means uncommon, and drunkenness and hooliganism were very much part of the sports scene throughout the 1930s.

By the end of 1935, it was clear that Soviet soccer had its share of problems on and off the field. It had become, by far, the Soviet Union's most popular sport, but clearly it could not continue along the semi-professional lines of the past.[93] A change in course was required. The leaders of the game finally took action early in 1936.

The Emergence of Modern Spectator Sports

The modern era of Soviet spectator sports began in May 1936. The previously haphazard and inconsistent structure of soccer, the most popular of all games, would now change. Instead of the occasional tournament, an All-Union league was established, in which permanently organized club teams, representing various sports societies, played each other on a regular seasonal basis. This more serious, systematic, and professional approach to the presentation of sports spectacles was characteristic of other changes then occurring in Soviet society, as the Party pulled back from a broad range of radical policies after the whirlwind of change that had taken place in the first half of the decade.

A More "Joyous" Life

At the end of 1935, Stalin made his famous proclamation, "life has become better; life has become more joyous." Among many other things, he meant that the fevered pace of industrialization was to slow down. During the First Five-Year Plan (1928–1932), a newly consolidated proletariat had worked so hard and so long that it had little time left to play or watch games; but by the second half of the decade, many workers had gained at least a measure of free time. Appropriate recreations had to be found to accommodate this relative increase in leisure, and spectator sports, as a modern, urban leisure practice, grew quickly.

The organizers of Soviet sports chose to establish a truly national league in order to accommodate the growing demand for sporting entertainments. This model had been developed by the highly successful professional soccer enterprises in capitalist countries, and it was the path now chosen by both soccer professionals and government organizers as the best way to develop the game in the USSR. It was also thought that by forming a truly all-Union soccer league, it would be possible to create yet another institution that could reinforce the less-than-firm sense of cohesion in the farflung multinational state that the Soviet Union had become.

By the mid-'thirties, the USSR had weathered the earliest and most wrenching phases of the industrialization drive. Millions of peasants had been uprooted from the countryside and thrown into factories, construction sites, and mines. Collectivization had caused famine, took countless lives, and left its survivors exhausted. Tens of thousands of workers had gone from the factory floor to positions of management and power. Within a few short years, much of the population found itself in new surroundings, performing strange and confusing tasks. The strenuous pace of these years cost an enormous human toll and left little time for games. All sports, both participant and spectator, went into eclipse during this hectic period.[1]

Once the tempo was moderated, however, it became possible to return to the playing fields. As a result, mass spectator sports were born in the USSR during the middle of the 'thirties, and soccer became a central part of this "more joyous" life. Soviet citizens were offered a variety of spectacles and festivals, sporting and non-sporting.[2] Some of them would be accepted with enthusiasm; others with indifference. Soccer had always been the favorite game of the working class, and the newly emerging proletarians of the 1930s, many of them fresh arrivals from the countryside, took to the game as eagerly as had their predecessors.

The Soviet sports system that the West came to know after the Second World War was put in place during the 1930s. Its emphasis on the many sports of the Olympic program, rather than on a relatively few commercially lucrative games, was also established during this period. This process would involve the creation and rewarding of indivdual heroes, and successful athletes were given special privileges. Their "work" was to act as heroes for the masses, a task that could not be achieved without specialization and professional training. The enthusiasm of the masses, acting on their own, was not sufficient to create this new elite. By the end of the decade, the Party leadership had learned this lesson In many fields of scientific, cultural, and economic endeavor. The leveling policies of earlier years were abandoned, to be replaced by highly stratified rewards, privileges, and salaries.

As the purges gathered momentum and the show trials grabbed the world's attention, the Soviet peoples were told that their life had become better. Sports were to be part of that improved life. In producing spectacles for the masses, the state had a clear set of utilitarian goals; primarily, the production of more efficient workers and fitter defenders of the nation. As in so many other areas of life, those aims were fulfilled only incompletely, as Soviet citizens accepted only some of the official meanings ascribed to sport. They did this by watching only the spectacles they chose to watch, and in doing so they behaved in ways that were not always envisioned by the organizers of those events.

The Creation of the Soccer League

As I have noted, both state and society in the mid-'thirties began to take a very different direction of development from the path followed during the period of "cultural revolution" that coincided with the First Five-Year Plan. In 1936, the new Stalin Constitution was published. It proclaimed, with little basis, the actual achievement of "socialism." The social engineering, icon-oclasm, and sheer ferocity of the First Five-Year Plan was abandoned. The strenuous efforts of these years had exacted an enormous human price, and it was now necessary to slow the pace of change. Moshe Lewin has described this shift, which had important consequences for the world of sports:

> After the early period of "proletarianization," two additional strategies were used to stabilize the body social: first, creation and consolidation of a network of supervisors in the form of hierarchies, apparatuses, and elites; and then from about 1934, the adoption of. . .a set of classical measures of social conservatism, law and order strategies complete with a nationalist revival, and efforts to instill values of discipline, patriotism, conformism, authority, and orderly careerism.[3]

In family policy, abortion was made illegal and divorce more difficult. Tra-ditional authority was restored in the classroom, and in a wide variety of cultural and scientific activities, trained professionals rather than underedu-cated workers were put back in charge. In return for not directly challenging the authority of the Party, educated and skilled elites were afforded lives of privilege and comfort; what Vera Dunham called the "Big Deal." This shift was, in turn, accompanied by a measure of professional autonomy for those who possessed the skills required by the nation.[4]

Sports and physical culture were not exempt from this process. On June 21, 1936, the All-Union Physical Culture Council was reorganized and ren-amed the All-Union Committee on Physical Culture and Sports Affairs. It was put under the direct authority of the Council of People's Commissars (*Sovnarkom*) and headed by I. I. Kharchenko, a protégé of Kosarev's. The old council was severely criticized for its poor organization of both mass and high-achievement sports.[5] Competitive sports were further legitimized and put in the hands of those who had devoted their lives to their practice. In the world of Soviet soccer, the game could now be put on a basis more closely resembling the practices of professional sports.

To be sure, official Soviet spokesmen still made the claim that sports in the USSR were strictly amateur, and it was not uncommon for those same sports authorities to complain often about excesses in the payment and privileges of players. Nor were these facts secrets. They were openly discussed in the press, and any serious fan was well aware of the paying of players. Yet, at this time, the people who had devoted their lives to soccer were given more control over the daily running of the game. It would now be possible to earn a living as a coach or player. This change, though, did not mean that soccer had achieved anything resembling true autonomy. Unlike most other sports, soccer was too attractive and too compelling for Party figures not to meddle with it. Soccer had become the passion of the Soviet working masses. Party leaders, many of them recently promoted from the factory floor, were not immune to its attractions.

Among soccer professionals, however, the decisive impulse for the reorganization of the sport came with the defeat of the Moscow selects by Racing Club de France on New Year's Day, 1936. Upon the return of the team to Moscow, Kosarev called a meeting of the central committee of the Komsomol to discuss the reasons for the loss. While a close defeat away from home by one of Europe's strongest club teams was no cause for shame, the soccer professionals at the meeting seized the occasion to call for reorganization. Nikolai Starostin proposed a course that had been discussed for some time. He told Kosarev, "We are stewing in our own juices."[6] The present system retarded the growth of soccer by limiting the opportunities for young players to improve themeselves against top competition. There was much to learn from "bourgeois" soccer. Even the "W" system was no longer dismissed.

The old format of competition was the cause of the presumed stagnation. Select teams everywhere, were they city or national, had a tendency to pick the same stars over and over, making it difficult for young players to develop. As select teams did not practice together on a regular basis, there was little opportunity for the young to impress coaches. In the West, new stars could emerge in domestic league competition. Teams that practiced together on a daily basis could more easily judge the development of talent and decide the moment to make changes in lineups; but without competition for places on teams, the development of a sport could stagnate. This was Starostin's main point, and it was broadly supported.[7]

The answer to this problem was a league organized along the lines developed by Western professionals. The championship was now to be contested by club teams, sponsored by the various sports societies in the main cities. The season would stretch out over the summer, as teams played each other in a regularly scheduled pattern. This change would provide a stimulus for the players and entertainment for the populace. *Krasnyi sport* foresaw "a huge interest in the games on the part of the broadest masses of the workers.''[8] This prediction proved fully correct, and Soviet soccer enjoyed its second birth in 1936, a date that also marks the true beginning of professional spectator sports in the USSR. Because of the irregularity of their organization and the episodic character of their important moments, all sports in the USSR before 1936 did not fit the definition of spectator sports I have advanced here. The occasional sporting spectacle now gave way to a regular diet of spectator sports.

In addition to the first league season, which was limited to seven top club teams, a cup competition was organized the same year. This practice, too, had become common in the West. National cups are usually open to any regularly registered team, regardless of its level. Over the course of the season, clubs would play an elimination tournament, leading to an annual final in the capital. One of the most attractive aspects of these competitions could come in the early rounds, when a famous team visited a smaller town to play the local side. These games were especially important in the Soviet Union for propagandizing the sport outside the major cities that had previously been the main centers of the game. Despite the swift, often chaotic, industrialization and urbanization of these years, sports outside urban areas were still weakly developed, and cup games were an excellent advertisement for soccer. While the league afforded an opportunity for the USSR's best players to hone their skills, the cup competition played a crucial role in expanding the mass base of the sport.[9]

Despite the hope engendered by the new form, soccer's organizers would continually struggle to find an optimal structure and schedule. The number of teams allowed to compete at the first-division level (called ''Group A'') changed every year, and there were constant disputes about proper and fair ways to arrange the schedule. The lower divisions were equally confused. Coordinating the demands of the league with those of the cup often proved troublesome, and it was not uncommon for the dates of matches to be changed with minimal notice. In fact, these problems bedeviled Soviet soccer throughout its history. In a vast land, with a still-inadequate railroad network, it was by no means a given that teams would show up for scheduled games, and when both teams appeared, the referees often were missing.[10]

Soccer in the late 'thirties was dominated by the rivalry of the two great Moscow sides, Dinamo and Spartak. Sponsored by the Ministry of Interior, Dinamo was known for its precise and technical game, which featured constant running and long passing. Spartak, supported by the wealthy *Promkooperatsia,* featured a more unpredictable and improvisatory style that stressed ball control and precise passing. These images—of Dinamo's rationalism and Spartak's romanticism—heightened the rivalry. Whether accurately or inaccurately, Soviet fans continued to hold to these images throughout the history of both clubs.[11] In 1939, after Lavrenti Beria assumed the leadership of the secret police, this rivalry took on an especially malevolent cast. An average soccer-player during his youth in Georgia, Beria wished to see the Dinamo teams, sponsored as they were by the Ministry of Interior, dominate the league, but Spartak and the Starostin brothers too often stood in his way. Eventually he would find decidedly nonsporting means to eliminate his rivals.

Among the Moscow teams, only the Central House of the Red Army (*TsDKA*), with its great star, the striker Grigory Fedotov, could challenge the Big Two. The Lokomotiv Society, representing transport workers; the Torpedo Society, sponsored by the ZIS automobile factory; and *Krylia sovetov,* from the aviation industry also fielded respectable teams that attracted smaller but loyal followings of Moscow fans. Outside the capital, *Dinamo Tblisi,* with its star Boris Paichadze, established itself as a power. *Dinamo Kiev* also enjoyed success with such players as Iosif Lifshits, Ivan Kuz'menko, and Boris Greber. *Traktor* of Stalingrad, *Selmash* of Kharkov, and *Stakhanovets* of Stalino were but a few of the other successful sides from the periphery.[12]

Both the league and the cup competitions proved attractive to the public, and soccer quickly acquired an even more sizable mass following. In 1938, first-division games averaged crowds of 19,000, and the next year ten million attended soccer at all levels of competition. Cup finals and meetings between Spartak and Dinamo could overflow Dinamo Stadium in Moscow, but less important games drew considerably smaller crowds. As few as five thousand Muscovites might watch Central Army take on Torpedo.[13] Odessa, Leningrad, Kiev, and Tblisi were hotbeds of soccer interest, and each town had a sizable stadium with a capacity of between twenty and forty thousand.

In general, attendance levels rose and fell in the same way they did everywhere else in the world. Leading Moscow teams drew the largest crowds when they played each other. They were also responsible for the biggest gates when they played in the provinces. Matches between weaker teams, whether in Moscow or the periphery, drew comparatively minuscule audiences of between one and five thousand. Soccer had become a mass phenomenon, but only its best attractions proved capable of filling arenas. There was still considerable room for growth, especially outside Moscow and Leningrad. Nevertheless, the game had found a place as one of the public's favorite amusements, and, as would prove true in other fields of popular culture, soccer's often-raffish public did not always take to heart the lessons the state sought to inculcate through sports.

The establishment in 1934 of the artistic doctrine known as Socialist Realism constricted the kinds of movies, art, literature, theater, and music that could be presented. The men and women who made products of mass culture now had to conform to an increasingly strict censorship. Many careers were ended and lives ruined. These tragedies did not mean, however, that Soviet audiences blindly accepted Stalinism's worst cultural excesses. Richard Taylor and Denise Youngblood have demonstrated that didactic films continued, more often than not, to fail to find ticket-buyers, while musical comedies and melodramas, foreign and Soviet, won large audiences.[14] In a somewhat different vein, Frederick Starr has shown how jazz and jazz-influenced popular music survived throughout this era, despite repression and severe official criticism.[15]

While not all official mass culture was didactic and formulaic, much of it was.[16] By comparison, soccer far more consistently provided a relatively honest performance that afforded its fans excitement and emotional release. In the midst of the fear of the purge period, soccer, unlike much art, was able to retain the moral core of its human attractiveness. Reminiscing on this phenomenon a half century later, Nikolai Starostin remarked: "Football was separated from all that was taking place around it. It was in some way not under the authorities, a healthy thought for a generation of sinners.... For the majority, football was the only, sometimes the last, possible hope for maintaining in one's soul some small piece of humane feeling and humanity."[17] This is not to say that soccer was an oasis of the apolitical. The Party always sought to use so popular a phenomenon for its own ends. One could even say that there was such a thing as a "socialist realist" approach to the game that would stress the official values the state wanted to teach through sports. Nevertheless, the attractions of the game were so great and its fundamental spontaneity so inescapable that the state never fully mobilized it as a tool of dominance and control.

While domestic competition had established a sizable audience, international matches proved to be the biggest attraction and the best advertisement for the game. In 1936, the Turks made their last appearance in Moscow before the war, and Dinamo Moscow played several games in Czechoslovakia. But the turning point for Soviet soccer came the next summer. At the height of the Spanish Civil War, an all-star team of Basque players, drawn from the leading clubs of Spain, toured Europe to raise funds for the Republican cause.[18] This was an extremely strong side. All of its players had at one time been Spanish internationals, and the center-forward, Langarra, was one of the greatest players in all of Europe.[19] While they were in Poland, the Basques agreed to come to the USSR as a gesture of solidarity and thanks for Soviet support of the Republicans in the Civil War.

The Basques arrived in Moscow on June 16, 1937, and were greeted by a huge crowd at the Bielorusskii train station. Their games were, in *Izvestia*'s words, "the most eagerly awaited matches ever to be seen in Moscow." The Basques were scheduled to play two games in Moscow (against Lokomotiv and Dinamo) and then tour Leningrad, Kiev, Tblisi, and Minsk. Two million ticket requests flooded in for the Moscow games, which were broadcast throughout the nation. On June 24 the Basques defeated Lokomotiv 5–1, prompting *Izvestia* to remark, "our fields have never seen a team of such high class."[20] Two days later, 90,000 overflowed Dinamo Stadium to see the Basques defeat Dinamo Moscow 2–1. They won easily in Kiev, Tblisi, and Minsk, and tied the Leningrad selects 2–2.

Everywhere they played, the Basques provoked great excitement and admiration, but the Soviet hosts wanted one last chance for a victory. Despite their fatigue, the Basques agreed to two more games in Moscow, one against Dinamo and the other against Spartak, which mysteriously had not been included in the original list of opponents. Following a practice that would become standard in the USSR's international games, both Moscow sides were strengthened by players from other teams. Spartak, in particular, was joined by Central Army's Fedotov. Dinamo was defeated 7–4, and the defense of the honor of Soviet soccer was left to Spartak. No chances were taken. The referee, Ivan Kosmachev, was an official of the Spartak Society. With the score tied 2–2, he awarded Spartak a disputed penalty. Even the Soviet fans booed the call. Spartak converted, while the Basques protested. The match soon got very rough, and the Basques, tired from a long tour and having nothing left to prove, decided to pack it in. They eventually lost 6–2.[21]

The victory gave an enormous boost to Spartak's popularity, and many longtime fans of the team still link their love of Spartak to the great victory over the Basques.[22] This was the first defeat of a first-class professional team by any Soviet side. The honor had gone to Spartak and not Dinamo. This fact did not sit well with Dinamo's patron, Lavrenti Beria, and other powerful police figures. Kosmachev was banned from refereeing ever again, an act that Starostin, perhaps self-servingly, attributes to the jealousy of the Dinamo society and their supporters in the secret police.[23] This kind of bureaucratic interference with soccer was by no means exceptional. The sport had become so popular that the Party could not ignore it. Yet the meddling of powerful figures did not involve the rigid control of the political meanings and ideological messages of soccer. Rather, Party officials were like children, unable to tear themselves away from a sweet but far too rich cake. They, too, loved soccer, and many chose to exhibit their power by interfering in the work of coaches, players, and officials.

Every Soviet stadium had its "government loge," and teams knew that it was necessary to cater to this privileged element. During the late 1930s, Spartak regularly gave out a thousand tickets per game. Many went to members of the Central Committee; others were given to important figures in the Moscow City Soviet.[24] For some members of the *apparat,* good seats were not enough. They named and dismissed coaches and sought to dictate team lineups, actions that were deeply resented by soccer professionals. Alexander

Starostin, who had been named the president of the soccer section of the Committee for Physical Culture and Sport, decried meddling by state and Party officials at a 1938 public meeting. He said the initiative of those who played and coached the game should be the determining force in deciding soccer matters and complained that the Sport Committee ignored professionals in determining policy.[25]

The next year, Starostin would find out just how blatant state interference could be. Spartak defeated Beria's favorite team, Dinamo Tblisi, 1–0 on a disputed goal in the cup semi-final. Two weeks later, Spartak defeated Stalinets of Leningrad 3–1 before 70,000 fans to take the cup. Soon thereafter, the Party Central Committee ordered Spartak to replay the semifinal against Dinamo Tblisi, even though the final had already been played. Nikolai Starostin used all his influence with friends in high places. He visited a member of the Central Committee, who told him the replay was ordered personally by Stalin's close associate Andrei Zhdanov. There was nothing to be done, and the first semifinal game in the history of soccer to be held *after* a final actually took place. Despite the machinations, Spartak did manage to win 3–2 and keep the cup.[26]

While some forms of interference were absurd, others were far deadlier. The leadership of the sports world did not escape the purges of the late 'thirties. Athletes, including even European record holders like the high jumper Nikolai Kovtun, were arrested in the hundreds. Soccer players were not immune, and Viktor Strepikheev, a former hockey star and head of the *Burevestnik* sports society was arrested, along with Viktor Riabokon, president of the Lokomotiv Society. Spartak came under special suspicion when Kazimir Vasilevskii, the head of its sponsor, *Promkooperatsia,* was arrested in 1939. Kosarev's arrest and execution similarly threatened Spartak. I. I. Kharchenko also was removed from the head of the sports committee, arrested, and executed.[27] In 1939, Beria attempted to have the Starostin brothers arrested, but Nikolai Starostin's daughter attended the same school as the daughter of Viacheslav Molotov, then the Prime Minister. The girls were best friends, and Molotov refused to sign the arrest order.[28]

Beria had accused the Spartak Society of running a professional sports operation along bourgeois lines, mishandling funds, and neglecting mass sports for the support of champions. While these activities can hardly be called capital crimes, it must be said that there was an element of truth to the complaints. In 1939, Beria called in one of Dinamo's coaches and demanded to know why Spartak had become more successful than Dinamo. The coach replied, ''Spartak pays more.'' This was true. Starostin had gotten the assent of Anastas Mikoian, by then a member of the Politburo, who had signed an order permitting Spartak to pay its players a monthly ''stipend'' of eighty rubles (for that period a very generous amount). This sum supplemented the players' salaries, which were also paid by the society for their work as "instructors."[29]

This situation was by no means exceptional. The Dinamo coach did not say Spartak paid while others did not pay, only that Spartak paid more. At the very minimum, players became semiprofessional once the league was organized. The top clubs were called "demonstration" (*pokazatel'nye*) teams and were distinguished in the press from "amateur" (*liubitel'skye*) teams. Newspapers consistently made this distinction, despite official claims that all Soviet sports were strictly amateur. Had the professionalism of the top teams been a special secret, one would not have expected the press to call lower-level teams "amateur," since all teams were supposedly amateur. For these collectives, the term "mass" (*massovoi*) would have been more precise, but it was rarely used in this context.[30]

Whether or not the public was fully aware of the payment of players, those within the sport knew full well what had become standard practice. In 1990, Evgenii Eliseev, a longtime coach and a player for Dinamo Moscow in the late 'thirties, recalled:

> With the very first league season of the USSR among club teams, players, in fact, became professionals. They received a wage for their labor. When, in the spring of 1936, I turned up as a player for Moscow Dinamo, I was registered as an instructor of physical culture [for the Dinamo Society], and for the first time in my life began to receive money for playing football. This kind of system existed in both army and trade union teams. . . . [31]

As James Riordan has shown, these practices were widespread and fully in keeping with the broader social phenomenon of what he has called "elite creation."[32] Soviet society was becoming deeply hierarchical, and the sports world was no exception. Cash prizes were not uncommon for competitions at lower levels, and sums as large as two hundred thousand rubles went to winning sports societies at various Spartakiads.[33]

The best-known soccer teams were able to make additional money by staging "comradely," i.e., exhibition, games outside the regular schedule.[34] Most often, one of the teams from the first division would play in a smaller city against the local side. The teams would agree to play "honestly," without unnecessary roughness, and an interesting match was usually provided for small-town fans who filled the stadium to see the stars of the game. A large portion of the gate receipts would not make their way into the official financial records for the game. Local courts, the NKVD, and police were all paid to look the other way. The big-city club would take the bulk of the money, which was then divided among the players.[35]

In 1936, *Krasnyi sport* related the story of the lower-division Lokomotiv Club of Sverdlovsk. The team's players had read of the profitable barnstorming tours of Europe regularly taken by the English national team. The Lokomotiv players, who dubbed themselves "Anglomaniacs," decided to do the same, organizing exhibitions with teams in Cheliabinsk and Perm. They did this, however, without the permission of the regional (*oblast'*) sports committee. They lost both games but made 1,500 rubles. The head of the Lokomotiv Society in Sverdlovsk was incensed to learn of the unauthorized tour. He told the players that the society took very good care of them, feeding them, housing them, and giving them "easy jobs." Some of the players, he said, "don't work at all." He also noted with displeasure the fact that the team had lost both games. One of the players replied that English professionals also did not have "real" jobs, to which the head of the society responded, "English players do not lose."[36]

Press accounts of the payment of players were common, although it must be said that no reporter approved of the custom. Thus, it is revealing that newspaper coverage of a 1940 congress of first-division players, coaches, and officials noted, without comment, demands for "higher wages" made by the players.[37] While it is hardly shocking to the present-day reader that such practices went on, it is quite surprising that so little was done to keep these things a secret. Soccer had become a full-time occupation. Teams came to spend as much as two months in southern towns for preseason training. The press reported these preparations in considerable detail. Clearly, these time demands, of which spring training was only one, made the holding of a regular job at best a formality.[38]

In 1937, Kosarev criticized the practice of hiring high-performance athletes as "instructors" who taught no one. Many of the societies spent far more on their soccer teams than on all other activities combined. The search for stars, he complained, led to a neglect of mass sports. "The masters of sport and champions are beyond any measures, and the mass of sportsmen is often forgotten." Kharchenko denounced the societies who sought out stars by offering to pay living expenses, while giving them "easy work or no work at all." In a 1936 speech, Kharchenko noted one factory in the city of Gorky that was offering soccer players four hundred rubles a month, plus a no-show job. "As soon as an athlete demonstrates a good result," complained Kharchenko elsewhere, "he becomes the object of buying and selling."[39]

Sports "businessmen" roamed the country in search of good soccer players. Athletes moved from team to team looking for better deals, and outside the big cities, it was rare for a team to start many locally trained youngsters. The sports societies were supposed to develop their own talent in special schools and programs that were to be made available to local youths. The search for success however, often overrode a society's sense of responsibility to its rank and file membership. Officials of the sport committee denounced the easy transfer of players. Loyalty to the collective was weakened by the phenomenon of stars' pursuing their individual ends. The press often criticized Western professional soccer for turning players into commodities, but a similar buying and selling emerged in the USSR even before the establishment of the soccer league.[40] The rules governing the movement of players remained extremely murky throughout Soviet history. They were the subject of constant discussion among professionals and in the press. Only the worst excesses were reported, but the truth was always difficult to learn.

Of all the societies involved in high-performance sports, especially soccer, Spartak was most often accused of fostering the practices of professionalism. In 1936, the Starostins and several other society officials were taken to court for misuse of funds and other improprieties. They were later accused of ignoring mass work and using the considerable means of the *Promkoop-eratsia* to purchase topflight athletes in a wide range of sports. These accusations would be repeated throughout the late 'thirties. While most of the charges would be dismissed when they went to trial, the accusation of running a bourgeois, professional sports operation would not go away. Eventually it became the basis for Beria's case against the Starostins, which led to their arrest in 1942.[41]

The hypocrisy of professionalism during this era was of a very different order than it would assume after the war. The various fig leaves used to disguise these practices gave something of a tinge of semiprofessionalism, rather than complete professionalism, to big-time soccer. To paraphrase a standard Soviet joke, the players at least had to *pretend* to work. Perhaps it is best to say that they were paid athletes rather than professional sportsmen in the full capitalist sense. Nevertheless, these practices did clash with offical claims that "bourgeois" professional sports did not exist in the USSR.

It is important, therefore, to remember that during the pre-war years it was less necessary to appear to be amateur. The Soviets were not part of the Olympic movement. They had rejected the aristocratic amateurism of the Games, refusing to participate. There was little need to twist reality to comply with prevailing international rules of eligibility. The participation of Soviet athletes in the equally amateur workers' international sport movement did not raise this issue. Most events Soviets took part in were controlled by their own Red Sport International, and by 1937 at Antwerp, the good feeling of the Popular Front years did not lead to much criticism when Soviet representatives such as the Spartak soccer team easily won their competitions. For these reasons, there was less need to be secretive about the payment of athletes. Party officials may not have been pleased by the phenomena engendered by big-time sport, but before the war, they had less need to hide them.

The rise in playing standards and the greater attendance at games did not, however, have a positive effect on players' behavior. If anything, the greater importance of soccer led to a decline in sportsmanship. The president of the Moscow college of soccer referees lamented the situation: ''Many players have introduced elements of crudeness and hooliganism into the game. To our shame, one often confronts these facts among players of the top teams who should be examples of irreproachable play.''[42] *Krasnyi sport* argued that ''Soviet soccer players must be the best in the world not only technically, but they should be models of discipline, culture, and high moral values. . . . Soccer is a wonderful way of teaching strength, dexterity, endurance, courage, and persistence. . . . However, many players are far from having an awareness of their duties and responsibilities.''[43]

After the first two months of the inaugural 1936 season, the Football Section's disciplinary committee was required to deal with forty-three separate incidents of ''hooliganism.'' It was not uncommon for players to kick an injured opponent who was lying on the ground in pain, and cursing referees was in no way exceptional.[44] Not all of this disorderliness was the fault of the players. Standards of refereeing were far from uniformly high. It was not uncommon for arbiters to lose control of matches, and often the referees, rather than the players, received suspensions. Teams were allowed to object to the naming of a particular referee. Before one 1939 game between Spartak and Central Army, eight candidates were rejected before the teams could agree on a referee. As *Izvestia* remarked, this situation did little to contribute to the authority of those whose task it was to control player behavior.[45]

During the late 'thirties it became common for the press and sports officials to attribute this poor behavior to a lack of ''political education.'' Insufficient political training, they said, contributed to the low cultural level of most players, leading to violent play and to poor results on the field, as well. When Dinamo Odessa plunged from the ranks of strong teams in 1939, *Krasnyi sport* attributed their decline to a lack of discipline and collectiveness caused by the collapse of educational work. Most teams had Komsomol cells, and one player was designated a ''political guide'' (*politruk*). In some cases, this education bordered on the simultaneously comical and sinister. Players of Selmash of Kharkov reported that their successes were the result of ''deep study'' of the notoriously falsified *Short Course of the History of the Communist Party*. Nikolai Starostin would claim that Spartak's disciplined behavior was the result of cultural education, including attendance at plays, museums, and lectures.[46] In fact, Spartak's players were as capable as any others of dirty play, and one can only speculate that this political and cultural training was window-dressing, given its minimal impact on ''hooliganism'' on the field.

If the players did not always approach the task of playing soccer with official values in mind, the same may be said of the fans who watched the games. Their love of the sport and the way they consumed it closely paralleled the experience of their counterparts in capitalist countries. Fans came to adopt favorite teams. Stars emerged who were heroes to the public. Fathers took their sons to games, as the sport became an important form of male socialization. Souvenirs were collected, and discussing soccer news with friends became a favorite leisure activity. More and more games were broadcast over the radio as millions listened. In the increasingly anomic and crowded world of the new Soviet cities, with so many recent emigrants from the countryside, a fan could attend a game and find an immediate sense of community. *Krasnyi sport* described the phenomenon: "You go to the stadium and sit in the stands and it seems as if you have known the person sitting next to you from childhood. You understand each other with a word."[47] This kind of spectating was not, by itself, necessarily a welcome phenomenon. The raw, potentially violent emotions often released by soccer were in direct contradiction to the values the state sought to ascribe to sport. For the authorities, the Soviet fan had to be different:

> Soviet lovers of football demonstrate an example of authentic culture by maintaining their objectivity from the beginning to the end of the match. The fan [*bolel'shchik*] of Spartak does not forgive his favorites for bad play just as the fan of Dinamo will not compromise with the errors of his team. The Soviet student of the game, whether he is for one or another team, is above all a patriot of Soviet football. Football in the Soviet Union is truly a people's game. This is why we have achieved such successes in this sport.[48]

Unfortunately, not all spectators fit this ideal type. Another article described the "*profany*" who were "hypnotized by the sensation and fashionability of the events inflaming the stands." On the days of big games, public order was not easily maintained. Crowds overflowed subways and trams. Pushing and shoving in disorderly queues were common.[49] Nor was it always clear that the demonstration effect of big-time soccer inspired those who watched to exercise themselves.

Passive spectatorship had its dangers, which were lovingly mocked by the famed satirists Ilf and Petrov. They described what it was like to be a soccer fan—going to games, talking about them with friends, and rooting for favorite teams and stars. They also denied that soccer fans were not fit. "The person who attends a soccer game," they said, "is able to do all the exercises for his GTO [physical fitness] badge." The exercises included:

1. Running for trolleys
2. Jumping onto moving subway cars
3. Seventeen rounds of boxing outside the stadium
4. Lifting heavy objects (like a wife or child)
5. Military swimming (sitting two hours outdoors in the rain without an umbrella)

Finally, they concluded, "there is only one thing the football fan cannot do— play football."[50]

In fact, it was difficult for spectators to act in an orderly manner when the atmosphere at the stadiums did not support such behavior. *Krasnyi sport* lamented in 1937, "to serve those watching in a cultured manner and give them maximum confort has not, up to now, been one of the first concerns of stadium directors." Most of the time only a few box office windows were open. "Gloomy and crude people" controlled the entrances. There were no ushers to show people to their seats; no guides or plans to help the fans find their places on their own: "If you try to get something to eat during half-time you stumble over a steeplechase of people and when you actually get to the buffet there is a long line and you risk missing the second half."[51] Most stadiums lacked scoreboards. Public address systems were equally rare. Programs were not usually available, and the few that were printed provided only minimal information. Cramped conditions and surly service did not contribute to public order. Fans often threw bottles and other objects on fields. At other times, they invaded the playing surface. Full-scale riots were rare, but some did occur. After one particularly violent disorder at a 1937 match in Leningrad, the authorities instituted the practice of ringing the field with soldiers. This approach to crowd control continued to the end of the Soviet period, despite the fact that at many matches soldiers outnumbered spectators.[52]

Clearly soccer's appeal went beyond the rational and utilitarian. The game excited emotions that were not always healthy, even if they were fully human. Only rarely did the press seek to illuminate soccer's irrational attractions. Evgenii Kriger's 1939 article in *Izvestia,* entitled "The Magical Sphere," was one of very few exceptions to this rule: "Thousands of people, regardless of sex, age or occupation, get up out of their places and head in one direction. Even those citizens who are distinguished by their seriousness and their spiritual equanimity begin to move around and gesticulate wildly under the influence of the soccer ball."[53]

The working class had found in soccer a spectacle that provided a satisfying emotional release and the possibility of identifying with heroes and teams. The creation of a mass-culture industry to entertain the citizenry was fully consistent with the conservative social and cultural policies of the late 'thirties. Providing a less-than-fully-politicized form of diversion from the problems of the moment was but one of the state's goals in this era. The authorities also sought to use sports as a tool for inculcating discipline, obedience, and public order. Of all games, however, soccer, with its potential for irrationality and romanticism, was perhaps least suited to this task. At the same time, that very irrationality and romanticism explain the sport's tremendous popularity. By the end of the decade, soccer in the USSR had taken on many of the characteristics of professional sports in the West. It was something that the Soviet public very much wanted and the state knew it had to provide, but in consuming this particular spectator sport, Soviet citizens ascribed to it very different meanings than did those who produced and supported it.

Other Sports—The Search for an Audience, 1917–1941

Before the war, only soccer achieved mass acceptance with the Soviet public. Quite a few sports won some public acceptance, but difficult material roadblocks hampered their search for an audience. During the prewar period, there were no indoor arenas with more than two thousand seats. As a result, most sports could only hope to attract large numbers of fans during the summer, while winter sports had to be held outdoors in often-numbing cold. Despite this problem, Soviet fans came to watch a variety of games other than soccer, but they did not do so in huge numbers.

Boxing and wrestling, with their ties to the great and less-than-noble Russian tradition of the circus, always had a sizable public. Professional boxing was a significant part of the "fast life" of the Soviet 'twenties, and bouts were usually held in theaters and circuses. National and city amateur championships also took place in these years, and intercity team competitons could fill these smallish arenas. As everywhere, inconsistent judging was common, and unpopular results touched off disorders. There was also considerable international competition. Delegations of boxers from France and Norway toured the USSR in 1935 and 1937, while Soviet journalists kept their readers up on the Western professional scene. *Izvestia,* for example, reported with satisfaction the triumph of the "Negro boxer, Joe Louis" over the German, Max Schmeling, a victory that dealt a blow to Schmeling's "fascist" supporters in America.[54]

The circus also kept alive the tradition of professionalism in wrestling. The sport had a following throughout the USSR, but it was especially popular in the Caucasus and Central Asia. Competitions usually took place in small gymnasiums, but as late as 1939, professionals were meeting amateurs in a special program held at the circus in Gorky Park.[55] The audiences at these events were fairly rough-and-ready, as were the wrestlers. *Krasnyi sport* reported that the 1938 Ukrainian championship held in Odessa broke down into a brawl between "drunken" wrestlers from Kiev and the home crowd.

Basketball had a limited public. Basically it was known as a "student" sport, with little acceptance throughout the broad ranks of the working class. It was also widely played, but little-watched, in the Red Army. The game was first seen in Petersburg in 1906, and the first Soviet championship took place in 1923. All-star teams from the major cities contested the title that year and again in 1924 and 1928. The national championship then lapsed, to be revived in 1934, after which it was held annually before the war, changing in 1937 to a competition of club teams rather than city selects. Most games took place in small halls, and crowds of more than a thousand were rare. Along with Moscow, Leningrad and Tblisi had strong basketball traditions.[56]

The sport received a boost in 1939 when the USSR forcibly annexed the three Baltic nations of Latvia, Lithuania, and Estonia. After World War I, the YMCA, under whose aegis the game had been invented, introduced basketball in Protestant Latvia and Estonia. Throughout the 1920s and into the 1930s, both republics regularly beat Catholic Lithuania. After the Berlin Olympics in 1936, however, the captain of the victorious American team, Frank Lubin, by nationality a Lithuanian, took a vacation with his family in then-independent Lithuania. While there, his sister-in-law broke her leg. During her convalescence, Lubin (''Pranas Lubinas'' in Lithuanian) began to coach the game. The next year, several Lithuanian-Americans were invited to play for the national team, which went on to win the European championship in 1937 and again in 1939. Basketball instantly became the number one sport in this small nation, which already had a proud tradition in many other sports, especially soccer, track and field, and Canadian-style ice hockey. The rivalry with Estonia and Latvia, which were both still strong in basketball, continued even after these nations fell under Soviet dominance, and over the years, the Baltic gave the Soviets many of their greatest players and coaches. Before the war, it was the one region of the USSR where basketball attracted crowds of several thousand.[57]

Tennis and volleyball had publics roughly similar to basketball's. Gymnastics, weightlifting, and speed skating also occasionally attracted sizable crowds. During these years, there were also several attempts to introduce baseball. The first games were played in Leningrad during 1928 at the Lenin Institute of Physical Culture. The opposing teams were English students on one side and Koreans on the other.[58] During the 'thirties many American Communists came to the USSR, either as émigrés or as temporary participants in what they thought was the construction of socialism. They brought baseball with them. In 1935, the foreign workers at Moscow's Gorky Auto Plant took on a team of other foreigners. Baseball was also played in Minsk and Karelia. The press praised baseball's grace and complexity, but the game failed to win a wide audience. One of the central problems was a lack of equipment, but the sporting authorities never opposed the game simply because of its American origin.[59]

In fact, only two sports could be said to approach the category of mass spectator pastimes. These were Russian hockey, played outdoors in the winter, and track and field, the favorite sport of the authorities. Both hockey and track were played by women as well as men, but the two sports were very different.[60] Hockey was often called "winter football," and many of soccer's greatest stars played hockey in the off-season. Hockey also exhibited many of the negative characteristics associated with soccer. Track, on the other hand, was seen as a "cultured" sport, highly technical, engaged in throughout Europe by "university" people, rather than the working class.

Russian hockey had a relatively short season. In the absence of any capacity to make artificial ice, cold weather was necessary. In Moscow, games usually began in early December and ended early in March. Hockey had gone into eclipse during the Civil War and reemerged only in 1923. Before 1936, club teams contested city championships, and select city teams competed for a national title, which was not contested every year. That year, when soccer reorganized, so did hockey. A cup competition was held, and club teams from various cities also played each other. Rather than travel for home and away games, several teams were gathered in a single city to play a series of matches. These mini-tournaments did not entirely replace either of the older structures of competition, especially the city championships.[61]

The same sports societies that dominated soccer fielded the leading hockey teams. Dinamo, Spartak, Central Army, Metallurg, Krylia Sovetov, and Lokomotiv were just a few of the stronger clubs, all of which supported women's teams as well. On the rare days with good weather, as many as thirty thousand might attend a game between top teams at Moscow's Dinamo Stadium or at Lenin Stadium in Leningrad, but these gates were extremely rare. If five thousand showed up for a match, organizers would be well satisfied, and crowds of a thousand or less were the norm for run-of-the-mill games.[62]

Russian hockey could get every bit as rough as soccer, and dirty play and "uncultured deportment" were common. Players might deliberately strike each other in the face with their sticks or engage in other acts of violence. Female hockey players also engaged in "crude play," and several had to be disqualified each season. Referees were constantly assaulted verbally. In some cases, the players' complaints were justified, especially when referees refused to postpone games despite temperatures as low as minus thirty-five degrees Centigrade. Bad player behavior inevitably had its effect on spectators, who could also get unruly, although far less often than in soccer. By 1940, however, the situation had become so serious that the Central Committee of the Komsomol issued a resolution demanding that the sports societies restrain their players from "rough play, lack of discipline, and the cursing of referees."[63]

Because hockey attracted smaller audiences, the impulse toward professionalism was far weaker than in soccer. Nevertheless, there was competition for the best players, and the phenomenon of "buying and selling" did go on in the sport. One celebrated incident occurred in Minsk during 1940. A "representative" of Moscow's Krylia Sovetov appeared in Minsk with the aim of attracting several players from the local Spartak team. When one of Spartak's players did not appear for practice, the Minsk coach sent out a search party, which soon found the player, utterly drunk, in the company of Krylia Sovetov's agent. They were at the train station, preparing to leave for Moscow. According to press accounts, a "pitched battle" took place over the pliable body of the player, whom Spartak managed physically to prevent from leaving.[64]

While "bandy," as it was called, was played in several Scandinavian countries, the Soviets were well aware that the Canadian version of the game was far more popular throughout the rest of the world. The Canadian team had created a sensation at the 1928 Winter Olympics in St. Moritz. As a result, hockey soon became popular in much of Western Europe, especially England and France, where it was played largely by Canadians.[65] In 1932, a German workers' team came to Moscow. They played and won several games against hastily organized local teams, one of which was composed of members from TsDKA's Russian hockey team.[66] Canadian hockey was then played in institutes of physical culture during the 'thirties, and throughout this period, many sports figures called for its adoption. In the press the game was always described positively as "intense and graceful," a "compelling spectacle that would interest both athletes and spectators."[67]

In December 1935 when the Moscow select soccer team was in Paris to play Racing, they took in a hockey game. The event had a particlarly strong impact on Mikhail Iakushin, who also played Russian hockey for Dinamo.[68] On December 28, 1935, he wrote in his diary, "The game was very interesting. How would we do against these teams? Surely we would lose. But if we were to cultivate Canadian hockey, we would soon reach the level of the European teams."[69] Toward the end of the decade, calls for the introduction of Canadian hockey became more frequent. Plans were drawn up for an intercity tournament in 1939, but the event never took place.[70] The forced annexation of the Baltic states then added several capable teams and players who had long practiced this version of the sport. Had the war not intervened, there probably would have been a Canadian hockey season in the winter of 1941–1942.

The sport that best fit official ideals, though, was track and field. Track's rationalism contrasted with the potentially dangerous romanticism of soccer. The highly technical nature of track made it seem more consistent than soccer with the goals of a "scientific" version of socialism. The precise measurement of time, distance, and height revealed success or failure just as production statistics had come to demonstrate the success or failure of "socialist construction.'' Track and field, a sport of specialists, could be seen as the sporting correlate of the newly empowered technical specialists who grew so swiftly in numbers during the late 'thirties. In Europe, track was a sport of the educated rather than the working class. It was practiced and watched with the kind of refined and "cultured" style that Soviet sport authorities wished to inculcate in their athletes and fans. Finally, the fundamental skills of track and field were closely tied to military fitness. In 1940, *Izvestia* noted: "It is one of the most basic of the applied-military forms of physical culture and sport. Walking, running, jumping, and throwing all develop endurance, strength, and speed, i.e., the basic qualities that are needed by every Soviet citizen in labor and in the defense of our great homeland.''[71] For all these reasons, track, not soccer, was the one sport that the state sought to popularize among the Soviet masses. To stretch an analogy, we could call track a "socialist realist" sport, while soccer was a sports correlate of the musical comedies and melodramas that attracted the bulk of the Soviet film audience.

As a sign of this emphasis, more track athletes were designated with the official title of "master of sport" than were soccer players. Track and field became the showcase of the Olympic Games, and it also was the most publicized element of the Spartakiad program. Track received as much attention as soccer in the Soviet press, despite the fact that far more people watched soccer. Important competitions were well publicized, but only the most compelling events attracted large crowds. Track stars became highly visible heroes whose exploits were detailed in the press. The pole vaulter Nikolai Ozolin, the high jumper Nikolai Kovtun, and the sprinter Maria Shamanova were three particularly famous figures, but the leading track athletes of the 'thirties were Serafim and Georgii Znamensky, middle-distance runners who between them held every Soviet record between 800 and 10,000 meters. They were extensively publicized heroes who traveled widely and were lionized by the workers' sports international wherever they went. While the vast majority of Soviet performances were well below world-class levels, Ozolin, Shamanova, Kovtun, and the Znamenskii brothers compared favorably with the best athletes in Europe. They toured abroad often, particularly in France, and always played the role of ideal spokesmen for the state.[72]

For all the official support of track and field, it only succeeded in finding a limited audience. During this period, the sport had attracted large crowds throughout Europe, but the Soviet fan proved resistant to its attractions. In 1936, *Krasnyi sport* ran an article entitled "Why Are There No Spectators?" They lamented, "Tens of thousands of spectators congregate for an interesting soccer match, but for a track meet, just a few hundred. Why is this so? Is track and field really less interesting? Of course not. In America [and Europe] fans storm the box office for a track meet. . . . Why in the Soviet Union are there so few spectators at track meets?''[73] For some, the Soviet public was insufficiently cultured to understand the sport, as *Krasnyi sport* suggested in 1926: "For our spectators a track meet is the same thing as putting a ram in a drugstore. There's lots inside but nothing to eat. The spectator watches and watches but does not understand.... Our public has not yet learned how to watch track and field."[74] The attendance problem was so serious that sports authorities often held races at the half times of soccer games in order to publicize track.[75]

Of course the Soviet fan had a good excuse. A track meet is far more difficult to organize than a soccer game. Much specialized equipment is needed. Many judges are required. Events must follow each other according to a precise schedule. Public-address announcers must inform the spectators of the names of competitors, results, and upcomimg events. The meet must start on time. The stadium must be ready. This sort of efficiency was rarely found at Soviet meets. Often, competitions deteriorated into incomprehensible mob scenes. At one marathon in 1937, a large number of competitors succeeded in breaking the national record. Only later was it revealed that the course was two kilometers short—as a result of which the race organizers were arrested.[76]

Izvestia complained that a 1935 meet that featured the USSR's leading stars drew few fans to Dinamo Stadium because the organizers had "again charged commercial prices for tickets." Two years later, at a similarly important meet, participants were not informed of upcoming events, an especially serious problem in view of the fact that a program had never been printed. The next year, Nikolai Ozolin, the pole vaulter, complained in print that the organizers of one meet had neglected to find an orchestra for the opening ceremonies, as a result of which the competitors had to parade ceremonially around the track in silence.[77]

Ironically, it would be the inadequacies of the organization of Soviet domestic meets that would lead to Nikolai Starostin's arrest. At a meeting of the Spartak Society, Starostin complained about the disorder at Soviet track events. He described a competition he had recently seen in Finland that was well run. Starostin suggested using similar methods for Soviet events. When he was later arrested, one of the charges against him would be the very "propagandizing of bourgeois sport" he engaged in at this meeting.[78]

In many ways, the values and norms that the state sought to ascribe to sport were better suited to track then they were to soccer, with its overt professionalism, crude players, and rowdy fans. One never reads, after all, of riots at track meets. It would, of course, be a gross distortion to suggest that the authorities sought therefore to repress soccer or that its fans in any conscious way saw themselves as in opposition to the Party and state. Nevertheless, the Soviet public's choices of sporting entertainment present a clear case (using the categories of Stuart Hall) of a "negotiated" response to the messages of a mass culture industry. Soccer proved to be a sport loved by the people, which the state was required to present, while track was a sport that the state presented but was neither required nor loved by the people.

The Soviet high-achievement sports system was born in the 1930s. It was inescapably a product of the period of Stalinism. It did not exist before the revolution, nor was it highly developed in the 1920s and early 'thirties. The track stars, weightlifters, swimmers, and gymnasts who come to our minds when we think of Soviet sports were first produced in Stalinist society by a state-supported system that paid and gave privileges to many of its top athletes. Spectator sports, however, were but a subset of high-performance sports. While most spectator sports are also high-performance sports, not all high-performance sports are spectator sports. Such was the case in the Soviet Union before the Second World War. Only soccer achieved the status of a mass phenomenon of popular culture. Nevertheless, the model had been established. An organized league gave Soviet fans a regular diet of entertainment. Once victory over Germany was won, other games would follow soccer's lead and become spectator sports in the same sense of the term.

4

Internationalism and High Stalinism

Germany's invasion of the Soviet Union in June 1941 began a process that would eventually end the diplomatic isolation of the USSR. Participation in the Allied victory over Germany brought the Soviets into the world community, and sports played a role in this emergence. The competitive, high-achievement system that was established in the 1930s was revived after the war, and Soviet athletes stepped onto the international stage as goodwill ambassadors whose talents had, until then, been largely unknown to most outsiders.

It would turn out that these spokesmen and spokeswomen came onto the world stage at a particularly complicated and difficult moment in history. As hopes for lasting peace faded with the emergence of the Cold War, both of the new great powers to emerge from the conflict went through difficult periods of internal political oppression. In the late 'forties and early 'fifties, the United States experienced the fear and paranoia of McCarthyism, while inside the USSR, the years between the end of the war and the death of Stalin were particularly dark and dangerous, as repression became even more severe and increasingly incomprehensible.

During the war, the Soviet government had relaxed ideological controls to win support. Nationalism, religion, and a general openness to the West had helped generate broad public acceptance of the war effort. In the aftermath of the nation's struggle for survival, many Soviet citizens inside as well as outside the Party hoped that the postwar USSR would be far less repressive than it had been in the 1930s. In 1946, Stalin himself still believed that peace could be maintained with the West and that more consumer goods and fewer ideological controls would characterize Soviet life in the near future. Those hopes would be scuttled by the worsening of the Cold War and the problems posed by the enormous tasks of reconstruction. The war had caused an enormous manpower shortage, and the economy revived slowly. Finally, intense rivalries among Stalin's underlings led to cultural and scientific policies characterized by xenophobia, chauvinism, and dogmatism.

Despite these difficulties, sports, especially spectator sports, received an enormous uplift in the afterglow of victory. The massive task of rebuilding a nation that had lost more than twenty-eight million people was truly daunting, but it was possible, after much suffering, to play once again. In the midst of continued shortages, fans flocked to the stadiums, and new sports joined soccer as attractions. Throughout the world, the postwar period was a time of spectacular expansion for spectator sports, and the USSR was no exception. This growing popular interest in big-time sport, however, took place against the background of Stalin's last years. In the politically supercharged atmosphere of this era, it was not sufficient for Soviet sportsmen and women to reach the level of the rest of the world. They now had to be the best.

In the immediate wake of the war, even before the Cold War began to set in after 1948, Soviet athletes began to venture into the global arena, and affiliations were established with the various international sports federations. As most of these organizations were formally amateur, it now became necessary to claim that Soviet athletes, too, were amateur. This step was taken in a 1947 government resolution officially banning financial rewards for competitors.[1] This would begin a corrosive hypocrisy that would bring the USSR enormous success in sports, while distorting the lives of generations of athletes who had to conform to a web of legal fictions that masked their true status.

The International Olympic Committee was not blind to this fact and had delayed an invitation to the 1948 Games in London. At the same time, the Soviets themselves were debating the question of participation. According to numerous accounts, Stalin would have entered a Soviet team in 1948, but before the Games, he gathered together the leaders of Soviet sports. They told him victory could not be assured, and without such a promise Stalin chose to wait until 1952. This version of events is indirectly confirmed by N N Romanov, then head of the All-Union Committee of Physical Culture and Sport, who, in his 1987 memoirs, recalled that he could send no delegation of athletes abroad without a note to Stalin guaranteeing victory.

At the end of 1948, the goal of world sports leadership was formally articulated in a public resolution of the Central Committee, calling for victory, not simply participation.[2] Since the Soviets had been hidden from the world sporting stage for so long, one might have expected Stalin to be satisfied with respectable performances, but this was not the case. The relative autonomy that sports had achieved before the war, while not obliterated, was reduced. High-performance sports became the weapon of Soviet foreign policy, through which the outside world would come to know it, and this politically sensitive role created enormous problems for the sports world.

To make matters even more difficult, coaches and athletes had to achieve these goals under the most trying of material conditions. The war had ravaged the nation, and sports facilities, always inadequate before the war, were in a state of extensive disrepair. Equipment, chronically in short supply, was even harder to find, and the government, facing the task of reconstruction, could not devote massive funding to sports in this early phase of revival. Finally, the huge loss of life fell most heavily on young men, the demographic base of the nation's talent for the most popular spectator sports.

Despite the conditions of political pressure and insufficient resources, Soviet sportsmen and women approached their tasks with both dedication and ingenuity. Although the sport world experienced material difficulties, the postwar period proved to be a time of growth for spectator sports. Far more people came to watch and interest themselves in big-time sports, and other games came to adopt the practices that had helped the development of soccer. At the same time, soccer dramatically expanded its audience. By the end of the 1946 season, *Sovetskii sport* (formerly *Krasnyi sport*) would write with full justification, "soccer was never as popular in our country as it is now."[3] Soccer was played in far more cities and in many more republics than it had been earlier. Even Moscow's Dinamo Stadium proved to be too small to accommodate the masses who wanted to watch the increased diet of games.

Because Soviet teams were now more involved in international competition, these contests were not simply games but rather "examinations" of the condition of Soviet sports. The Party and the state had passed the ultimate test of war. Now new, safer, but still important battles were to be fought. These international contests exposed the world to Soviet sports and outsiders were struck by an athletic system that seemed very new and different. Yet the structures they saw for the first time after 1945 were established well before the war and had survived more or less intact. Four years of titanic struggle had left their mark on all of Soviet society, but, in the very midst of the war's massive destruction, Soviet sports demonstrated a strong capacity for survival. When Soviet athletes stepped out onto the world stage, the arena was new but the systems and structures that supported them were not.

Taking Time Out from War

In the catastrophic early years of the war, leisure and play could easily have lost their pleasure and meaning. With Leningrad starving through the nine hundred days of blockade and much of the USSR occupied by the Nazis, it is difficult to imagine that Soviet citizens had either the time or the desire to play and watch sports, but play and watch is precisely what they did. The sporting activity that took place during the war was by no means mindless frivolity in the face of a nightmare—an effort to escape each day's new horrors. Instead, playing and watching were an attempt to maintain morale and a shred of normalcy; to affirm the tiniest glimmer of humanity in the face of so much death and privation. During 1942, in blockaded Leningrad, with thousands dying of starvation and a daily bread ration of 125 grams, (less than 4 oz.) a day, soccer games were organized, and as many as eight thousand fans attended.[4] The first of these games took place on May 2, the traditional start of the summer sports season. These matches were broadcast with the intention of assuring Leningrad's citizens that life could go on. The games were supposed to intimidate the Germans by demonstrating the city's capacity to maintain the trappings of normalcy. That same year a city championship was organized in Moscow.[5]

No sooner would territory be regained than sporting activity would revive. On May 2, 1943, in the immediate wake of the bloody but decisive Battle of Stalingrad, a hastily reassembled Spartak team was invited to play a side of local all-stars before ten thousand at a hastily reconstructed stadium.[6] Even in occupied Kiev, Soviet citizens organized and in sizable numbers (five to eight thousand) attended many games. Watching such events was an act of no small bravery, as the audience consisted largely of the very sort of younger men the Nazis so often forcibly took to Germany for unpaid factory work. Numerous spontaneous games were also played by German troops, and contests between the occupiers and the residents of Kiev were not uncommon. In this context, the legendary confrontation between members of Dinamo Kiev and officers from the Luftwaffe loses some of the great drama that came to surround it. According to the standard account, the Dinamo players knew full well that the Germans could react to the humiliation of defeat by executing them. As professional athletes, they certainly could have been expected to defeat even a strong group of amateurs. Nevertheless, Dinamo Kiev's players fought to the maximum of their abilities and defeated the Germans 5–3, a victory that was supposed to have led quickly to their executions. One veteran Soviet sports journalist who lived through the occupation of Kiev, however, has claimed the incident has been over-dramatized. As it turns out, only a few of the Kiev players were actually from the Dinamo team. While many of them were executed, the sequence of their executions was not clearly related to the "match of death."[7] Nevertheless, the larger lesson associated with these games can be said to be true. The popular love of soccer was so strong that even in the most inhuman and tragic of circumstances people still played and watched it. To do so was to snatch some small piece of humanity in the midst of misery. In playing, Soviet citizens were able to remember something joyous, a reason to hang on to life, despite the terrors of each day.

By 1943, the tide of battle had turned. In the rear, life began to take on a few of the trappings of the everyday, and the sporting life of the country slowly and tentatively resumed. Early in the spring, the leading sports societies of Moscow began to prepare for a city soccer championship that started in a packed Stalinets Stadium (20,000). Moscow's top teams played a reduced schedule throughout the summer, ending the season in a repaired Dinamo Stadium before a crowd of slightly more than 20,000. Difficulties of transport made it impractical to resume a full national schedule, but a few intercity exhibitions were also organized. With eventual victory assured, hockey was also revived in Moscow as early as January 1943. Track and field reappeared in the summer, highlighting a subdued celebration of Physical Culture Day, restricted to Dinamo Stadium. By 1944, basketball was again played, attracting far larger crowds than it ever had done before the war. The Moscow city soccer championship was again contested in 1944, but Spartak and Dinamo were unable to dominate as they had in the past. Instead, Torpedo won the title in a season of fourteen games. Their strongest competition now came from TsDKA. International links were also revived in 1944, when Dinamo Tblisi toured Iran.[8]

With victory expected soon, the military came to enjoy the admiration of nearly all citizens. The army's triumph and sacrifice had increased its popularity, and a great deal of the public adulation washed over onto its teams. TsDKA now found it easier to attract players, coaches, and financial support. Strong before the war, the army team now became a leader. By the end of the war, they had emerged as the coming power in Soviet soccer, replacing Spartak as Dinamo's main rival.[9] The revival of the sport also meant a return to many of the less-than-savory practices that had characterized the prewar period. The patriotic upsurge of the war years did not raise the level of morality in the sport. As soon as the city championships revived, the buying and selling of players resumed. The famed film director Mark Donskoi publicly decried the practice, especially in time of war. It was the task, he said, of each team to develop its own talent. The "purchase" of players from elsewhere, Donskoi claimed, could only lead to temporary success.[10] He noted one of the iron laws of professional sports had come to apply to the Soviet scene, as players were kept around only as long as they were useful. Those who engaged in these practices were, in Donskoi's eyes, "traders and not educators of young sportsmen."

Both the rise of TsDKA and the decline of Spartak had roots in events outside the field of play. Spartak's ability to compete in these years was severely crippled. The team had been cut off at the head. On March 20, 1942, Nikolai Starostin was arrested along with his brothers. Lavrenti Beria had finally succeeded in gaining the assent of another Central Committee functionary, Georgii Malenkov, who signed the arrest order that Molotov had refused to support in 1939. Nikolai was taken to the headquarters of the secret police, the Lubianka prison in the heart of Moscow. He was told that as a result of Kosarev's "confession" at the time of the Komsomol leader's show trial, Starostin had been implicated in a conspiracy. Kosarev was said to have organized a group of athletes to engage in antistate terror. Starostin was supposed to have planned a terrorist act against the leadership in 1937, while playing soccer before the mausoleum during that year's Physical Culture Day Parade. He was also accused of "propagandizing bourgeois sport."[11]

After spending two years in the Lubianka, where he was repeatedly interrogated but not tortured, Starostin was given ten years in a labor camp at Ukhta. For many of those sent to such a place, ten years could easily be a death sentence, but this would not be Starostin's fate. After an arduous journey of three months, he arrived in Ukhta to be met by several soccer players of the local Dinamo team, some of whom had also been exiled. They told him that the commandant in charge of the region, Lieutenant General Burdakov, wanted Starostin to coach the Dinamo team of Ukhta. Starostin was given a day pass outside the camp, and this archenemy of Dinamo was now coaching one of its teams at Soviet soccer's lowest level. This fact was not known to Beria, but Starostin credits it with saving his life. He coached in Ukhta for a year, after which he was sent to Khabarovsk. He arrived there just one day before the end of the war and soon found himself performing the same coaching duties, again unbeknownst to Beria.[12]

As was the case with so many others who were arrested, Starostin's name disappeared from the sports pages. Yet he clearly was missed, and in 1943, *Krasnyi sport* went as far as to make a veiled reference to the absence of the Starostins by attributing Spartak's continuing poor results to a lack of "qualified leadership."[13] So great was the passion of the local police commanders for soccer and so widespread was Starostin's reputation that he was able to escape the likely death of the labor camps. Much the same good fortune befell his brothers, all of whom would survive their exile. Nevertheless, they were not able to return to live in Moscow until 1955, when Nikolai again took up leadership of Spartak and Andrei started a successful career as a sportswriter and soccer bureaucrat. Despite the fact of their rehabilitation and their renewed visibility in the world of sports, journalists could make only oblique mention of the Starostins' exile until 1989. Even in Andrei's own 1964 book, *Bol' shoi futbol,* he refers only to time "spent in the north."[14] As late as 1970, a *Sovetskii sport* article about the history of the Spartak Society, written by the respected journalist Lev Filatov, ommitted any mention of the brothers' exile. Eventually three of the Starostin brothers died natural deaths, all of them respected figures. As of the writing of this book Nikolai remained alive. Well into his nineties, he continued, quite successfully, to manage the fortunes of Spartak's soccer team.

In 1948, Stalin's son, Vasillii, secretly flew Nikolai from exile back to Moscow. It was the younger Stalin's intention to install Starostin as the coach of the struggling Air Force team (*VVS*). There was, one obvious problem with this plan. As an exile, Starostin was not allowed to be in Moscow. He was therefore forced to live for three months with Vasillii, who had to accompany Starostin everywhere in public for fear that the secret police would arrest his coach. This charade enraged Beria, who was an intense personal rival of Stalin's son. One time, Starostin made the mistake of sneaking out of Stalin's house to spend the night with his family. The next day he was arrested and deported from the city. Stalin brought him back again, but it soon became clear that Beria still enjoyed too much power and influence with Joseph Stalin to let Starostin stay and coach a rival. Reluctantly, Starostin went to Alma-Ata in Central Asia, where he spent the rest of his exile coaching the local team, *Kairat* of the second division.[15]

Soviet Soccer's Golden Age

In the wake of the war's devastation, the USSR faced an enormous task of reconstruction. Much of the infrastructure that had supported the industries of mass culture was crippled or destroyed. Theaters and arenas were in ruins; electricity and equipment were once again scarce. Of all the entertainments available to the public, sports, especially soccer, were the quickest to revive, as spectators rushed back to the stadiums to partake in guiltless pleasure. Soon, however, many elements of culture—mass, middle-brow, and elite— would be stifled by the grip of intensely conformist policies. This clampdown was initially associated with Andrei Zhdanov, who had become a secretary of the Central Committee after years as head of the Leningrad Party organization. Zhdanov sought to have the arts and sciences adhere to a strict "Soviet" standard, and the term "Zhdanovism" would eventually enter English to signify an especially high level of cultural repression.

It has, however, been argued that Zhdanov's positions on cultural matters, while obviously highly conformist, were actually less extreme than those of his competitors for power at the Party's highest levels. He was embroiled in an intense struggle with such rivals as Georgii Malenkov and Mikhail Suslov, and his criticisms of ideological laxness in literature and culture were possibly an attempt to forestall the even more repressive views and policies of his opponents. Zhdanov began his campaign in late 1946. Two years later, however, he had lost favor with Stalin. He and his allies were deprived of their power, and an even more chauvinistic and dogmatic group, which included Beria, gained ascendancy.[16] Spectator sport had been relatively untouched between 1946 and 1948, the period of the *Zhdanovshchina,* but when

Malenkov, Suslov, and Beria gained the upper hand, athletes, coaches, and officials could no longer escape severe ideological controls.

This intraparty power struggle took place against the background of steadily worsening relations with the West. As a result, attending the movies, ballet, theater, or concerts in the late 'forties became tedious, even depressing. Many who lived through these years say that soccer, comparatively untouched, was their only spectacle. Sports were, of course, effected by the repressive currents of this era, but their fundamental core was not subverted. They maintained their attractiveness, and in the glow of the nation's victory, Soviet citizens flocked to stadiums and arenas as they never had before. The range of sporting entertainments increased, as fans came to watch, not only soccer, but hockey, basketball, track, and many other games. Almost every contest drew a crowd. Beyond mere numbers, the social base of sports, including soccer, was now broadened. Intellectuals, professionals, industrial managers, and their patrons in the middle and upper reaches of the Party began to interest themselves in pastimes that previously had been the province of the working classes.

The author Lev Kassil, who often wrote about sports, described a day in the stands of Dinamo Stadium during the fall of 1945, "I had conversations with many authoritative 'fans' who came from the broadest variety of life's professions."[17] Mark Donskoi similarly sought to associate soccer with Soviet culture's most eminent figures: "You can meet people of all professions and ages at sporting events. There's the composer Dmitri Shostakovich, rating the chances of the teams. He understands the game well and knows the coaches and players by sight."[18] Donskoi's purpose was not to praise the composer but to associate the sport with high culture and, therefore, civilization.

At the beginning of the 1952 season, *Sovetskii sport* described soccer's new social base: "There was a time when football was thought to be a game played by youths for youths. Now Dinamo stadium encompasses the population of an entire city.... Here you can meet people of all ages and the widest variety of professions. A young Stakhanovite sits next to a composer who is known to all the people. A Pioneer sits next to a famed artist; an old worker next to someone with a university pin in his lapel."[19]

In a society that had become hierarchical, this new interest of the powerful and privileged heightened the political and social role sports were to play. As they had been in the West, big-time spectator sports in the USSR were now to be a social leveler, providing a common discourse for all Soviet men (though not many women), while obscuring differences in their social stations. Soviet citizens had lived through the horror of real battles, and the mimetic struggles that took place on playing fields must have provided citizens of all social levels with an especially compelling combination of both safety and excitement. With the war over, it was now possible to play. Before the war, soccer had been described as the favorite sport of the working class. Now it was supposed to provide healthy leisure for the entire population.

On May 13, 1945, four days after the declaration of victory over Germany, the national soccer championship began its seventh season. The league was revived with twelve teams—six from Moscow, two from Leningrad, and one each from Kiev, Tblisi, Minsk, and Stalingrad. Instantly, arenas all across the Soviet Union were filled beyond their capacities. In June, more than eighty thousand stuffed their way into Dinamo Stadium to see newly powerful Dinamo Tblisi take on Spartak. As many as forty thousand attended games in Kiev, Tblisi, and Leningrad. Dinamo Moscow won the first postwar championship, and three weeks later, Central Army would defeat Dinamo in the cup final.[20]

Mikhail Iakushin had now become Dinamo's coach, replacing Boris Arkadiev, who moved on to Central Army in 1944. On the field, Dinamo was led by its new star, Konstantin Beskov, but the greatest discovery of the first postwar season turned out to be Central Army's twenty-two-year-old striker, Vsevolod Bobrov. The league's leading scorer, with twenty-four goals, Bobrov would go on to become the greatest, and certainly the most visible, multisport athlete in Soviet history. Not only was he one of the leading soccer players of his day, but he also became the dominant star of the earliest era of ''Canadian'' hockey. Early in his career, Bobrov received a serious knee injury that required four complex surgeries, the first in 1947, the last in 1953. While he returned to his previous level of excellence, he played in pain for the rest of his career, receiving injections before virtually every game.[21]

As for Spartak, in the first postwar years it would suffer from the loss of the Starostins' leadership, but by 1949, the team would begin to recapture some of its former glory, adding such stars as the halfback Igor Netto, and a blazingly quick striker from Abkhazia, Nikita Simonian, who would score thirty-four goals in the 1950 season, a record that stood for thirty-five years. Spartak would twice win the cup, and in 1952, with TsDKA disbanded, they were once again champions. Throughout this period of temporary and comparative decline, however, Spartak remained a fan favorite, playing attractive soccer and continuing to draw large crowds.

Dinamo Tours Great Britain—Soviet soccer received its biggest boost in mass popularity at the end of the 1945 season. Dinamo Moscow received an invitation to play several games in the United Kingdom. For the Soviets, Britain had remained the center of world soccer, and the invitation was treated as a call to an initiation. In the fall of 1945, the goodwill generated by common victory over the Axis had not yet dissipated, and Dinamo's tour was undertaken in the spirit of shared triumph. While the excursion had the direct political purpose of spreading a spirit of friendship that would not last very long, the trip, from the sporting point of view, would prove to be a decisive turning point in the history of Soviet soccer.

Long deprived of competition with the best professional teams of Europe, Soviet soccer was now given a chance to test itself against clubs from the nation the Soviets thought to be the world's strongest soccer power. For Soviet players, coaches, officials, journalists, and fans, all of whom had been reading about British soccer for years, the anticipation of this confrontation was enormous. How would the Soviet "school" of soccer fare? Would the much-touted "collectivism" of the Soviet style be able to withstand the onslaught of the bourgeois professionals? The game against Racing Club de France in 1936 had been an important moment in the history of Soviet soccer; so had been the tour of the Basques, but the Soviets had lost those games. Now they were going against clubs from the nation that enjoyed the greatest reputation among Soviet fans and specialists.

When Dinamo left Moscow on November 4, 1945, they took with them Vsevolod Bobrov and two members of Dinamo Leningrad. The Soviets were following their well-established practice of strengthening touring clubs with stars from other teams. Soviet fans certainly knew that Bobrov was not a *Dinamovets*. The fact could hardly have been kept a secret. Nevertheless, there were no public objections from partisans of Spartak or TsDKA. Bobrov's presence greatly enhanced Dinamo's chances of being the first Soviet team to defeat the British. If there was any jealousy from other Soviet teams, it did not appear in the contemporary press, nor has it seeped into the more candid memoirs that have appeared in recent years.

At the same time, contemporary English accounts showed little awareness of the fact that their clubs would have to go against a side that was considerably more powerful than the team that had just won the Soviet championship. The *London Times* freely admitted its ignorance before the first game in London on November 13: "Some of the mystery which seems to follow everything connected with the Soviet Union will follow the Moscow Dynamo footballers on to the field at Stamford Bridge for their match aganist Chelsea this afternoon.... If there is any mystery about Moscow Dynamo, it lies chiefly in its style and quality of play."[22]

The intrigue attracted a huge crowd to see Dinamo play Chelsea, which was led by the great Tommy Lawton and strengthened by two players from Fulham. As many as 85,000 filled every available viewpoint well before the beginning of the match. The liberal *Manchester Guardian* described the mob scene: "There have never been such scenes at Chelsea. Some of those unable to get a view climbed up the tall stand from behind. The glass and iron corrugated roof creaked to the alarm of those sitting underneath. At least two people fell through the glass and dropped among other spectators. Thousands swarmed round the touch line. The police repeatedly had to clear a way for the players to take corner kicks.''[23]

In the first half, Dinamo had much the better of the play, but failed to realize numerous possibilities, even missing a penalty kick. At halftime they found themselves down 2–0, and had the Dinamo goalie, Aleksei Khomich, not made a brilliant save against Lawton with eight minutes left in the half, the damage would have been even greater. Finally, in the sixty-fifth minute, Vasilii Kartsev took a pass from Beskov and scored. Six minutes later, one of the players on loan from Dinamo Leningrad, Evgenii Arkhangelskii, evened the score after being set up by Beskov. In the seventy-seventh minute, Lawton put Chelsea out in front, but two minutes later, Bobrov, with yet another pass from Beskov, finished the scoring.[24]

The 3–3 tie did not reflect the run of play, which had been heavily in favor of Dinamo. The *Manchester Guardian* remarked on the scene:

> Thousands of people swarmed on the field and tried to chair the Russian team to the dressing room at the end of their great match with Chelsea at Stamford Bridge yesterday. The result was a draw of three goals each but on the day's play Dynamo should have won with a comfortable margin to spare. . . . Apart from weak finishing the Russians surprised everyone by their skill. They are up to the highest international standard.[25]

Even the more conservative *Times* was impressed: "Altogether, the first appearance of a first-class Russian football team in Britain produced a memorable occasion. Moscow Dynamo not only played fully as well as any reasonable person had expected; they also drew a monster crowd, some thousands of whom overflowed from the mighty banks of Stamford Bridge. . . . ''[26] The impact was even more sensational back home. The game was broadcast live to the Soviet Union by the first of the great sports broadcasters, Vadim Siniavskii. Press accounts were extremely enthusiastic.[27] Four days later, Dinamo journeyed to Wales where they overwhelmed a young Cardiff City team by a score of ten to one.[28] Beskov had four goals while Bobrov and Arkhangelskii had three each. The crucial match of the tour, however, was four days away. Dinamo was to return to London to face Arsenal.

The composition of Arsenal's team became the subject of some controversy, however. Arsenal's manager, George Allison, argued that his team, weakened by the call-up of its players during the war, could not adequately play at the high standard Arsenal had established before the war, so he invited several players from other teams. The Soviets protested, and a public statement was issued over the signature of Dinamo's captain, Mikhail Semichastnyi, who claimed that his team had not agreed to a strengthening of Arsenal. The Soviet delegation contended that Dinamo would, in fact, be playing a team representing all of England. No one from the Soviet delegation, however, mentioned the fact that eight of Dinamo's thirteen goals had been scored by men who were not regular players for Dinamo, nor did the British press show any awareness of this fact. Instead, the *Times* took Arsenal to task for using the war as an excuse. "The Russians also have been at war," they argued, "but their football is not bad in consequence."[29]

The game against Arsenal was played under the most bizarre of conditions. November 21, 1945, witnessed one of London's famed pea-soup fogs. No one could see more than halfway across the field. Under normal circumstances, the game would have been postponed, but so great was the anticipation that huge crowds massed early in the morning outside Tottenham's north London stadium where the match was held due to bomb damage at Arsenal's nearby home ground in Highbury. The police decided to admit the crowd of more than 50,000 at 10:30, four hours before kick-off. By then, it proved impossible to call off the match, and so the most important game in the history of Soviet soccer was held in conditions that greatly enhanced the possibity for strange and accidental occurrences.

Arsenal's hastily assembled collection of stars lacked the cohesion needed against as formidable an opponent as Dinamo. Bobrov opened the scoring, but Arsenal, led by the borrowed Stanley Mortenson of Blackpool, answered with three goals. Beskov then got one goal back before the half. Three minutes into the second half Sergei Soloviev tied the score, and fifteen minutes later Bobrov, on yet another pass from Beskov, scored a winning goal that most of the crowd and many of the other players did not even see. Iakushin, standing, as was then the custom, behind his own goal, saw none of his team's scores. Despite the strange conditions and the hastily organized character of Arsenal's team, the English press gave Dinamo its due. The *Times* remarked:

> What was clear was the Russian superiority in collective ball-control—in other words passing—and their amazing speed in midfield when a sudden breakthrough was effected. Individually the Moscow side had no player of the football stature of Matthews, nor indeed were they noticably cleverer in one position or heavier and tougher men. But, compared with their team-work that of the Arsenal was painfully ragged and uncertain.[30]

The reaction back home was ecstatic. Siniavskii, noting the dispute over the composition of Arsenal's side, told his audience that Dinamo had beaten an "all-England" team.[31] Dinamo's victory won a huge audience for soccer inside the Soviet Union, as millions listened to the broadcasts and read the extensive press coverage. Soviet fans now had an excellent reason to believe that the soccer played in their own stadiums was as good as any in the world. The belief that they could watch a superior product caused Soviet citizens to flock to matches as never before. One week after defeating Arsenal, Dinamo journeyed to Scotland where they played a 2–2 tie against Glasgow Rangers before 90,000 at Ibrox Park.[32] Playing away from home, using British referees in all but one game (against Arsenal), Dinamo had more than held its own, as Soviet soccer entered the world stage triumphantly.

Iakushin attributed much of his team's success to the tactical variation he introduced on the previously "bourgeois" "W" formation. His five attackers constantly shifted their positions. The inside left could wind up on the right wing; the center forward might appear anywhere along the front. Beskov would later claim that Iakushin's innovation anticipated the 4+2+4 formation that the Brazilians later made popular. Regardless, the Soviet approach did confuse British defenders, and many of them mentioned this particular tactic in their interviews with the press. The British were also impressed by the great speed and excellent conditioning of their opponents. As such, Dinamo's victory became a triumph not just for the team but for all of Soviet football. The Soviet press was quick to take the lesson several steps further and draw the conclusion that a team such as Dinamo could emerge only in a very special society.

As much as any single event, Dinamo's tour demonstrated sport's international political potential to the Party leadership. Soviet athletes were to be carriers of "peace and friendship," and their successes could be seen as proof of the superiority of the society they had emerged from. While it is fair to say that sports played a fairly limited political role before the war, their importance increased after 1945, and during the early years of the Cold War, the Soviet sports system came to take on many of the trappings that those outside the USSR would soon find all too familiar.

Building the World's "Leading School" of Soccer—The postwar period witnessed a boom in soccer attendance. Important games between Moscow's leading teams and matches against such top provincial contenders as Dinamo Tblisi regularly packed Dinamo Stadium with crowds of between seventy and ninety thousand. Since Dinamo Stadium's capacity had been listed as only fifty thousand, one can readily imagine the crush and intensity on big game days. In the first two years of postwar soccer, an estimated twelve million attended first-division games. With a twelve-team league, this meant that the average gate was 45,000. Even allowing for the relative cheapness of tickets, this was an impressive figure, and large crowds were no longer limited to the capital. When Dinamo Leningrad or its local rival *Zenit* played each other or either team took on a well-known opponent, thirty thousand or more would fill Lenin Stadium, tickets selling out several days before the game.[33] The demand, in fact, was so great that city officials revived the construction of the 74,000-seat Kirov stadium that had been begun before the war.

Dinamo Tblisi could fill its 40,000-capacity stadium even on rainy week-days, and fans came from the city and from all over the southern republics as well for big confrontations against Central Army or Dinamo Moscow. The same phenomenon occured around such cities as Stalino and Kuibishev, as interest spread from the centers where the game had first been popular.[34] Once soccer expanded its base outside the main cities, it could finally assume the role of a truly national pastime, one that could unite an immense multi-ethnic state. The increasingly common broadcasting of matches also spread interest in soccer into the countryside and into many of the eastern republics that had previously ignored the game.

Significantly, more than just the big games were attracting sizable crowds. In Kiev, thirty or forty thousand would turn out to see a then-weak Dinamo Kiev take on such middle-level sides as Dinamo Leningrad or *Trak-tor* of Stalingrad. While Spartak lost some of its strength during the postwar era, it was still a respectable team that retained much of its popularity, reg-ularly drawing thirty thousand for weak opponents and filling Dinamo Sta-dium against strong sides.[35] Even the less-popular Moscow teams like *Krylia Sovetov* and *Torpedo* could attract ten or fifteen thousand when they played each other. Before the war, only important matches had been witnessed by large numbers of people. There had always been a huge dropoff in interest when lesser teams played each other. Ordinary contests had rarely drawn more than five thousand; sometimes, just a few hundred. Immediately after the war, hardly any game either in Moscow or the periphery failed to draw a decent crowd, demonstrating a new and fundamentally different depth of interest in soccer.

The increased level and wider distribution of attendance marked a cru-cial watershed. Earlier, soccer had been the most popular of sports, but its public was still limited numerically and socially. After the war, the sport moved to a new level as a phenomenon of popular culture. To recall Stuart Hall's definition of popular culture, soccer was no longer simply one of the many products of mass-culture industries. It now had a broad and committed audience, and that audience followed the sport on its own terms, rather than those of the government—a "negotiated" rather than "dominated" response to the state's attempt to control mass culture. Soccer became a regular daily concern, even passion, for most Soviet males. While they may have accepted the fundamental legitimacy of the political and sports systems, they did not always respond unquestioningly to the particular set of messages the Party and state attached to the sporting events that were made available.

Soccer's appeal was now universal. This fact would, however, prove to be a mixed blessing. While fans would continue to contest, consciously and unconsciously, the meanings the authorities sought to attach to soccer, those same authorities were now even more interested in the sport and its uses.

With increased attention came greater responsibility. The political tasks of big-time sports became more important, and the drive for success became even more intense. Soccer's increased visibility made it a riper object for political interference, and in the context of the increasing cultural conformity of this era, the struggle for control of soccer's meaning became more serious.

In the postwar period, especially after Dinamo's victories in England, Soviet journalists, coaches, and officials laid claim to the global superiority of Soviet soccer. In any team sport in any social system, capitalist or Communist, teamwork has always been an essential element of success. There was nothing particularly new or especially political about this fact, but the Soviet press argued that such cohesion was more easily achieved in a society that valued the collective. In 1950, *Sovetskii sport* summed up the results of the past soccer season: "The discussion is about collectivism—the distinguishing characteristic of our football, the leading school of football in the world.... What is the basis of the Soviet style? The answer lies in collectivism, in close interaction; in the absence of 'me-ism' [*iachestvo*]." Furthermore, it was the job of the players to inculcate these values in the rest of society: "The sacred task of our masters is to be an example of discipline and high moral character for players at all levels, to develop in them the best features of the Soviet style of soccer."[36] The coach of TsDKA, Boris Arkadiev, argued the superiority of Soviet soccer even more specifically:

> Our players not only beat the strongest English teams, they brilliantly demonstrated the original Soviet school of football which is so sharply distinct from foreign approaches. What are the distinctive features of the Soviet school of football? Above all it is the high moral and physical character of the players. It is a spiritual collectiveness of play. It is the effort of will of the players. It is the tactics of widely maneuvering attackers and a mobile and impenetrable defense.[37]

The new importance that was accorded to soccer precipitated a rise in criticism of the sport. Every contest, no matter how insignificant, now had to be analyzed for its possible contribution to the development of Soviet soccer. In the process, sports journalism's autonomy was diminshed. Game accounts, which had in the past been straightforward and descriptive, now had to evaluate the quality of play as well. Long analytical articles, a relative rarity before the war, became a journalistic staple in the regular as well as the sports press. Coaches, officials, and referees, not to mention academics, actors, composers, and writers, increasingly expounded on the state of the sport. Previously, fans had been able to draw their own conclusions about the significance of games described in *Sovetskii sport*. After 1948, spectators may have continued to make independent evaluations, but journalists now had to instruct their readers about the consequences of what had transpired on the field.

In other cases, the pressure on sports journalists took more direct forms. Nevertheless, small acts of resistance were still possible. One such story, perhaps apocryphal, circulated for years in the offices of *Sovetskii sport*. During the late 'forties, a night editor was alone in the offices, waiting for the late soccer results. Around midnight, he reportedly received a call from Beria, who wanted to know the score of the Spartak-Dinamo Tblisi game. The editor replied, "1–0, Spartak." Beria then said, "Print the score 1–1." Faced with this crisis, the sportswriter, rather than print a falsehood, ommitted the score from the next day's paper.[38] Perhaps Hall's concept is used too literally here, but it is difficult to think of a clearer case of a "negotiated" response to the government's message.

Another common theme of sports commentators was the chronic lack of facilities, exacerbated by the destruction of the war. Many playing fields had been destroyed; others had been neglected and were in poor condition. In soccer, as in every other sport, places to train were hard to find. As a result, Soviet soccer coaches had their players run, swim, or play basketball in order to get in shape. The long winter required ingenuity as well. Indoor arenas were nonexistent, and gymnasiums were few and often too small. Many coaches went so far as to have their players cross-country ski in order to reach peak condition.[39] Hockey players had a similar problem. The extreme shortage of rinks and the absence of artificial ice until 1956 necessitated a great deal of land training.[40]

The practice of having athletes in one sport train by playing other sports was an adaptation to the chronic lack of training facilities. This approach did turn out to have certain advantages, though. Constantly varying practices were more interesting for the athletes, who dreaded repetitive drills and exercises. Eventually what today is known as "cross-training" became one of the basic methods used by Soviet coaches to condition their charges. Necessities of this sort required Soviet coaches to adapt and innovate constantly, and many of their responses to a strapped situation were highly original. Indeed, those who could not innovate were rarely successful. Thus Arkadiev's claim about the "originality" of the Soviet school was by no means mere boasting. It is, however, significant that this originality was the result of a lack of resources, rather than the product of a well-endowed system.

Increased international competition would give Soviet soccer many more opportunities to test the value of its methods. In 1946, the Soviets joined international soccer's governing body, FIFA (Federation Internationale de Football Association). Membership meant they were now able to schedule sanctioned exhibition games with foreign professionals, and considerable care was taken in the selection of their opponents. Teams from Eastern Europe provided the bulk of the competition, and no team the caliber of Dinamo's British opponents would be faced until after Stalin's death. In 1946, Lokomotiv of Sofia played two games in the USSR, as did the Yugoslavian army team, *Partizan* of Belgrade. Spartak, no longer one of the favored teams, got to tour Albania.[41] The next year brought more serious tests. In August, Torpedo won two games in Hungary. Dinamo Moscow toured Scandinavia in October, where they defeated a series of professional opponents, the strongest of which was Norkopping.[42] At the same time, Central Army journeyed to Prague, where they got to play and defeat the same *Sparta* team that the touring Moscow selects had not been allowed to face in 1934.

By 1948, however, international competition became much less frequent under the impact of increasingly xenophobic internal repression. The postwar era of peace and friendship was now over, and games against foreign opponents did not revive until 1950, when Spartak defeated three weak Norwegian opponents. In 1951 and early 1952, strengthened Soviet club teams played the national teams of several Eastern European countries, dominating all of them, but no Soviet national team was formally organized in these years. In addition, no Western European team of any stature was defeated between 1948 and 1953.[43]

Accordingly, it is difficult to share the view of one Soviet specialist from this era who boasted about Soviet international success:

> The many victories of Soviet teams in international competition demonstrated the advantages of our school over all others. . . . Soviet football serves the people, the task of communist education, and the improvement of the workers' health. Soviet football develops on the basis of the latest achievements of science. Our methods of study and training have a marked advantage over methods used in capitalist countries. . . . [44]

Rarely has so much been made of so little. Aside from Dinamo's successes in England and TsDKA's defeat of Sparta, the Soviet international record was one of well-prepared episodic triumphs against opponents who were hand-picked and often far less motivated than their Soviet counterparts. The leaders of Soviet soccer had reason to feel proud of the progress they had made, but the claims quoted above had little justification. Soviet soccer had reached a high level, but it was still far from the world's best. The danger, however, came from the fact that Soviet political figures believed this rhetoric. As a result, Soviet soccer became the object of unrealistic expectations that would soon lead to severe disappointment.

Fighting Hooliganism—The Political Education of Players and Fans—
Success and visibility did not breed discipline and order among players and

fans. The problems of violent play, attacks on referees, disobeying of coaches, the breaking of training, and a star syndrome (*zaznaistvo*) persisted throughout the immediate postwar period, despite the increased attention soccer now received from the Party. In 1946, players of Dinamo Kiev rarely showed up on time for meetings and practices, and neither did their coach. After a particularly violent 1946 match between Dinamo Leningrad and Torpedo, several players lost their "master of sport" titles and were suspended for a year, while the referee was suspended for two years. In just one month of the 1947 season, seven first-division players were disqualified for rough play. The situation was, if anything, worse at the lower levels. During the 1948 Moscow local season, 230 players had to be sent off, and similar incidents occurred in many other towns.[45]

The Party's December 27, 1948, resolution on sport focused further attention on these problems. The achievement of world sports superiority was now an explicitly stated task, and ungentlemanly play did not advance the cause of Soviet sports. In the years before Stalin's death, both the sports and non-sports press repeatedly discussed "hooliganism" among soccer players, but dirty play and other forms of "unethical behavior" persisted. Even team captains, who should have been models of solidity, became involved in brawls. Coaches and referees maintained their authority only with difficulty, despite strenuous efforts by sports authorities to inculcate order and discipline in the players.[46] The problem, as sports and Party officials saw it, was a lack of "political-ideological" education (*vospitanie*). One finds a few references to this matter during the prewar period, but after 1948, with Zhdanov's demise, it became an obssession in the press.[47]

Between 1948 and 1950, Soviet teams ceased to play foreign opponents, and an attempt was made to find Russian-language equivalents for the many English words that had slipped into the sports vocabulary. "*Khavbek*" (halfback) now became "*poluzashchitnik*," and "*offseid*" became "*vne igry.*" There was even an unsuccessful attempt to change "*futbol*" to "*nozhnoi miach.*" Political-ideological education, as a postwar weapon against insufficient sporting discipline, was first discussed at a February 1948 gathering of the coaches of Dinamo Society soccer teams. *Sovetskii sport* reported on the eve of the 1948 season that this important element of team preparation had previously been limited to the occasional lecture. It argued that these political inadequacies were the result of weak ties between the teams and the organizations they represented.

When teams played poorly, therefore, failure was attributed to a lack of political-ideological work. Successes were similarly explained by a high level of such training. Mikhail Butusov, one of the great stars of the earliest era of Soviet soccer and the coach of Dinamo Leningrad, detailed his team's activities in the area of "mass cultural and political educational work." All his players, he claimed, were required to read Stalin's biography and study both the history of the Bolshevik Party and the theory of Marxism-Leninism. Team excursions to films, museums, and historic sites took place often, as did lectures by players to their fellow team members. One forward gave a speech called "The Leading Position of Soviet Scholars in the Development of World Science and Technology." Other players, Butusov continued, gave reports on Russian classical opera, Soviet foreign policy during the war, and the works of the great prerevolutionary playwright Ostrovskii.[48]

At the 1948 plenum of the All-Union Football Section, *Krylia Sovetov* of Kuibishev was praised for its work: "The players of this team seriously study the history of the Bolshevik Party and regularly attend lectures and museums. Many of them read. The collective regularly discusses such marvelous works of Soviet literature as Fadeev's 'Young Guard,' Ehrenburg's 'Storm,' and Adzheev's 'Far From Moscow.' "[49] Intellectuals who were fans of TsDKA were regularly invited to address the team on such topics as "The Degeneration of Contemporary Bourgeois Art," "Soviet Patriotism and Literature," and "Military Operations of the Popular Democratic Chinese Army." For two hours each week, players were required to discuss sections of the infamous *Short Course* of the history of the Party. The coach, Boris Arkadiev, was described as a lover of art and literature (he truly was) who often advised his players on their reading choices.[50] One press account even had Arkadiev reading to his players from the prerevolutionary poetry of Alexander Blok.

The reality of these claims can obviously be questioned, and even if they did take place, one can easily imagine that many players took their lessons less than seriously. An educated guess might suggest that Soviet players approached these classes with roughly the same level of sincerity that present-day American college athletes tackle their own studies. Some players certainly saw this education as an attempt raise their cultural horizons. Others probably simply went along with what they saw as a charade. Certainly if political-ideological education had been as effective as its originators had wished, there would have been far fewer subsequent complaints about the phenomena it was supposed to combat.

Changing the Soviet footballer from a roughneck into a cultured person, however, was probably the least important goal of this program. Educated athletes were supposed to be disciplined athletes who obeyed their coaches and did not beat each other up. Better behavior was only one goal of political education, but the ultimate stated purpose of the ideological campaign was the improvement of performance on the field. *Vospitanie*, was directly linked to a team's results. One sports official commented near the end of the 1948 season, "Without the ideological hardening of the football cadres, it is impossible to reach the heights of sporting mastery. The higher the level of an athlete's ideological consciousness and political activity, the more productive the work in achieving sporting mastery and the better the results."[51]

Actual experience, however, demonstrated that success on the field could, in fact, be achieved without the necessary changes in attitude. At the end of the 1948 season, Central Army had won both the league championship and the cup, but its players were taken to task by *Sovetskii sport* in an editorial that claimed "success had turned their heads." TsDKA's behavior on the field and in practices had not been exemplary. They had been guilty of breaking both training regimes and opponents' bones. The press demanded that the champions improve their ideological and political work. Bobrov, who was known for his relaxed approach to training, was singled out as a particularly guilty party.[52] Lectures on the degeneration of bourgeois art and reports on the tactics of the Chinese Communist Army had not had much effect on team play, positive or negative. In fact, two years later, Central Army, still the champion, was taken to task again for crude behavior.

By 1950, the campaign began to peter out, as the intra-Party power struggle took on new and more opaque forms.[53] Educational work was said to have weakened on many teams. The press criticized Iakushin for neglecting his cultural duties, which, it was argued, had hurt Dinamo's play on the field. Similarly, Spartak's troubles during the 1951 season were ascribed to the failure of its ideological work. Ultimately the campaign had little, if any, success. Among it many goals, political education was supposed to instill loyalty to the collective and thus stop the undesirable phenomenon of transfers. Yet players were changing teams in 1950 as often as they had ever done. Dirty play, too, continued unabated, and teams often made no attempt to discipline players who had trangressed standards of fair play.[54] The campaign had the goal of "civilizing" the players who were drawn from the working class. They were to be exposed to "culture" through contact with the many nonproletarian figures who had been drawn to the sport in the wake of the war. Much of the impulse for the campaign, however, appears to have diminished after 1950, and soon thereafter the press came to report far more failures than successes in the sphere of political education.

While the campaign to insert ideological-political education into sports was supposed to improve players' behavior and raise the level of play, the entire exercise had even more importance for the audience. Lectures to players on the degeneration of bourgeois art and on Russian opera may never have taken place, but it was important that the fans thought they occurred. Even if the players never read a book, it was crucial that the link between ideology and victory, politics and order should be firmly established in the minds of those who watched the games. Player behavior was therefore the key element. If soccer were gentlemanly, then the audience could perhaps be persuaded to take seriously the lessons the authorities sought to inculcate. If, on the other hand, players regularly acted like louts, spectators could not be expected to accept the imputed link between the reading of the *Short Course* and success, not only on the field, but in life.

Before the war, soccer crowds had not always behaved in a manner that could be called refined and civilized. The postwar Soviet spectator, on the other hand, was supposed to be an orderly, fair, and informed observor of the game. As it turned out, postwar Soviet fans acted much like their counterparts in other countries, for better and for worse. The fundamental difference was in the minds of the organizers of Soviet sports events. Those who presented capitalist sports spectacles were far less concerned than were Soviet officials with the moral, cultural, and political lessons of the spectacles they were presenting.

Otherwise, the phenomenon of fanship was much the same regardless of the social system. The Soviet fans' attraction to sports, including the choosing of favorite teams and players, was not much different from that of fans in capitalist countries. Even the Stalin-Prize-Winner Donskoi in 1949 described Soviet "lovers of sport" in tones that ring true for any sports fan, "Each of them roots for his own team; for his favorite athletes to whom he gives sympathy and with whom he shares victories and defeats."[55] *Sovetskii sport* used similar words: "They are joyful to the depths of their souls with the victory of their team, and they suffer with each of its defeats. They are open in the expression of their feelings. Everyone can see their joy and their pain. But, loving their team, they are harsh and demanding toward it."[56] Lev Kassil even described feeling compelled to hide his sports sympathies while sitting precariously at Dinamo Stadium between one group of Dinamo fans and another group of Central Army supporters.[57] Rooting for particular teams and players one could identify with had been one of the universal attractions of spectator sports. The aesthetic beauty of the contest was not always a sufficient reason for a sports fan to make the choice of attending a game. Here Soviet fans were no exception.

During these years, many Soviet writers claimed to have found a certain objectivity in their spectators, and there is certainly no shortage of well-documented incidents of visiting teams receiving applause and praise for good play. This fairness, however, was largely a Moscow phenomenon. The capital had several teams, and fans based their loyalties on a complicated mix of motives, reasons, and values. In the provinces, however, it was rare for a city to have more than one first-or second-division team in any sport. On the periphery, loyalty was based on a less reflective and far less gracious rooting for the home side. Fanship was not the result of choice, rational or irrational. Thus the objectivity that Moscow-based journalists thought to be universal turned out to be a great deal harder to find outside the capital.[58]

Going to a game in Moscow during this era was not all that different from the experience of going to a game in any major world city. A Western spectator would find familiar the descriptions of packed subway cars filled with fans discussing and arguing about the game they were about to see. Another Stalin Prize-winner, Leonid Maliugin, wrote, "Already in the metro they are exchanging football prognoses and engaging in hot arguments."[59] With each stop before the "Dinamo" station, more fans, most of them male, would squeeze into the cars, only to explode through the open doors at their destination. This "march" on the stadium was not always orderly and refined. Sports crowds, especially for soccer, have hardly been paragons of propriety in any country, but the jostling, pushing, and shoving typical of any pregame crowd were probably more intense in the USSR than elsewhere. Anyone who has spent time on Soviet transport knows that passengers have rarely made a fetish of avoiding bodily contact. Ilf and Petrov were probably far from wrong when they compared entering a Soviet stadium to "ten rounds of boxing."[60]

In 1949, *Sovetskii sport* described the scene at the "Dinamo" metro station before a big game: "Even the metro has sometimes turned out to be helpless before the unstoppable avalanche of football lovers. Quite often on the days of interesting matches the flow of passengers was so great that it was necessary to close the car doors at 'Paveletskaia', 'Belorusskaia', and several other stations."

The station managers, however, eventually figured out an obvious way to deal with this problem. They went as far as to obtain a schedule of games and anticipated big crowds. They knew that Soviet fans followed the universal rules of attendance—games between the best teams attracted big crowds; those between weaker opponents were rarely big draws: "On the work desk of A. K. Smirnov, chief of the Gorky metro region, lies a schedule of games. It is his meteorological code. The subway staff knows precisely that a meeting of VVS [Air Force] with Krylia Sovetov of Kuibishev means 'light cloudiness,' Spartak and Zenit means 'occasional rain', but Moscow Dinamo versus TsDKA means 'thunder and rain.' "[61] For big games, a metro worker stood at every car entrance, and the number of trains per hour was raised from the normal forty-four to fifty-two. The number of open change booths was quintupled, and all escalators went up before the game and down after it.

Once they were above ground, the spectators' situation did not become any easier. If they had not yet purchased a ticket, they were in for a new round of pushing and shoving. Stadium directors were often criticized for failing to open enough box office windows on game days, causing many fans to enter the stadium after the game had begun.[62] In 1946, *Sovetskii sport* asked children to send letters about their problems in attending games. One

"Looks like we sold three tickets for each seat"

"I hope there's no more goals. I can only count to nine."

"No need to find the buffet"

"The only commentator and public address announcer"

nine-year old named Vitia Brokov wrote, "It's practically impossible to get a ticket for a big game at Dinamo, even if we show our 'Young Dinamovets' cards. You can't even line up for tickets when they go on sale. Adults threaten us and run us off." A teacher also wrote that twelve- and thirteen-year-olds simply did not have the strength to "fight the crowds" on ticket lines where they were "pushed and cursed by hooligans."[63]

Getting a ticket in advance for a big game also was no easy task. The day before one important match in 1947, reporters for *Sovetskii sport* went around to the booths in metro stations that sold tickets to theatrical, musical, and sporting events. At their first stop, they were told no tickets were available. At Dzerzhinskaia station they were told they could buy soccer tickets only if they purchased theater tickets. At the Sverdlov station they found a ticket window with the sign "No tickets for Dinamo and there never were any." They then questioned the director of the ticket distribution system, who told them that the day before the game he had been given only three thousand tickets for public sale and that they would be available at nine o'clock the next morning. The next day the reporters appeared at the Lenin Library Station ticket window to be told all tickets had been sold to "organizations." They then went to the stadium where they found a large crowd pushing and shoving around the only two open ticket windows. Police stood by and did nothing while this crowd of "hooligans and speculators" bought up all the tickets for scalping purposes.[64]

Stadium directors were continually criticized for providing poor service to spectators. Public address systems were rarely used to provide fans with information before and during games, and programs were hard to find. While food and drink were usually available, obtaining them involved long waits on line and sometimes more of Ilf and Petrov's "boxing." Journalists had the delicacy to omit criticism of toilet facilities, but one can easily extrapolate from their descriptions of other elements of stadium service. Clearly attending a game in postwar Moscow was far from a "cultured" activity. Nor could these conditions have improved the disposition of spectators who still had occasion to invade the field or throw rocks and bottles.[65]

It should then be clear that the Soviet sports spectators, even at the height of Stalinism, did not consume their soccer diet in the same spirit and with the same values as the sport's organizers. If sports were to be an icon of discipline, the players were refusing to worship, and this lack of "civilization" had an impact on the audience, which was forced to attend sports under conditions guaranteed to bring out the worst possible behavior. If watching sports was supposed to be an arena of order, the Soviet spectator in the early postwar era still required further "education."

The "Secret" of the Team of Lieutenants—As I have already mentioned, postwar Soviet soccer was dominated by the team representing the Central House of the Red Army (*Tsentral'nyi dom krasnoi armii*). Coached by Boris Arkadiev, Central Army won five of the seven league championships between 1945 and 1951 (Dinamo Moscow won the other two). In the wake of victory over the Nazis, the army had come to enjoy unparalleled popularity in society, and its sports organizations were able to translate this support into strength on the playing field. The army had always been able to draft (in the military sense) promising young players from other clubs. The various teams of the Dinamo society had been able to do the same, although to a lesser degree. New sports priorities gave the armed forces an even greater advantage. With the Soviets about to join the officially amateur Olympic movement, it was now necessary that their sportsmen appear to have work outside the world of athletics. No better model could be found than the "soldier-sportsmen" of Central Army's soccer team.

With one exception, all team members were officers, despite their lack of military training. From this fact came their nickname "the team of lieutenants." Aside from Grigorii Fedotov (the first Soviet player to score 100 goals) and Vsevolod Bobrov, TsDKA's stars included their goalie, Vasilii Nikanorov, and the defender, Anatolii Bashashkin, the team's only sergeant. TsDKA's most dramatic moment of the postwar era came at the end of the 1948 season. They had started the season poorly but had won twelve games in a row to pull even with Dinamo. As so rarely happens during a league season, the two leading contenders met in the final game. A win or tie would have given the championship to Dinamo. On a typically cold and rainy late September afternoon, an overflow crowd in Dinamo Stadium watched as Bobrov opened the scoring on a header off a pass from Viacheslav Soloviev. Ten minutes later Beskov tied the match at 1–1, but just before the half,

TsDKA went ahead 2–1. But in the second half of an intense battle filled with ebb and flow, TsDKA's veteran defender Ivan Kochetkov gave up an own goal. The score remained tied as the traditional gong sounded with five minutes to go in the game. On the verge of injury time, Soloviev would hit the goalpost with a shot from long distance only to have the rebound come out to Bobrov, who scored the championship-winning goal as the referee's whistle blew and fans flooded the playing field. The press was filled with praise for this victory. Never before had a Soviet soccer season actually gone beyond the end of the last game before a champion was decided, and TsDKA was flooded with three thousand congratulatory telegrams.[66] As much as anything, this victory would contribute to their legend.

The Soviets were to take part in the 1952 Olympic soccer tournament, the first international test of the power of the "Soviet school." Possessed of such a team, sports officials and Party leaders were extremely optimistic about their chances. Because the leading capitalist professionals did not take part in Olympic soccer, the Soviets' strongest opponents came from the other "amateur" teams of Eastern Europe. In 1951 and early 1952, strengthened Soviet club teams and Moscow select teams had successfully played against all of Eastern Europe's national teams, with the sole exception of the "revisionist" Tito-ites of Yugoslavia, who had rebelled against Soviet control in 1948. Many of the Eastern European teams had been built around prewar professional clubs and were quite powerful, leading some observers to argue that the Helsinki competition was the strongest of all Olympic soccer championships.

While the press had begun to express reservations about the progress of Soviet soccer by 1951, sports officials and political figures were expecting victory. If Soviet soccer were, as claimed, the "leading school of football in the world," then surely its most outstanding representative had to be the world's best team. In 1952, the leaders of Soviet soccer were faced for the first time since 1935 with the task of assembling a national team. Many specialists, officials, and fans thought the best approach was to build the *sbornaia* around TsDKA. Despite the many complexities of choosing and organizing a national team, the formula for triumph seemed simple to inexperienced Soviet organizers. Yet victory would elude the Soviet team, and this defeat, sometimes called "the secret of the team of lieutenants," is one of the most mysterious and controversial episodes in the history of Soviet sports.

For many, Central Army's fate represents the height of political meddling and interference in the sporting process, but this is not a view universally accepted by journalists, historians, and veterans of the game. Precisely because this controversy involved figures at the highest levels of the Party hierarchy, it is particularly difficult to find conclusive evidence on the roles of Party leaders. The relevant archives have been closed, and the historian is forced to rely on memoirs and press accounts. Some observers have described a conspiracy surrounding the team involving everyone from Stalin and Beria to the army High Command. Others have contended that the causes of the Soviet defeat at Helsinki can be more easily explained by events limited to the world of sports. They argue that the political explanation does not hold up under detailed scrutiny.

The facts there is universal agreement on are as follows: The 1952 Olympic soccer tournament was the largest in the history of the Games. Twenty-seven teams had chosen to contest the title. Arkadiev was named the team's head coach. Iakushin, who had moved to Dinamo Tblisi, was appointed as his assistant fairly late in the preparation process. In their first game, the Soviets had to go into overtime to defeat a highly capable Bulgarian side by a score of 2–1. Only three of the starters in the first game actually came from Central Army—Anatolii Bashashkin, Iurii Nyrkov, and Alexander Petrov. Bobrov, as noted, had switched to the Air Force team, and he was joined by such new stars as Spartak's great halfback, Igor Netto. Beskov, of Dinamo Moscow, would start the next game. Dinamo Tblisi also contributed two men to the squad—Avtandil Chukaseli and Avtandil Gogoberidze—both of whom would later make appearances. To be sure, Central Army had the largest delegation on the national team, but it is impossible to argue that the "lieutenants" alone were representing the USSR at Helsinki.[67]

Yugoslavia was to be the second-round opponent. This match-up presented a problem. Due to the collapse of relations with the Tito government, the Soviets had not played any Yugoslavian team since 1947. Bulgaria had been a known quantity, but no one had any idea what to expect from the Yugoslavs. To make matters worse, no one from the Soviet delegation— neither Arkadiev; nor Iakushin; nor the head of the Football Federation, Valentin Granatkin—had bothered to see the Yugoslavs' first-round match, in which they defeated India by a score of 10–1. By half time, Yugoslavia, using tactics completely unfamiliar to the Soviets, was leading 3–0. When play resumed, the score quickly became 4–0. Bobrov soon managed a goal, but before the Soviets could celebrate, the Yugoslavs retaliated, two minutes later. The score remained 5–1 until the seventy-fifth minute, when Vasilii Trofimov of Dinamo Moscow brought his team back to life with a goal. The Yugolsavs had retreated into a defensive mode, but they failed to prevent Bobrov from scoring just two minutes later. The Soviets continued to attack furiously, but only in the eighty-seventh minute did Bobrov strike again. With the score 5–4 and one minute to go, the cause still seemed hopeless, but TsDKA's Alexander Petrov headed in a corner kick to tie the game. Half an hour of overtime yielded no scoring, and a replay was scheduled for two days later.[68]

Having staged one of the greatest comebacks in the history of the sport, the exhausted Soviet players were put through a heavy practice the next day. For the replay, the Yugoslavs fielded the same players. Arkadiev and Iakushin made one change, replacing Leningrad Zenit's Mariutin with Chukaseli from Dinamo Tblisi, a switch that would later prove to be controversial. Bobrov scored the first goal of the replay, but the younger Yugoslavs soon overpowered their fatigued opponents, winning by 3–1. The defeat was so shocking and deemed so shameful that it was not even reported in the Soviet press. The Olympics had received extensive coverage in regular newspapers as well as in *Sovetskii sport,* but the loss to the Yugolavs went unmentioned. Hungary's triumph over Yugoslavia in the final was covered, and those who remembered Soviet victories over the Hungarians in pre-Olympic "friendlies" were able to draw the conclusion that something strange and unpleasant had occurred. Only after Stalin's death did histories of the sport even mention the Olympic defeat.[69]

The players and coaches returned home to resume the regular season, only to find their play receiving far less press coverage than before the Olympics. Descriptions of matches that did appear were uniformly critical of the level of play. Finally, in September, after avoiding the issue for several weeks, *Sovetskii sport* ran the league standings. Central Army was missing.[70] The team had been disbanded. VVS, the Air Force team, would soon meet the same fate, its players distributed to other teams. In addition, Arkadiev, Beskov, and Valentin Nikolaev lost their "Honored Master of Sport" titles, while Bashashkin, Konstantin Kryzhevskii, and Alexander Petrov had their "Master of Sport" honors taken away. While the army team was disbanded, not all those who lost official honors were members of TsDKA; notable exceptions were Beskov and Kryzhevskii. The punishments stopped there, however. No one was arrested, sent into exile, or executed. It would, however, be two years before any team from the armed forces again appeared in first-division play. In the interim, Stalin, of course, would die.

All of Soviet soccer came in for severe critcism in the wake of the Olympic defeat. Even Soviet hockey's founding father, Anatolii Tarasov, attacked club soccer coaches for failing to develop younger players. Left unsaid was the fact that many of the players on the Olympic team were past their primes. Bobrov was 30; Beskov, 31; Trofimov, 33; and Valentin Nikolaev, 31. They were four of the five starting attackers. Their age limited their ability to return to full form only two days after a titanic struggle. Had they been defenders, this feat might have been possible, but it was harder to come back quickly playing a position that demanded speed. In his memoirs, Iakushin cites this fact as one of the central reasons for the loss to Yugoslavia, and he admits his mistake in forcing these veterans to practice on the day between games.[71]

Subsequent accounts of the Olympic debacle emphasized the decisive importance of political meddling. In 1988, two Soviet sportswriters, the veteran Stanislav Tokarev, and the younger Alexander Gorbunov, writing in the monthly *Sportivnye igry,* stressed the role of this interference. Rather than allow Arkadiev to take his powerful "lieutenants" to Helsinki, every "patron [*metsenat*] of the game" sought to pressure the head coach into taking men from his own team. Beria, Vasilii Stalin, and many generals were constantly offering "advice" to the coaches. Komsomol secretaries were also said to have interfered in the selection process. The suggestion made in this series of articles is that TsDKA was strong enough to have won on its own. Instead, as many as sixty players passed through the various training camps and exhibition games, preventing the development of the necessary level of cohesion. The political "agiotage" around the composition of the squad was supposed to have destroyed morale. In particular, Gorbunov and Tokarev suggest that the replacement of Martiunin by the young and inexperienced Georgian, Chukaseli, was the indirect work of his fellow Georgian, Beria.[72]

Citing the memoirs of Iurii Nyrkov, one of TsDKA's stars, Gorbunov and Tokarev emphasize the enormous political pressure put on the players by various figures in the Soviet Olympic delegation. They make reference to, but doubt the likelihood of, a pregame telegram from Stalin, in which "the greatest friend of Soviet physical culture" emphasized the enormous significance of a victory against the enemy Yugoslavs. All of this attention, contend Tokarev and Gorbunov, made it impossible for the Soviet players to approach their task with any equanimity or strength of will. The pressure was simply too great.

The authors also argue that the decision to disband the Central Army team as punishment for "their" Olympic failure, was made by Stalin personally.[73] For this assertion, however, they are not able to present direct evidence, given the present state of archival access. Gorbunov and Tokarev do, however, describe a meeting held in the Kremlin immediately upon the return of the entire Olympic delegation on August 6, 1952. The purpose of this secret gathering was to allow top Party and state officials to evalaute the overall Olympic performance. Georgi Malenkov chaired the meeting, which was also attended by Beria and the sitting head of the All-Union Committee of Physical Culture, N. N. Romanov, among others. No account places Stalin at this gathering.

Basing their story on Nyrkov's undocumented secondhand memoir account, Gorbunov and Tokarev relate that Malenkov asked Romanov if the Olympic soccer team had been based on Central Army. Romanov, who clearly knew better, incorrectly replied "yes," and Beria supported this distortion in order to deflect blame from the several representatives of both Dinamo Moscow and Dinamo Tblisi who had played in Finland. All the guilt then fell on the army team, even though it was clear to many inside and outside the sports world that TsDKA was not the core of the Olympic team. Indeed, Beria's attempt to divert the blame from his institution failed, as one of those who lost his "Master of Sport" title was Beskov, a Dinamo man.

Using more reliable evidence and more plausible arguments, Gorbunov and Tokarev then go on to cite archival material from the All-Union Committee of Physical Culture concerning a January 15, 1953, meeting of the "All-Union Scientific-Methodological Conference on Football." Held in the supercharged atmosphere generated by the announcement of the "Doctors' Plot" two days earlier, the gathering turned into an orgy of denunciation directed at Arkadiev. TsDKA's coach was described as an "apolitical intellectual" who, it was said, held himself above his players, none of whom could understand their coach because of Arkadiev's "constant use of foreign words." No doubt the highly cosmopolitan term *"khavbek"* was among those words. One representative of the coaches' council went as far as to suggest that Arkadiev's failures were rooted in his ignorance of Stalin's recent "masterpiece," *Economic Problems of Socialism in the USSR.*

In the context of the time, these sorts of attacks, absurd as they may seem, surely must have occurred. Stalin had, after all, sought to establish himself as the last word on a wide range of subjects beyond sports, including economics, linguistics, music, and biology. He had established the quack scientist Lysenko as the nation's leading authority on genetics, and many fully competent professionals in a wide variety of fields had been denounced and dismissed from their jobs. Yet, in describing these meetings of soccer specialists, Gorbunov and Tokarev do not cite specific documents. Instead, they merely mention, at the outset of their piece, the numbers of the archival files from which this material was drawn. Their imprecision makes it impossible to verify their account.[74]

Two years later, their version of events was disputed both by Iakushin (in his memoirs) and by the veteran sportswriter Arkadii Galinskii. Both men found sufficient reasons within the sports sphere to explain the Soviets' quick exit from the Olympic soccer competition. Iakushin accepts responsibility for both himself and Arkadiev, who died in 1986. He cites their inexperience in international competition as the reason for the many errors they made. Iakushin admitted that he did not know that in the Olympics, games followed each other more quickly than the weekly pace of a regular domestic soccer season. Had he realized this, he and Arkadiev would have chosen more young players.[75]

In a series of articles published in *Sovetskii sport* during 1990, Galinskii debunked the theory of a political conspiracy. A maverick who had his share of difficulties with the authorities over the course of a long career, Galinskii was not seeking to defend the high Party officals accused of meddling, and his own past gives a certain credibility to his account. Galinskii argued that by 1952, Central Army was no longer the team it had been in the late 1940s. Fedotov had retired. Bobrov, oft-injured, had moved to VVS, and many other stars were getting older. Throughout 1951, these facts had been noted often in the sports press in both analytical articles and game accounts. Not only TsDKA but all of Soviet soccer came under increasing criticism for "stagnation."[76]

Galinskii stated that Arkadiev understood the impossibility of basing the Olympic team on TsDKA. Galinskii also noted that Arkadiev, throughout his career, had resisted attempts by political nonspecialists to name his squad. He had quit Dinamo in 1944 over this issue, and in his time at Central Army, he had repeatedly ignored the "advice" of generals and colonels.[77] Thus the team that finally did go to Helsinki was by no means the "team of lieutenants," and according to Galinskii, this choice was Arkadiev's professional decision. It is important to remember that this was the first time since 1935 a Soviet national team had been organized. In all countries at all times, the politics of putting together national teams have been terribly complex, and coaches have always been subjected to extensive and unwanted advice, interference, and pressure. In this sense, the attempts of powerful nonspecialists to influence the composition of the Olympic squad were not all that different from the practice in the West, and the meddling by Soviet political figures was not the first such case in the history of the sport of soccer.

Galinskii also cited and supported Iakushin's account of the errors made by Soviet coaches. The Yugoslavs were an extremely strong opponent who would go to the final, only to lose to an excellent Hungarian team.[78] Galinskii also discussed the controversial decision to put the young Georgian attacker Chukaseli into the lineup for the replay. In Galinskii's version, Iakushin decided that Chukaseli, who played on Iakushin's club team, possessed the particular qualities to pressure the Yugoslavs' strong defender, Branko Stankovic. Chukaseli was inexperienced, but he was young and strong. Iakushin then discussed the matter with Arkadiev, Bobrov, Beskov, Trofimov, and Nikolaev, none of whom objected. Galinskii made no mention of Beria's role, but Galisnkii tried to suggest that a reasonable argument for the switch could be made on exclusively professional grounds.[79] The fact that Chukaseli did not play well did not, by itself, mean that the decision was made for the wrong reasons.

Finally, Galinskii raised doubts about the likelihood that Stalin personally made the decision to break up Central Army's team. The Olympic squad had, after all, not been based on TsDKA, and those who lost their titles were also not exclusively "lieutenants." In the absence of definitive archival evidence concerning political history at so high a level, however, Galinskii could only guess at other possible scenarios. He suggested instead that the decision to disband TsDKA was more likely made by the Minister of Defense, A. M. Vasilevskii, than by Stalin personally. Vasilevskii may have been taking a cue from Stalin, but Galinskii claimed that Vasilevskii had, at this time, broken up a number of the armed forces' teams in a variety of sports. The Air Force soccer team, after all, met a similar fate. Vasilevskii was an opponent of elite sports and preferred that the military give priority to mass physical culture. Only after Stalin's death, when Nikolai Bulganin was appointed Minister of Defense, were big-time sports revived in the armed forces.[80]

While Galinskii offered little more direct proof on this matter than Gorbunov and Tokarev, his explanation has a certain plausibility. If TsDKA's players only composed a minority of the Olympic team, why should Central Army have borne the brunt of the blame for the defeat? Galinskii at least suggests Vasilevskii's prejudices as a possible alternative explanation for the disbanding of the team. This analysis has the merit of going beyond Malenkov's garbled questioning of Romanov at the Kremlin, a conversation that itself may never have taken place.

While Galinskii's account offered a more credible reading of these events, it cannot be said that he directly disproved the version presented in *Sportivnye igry*. Nor did he bring a historian's perspective to the evidential weaknesses of that account. Instead, Galinskii presented a counterexplanation that left out possible political interference. I have presented both versions here at some length in order to show the kinds of myths, rumors, and accompanying controversies that have circulated around Soviet sports. True or false, these legends are part of the discourses of both specialists and nonspecialists, and over the years they have taken on a reality of their own. Every Soviet fan has his "secrets" learned from "insiders," and nearly all Soviet journalists have their stories that they "know" but cannot print.

In some sense, things are not that different in the West, where reporters know much more than they can confirm and print. Additionally, the highest level of Soviet politics was always a source of rumor and speculation. Indeed, much of what has passed for the history of so-called high politics in the USSR has been based on rumor and speculation. At the same time, big-time sport in any nation at any time has always been a repository of myths and legends. Thus, the combination of high politics and elite sport can be seen as particularly fertile territory for rumor, gossip, and conjecture.

Galinskii's version may be more plausible than that of Tokarev and Gorbunov, but one must remember that Stalin's last years were a period of Soviet history during which much occurred that was utterly implausible. Galinskii demonstrates that, even in this time of high Stalinism, sports could attain some measure of autonomy. Not every kick or save was foreordained at some Party congress. Yet clearly, soccer, like many other spheres of Soviet life, could not entirely escape the interference of the powerful. While it is likely that the realities of this and similar episodes will turn out to be considerably less bloodcurdling when they are examined in detail, it is nevertheless important to note that such myths may persist in the minds of sports fans.

Every game has its legends, both positive and negative. Babe Ruth probably never really promised that poor little sick boy he would hit a home run, nor is it likely that he really did call his famous "shot" in Wrigley Field. Yet such myths, even if they contain distortions of history, both explain the attractions of sport and generate its ideologies. The "Secret of the Team of Lieutenants" remains for many Soviet fans the quintessential case of political interference in sport. Stalin's last years were a time of enormous state meddling in all areas of cultural life, but it is difficult to prove that events of this sort actually took place. At the same time, the rumors remain so strong that it is hard to imagine that any type of presently unobtainable documentary evidence could ever change the minds of the convinced.

The Birth of Soviet Hockey

Canadian hockey had been played in the USSR during the 1930s in physical culture institutes. Before the war, the sport had many strong advocates, and interest in it quickly resurfaced. Very soon Canadian hockey would come to occupy a leading place in the sports life of the nation, overtaking Russian hockey and becoming the USSR's second true spectator sport. This shift to the Canadian version of the game, however, greatly taxed the limited resources that were then available for sports. Compared to soccer, hockey was expensive. In Europe and North America, the game was played on artifical ice in large, heated buildings, many of which had more than ten thousand seats. Players had to be covered with expensive and elaborate protective equipment. Goals and boards had to be built. Sticks and pucks were used up at a furious pace.

When they began playing Canadian hockey, the Soviets possessed none of these necessities, nor did they have the means of obtaining them quickly. There was still no indoor arena anywhere in the country. The first artificial rink was not built until 1956. In the absence of a well-developed sporting goods industry, many players had to make their own uniforms and equipment. The only helmets available were for bicycle riders or boxers. Teams had to share the few available rinks, and the lack of ice time required extensive on-land training, a necessity Soviet coaches would soon make a virtue.

Despite these obstacles, the Soviets quickly reached world-class levels. While the material obstacles were formidable, it should be remembered that the task, in sporting terms, was not as difficult as many have thought. Western journalistic descriptions of the Soviet hockey program have usually ignored the enormous importance of Russian hockey. The Soviets did not start from scratch, as many accounts have suggested.[81] Such claims ascribe subsequent Soviet success in hockey to the power of the sports system, with its scientific methods and lavish state support, fueled by ideologically generated political fanaticism. By ignoring the prehistory of hockey, one can be easily led to the far-from-correct conclusion that such a system could achieve similar goals in other sports, given the putative superiority of Soviet methods. In fact, Soviet hockey players simply adapted to a different version of a game that was fundamentally similar to the Russian hockey they had played for decades.

Many Soviet players had been familiar with Canadian hockey for more than a decade, and the recently conquered Baltic states had also played Canadian hockey during the period of their independence. The athletes who had enjoyed success in Russian hockey already knew how to skate, stick-handle, and pass at a very high level of skill. Virtually the entire first generation of Soviet hockey stars began their careers playing the Russian version of the game. Additionally, many of these athletes had played soccer during the summer.[82] When they switched to Canadian hockey, they not only adapted many tactics from soccer, they also preserved many of the most important characteristics (primarily speed and passing) from the earlier Russian game. In reporting on the the first season of hockey, the veteran sportswriter Iurii Van'iat stressed the importance of this transition: "Many of our authorities justifiably point out that a player who passes through the school of Russian hockey has all the bases for becoming a first-class player of Canadian hockey. It is entirely likely that Russian hockey will turn out to have an influence on the tactics of Canadian hockey."[83]

On February 17, 1946, after a game of Russian hockey, a primitive Canadian-style rink was set up, and students from the Moscow Institute of Physical Culture played before a crowd of several thousand, who applauded heartily at the end of the contest. That fall a ten-day crash course for coaches, players, and officials was held in Leningrad.[84] Early in December, teams representing most of the sports societies that had dominated soccer began to play a series of exhibitions in Moscow in preparation for the sixty-day season that would begin later that month. In the first of the exhibition games, on December 10, 1946, Spartak defeated Dinamo 9–1. The event impressed not only the fans but the press as well. *Sovetskii sport*'s account predicted quick popularity for Canadian hockey. "This first game showed that Canadian hockey can swiftly gain the sympathy of fans and players, with its tempo, quickly changing momentum, and intensity of play."[85] The first official games took place on Decmeber 22, 1946, in Leningrad, Moscow, Riga, Archangel, and Kaunas. Five thousand fans showed up at Dinamo Stadium in Moscow to watch a double-header, played inside six-inch-high boards. Spartak defeated Dinamo Leningrad, and TsDKA won 5–1 over their army club mates from Sverdlovsk.[86] In Riga, 2,000 saw Dinamo Riga beat Kalev of Tallin.

The season lasted two months, with a total of seven clubs contesting the championship. The teams were small with no more than twelve members. One of the leading players on each team served as coach. Arkadii Chernyshev played this role for Dinamo Moscow. His counterpart on TsDKA, Anatolii Tarasov, would go on to become the most important figure in the history of Soviet hockey. Tarasov was a gifted and highly original tactician and team leader, but he would prove even more effective in popularizing the game and spreading awareness of its intricacies to teams, players, coaches, and fans. He performed this task by regularly publishing detailed and lengthy critiques of the development of the game, and he is largely responsible for both the originality of the Soviet style of hockey and the inventiveness of its training methods. In all these endeavors, he worked closely with Chernyshev, and the two served virtually as co-coaches of the national team for two decades, with Chernyshev's steadiness and calm balancing the more ebullient but difficult Tarasov.

At this early stage, play was characterized by energetic skating and extensive passing. The players did, however, have some difficulty mastering the details of the rules. Offsides were common, as was icing the puck. Individual rushes were few, and hardly any defensemen learned to use their bodies in order to liquidate attacks. From the earliest days, most Soviet forwards demonstrated a reluctance to shoot that would continue to characterize their play. Only the Baltic clubs showed much tactical variation, but they were not able to match the athleticism of the top Moscow teams.[87]

Dinamo Moscow, which included Mikhail Iakushin in its defense, was the first champion, defeating TsDKA and Spartak on goal difference. Tarasov was the leading scorer, getting fourteen goals in seven games.[88] This first, brief season proved to be a great success. For all their technical flaws, the speed and skill of the players made for an exciting spectacle. Several of the more important games in Dinamo Stadium attracted five thousand, and ten thousand fans sat through the final match between Dinamo and TsDKA, despite weather of minus eleven degrees Centigrade. Press coverage was also extensive, with articles on the games as lengthy and detailed as those on soccer.

Hockey specialists were highly pleased that the players adapted to the new game so quickly, but it was feared by some that Canadian hockey would come to replace the Russian game. For the next season, players were required to specialize in one type of hockey, and most of the leading players chose the Canadian variant. On January 11, 1948, *Komsomolskaia pravda* decried this shift: "Canadian hockey, with its unusually crude play, is typical of the bourgeois West.''[89] *Sovetskii sport* responded to this criticism by noting that many sports popular in the West were also played in the USSR.

> But what a huge gulf lies between Soviet and bourgeois football, boxing, and basketball. The morals of bourgeois sport are deeply alien to Soviet sportsmen. ...We have created our own Soviet style in sport, the superiority of which has been demonstrated by our football, basketball, and water polo players, gymnasts, boxers and wrestlers in the biggest international competitions. Our goal is to create in this new sport for us, Canadian hockey, our advanced Soviet style, in order that our hockey players, in a short time, will become the strongest in the world.[90]

By the 1947–1948 season, the league had expanded to ten teams, playing an eighteen-game season. Moscow again dominated the league, with five clubs. Each Baltic republic had a representative, and there were two teams from Leningrad. As the players improved their technique, scoring increased, and so did the crowds. By the end of the season, Central Army emerged as the champion, led by the unstoppable Bobrov, who joined them after sitting out the first season. He scored 52 of his team's 108 goals to lead the league, teaming on a line with Tarasov and Evgenii Babich.[91]

Immediately after the completion of the season, Soviet hockey underwent its first international examination. Late in February, the LTC club from Prague came to the USSR to play three games against a select team of ''Moscow'' stars drawn from TsDKA, Dinamo, and Spartak, as well as one player from Dinamo Riga. In effect, a Soviet national team was playing a foreign club. LTC was a Czech power, including many players from their national team, which had just finished second to Canada at the Winter Olympics and had won the world championship the year before when the Canadians had stayed home. As no one knew exactly what to expect, the games were not extensively publicized, but word of mouth led to 25,000 spectators showing up at Dinamo Stadium for each game. Nor were they disappointed, as the results proved highly encouraging. The Soviets won the first game, lost the second, and tied the last. Having played one of Europe's powers on equal terms, the young Soviet coaches felt affirmed in having chosen the particularly original approach they had taken to the game, and their Czech counterparts were especially impressed by the speed and maneuverability of the Soviet skaters. Stick-handling and defense were still weaknesses, but the Czechs predicted that the Soviets would soon play an ''outstanding'' role in world hockey. A year later, the weaker Polish national team came to play Dinamo, TsDKA, and a combined Spartak and Krylia Sovetov squad. All three matches were routs.[92]

Given the importance then attached to achieving world superiority, these successes provoked great excitement, but, predictably, they also gave rise to continuing and intense criticism. The leading hockey referee, Sergei Savin, often appeared in print to evaluate successes and failures, and he attributed the recent successes to a higher level of preparation than had been previously achieved. By 1950, Moscow teams began their conditioning in August, and early in November they journeyed to colder regions to begin on-ice training as soon as possible. At the same time that he praised this new seriousness and professionalism, Savin repeated his criticism of most teams' defensive weaknesses, especially the unwillingness of most Soviet defensemen to use their bodies against opponents.[93]

Most of the swift early progress of Soviet hockey was the result of Tarasov's special coaching brilliance. In evaluating the results of the 1951 season, Tarasov praised the "high class" of play demonstrated against the Czechs and Poles, and also in domestic competition. He would attribute this development to the fact that Soviet hockey players now trained "the year round. "The convincing victories of our teams in international meetings shows the correctness of the direction of development taken by the Soviet school of hockey. The techniques and tactics created by our players and coaches are based on high physical and moral preparation."[94] Tarasov, however, also decried the continuing tendency of offensive players to over-pass in search of the perfect opportunity. "Attacking teams," he protested, "must learn to shoot from farther distances."

All this attention and analysis testified to the swift growth of Soviet hockey, but it must be noted that these successes were achieved on a shoe-string. The first generation of Soviet players had to labor under difficult conditions. Dinamo Stadium was the main venue for hockey in Moscow. A rink was set up at the east end of the arena, inside the running track, allowing half the stadium's normal 55,000 capacity to have an acceptable view of play. But, all of these seats were on one sideline and the end-zones. There were just a few places set up on the sideline that opened out to the rest of the stadium.[95] The first playing surface was quite primitive, lacking even rounded corners. The quality of ice was entirely dependent on the outside temperature, and more than a few matches had to be called because of good weather. Snowstorms and blizzards were rarely deemed sufficient reasons to stop a match. To assure sufficient cold, most games were played at night, putting a special burden on Dinamo Stadium's less-than-brilliant lighting system. In the pinched conditions of the postwar era, stadium officials, to save electricity, often turned off the lights between periods, plunging the entire arena into complete darkness.

This unusual venue did, however, have a special magic. One Soviet journalist has reminisced about those early days: "Oh, those hockey vigils on the east tribune of Dinamo under the soundless implacable tramping of thousands of boots! No frost could stop the movement on the floodlit rink, surrounded by snowdrifts, where athletes, wearing biking helmets, since we had no hockey helmets at the time, created a game.'"[96]

Equipment, as already mentioned, presented enormous problems. These difficulties were faced not only by teams on the periphery but also by the elite Moscow clubs. Tarasov complained about this situation often and at great length:

> Our hockey players are awaiting high quality equipment. However, we unfortunately do not have enough. Take, for example, the stick, the player's main weapon. The majority of them are made at factories, in an off-handed way and not from the correct materials. As a result, these kinds of sticks break after a few minutes of play. The directors of plants that make sports equipment must supply hockey players with the kinds of sticks that are made of durable materials. . . . Much of the equipment of the hockey player must be made by the athlete himself.[97]

These problems did not prevent hockey from finding a mass audience. Tarasov, Chernyshev, and their colleagues quickly succeeded in producing a highly attractive version of a game that in North America and Europe had already become an important spectator sport. The few games of the first season averaged 2,500 spectators, with Dinamo and TsDKA attracting the largest audience—10,000. The next year, crowds grew larger. Spartak, still the most popular of the sport societies, attracted 15,000 for its match against Central Army and 18,000 when it played Dinamo. By contrast, Dinamo versus TsDKA, two stronger teams, brought only eight thousand fans to Dinamo Stadium. In the provinces, crowds were considerably smaller, with audiences of 100 to 1,500.[98]

The next season, Bobrov had switched to Vasilii Stalin's Air Force team (*VVS*), adding yet another gate attraction. When they played in Riga, over eight thousand showed up. Games against his old team drew over twenty thousand, as did matches of both military teams with Dinamo. By 1951, games between these leaders were drawing thirty thousand spectators on a regular basis. That same year the season was capped off with two games between the Moscow selects and the Czech national team. The Soviets won both contests, each of which took place before audiences larger than thirty thousand. These matches made especially compelling sights. The large crowd surrounded the small rink, which was separated from the audience by snowbanks. The scene took on an especially magical quality in the cold night air, illuminated by the immense but still inefficient light towers of the stadium.[99]

Given the violence that is innate in the game, it is perhaps surprising that denunciations of rough play, so common for soccer, were comparatively rare for hockey. This gentlemanliness may have had something to do with a desire to contrast the Soviet style with the cruder, brawling approach so common in North America. Indeed, the fighting that typified Canadian hockey had led many observors before 1946 to resist its adoption. Soviet hockey had therefore to be utterly clean by comparison. Savin repeatedly stressed the difference: "Hockey in our country develops by its own path and has nothing in common with foreign versions of the game. There, players follow the worst example of Canadian professional hockey, try always to fight, and replace technique with crude physical force."[100] It had been difficult to find a corps of capable referees who could keep rough play in check, but despite a common uncertainty about the rules, all officials frowned on fighting from the very beginning. Their work was made somewhat easier by the fact that Russian hockey did not stress the intense body-checking of the Canadian game, and Soviet players actually had to acquire the ability to use their bodies in ways that the more liberal Canadian rules allowed.

This emphasis did not mean that Soviet hockey was free of dirty play. The disciplinary committee worked regularly, disqualifying players for several games at a time.[101] Yet contemporary press accounts of hockey were characterized by far fewer complaints about player violence. In part, this contrast may be the result of the differing expectations observers brought to hockey, as opposed to soccer. A certain amount of contact was supposed to occur in hockey, while similar roughness in soccer destroyed the game's flow and beauty. More likely, the comparatively low level of dirty play in hockey had to do with the fact that there was simply a great deal less hockey played than soccer. The season was shorter. It could only be played in colder regions, and fewer groups could afford the comparative expense of fielding and equipping a team.

As in soccer, the guardians of the sport's welfare saw the answer to violent play in ideological-political education. In 1949, Savin attributed a rise in the number of players breaking training to "unsatisfactory" political work. As late as 1951, Bobrov, whose own regimen was known to be less than spartan, told an interviewer that the success of his new team, VVS, was the result of "systematic political-educational work."[102] Tarasov, who often attributed his success to the Party and the government, also paid homage to the prevailing spirit of cultural conformity:

> The main condition for raising the class of play of our teams is well-run political-educational work. Thorough, systematic political study broadens the athletes' horizons and educates them about the highly conscious, cultured patriots of our homeland.... In the course of the season Central Army's players studied the *Short Course of the Histor of the Communist Party (Bolsheviks)* and listened to a series of lectures and reports on current politcal affairs.[103]

The reference to "highly conscious, cultured patriots" suggests that educational work was to play the same civilizing role among hockey players as it did among those who played soccer. The available sources do not comment on the matter, but they give no reason to believe that the stars of Soviet hockey did not come from the same social strata as their football counterparts. Nor is there any evidence that the hockey audience was different in social composition from the public for soccer. Some sports were seen as the games of the "intelligentsia" (tennis and sailing), and others were called "students' games" (track, rowing, swimming, volleyball, and basketball). Thus there is every reason to believe that hockey players and hockey spectators came from the same milieu as the practitioners and fans of soccer. As a result, the need to struggle against this "lack of culture" (*nekulturnost'*), while less visible than in soccer, persisted in the world of Soviet hockey.

Because they did not start from scratch, the Soviets quickly rose to the top levels of world hockey. They did this without a massive influx of resources and without elaborate facilities. Their success was in large measure the result of an ability to attract many of the best representatives of a vast talent pool to the sport of hockey. The growing size of the audience and the great potential rewards made hockey an attractive choice for athletes. At the same time, Soviet hockey had the good fortune to find in Anatolii Tarasov a coach of true genius. Perhaps his greatest gift was an ability to turn disadvantages into advantages. He overcame the Soviets' ignorance of traditional tactics by developing an entirely new style of play. Similarly, he was able to surmount the lack of training facilities by inventing a wide variety of cross-training routines. Finally, he was able to articulate his ideas in written form so that the first generation of Soviet coaches, players, and fans could apply them relatively quickly throughout the entire country. So great was Tarasov's influence that one journalist recalled his own youth playing hockey on ponds with his friends: "Already back then you heard on these improvised rinks, 'Tarasov said . . .' 'Tarasov thought up,' 'Tarasov promised to call [some player] to the team.' "[104] On the eve of Stalin's death, after just six seasons of league play, Soviet hockey was ready to step onto the world's stage.

Olympic Sports and Olympic Games

Throughout Europe and North America, the postwar period was a time of great excitement and achievement in sports. A world at peace was a world that could play, and millions flocked to stadiums, others listened on the radio, and a few would come to watch on television. The USSR was no exception to this phenomenon. The audience for all sports expanded. The growth of soccer and hockey attested to this fact, and much of the excitement extended to other games. Despite all the difficulties of reconstruction, it was also now possible to expand the facilities available for sports spectacles. Pishchevik

Stadium in Odessa was restored and a new sports complex was built in Erevan. Construction was resumed on the giant Kirov stadium in Leningrad. It
opened in the middle of the 1950 soccer season, and its 74,000-seat capacity
made it the largest arena in the nation. In Kiev, Dinamo Stadium was restored, expanded to 50,000 seats, and named after the sitting head of the
Ukrainian Communist Party, Nikita Khrushchev, himself a former soccer
player of little distinction. Construction began in 1949 on a 45,000-seat arena
in Baku, and even such smaller cities as Vladimir got a stadium holding
15,000. In Leningrad, a Tsarist *manège* was turned into an indoor sports
facility in which as many as three thousand could watch track, basketball, or
volleyball.[105] All this growth would expand the number of places for Soviet
fans to watch sports events. Yet the USSR still lagged far behind the West
in the facilities available for spectator sports.

Track, swimming, basketball, and boxing, all of which received the bulk
of attention in such multisport competitions as the Spartakiads and the Olympic Games, were also affected by the broad growth of popular interest in
sports. While these sports still trailed the Big Two for the loyalty of Soviet
fans, they were not immune to the general rise of interest in spectator sports
during the postwar period. Of all these games, basketball enjoyed the biggest
increase in popularity. Before the war, the game had attracted many participants but only a limited audience. After 1945, there still was no basketball
league, but the national championship, an annual tournament, came to be
contested by club teams. Unlike in soccer and hockey, Moscow did not dominate. To be sure, Central Army, Air Force, and Dinamo Moscow had strong
teams, but they were severely challenged by clubs from the three Baltic
republics, as well as teams from Georgia and the town of Sverdlovsk in the
Ural Mountains. Leningrad also had a strong basketball tradition.

In 1946, basketball tournaments held in Leningrad and Kiev attracted
thousands of fans. The 1947 national championship, which took place in
Tblisi, was won by the local Dinamo club, led by their star center, Otar
Korkia. All of these events were held outdoors due to the lack of arenas, and
even these venues proved unable to accommodate all those wishing to take
in the games. At Tblisi, only three thousand seats surrounded the outdoor
court, but, according to press reports, as many as ten thousand viewed the
games from every nearby rooftop and tree. Even larger crowds had attended
outdoor games in Kaunas and Vilnius, Lithuania. But the sport's potential as
a spectator attraction was severely hampered by the fact that there were no
large indoor arenas in which the game could be played during the long winter.
At times Leningrad's *manège* could accommodate three thousand viewers,
but there was no comparable facility in Moscow.[106]

All accounts of postwar basketball remark on the enormous advance in
the quality of play. This improvement was, by and large, the result of the

addition of the Baltic teams. Zhalgiris of Kaunas, Kalev of Tallin, and later the Army Club of Riga provided strong competition for the Moscow, Leningrad, and Tblisi teams. The Baltic clubs also gave Soviet basketball a technical sophistication that was the result of many years of high-level basketball played during their period of independence. Aside from the excitement added by teams representing different national groups, Soviet basketball fans found the contrast in styles especially compelling. When Baltic skill and precise shooting were combined on national teams with the athleticism of the Russians and the intensity and quickness of the Georgians, they produced a particularly powerful brand of basketball that could in all truth be called "Soviet." When a Soviet team composed of two Georgians, two Lithuanians, two Estonians, and five Russians won the European championship at Prague in 1947, the Soviet press was ecstatic in praise for their triumph. In distinction to the other teams, the Soviets played a constantly fast-breaking style combined with a man-to-man defense that none of their opponents employed. In those days, it was possible to use such an approach only if one had the extremely fit athletes and great depth possessed by the Soviets.[107]

The victory of the men's basketball team seemed a perfect micrcosm of the vast and fraternal multiethnic union. Accordingly, the press gave added attention to basketball, further expanding its popularity. When the Soviets won again at Paris in 1951, *Sovetskii sport* was now ready to claim that the nation's progress in basketball had fulfilled the goals of the 1948 Party resolution that called for world preeminence: "The Soviet basketabll team, sent by the army of our physical culturalists to the European championship, convincingly demonstrated in the capital of France the advantages of the Soviet school of basketball, the most progressive and advanced in the world."[108] As a sign of the game's new importance, the team was greeted on its return to Moscow by Party leaders and marching bands at Vnukovo airport.

Having achieved international success, basketball would also begin to receive greater support, but its appeal was still limited. Outside the game's hotbeds it was little played, and its social base did not go much beyond university graduates and other educated sectors, a fact that some journalists attributed to the game's "complicated rules."[109] The lack of suitable venues also constrained basketball's growth. Large crowds could only watch in the summer, but everywhere else in the world basketball was a winter sport made compelling by the comparative intimacy of closed arenas. In the USSR, basketball's growth had been considerable, but it was not able to make the breakthrough in these years that was achieved by hockey.

Despite Dinamo Moscow's 1945 tour and despite the success of the men's and women's basketball teams, the outside world would come to know the Soviet sports system best through track and field. Because the sport was organized globally on an amateur basis, there were no institutional barriers to confrontations between Soviet and foreign athletes. The Soviets joined the International Association of Athletics Federations (IAAF) in 1946, sending a small but powerful delegation to the European championships in Oslo.[110] This event marked the first officially sanctioned participation by Soviet athletes in any international competition. The visibility of Soviet track athletes was also enhanced by the sport's place as the centerpiece of the Olympics. Domestically, track had also been the most publicized of the events at the Spartakiads, and leading up to the 1952 Helsinki Games, many Soviet performers, male and female, achieved world-class results. Nevertheless, the sport still struggled to find a constant and sizable audience inside the USSR, although interest in it did rise as a result of the general sports boom of the postwar period.

Accounts of track meets rarely mentioned either the size or the composition of the audience. Newspapers covered a wide variety of city, intercity, and national meets, which they described with heavy reliance on statistics. Such top performers as the still-active Nikolai Ozolin, the Estonian shotputter Heino Lipp, and the Georgian discus-thrower Nina Dumbadze were given star treatment. Their training methods were dissected and were offered as examples for others. They also gave interviews describing the human qualities needed for sports sucess. Despite all this attention, track and field's successes at the gate still were only episodic. Kharkov in the Ukraine was an exception. There important intercity meets regularly filled 20,000-seat Dinamo Stadium, as a result of which the city was often rewarded the national championship.[111] Moscow did not dominate track as it did soccer and hockey, as good athletes could be found and trained everywhere. Because track was, by and large, not a team sport, athletes did not have to be part of well-equipped clubs. For runners in particular, elaborate training facilities and first-class equipment, while helpful, were not absolute necessities.

In this sense, track and field was more nationally representative, even more democratic in its internal organization, than the most popular spectator sports, with their hierarchies of coaches, officials, and sponsors. As a result, track's ties to mass sport and the practices of physical culture were especially close. Many of the tests for the national physical fitness badges were track events. These factors put track and field in a different category from the successful spectator sports, which had fewer ties to mass physical culture and participation. Nevertheless, sports authorities continued to try to popularize what the press always called the "king of sports."[112]

To publicize track and field, events were often sandwiched around soccer games that were guaranteed to draw large crowds, but these combinations did not always go smoothly. In 1947, a Moscow meet was scheduled to begin two hours before a soccer game between TsDKA and Dinamo Tblisi. The same ticket entitled the bearer to watch both events, but those who had come to watch the track meet were forced to leave the stadium an hour before the soccer game was to begin, despite the fact that all the scheduled events had not yet been run. Worse still, the participants in the meet were similarly banished. As if that were not bad enough, those leaving the stadium were forced to give up their tickets, which were not returned, making it impossible for those who had watched the track meet to attend the soccer game.[113]

Organizational difficulties continued to plague the sport. Some meets were poorly advertised. Others were not provided with sufficient equipmemt. Judges did not always appear. Meet schedules were often improvised. Public-address systems remained a problem, and even when announcers were used, they had much difficulty performing their tasks with efficiency, given the prevailing bedlam. Yet these failings did not prevent many talented athletes from emerging during these years. The Soviets were able to enter strong track and field delegations in a variety of international competitions leading up to 1952, and they would make a good showing at Helsinki.[114]

Other sports also had some success in attracting audiences. The late 1940s were a golden age for boxing in Europe and North America, and the same may be said for the Soviet Union. The only available venues were still circus buildings that rarely held more than 1,500, but these buildings were regularly filled for important competitions. Whereas professionals had appeared on some occasions before the war, now all shows were strictly "amateur." At the same time, *Sovetskii sport* closely followed Western professional boxing, paying special attention to the triumphs and tragedies of Joe Louis.[115] Figure skating and speed skating had episodic successes in attracting large crowds, and in 1949, 100,000 Georgians watched a traditional equestrian competition.[116]

When the USSR joined the Olympic movement, it had long been practicing the various sports on the Games' program, even in its earlier isolation. Now, however, the USSR was far from isolated. In the interim, whether through takeover or genuine revolution, many nations in Eastern Europe and Asia had become Communist. The idea of international competition took on an entirely new meaning for the Soviets. This change also affected the sports rituals through which the Party ascribed meaning to sports and physical culture. The defiant nationalism of the prewar Physical Culture Days would eventually be replaced by a defensive internationalism that was more consistent with participation in the Olympic movement. During Stalin's last years, the parades themselves became increasingly less important, and their slogans changed with the new needs of the Party. The concern for mass sports and physical culture also diminished with the need to divert resources into the varieties of high-performance sports that would increasingly be measured in international competition.

In the flush of victory, the first postwar parade in 1945 was every bit as large and as oriented toward military concerns as any of the rituals of the 1930s. Two years later, however, the celebration of the holiday was restricted to Dinamo Stadium. Stalin, Molotov, and the Party leadership still attended, and they were joined by an invited audience of generals, admirals, Stalin Prize-winners, scholars, artists, and Stakhanovites.[117] In his speech, N. N. Romanov, then head of the Sport Committee, made clear that mass sport was no longer simply a way to prepare better workers and soldiers: "Our goal is to unceasingly develop physical culture and sport. It is a mass, popular movement with the goal of establishing the capacity of Soviet athletes to struggle for national and world records for the glory of our homeland."[118] Holding the event in a stadium made it possible to include competitive events on the program, along with the usual mass gymnastic displays and card sections. Significantly, the sport chosen for this purpose was usually track and field. Yet these events would be something of a last gasp for Physical Culture Day. By 1951, the holiday had been downgraded even further. There was no longer a gathering of the leadership for a grand parade in a stadium. Rather, a series of field days and participant events were organized at venues throughout the city and the nation.[119]

The sports movement now had a new goal, the winning of prestige and glory in Olympic competition. The Soviets' debut in 1952 represented a culmination of practices that had been put in place during the 1930s. While the public had shown interest in a narrow range of sports, the state had continually supported the broadest possible range of athletic activities. From the first days of the revolution, the authorities had embraced the multi-sport Olympic model, even as they rejected the socially aristocratic Olympic movement. After 1945, Soviet athletes began to appear in a variety of international competitions, and much of the outside world was stunned by the Soviet success at Helsinki. Yet both the Soviet public and the authorities understood their victories to be the result of many decades of preparatory work.

In 1948, the possibility of participation in the Olympics had provoked uncertainty and concern, but no formal invitation was ever offered by the International Olympic Committee. An observer delegation was instead sent to London. Soon thereafter, the Soviets appear to have changed their minds and decided to take part in 1952. Avery Brundage, the longtime president of the International Olympic Committee, and many of his associates were well aware that Soviet athletes were state professionals who did not conform to the Games' amateur code.[120] Ultimately, however, they came to decide that excluding one of the world's two new great powers would hurt the Games more than sullying the tradition of amateurism, and in January 1952, the Soviets announced their preliminary decision to take part in Helsinki.[121]

Because the many sports of the Olympic program were never mass spectator attractions in the Soviet Union, and because the only way the Soviet public could even watch the Games was on television (until 1980), the Olympics have not been at the center of this study. Yet to ignore Soviet participation in the Olympics would also distort reality. The system that was organized to turn out so many champions represented Stalinist sports in their purest form. Initially, the Soviet audience may have been relatively indifferent to the sports in which their comrades were triumphing, but there can be no doubt that the cumulative effect of so many victories, combined with the incessant trumpeting of the media, did generate more than a small measure of patriotic pride.

Soviet fans were disappointed by the failure of the soccer team at Helsinki, but sweeping victories were achieved in men's and women's gymnastics, wrestling, and weightlifting. Several female track athletes performed well in the throwing events, with Nina Zybina setting a world record in the shot-put. The men's basketball team won a silver medal, losing to the United States in the final. Earlier claims that the Soviet school of basketball was the "most advanced in the world" were ignored, and second place was deemed a great success. In basketball, unlike soccer, it was sufficient that the Soviet team be "one of the strongest in the world." The cycling, swimming, and water polo teams, however, did not perform well. Without fanfare, soccer was listed in N. N. Romanov's summary of the results as one of several sports in which "our sportsmen performed below their possibilities."[122]

In the unofficial national point totals, the Soviets initially claimed victory, then admitted that the United States' team had tied them. Later Western counts would suggest a small margin for the American team, but the larger point had been made. In their first Olympic appearance, the Soviets had proven the equal of the Americans. The very idea that their nation could perform as well as the United States in any field of human endeavor had great resonance with the Soviet public. In 1952, the Soviet Union was a much poorer country than the United States, and it had only just begun to recover from the devastation of the war. Parity in this international test was seen as a great victory. Soviet citizens knew very well that the best Western athletes were professionals who could not take part in the Games. This was hardly a secret. The Soviet sports press had reported the exploits of foreign professionals in great detail for many years, but these facts were ignored at this moment. *Sovetskii sport* did not hesitate to draw the boldest of conclusions: "The victory of Soviet athletes at the Olympic Games is a sharp demonstration of our enormous advances forward; of the development of culture among our people. This kind of growth of talent is inconceivable in any capitalist country."[123] This first step was merely a prelude to Soviet domination of both the winter and summer Games. The Helsinki "victory" had been achieved despite limited funding, inadequate facilities, and considerable public indifference. In part, the Soviet triumph probably had less to do with Soviet strength and more to do with the comparative inefficiency with which Western nations then organized their participation in the Games.

I have tried to suggest that the athletes and sports exposed to the outside world at the Olympics represented only a fraction of the entire world of Soviet sport. Even during the height of Stalinist interference in every corner of Soviet culture, the sports-watching public demonstrated an ability to choose what it wanted to see and to see what it wanted in a manner not always palatable to the authorities. Spectator sports may not have been an apolitical oasis in the desert of high Stalinism, but it can fairly be said that, despite all the interference, spectator sports' essential core remained uncorrupted. The competition may not always have been fully honest, but it was honest enough to build a large and loyal audience.

Moscow soccer fans on the way to a game in the 1920's. Source: M. Iakushin, *Vechnaia taina futbola*, Moscow, 1988

The famous 1937 soccer game played in Red Square. Source: N. Starostin, *Futbol skvoz' gody*, Moscow, 1989

Source: Starostin

Scenes from Physical Culture Day parades.

Source: *Olympic Moscow*, Moscow, 1980

Source: *Pageant of Youth*, Moscow, 1939

Source: *Pageant of Youth*,
Moscow, 1939

Source: *Pageant of Youth*,
Moscow, 1939

Scenes from Physical Culture Day parades.

Source: *Pageant of Youth*, Moscow, 1939

The legendary goalie, Lev Iashin. Source: Lev Iashin, *Schast'e trudnykh pobed*, Moscow, 1985

The greatest of all Soviet athletes, Vsevolod Bobrov. Source: *Sovetskii sport*, December 4, 1992

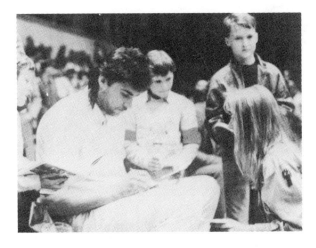

Young fans are the same all over; Lithuanian basketball star, Arvidas Sabonis, gives autographs. Source: Igor Fein, *Arvidas Sabonis*, Moscow, 1988

Moscow's Palace of Sport, opened in 1956. Source: *Sovetskii sport*, December 15, 1956

The Leningrad Winter Stadium, a converted eighteenth-century manège, the city's only venue for indoor sport until the 1960's. Source: *Sovetskii sport*, October 18, 1949

The magic of hockey played outdoors at night in Dinamo Stadium. Source: *Sovetskii sport*, January 25, 1951

Despite the difficult climate, no Soviet stadium had a roof. Source: *Sovetskii sport*, August 27, 1970

The most famous of Soviet sportscasters, Nikolai Ozerov. Source: *Sovetskii sport*, August 30, 1970

In the late 'forties, basketball was played outdoors on dirt courts. With the ball, the first great Soviet center, Dinamo Tblisi's 6'4" Otar Korkhia. Source: Alexander Gomelskii, *Tsentrovye*, Moscow, 1987

Dinamo Moscow in London during their 1945 triumphal tour. Source: Iakushin

Uruguay's shocking overtime goal that eliminated the Soviets from the 1970 World Cup. Source: *Sovetskii sport*, July 18, 1970

Central Army's "Team of Lieutenants." Left to right: B. Arkadiev (coach), V. Nikolaev, G. Fedotov, V. Nikanorov, V. Soloviev, A. Grinin, I. Kochetkov, A. Vodiagin, V. Bobrov, V. Demin, V. Chistokhvalov, A. Prokhorov. Source: *Sovetskii sport*, Oct. 14, 1947

5

Professionals and Amateurs— International Competition

When Stalin died in 1953, relations with the West had deteriorated to a state of harsh and dangerous confrontation. In the next decade, though, the tone of Soviet foreign policy became less antagonistic. A policy of "peaceful coexistence" would evolve, as Nikita Kkrushchev consolidated his power in the course of a far less deadly succession struggle than that which followed the death of Lenin. In this new era, Communism and capitalism were still to compete with each other, but that competition was now to take on peaceful as well as more dangerous forms. The Olympic Games, with their historically militaristic overtones and controlled opportunities for state nationalism, soon became one element of that competition, and the quadrennial event was transformed into a surrogate for the Cold War. In the light of these developments, the Party sought to portray subsequent Soviet dominance of the Olympics as proof of the superiority of Communist methods, not only in sports, but in all areas of human endeavor. For many years these efforts would appear to be successful.

Sports and the Cold War

In the post-Stalin era, the high-achievement, multisport system that was established in the 'thirties continued to play the same domestic and international roles it had always played. While Soviet foreign policy under Khrushchev and Leonid Brezhnev was more benign than it had been under Stalin, the structural relationship of the Olympic sports system to both foreign policy and domestic society did not change after the death of Stalin. It remained much the same even after the coming to power of Mikhail Gorbachev in 1985. That system, however, was but a part of the entire Soviet sports scene.

In coming to dominate the Olympic Games, the USSR staked out only a limited portion of the total territory of world sports. The Party consciously chose to emphasize success in the full range of Olympic sports, many of which had limited publics both inside and outside the Soviet bloc. In addition, the Soviets participated under eligibility standards (their quasi-professionals against the West's quasi-amateurs) that gave them an enormous advantage over their capitalist opponents, whose best athletes were openly professional.

When the Soviets came to play Western professionals in the more popular spectator sports of soccer, hockey, and basketball, the overall record of the USSR was far less impressive than it was in the Olympics. When they ventured outside the officially amateur ranks, the Soviets lost almost as often as they won, and this mix of success and failure, as opposed to nearly total Olympic dominance, more accurately reflects the limited place sport actually came to assume in postwar Soviet society. Only by constraining the types of competition and eliminating much of the West's sporting talent were the Soviets able to appear as dominant as they seemed.

Throughout the years of superpower confrontation, the USSR was always a considerably poorer country than the United States. Big-time sports continued to grow in the USSR throughout the post-Stalin years, but the comparatively low level of national wealth and the limited commitment of resources meant that spectator sports, as distinct from Olympic sports, never developed on the scale they did under capitalism. By using limited resources efficiently, the Soviets were able to achieve their Olympic triumphs, but this success did not mean that the entire nation was "sports crazy," nor did it signify that sports had assumed an unusually dominant, even pathological place in Soviet society. While sports and physical culture were supposed to play their assigned roles in furthering the goals of the state and Party, they remained less than central to Soviet life.

Between 1953 and the ascension of Mikahil Gorbachev in 1985, the international posture of the USSR oscillated between confrontation and détente, and sports continued to be one way of enhancing that posture. Because of these continuities, the Olympic sports system the world came to know was something of a Stalinist remnant, even an anachronism, changing little from Olympiad to Olympiad. By contrast, the practices surrounding the most popular spectator sports were profoundly affected by the rapidly evolving world market for sports spectacles and also by the many changes Soviet society passed through between 1953 and 1985.

While the world of elite sports in the USSR was relatively isolated from these phenomena, spectator sports were not. Olympic sport was a creation of the state and could be molded regardless of the evolving tastes of the public.

Spectator sports were different. Their audiences were the very same members of Soviet society whose lives had been affected by the significant developments of the post-Stalin years. As their lives changed, so did their consumption of spectator sport.

After 1952, Soviet sports emerged on the world scene, and many of their leading figures became household names in the West. Televised Olympic competition brought many Soviet athletes into millions of homes in capitalist countries, and Soviet sports heroes became world-famous. As a result, the events of these years will be more familiar to readers than those of the era preceeding Stalin's death. Accordingly, I will not attempt in this chapter to offer a complete history of Soviet participation in international sports during the post-Stalin period. I intend instead to take a more topical approach, concentrating on the issues that have already emerged in our examination of events before 1953. While this strategy may do damage to chronology and undermine a clear narrative, it allows me to answer with greater clarity the questions posed at the outset of this study.

Competition on the international level inevitably led to entanglements with the contradictions of the Cold War.[1] The Soviet government used these events to make political points, but it was as often the target of protests as it was the instigator. In 1959, the Soviets were stripped of their victory in the world basketball championship because they had refused to play the Taiwanese team in a preliminary game.[2] The next year the tables were turned. The Soviets were to play Spain in the semifinal of the European soccer cup. In those days a home-and-home series was played, and the Soviet and Spanish federations communicated and agreed on dates. On the eve of the first game, however, the Franco government forbade its team to play. The Soviets went through the ritual protests but gladly accepted a free trip to the final in Paris, which they won.[3] In 1962, retaliating for the construction of the Berlin Wall, NATO's Allied Travel Board refused to grant travel documents to the East German hockey team for the world championship, held that year in Colorado Springs. The Soviets refused to participate, and *Izvestia* published a letter of protest signed by, among others, Iurii Vlasov, Valerii Brumel' and Igor Netto, attacking what they called the "championship of what world?"[4]

In 1973, the Soviet soccer team was placed in a World Cup elimination group that required its winner to play the winner of one South American group for a place in the 1974 final stage. This procedure was unusual, but when the Soviets won, they were glad to play Chile, then under the socialist government of Salvador Allende. Chile came to Moscow and lost the first game, but before the return leg could be played, the Allende government was overthrown in a coup d'état led by the army. Worse yet, the site of the game, the National Stadium in Santiago, was used as a giant prison, and many socialists, Communists, and others were executed there. The Soviet federation petitioned FIFA to move the game to a neutral site, but FIFA refused. The Soviet government then decided not to play the game, and, as a result, the soccer team lost the opportunity to play in the final round.[5] Given the importance of soccer and the enormous significance of participation in the World Cup, the government's decision greatly disappointed even the most politically committed of sports fans.

All of these acts were preludes to the reciprocal boycotts of the 1980 Moscow and 1984 Los Angeles Olympics. The United States, which had participated in the 1936 Berlin Olympics, found the Soviet invasion of Afghanistan sufficient reason not to take part in the Moscow Games. The Soviets, who had summoned the courage to send teams to Hungary and Czechoslovakia not long after they had invaded each nation, gave security concerns as their reason for not sending a team to Los Angeles. These events were cited by observers everywhere as sad examples of political interference in sports, and even the Soviets trotted out this hoary idealist lament on occasion. In fact, the Soviets always understood that international competition at the highest levels was tied to the complexities of world diplomacy, and the Olympics continually played just such a role in Soviet foreign relations.

Fielding National Teams

In the individual sports on the Olympic program, the gathering of national teams was not a problem. In team sports, for which the Olympics were not always the most important competition, this process proved far more difficult. In many cases, Soviet opponents were not amateurs. Soviet soccer teams had played against Western professionals from the very first moments after the war, and later Soviet athletes would take on professionals in hockey and finally in basketball. Victories against these kinds of opponents would prove a great deal more difficult to achieve than Olympic medals.

Throughout the world, the organization of national teams in major sports has always run into conflict with the needs and demands of domestic competition. Schedules have to be coordinated, and clubs have often been reluctant to release players for anything but the most significant games. There are always public and private debates about who should be selected, what type of tactics should be pursued, and who should coach. Aside from the political pressures within the sports world, competition on this level has always been inextricably entwined with international diplomatic issues, as results have been viewed by leaders everywhere, not just Communist countries, as examinations of national worth. In bringing together their national teams, the Soviets escaped none of these problems.

The Search for Soccer Happiness—In prerevolutionary Russia, intellectuals were obsessed by a series of what were called "cursed questions." There was the "peasant question," the "women's question," and many others. In the postrevolutionary world of Soviet sports, there was no question more cursed than the ongoing failure of the national soccer team to live up to the hopes and expectations of its millions of fans, both inside and outside the government. The death of Stalin did have the positive effect of allowing discussion about the team's performance to be more open and measured than the discussion about the "team of lieutenants." Nevertheless, such talk was cheap, and defeats were still as common as victories. Given the immense popularity of soccer and the importance of international success, the star-crossed record of the national team proved a source of persistent criticism and blame.

The Soviets faced three enormous handicaps in seeking international soccer glory. The first problem was the weather. In most of Europe, the soccer season has started in late summer and continued through the relatively mild winter until sometime in May. The harsh Russian winter has made such a domestic schedule impossible. Because most international competitions have culminated in the late spring or early summer, a time when Soviet players are only just getting into shape, they have had enormous difficulty with opponents whose schedules have led up to these decisive moments. There were numerous attempts to adjust the domestic soccer calendar to accommodate the needs of the national team, and all sorts of experiments were tried. The question of the schedule was constantly debated, and it was changed from year to year, creating chronic and ennervating confusion among coaches and players.

The second factor hampering Soviet soccer was discussed far less frequently than the problems caused by climate. For the fans, soccer was always their greatest love, but for the authorities, soccer was only one of several sports on the Olympic program. The official insistence on the across-the-board excellence needed to dominate the medal counts restricted soccer's capacity to attract the nation's best athletes. At some point in their early teens, talented Soviet youngsters had to choose the sport they would specialize in. Until the late 1980s, the rewards in soccer were not that much greater than those in other sports. As a result, the talent pool was spread more thinly over a wider variety of sports than was the case in non-Communist countries.

In other parts of the world, the most remunerative sports, by and large, attracted the best athletes, but in the USSR the popular dream of soccer glory was undermined by the official emphasis on Olympic victory. In a sense, the state's sports priorities mirrored its historic economic and political concerns. The goal of achieving military parity with the West deprived the consumer sector, making it enormously difficult for Soviet citizens to take care of their personal needs. The popular spectator sport of soccer suffered similarly, unable to mobilize enough of the scarce resources the state directed toward other, more controllable sports.

The third and final reason for Soviet soccer's failures is painfully obvious, but it does need to be stated. Soccer is the only sport in which Soviet teams played against professionals from the earliest days of the postwar era; indeed, even before then. This was not the case for most of the other sports on the Olympic program. The best athletes in capitalist countries were always professionals, but by claiming to be amateurs, the Soviets were able, in many sports, to limit the talent pool available to their opponents. This would never be the case in soccer.

The Soviets did not enter the World Cup, the ultimate test of soccer success, until 1958. Before then, the national team and several of the leading clubs played numerous "comradely" games against a carefully chosen roster of opponents, picked for the often-contradictory concerns of their prestige and defeatability. In 1953, Soviet club teams again began to play foreign opponents, both at home and abroad. These contests occurred in the late summer before the opening of the European season and in the fall after the end of the Soviet season. Among foreign clubs, the most important to visit the Soviet Union that year were Ujpest Dosza of Budapest and Rapid Vienna, both of which toured with mixed success against Dinamo Moscow, Spartak, and Dinamo Tblisi.[6]

The 1954 international calendar was also dominated by club teams. England's Arsenal returned Dinamo's 1945 visit with an October game in Moscow, won 5–0 by Dinamo. One month later, Spartak played Arsenal in London and won, 2–1. Just two weeks earlier, they had beaten Anderlecht in Brussels by a shocking 7–0 score. That summer, the national team was finally reassembled for the first time since the Olympic defeat. Headed by their new coach, Gavril Kachalin, they played to a 1–1 tie in Moscow against a powerful Hungarian team led by Ferenc Puskas and Sandor Kocsis.[7] This result was particularly gratifying. Known as the "Mighty Magyars," the Hungarians had won the last Olympic title and were defeated 3–2 in the 1954 World Cup final by West Germany when Puskas was hampered by an ankle injury.[8]

Under the guise of the Moscow selects, the Soviets also played Bulgaria (a tie and a loss) and Poland (a win and a loss). These games marked the international debut of the twenty-five-year-old Dinamo Moscow goalie, Lev Iashin, who would go on to become one of the greatest players in the history of the game and the most honored of Soviet soccer's postwar stars.[9] The peak of pre–World Cup international activity came in 1955. Dinamo Moscow and Spartak toured Italy and England, where they took on such celebrated teams as Wolverhampton Wanders, A.C. Milan, and Fiorentina, but the highlight of the year came that summer when the national team, playing in Moscow, defeated the recently crowned world champions from West Germany.[10]

This victory gave Soviet coaches enough confidence to schedule games with other strong national teams. Not all of these confrontations were wins, but they were the necessary prelude to success at the highest levels of the sport. Failure to give the team experience against other national sides was thought to have contributed to the defeat in the 1952 Olympics, and this series of difficult games prepared the Soviet team well. In 1956, at the Melbourne Olympics, the Soviet team, with eight players from Spartak, defeated Yugoslavia 1–0 in the final to take the gold medal. The Olympics, however, were far from the ultimate test.[11] The World Cup now awaited.

The Soviets' first appearance in the World Cup began a series of frustrations that were relieved only by occasional good results in the less prestigious, but still important, European Cup. This extremely limited record of international success was not for want of trying. In the inevitable tensions between the demands of the national team and the needs of the clubs, the national team was always given preference. League schedules were continuously disrupted, and the clubs had no choice but to release their players for international events. Coaches of the national team were replaced at a dizzying pace, with thirty-one changes between 1952 and 1983. In all, fifteen men held the job, with Kachalin and Beskov each having four turns at the helm.[12] Congresses of specialists were held. Players, coaches, and team officials were brought together to discuss the state of the sport. Scientists were consulted. The press was filled with analysis, criticism, and recrimination, but aside from the European title in 1960 and a semifinal World Cup appearance in 1966, there was little to show for all the effort and discussion.

It was a source of continuing frustration that so large a nation with so much sporting success should not be able to achieve equally good results in its most popular sport. But this record should not be seen as anomalous. These failures are as much a reflection of the weaknesses of the Soviet sports system as Olympic victories are signs of its strengths. When competing against professional athletes who enjoyed the full support and resources of powerful capitalist nations, the Soviets had difficulty winning consistently. It would have been better for the state if the people had preferred a sport in which the international record was more successful, but that was a choice the authorities could neither make nor impose.

Soviet performances in the World Cup followed a familiar pattern. The team would make the final stage of the competition in the host country and play well in the opening round-robin groups. They then would advance to the quarter-finals, where they would be eliminated, often under bizarre circumstances. Only in 1966 did they get as far as the semifinals. Each time the national team failed to perform well, there was a hail of criticism, proposals, coaching changes, recriminations, and excuses. Bad luck even played a role.

In 1958, when Kachalin, with the assistance of Mikhail Iakushin, took the team to Sweden for the Soviets' first World Cup, no one knew exactly what might happen. Mercifully, the false hopes and inflated expectations of 1952 were not repeated. The team had survived the elimnation rounds to get to the final stage. Once they arrived in Sweden, they played well in the first round, despite the loss of Netto to injury—tying England, beating Austria, and losing to the powerful and ascendant Brazilians, led by Garrincha, Didi, and a young Pele. The Soviets then survived a second-place playoff with England. But in the quarter-finals they had to play the host country, Sweden, and lost 2–0. Subsequent discussion of the team's performance centered on "lessons" rather than recriminations. Kachalin and Iakushin accepted blame for failing to find enough young players to push the veterans, who had been together since 1955. As a result, there had been less competition for places on the team and reduced dedication to training. As the Soviets' greatest strengths were speed and endurance, these failures had serious consequences.[13]

The press, however, did not mention one particularly serious handicap facing the team in Sweden. Their performance might have been stronger had one of their best players—the young, talented, but troubled Eduard Strel'tsov—not been arrested on a rape charge when the team was supposed to be sequestered at its training base, preparing for the World Cup. Strel'tsov had first played for Torpedo Moscow in 1954 at the age of seventeen. He quickly acquired a reputation as one of Soviet soccer's most prolific goal scorers and most difficult personalities. A world-class carouser, Strel'tsov fought often, with opponents and teammates alike.[14] Subsequently, Strel'tsov would spend six years in prison, eventually returning to both Torpedo and the national team, playing brilliantly and acting poorly. In all, he scored one hundred league goals and appeared with the national team thirty-nine times during a career that ended in 1970. One can only imagine what this most talented but difficult of performers could have meant to Soviet soccer had he not wasted the best years of his career.[15]

In the wake of the 1958 defeat, the team was reorganized. More young players from provincial teams were selected. The veterans Iashin and Netto were joined by such figures as Mikhail Meskhi of Dinamo Tblisi and Viktor Ponedel'nik from second-division Rostov. These choices would prove fortuitous. In 1960, Ponedel'nik would score the winning goal against Yugoslavia in overtime of the first-ever European Cup final on a pass from Meskhi. Much was made of this victory at home, but in its initial edition the European Cup was not yet the major competition it would become. The leading teams of Europe would come to participate only in the late 'sixties, and all of the Soviets' opponents in 1960 were from Eastern Europe.[16] Nevertheless, expectations for the 1962 World Cup were considerably higher than in 1958. This optimism was fueled by a successful exhibition tour of South America prior to the Cup. Thus the disappointment was all the greater when the 1958 scenario was repeated in 1962 in Chile, where the team lost once again to the host country in the quarter-finals.[17]

Kachalin was formally taken to task by the Football Federation for failing to develop "individualists" who could take on "risk and responsibility" in tense moments.[18] Andrei Starostin, who was the team's general manager, admiitted that it had been a tactical mistake to try for a big victory margin against Colombia in order to rest the starters in the next game against Uruguay. After leading at half time 3–1 against Colombia, the Soviets relaxed and were tied 4–4, which meant they had to make an all-out effort against Uruguay for a victory that was won only in the eighty-ninth minute. While the Soviets made the quarter-finals, they had little energy left to play against the weaker Chileans. Kachalin had hoped to employ one of the lessons learned at Helsinki. Because games came more quickly than once a week in such tournaments, he had decided to find ways to rest his stars; but the strategy backfired.[19]

Much of the blame for these defeats fell on Iashin. With no telecast of the game back to the USSR, Soviet fans relied on press accounts. Several journalists criticized Iashin's performances against both Colombia and Chile. Later in Iashin's life, however, it became fashionable among Soviet sportswriters to discount these reports. A subsequent generation of reporters would claim that the observers who sent dispatches back to Moscow were not specialists in sports matters. Most neutral observers, however, also gave Iashin poor reviews. Against Colombia, he had allowed a score directly from a corner kick, and in the match with Chile, Iashin surrendered two goals from far out.[20] The French sports daily *L'Equipe* lamented that Iashin's performance "certainly marked an historic date, the end of the greatest modern goalkeeper, if not of all time, Yachine."[21] On his return to domestic play, Iashin was mercilessly booed. Irate fans left threatening notes on his car, and several times the windows of his apartment were broken by rock-throwers. So great was the pressure that Iashin considered retirement, taking a lengthy hiatus from the game in order to contemplate his future.[22]

In 1964, the national team, now under Beskov, made it to the finals of the European Cup, only to lose to Spain at Madrid. This time, the Franco government agreed to meet the representatives of Communism. While the result restored Soviet international prestige, it was not enough to keep Beskov in his job. Despite the obvious difficulty of defeating one of Europe's greatest soccer powers on its home turf, Khrushchev was personally dissatisfied with the result.[23] Along with Andrei Starostin, who had been the general manager of the team, Beskov was dismissed.[24] Nikolai Morozov was now named to the coaching position, and he would lead the team in 1966, when it would achieve its best result.

In England, the Soviets again made it to the quarter-finals, dispatching Italy, Chile, and the surprising North Koreans along the way. Having once again reached the hurdle of the quarter-finals, this time they managed to defeat Hungary 2–1, moving on to a confrontation in the semifinal with a West German team, led by the young Franz Beckenbauer. This game proved to be particularly rough. The Soviets' left-winger, Igor Chislenko, was sent off in the first half, forcing his team to play down a man for the rest of the match, which they lost 2–1. Had it not been for Iashin's brilliance, the disparity in the score would have been even greater.[25] The *London Times'* Brian Glanville described the game against Germany as a "sour, ill-tempered match, refereed without illumination. . . . It was only the majestic goal-keeping and incomparable sportsmanship of Yachine that gave the game any distinction."[26] While Morozov would publicly criticize Iashin for letting in the winning goal, the critics back home were at last satisfied.

The 1966 World Cup proved to be the shining moment of Iashin's long career. For some time, he had been recognized as soccer's greatest goal-keeper, winning many honors and revolutionizing the nature of goalkeeping. He was among the first to roam far outside the penalty area to liquidate threats and start quick counterattacks that took advantage of the Soviets' great speed. He also studied his opponents' tendencies on penalty shots, guessing which direction to dive in, instead of standing by passively and relying solely on his reflexes. Iashin became a beloved figure who happily played the role of the Soviet sports hero. He would retire in 1970 at the age of forty, the favorite not only of Dinamo Moscow's fans but of all those who considered themselves "lovers of football." He died prematurely in 1991, a much-admired and decorated figure.

After their success in England, expectations were high for the 1968 European Cup, but the team, now coached by Iakushin, would tie Italy in the semifinals, only to be eliminated by a coin toss. They would, however, lose the third-place game to England.[27] Iakushin was accused of scheduling too many exhibitions with weak opponents and inviting too many players to the training camps that preceded these games. Iakushin's critics charged that this practice tore players away from their clubs, which were the proper place for them to develop their skills. Domestic Soviet competition, they argued, was often stiffer than that faced in the exhibitions, while too many players had to be left on the sidelines during these games, depriving them of the chance for development only serious matches could provide.[28]

Kachalin was put back in charge of the team that went to Mexico in 1970. A new generation of players was recruited, but yet another fiasco ensued. The Soviets played brilliantly in first-round games, despite the difficulties posed by the unfamiliar heat and altitude. Anatolii Byshovets of Dinamo Kiev scored four goals in three games. They then met Uruguay in the quarter-final. While the Soviets dominated in regulation time, they were unable to pierce the strong Uruguayan defense. In overtime, however, the heat took its toll of the Soviet team. The Uruguayans came on, but against the run of play, Byshovets scored, only to have the goal disallowed on an offside. This turn of events took much of the remaining fight out of the Soviets. With three minutes to go in overtime, the Uruguayans' winger, Luis Cubilla, brought the ball up the right flank. He evaded a defender and chipped the ball far ahead, close to the corner. It appeared to the Soviets and many of those watching that the ball had gone out of bounds. The Soviet defenders raised their hands, expecting a whistle, but the view of the Dutch referee, Laurens van Ravens, was blocked by a group of players near the goal mouth. The linesman at that end of the field was on the opposite sideline and could not see what had transpired. Hearing no whistle, Cubilla crossed the ball into the middle where a fresh Victor Esparrago, who had come on as a substitute, put the ball in past a stunned and surprised Soviet team.[29]

The criticism this time was louder and longer than ever before. *Izvestia* said it received almost 300,000 letters about the team's performance. The outpouring was a reflection of soccer's enormous popularity, and it is difficult to imagine similar hand-wringing for any other sport, with the possible exception of hockey. For months afterwards, *Sovetskii sport* was filled with analytical and critical articles discussing the disaster. The paper organized a series of round tables at which everyone from Andrei Starostin to steelworkers appeared. The optimism that had been fueled by the successes of the 'sixties was now crushed. The players subsequently complained that it was impossible to sustain the typical fast-paced Soviet game in the hot conditions they faced in Mexico. Other critics attacked the level of play in the domestic league that provided the national team with its players. Many argued that the 1970 team did not have the talent of some of its predecessors.[30] In response, the Football Federation called a national congress of all those involved with the sport. The federation announced a number of reforms to improve domestic competition, but these changes would ultimately would have little impact on play at the international level.

After the Mexican disaster of 1970, the Soviet national team did not appear in another World Cup until 1982. The only bright spot during these years was a European Cup final appearance in 1972, where they lost to the powerful West Germans. In 1974, their refusal to play Chile cost them a place in the finals, and in 1978, the team did not even qualify to go to Argentina. This last catastrophe marked the failure of the great experiment in which the highly successful Dinamo Kiev club of the mid-'seventies served as the basis for the national team. Under the hyper-rational coaching of Valerii Lobanovskii, Dinamo Kiev had become one of the strongest teams in Europe, winning the Cup-Winners Cup and then the Super Cup in 1975. This last victory came against Beckenbauer's Bayern Munich club, a team that included many stars of West Germany's world champions. Dinamo Kiev's great striker, Oleg Blokhin, performed brilliantly in both legs of this competition and was voted European Footballer of the Year. The team played an extremely controlled style that, it was hoped, would give it greater cohesion than the more hastily assembled all-star teams that most nations put forward. But this approach required Dinamo Kiev to play league games, national cup games, European club games, elimination games for the World and European cups, and Olympic games as well. The inevitable result was exhaustion and disaster.[31]

In 1982 and 1986, the Soviets made it back to the final stage, but the classic pattern was repeated. Fine play in the first-round games only created anticipation that turned to disappointment with later bizarre losses. In 1982, in Spain, the Soviets were eliminated in the second round, failing to beat a strong Polish team that would eventually finish third. In 1986 in Mexico, strange tactical choices combined with odd refereeing to cause a 4–3 overtime defeat against Belgium in the quarter-final after a strong showing in the opening round against Hungary, Canada, and France, the eventual third-place winner.[32] By this time, however, journalists, officials, and other critics had such low expectations that they actually expressed a measure of satisfaction with the attractive brand of soccer shown in the early games.

In other international competitions, the record was also less than sterling. In the three European club tournaments, Soviet teams won a total of three times. Dinamo Kiev took the less competitive Cup-Winners Cup twice, while Dinamo Tblisi won it once. In 1970, Dinamo Moscow played in the Cup-Winners' final only to lose to Glasgow Rangers in a game that was marred by Scottish fans' invading the field. The summer schedule, the cause of so many of Soviet soccer's problems, had a particularly deleterious effect in these tournaments, which began in the fall and resumed in the early spring. In the fall, Soviet teams were quite successful. After playing an entire season, they were in good physical condition and the level of their team play was quite high. Few Soviet teams, however, managed to clear the hurdle erected by the resumption of the tournaments in early March when the weather in the USSR was still harsh and teams were coming off their winter vacations.[33]

Olympic victories also became harder to achieve after the triumph of

1956. In 1958, FIFA attempted to minimize the advantage of the officially amateur teams from the Soviet bloc. No player, professional or amateur, who had taken part in any World Cup game could now participate in the Olympics. While this change hurt the Soviets, it did not have the predicted effect of preventing the other Eastern European teams from dominating Olympic competition in the interim. In 1976, the Soviets were able to send an especially strong team, precisely because they had not taken part in the 1974 World Cup. Blokhin would lead many of his Dinamo Kiev teammates into Montreal, but they could do no more than bring home the bronze.[34]

The contrast between Olympic victory in so many sports and international defeat in soccer troubled Soviet bureaucrats, fans, players, coaches, and journalists.[35] A resolution of the 1975 All-Union Congress of soccer players and coaches made the comparison clear: "At the last Olympics and at many world and European championships, our colleagues—the representatives of other sports—have won tens of gold medals and held the banner of Soviet sport high. The results of our appearances on football fields have been a good deal more modest, causing anxiety and concern among the many fans of football."[36] Sports officials had to learn the painful lesson that they could not have it all. The same could be said for the larger needs of Soviet society, which were always subordinated to the military and geopolitical concerns of the state. If Olympic sports were a correlate of the heavy industry long favored by the government, then soccer can be said to represent the long-suffering and neglected consumer sector.

Olympic triumphs actually undermined the chances for domination in soccer. All of the scientific, psychological, medical, technical, tactical, and intellectual resources of the Soviet sports system were not enough to produce consistent international success in both Olympic sports and soccer. From the vantage point of the Olympics, the "Big Red Machine" seemed like a juggernaut, but in the larger context of world sports, those victories must be weighed against the results of Soviet soccer teams. This combination of success and failure more accurately reflects the limited support for sports in a nation that had far fewer resources to spare for matters that were not of primary importance. There may have been a broad popular desire for soccer success, but the state always had other sports concerns.

"Our Hallowed Ice Militia"—In contrast to soccer, Soviet hockey teams enjoyed enormous success at the international level. Most of these victories, though, came against other nations whose teams were officially amateur. For the Soviets, the annual world championship and the winter Olympics were the most important competitions. Professionals did not take part in the world championships until 1977, and they were allowed in the Olympics only in

1988.[37] Additionally, the balance of power in world hockey differed sharply from that in soccer. In Europe, only Czech and Swedish teams could challenge the Soviets at the club and international levels. The true center of the hockey universe was in North America; specifically, the professional National Hockey League.

Until the mid-'sixties, the NHL had only six teams. As a result, many talented players were still available to fill the rosters of several Canadian amateur teams. For many years the Canadians were able to dominate the world championships simply by sending their best amateur team, but this approach would be undermined by two developments. In the 1950s, the Soviets emerged to pose a severe challenge to Canadian hockey hegemony, and in the late 'sixties, the NHL expanded, creating more job opportunities for players and weakening the standards of Canadian amateur hockey.[38]

In further contrast to the uncertainty and experimentation seen in soccer, the Soviet hockey program was characterized by continuity of leadership and confidence in its methods. The coaching leapfrog seen in soccer never occurred in hockey. Tarasov and Chernyshev, their responsibilities often shifting, headed the team from its inception until 1972. There was then a brief interregnum, during which Vsevolod Bobrov and Boris Kulagin were at the helm. Finally, in 1977, Viktor Tikhonov moved from Dinamo Riga to take over both the national and the Central Army teams.[39]

There was another important difference from the situation in soccer. Moscow maintained its position as the center of Soviet hockey, and its four leading teams (TsSKA, Spartak, Dinamo, and Krylia Sovetov) usually occupied the top positions in the domestic first division. This fact gave Tarasov and Chernyshev ample opportunity to monitor the play of all candidates for the national team, picking them for performance rather than reputation. The successes of provincial hockey teams, by contrast, were never more than episodic, and most promising youngsters from the periphery usually received and accepted invitations to join one of the capital's clubs. In some cases, the invitations were harder to refuse, as many young stars were drafted into the army and soon found that their duties consisted of playing for TsSKA.

The severe shortage of artificial rinks had the effect of restricting the game to the nation's coldest regions in Russia, Bielorussia, and the Ukraine. While the leading soccer teams of many republics became surrogates for nationalist sympathies in the pre-glasnost era, Soviet hockey was not riven by such divisions. Additionally, the various clubs proved willing to make sacrifices for the good of the national team. In fact, the structural tensions between the needs of the *sbornaia* and the clubs were minimal compared to the situation in soccer. Finally, there was no problem of scheduling caused by the climate. As elsewhere in the world, hockey in the USSR was always a winter sport.

In 1953, when the Soviets returned to international competition, hockey officials initially followed the example of their counterparts in soccer. Several exhibition games were organized with a variety of foreign opponents, but the Soviets quickly found out that only the Czechs and the Swedes could give them a game. As a result, Tarasov and Chernyshev were confident when the decision was made to enter the team in the 1954 world championships to be held in Sweden. In fact, Tarasov has contended that he was fully prepared to enter the 1953 championship in Zurich; only Bobrov fell ill, causing the sports authorities to postpone the debut for a year.[40]

The Soviets defeated Canada 7–2 in the final of the 1954 championship, and the score was greeted with astonishment throughout the hockey world. The game was played on an outdoor rink in Stockholm, conditions that favored the Soviets, who always played outdoors; but still the result was shocking. That year's Canadian representative was not considered to be particularly strong, a fact noted even by the Soviet press, but in the past, almost any Canadian team had been good enough to win.[41] Additionally, the Soviets' style of play proved to be almost as stunning as their triumph. They eschewed the Canadians' characteristic use of individual stick-handling, checking, grabbing, and long-distance shooting for an attacking style that placed primary attention on the men without the puck, whose job, like a soccer player's, was to find empty space in order to receive penetrating passes.

It was thought that order had been restored the next year when the Canadians easily defeated a Soviet team that played without an injured Bobrov, but the Soviets' triumph over Canada's Kitchener Dutchmen at the 1956 Winter Olympics made it clear to all that the earlier victory was no accident. While the 1954 defeat had been shocking, Canada viewed the loss at the Olympics as a national disaster.[42] The Soviets, however, were not able to sustain their success. The first hockey stars were nearing the end of their careers, and a new group was yet to come of age. At the same time, the Soviets' emergence had caused other nations to take the world championship more seriously than ever before.

The 1957 competition, held in Moscow, was boycotted by the United States and Canada because of the invasion of Hungary, but Sweden, rather than the favored Soviets, emerged victorious.[43] In the next six years, the Soviet team won no gold medals, losing to the Canadians or Swedes at ensuing world championships and to the U.S. at the 1960 Winter Olympics. Tarasov was criticized for staying too long with veterans and for failing to advance the technical level of his players.[44] The Soviets were great skaters and passers, but they suffered from weak shooting, a limited tactical arsenal, and an inability to use their bodies on defense. By the early 1960s, the rest of the world had begun to adjust to the Soviets' free-flowing passing style, and Tarasov came to understand that his team now had to develop new strategies while improving their ability to stop opponents.

It would take until 1963 for the Soviets to return to the peak of amateur hockey. When they did, they began an unprecedented record of domination that would ultimately change the entire structure of international competition. They won every world championship between 1963 and 1971, losing finally in 1972 to the Czechs at Prague. During the rest of the 'seventies and early 'eighties, the Soviets enjoyed further success at the World Championship even after professionals began to compete in 1977. In Olympic competition, which barred professionals until 1988, the Soviet record was even more dominant. Starting with 1964, they won every competition, with the notable exception of the loss to the United States in 1980.[45]

Beyond Tarasov's tactical adjustments, Soviet fortunes were revived by a new generation of stars who emerged during the 'sixties. The program of talent development had spread its tentacles far outside hockey's original Moscow base. Increased televising of the game helped turn it into a truly national sport, and more and more young athletes chose it as their specialty. Spartak gave the *sbornaia* its brilliant line of Viacheslav Starshinov and the Maiorov brothers, Boris and Evgenii. Alexander Ragulin, Anatolii Firsov, and Konstantin Loktev came from TsSKA. By the end of the 'sixties, Chernyshev and Tarasov had discovered an even stronger group of players, including TsSKA's powerful line of Boris Mikhailov, Vladimir Petrov, and the unstoppable Valerii Kharlamov. Dinamo's Valerii Vasiliev and Alexander Mal'tsev along with Spartak's Alexander Iakushev and Vladimir Shadrin would join this group to lead the national team through the 'seventies.

Tarasov, who would leave his post in 1972, found the last piece of the puzzle in 1965 with the discovery of a fifteen-year-old goalie named Vladislav Tretiak. Tretiak was carefully groomed and made his debut for TsSKA in 1969.[46] He soon joined the national team and went on to become the greatest of all Soviet goalies. This crucial position had been a chronic Soviet problem, exacerbating the normal defensive weaknesses caused by the team's attacking, nonphysical style, but Tretiak's brilliance proved to be the perfect antidote to the many transgressions of Soviet defensemen.

By the late 'sixties, Soviet domination of world amateur hockey became so complete that in 1969 the Canadians refused to participate in further world championships unless professionals were allowed. Their amateurs could no longer compete with the best European teams, and they wished to send professionals. The International Olympic Committee, however, headed by Avery Brundage, refused to allow them into the world championships, warning that any amateurs who played against professionals would be barred from the

Olympics. The Canadians then withdrew from international hockey, not participating in any world championship between 1970 and 1972 and staying home from the Winter Olympics at Sapporo, Japan. By this time, the Soviets were also becoming bored by the constant winning and were curious about their ability to compete against players from the National Hockey League. Beginning in 1969, both publicly and privately, Tarasov began to raise the question of finding some way for the Soviets to take on Canadian professionals. Since 1957, Soviet teams had been touring Canada, playing and usually beating amateur clubs. Canadian amateurs had also journeyed to the USSR, where they had difficulty with various Moscow teams. By the beginning of the 1970s, however, the Soviets had only one world left to conquer, and the Canadians were certain that their dominance could be restored only if the Soviets were to play the best Canadian pros.[47]

After three years of public and private jockeying, both sides reached an agreement during the 1972 World Championship in Prague. A delegation representing all the groups involved in Canadian hockey made a proposal the Soviets could accept, and the Soviet team was so excited with the announcement that they promptly went out the next night and lost their title to the Czechs. That September the Soviet national team would play eight games against an all-star team of NHL Canadians. The first four games were to be held in Canada and the last four in Moscow. Given the different approaches to the game, the issue of refereeing would prove crucial. The Canadians wanted to bump and fight; the Soviets wanted to skate and pass. Neutral referees were to be used, Americans in Cananda and Europeans in Moscow, but the home team was to nominate the specific individuals, subject to the confirmation of the other side. Some of Canada's greatest stars would, however, not be able to play. Bobby Hull had signed with the rival World Hockey Association, and Bobby Orr was recovering from one of his many knee injuries. Nevertheless, the organizers of Team Canada were confident that enough talent remained, and the Canadian press, with virtual unanimity, predicted easy victory. Canadian coaches, sent to the USSR to scout their opponents, were able to see the national team in only one exhibition. On that night, Tretiak let in nine goals, and the scouts reported back that the Soviets had not solved their chronic problem in the nets. They did not know, however, that Tretiak's mind was elsewhere that night. He was to be married the next day.[48]

For their part, the Soviets publicly stated that they were glad simply to have the experience of playing and learning from professionals. They did not expect any wins, especially in Canada, with the smaller rinks used in the NHL. Privately, Soviet fans and players simply hoped that they would not be defeated by too large a score. Soviet press accounts were equally cautious, and the series was buried under the quadrennial attention given to the Olympics, which were occurring at the same time.

The Soviet players were confident in their methods and abilities, but they, too, were completely uncertain about what might await them, since the men who had built Soviet hockey, literally from the ground up, were no longer coaching them. In the wake of the victory at Sapporo, Tarasov, so the rumor went, had asked the sports committee for financial rewards comparable to those given the players. Chernyshev supported his demand, and both threatened to quit. Their superiors called their bluff, and it fell to Vsevolod Bobrov to lead Soviet hockey in its greatest test.[49] At this historic moment, one he had done so much to create, all Tarasov could do was watch from the stands.

The first game was played September 2 at Montreal. The Canadians' confidence seemed fully justified when the Boston Bruins' center, Phil Esposito, scored thirty seconds into the game. Six minutes later the Canadians scored again, and it seemed the rout was on. From that point, however, the Soviets seized the initiative and forced the Canadians to play their game. They tied the score at the end of the first period, and in the next twenty minutes Valerii Kharlamov scored two goals to change the momentum. By the end of the game the Soviet team was in full control, triumphing by 7–3. To compound their embarrassment, the Canadians had not been told that international matches ritually ended with a ceremonial handshake, and so it appeared they were acting boorishly when they left the ice with the final siren.[50]

For the Canadians the result was shocking, but Soviet press reaction, while pleased, was actually muted. An account of the game appeared only on the last page of *Sovetskii sport,* unable to compete for space with the simultaneous successes at Munich. This guarded optimism seemed justified when the Canadians got revenge, winning 4–1 two days later at Toronto. *Sovetskii sport* attributed this success to the Canadians' well-advertised ''dirty play.''[51] Buoyed by their victory, Team Canada approached the next two games with restored confidence. They had been caught napping by the better-conditioned Soviets, but they were now ready to assert their superiority.

Order, however, was not restored. The Soviets tied the next game 4–4 and won the last, with Tretiak emerging as the star of the series. Once back home, Bobrov tried to dampen the excitement generated by these unexpected triumphs. He noted in the press that the Canadians had not yet reached playing condition and cautioned that they would feel far less pressure in the Moscow games. Bobrov's fears were justified. According to Tretiak's later account, the victories in Canada had bred overconfidence, and Iakushev expressed similar fears. The Soviets would win the first Moscow game, but the Canadians, playing in a frenzy, took the next two games as the Toronto Maple Leafs' Paul Henderson scored the winning goal in both games to set up a final showdown on September 28.[52]

The series had provoked enormous interest in Moscow. The Palace of Sport was filled to overflowing for all four games. Additional thousands gathered outside the arena to somehow be near the scene of the action, while tickets fetched record sums on the black market.[53] Before the series had started, no one had thought the last game would be decisive, so great had been the expectation of Canadian dominance. After the Soviets' victories in Canada, the tables were turned. Soviet fans assumed the Moscow games would be easy wins, but the Canadians' brilliant and desperate play had proved these revised predictions wrong.

The last game was played at a fever pitch. Soviet fans, quiet by Western standards, could not believe the actions of Canadian tourists, players, and officials. Chairs were thrown on the ice, referees were threatened, and Canadian team representatives rushed goal judges. After two periods, the Soviets, playing without the injured Kharlamov, appeared to be in control, leading 5–3. The Canadians, however, rallied to tie the score with seven minutes to go. At this point, the Soviets went into an uncharacteristic defensive shell, a tactic ill-suited to their abilities. They realized, though, that while a tie would have left the series even in games, they led by total goals. By European custom, this margin would have allowed them to claim victory.[54] But with less than a minute to go, the crowd in a frenzy, and the players near exhaustion, Phil Esposito took a shot on goal that Tretiak blocked. Henderson, who had been knocked down behind the goal, got to his feet. He picked up the rebound and shot. Tretiak blocked this shot as well, but he could not prevent yet another rebound. With thirty-four seconds left, Henderson got his stick on the puck and nudged it under Tretiak.

The Canadians had saved face and in the immediate aftermath were pleased with their victory. The Soviets, disappointed that they had come so close, expressed outrage at the Canadians' goonish and crude play. Everyone soon realized, though, that international hockey had been changed forever. The Soviets had played the Canadians evenly, when few, including their own specialists, gave them any chance.[55] Subsequent Canadian accounts made it clear that they had won the battle but lost the war, while most Soviet observers came to express satisfaction with what was called a moral victory. Yet the fact remained that in this first confrontation with professionals, the Soviets had actually lost. They had proved they were as good as the Canadians but not better.

In the wake of the series, Canadian journalists and officials claimed that the Soviets' excessive emphasis on the national team meant that their hockey lacked depth. A truer test of each nation's hockey, they argued, would be a series of games between Soviet and NHL clubs. At the end of 1975, Central Army and Krylia Sovetov played a number of exhibitions in Canada and the United States. As had long been the custom in Soviet sports, both teams were strengthened by players from other teams. Thus the two teams sent to Canada each represented one-half of the Soviets' national team. TsSKA beat the New York Rangers and Boston Bruins, but they tied Montreal and lost to the Stanley Cup champions, the Philadelphia Flyers, in a game that was marred by such brutal tactics by the "Broad Street Bullies" that the new TsSKA coach, Konstantin Loktev, took his team off the ice for half an hour.[56] Krylia Sovetov beat Pittsburgh, Chicago, and the New York Islanders, and lost to the Buffalo Sabres. In subsequent years, these games became a staple of the year's schedule. Soviet teams won far more often than they lost, but eventually these confrontations became less important as NHL clubs, whose first concern was with their domestic seasons, ceased to prepare seriously for games that did not count in the standings.

In 1976, the Canadians proposed yet another competition. This event, called the Canada Cup, was to involve the world's best national teams and take place at the beginning of the season, unlike the world championship. All professionals could now take part. In the first tournament, the Soviets, coming off a poor performance at the world championships and choosing to send a so-called experimental squad finished third.[57] In subsequent renewals of the Canada Cup, playing on smaller rinks with NHL referees, the Soviets won in 1981 and demonstrated excellent hockey, even though they would lose the next renewal in 1984. Additionally, they would win a special three-game Challenge Cup held in New York during 1979, in which the national team defeated a group of NHL all-stars drawn from all the other nations with players in the league.

Over the years, the Soviets demonstrated that they could play on a level with the world's best. They brought a new and exciting style of play to the attention of the hockey world and revolutionized the game everywhere. Yet they could not repeat the dominance that characterized both their Olympic performances and their earlier results against amateurs at the world championships. Playing against a nation whose best athletes were funnelled into one sport proved a difficult challenge. While victories still came more often on the ice than on the soccer field, there were defeats as well.

Reds on Roundball—Throughout Soviet history, basketball was called a "student sport," played more in schools than in factories. This description meant that the game's social base was more circumscribed than soccer's or hockey's, a fact Soviet journalists ascribed to the complexity and variability of basketball's rules. But if basketball was not deeply rooted in the affections of the working masses, it was more widely played throughout the various national republics than any sport except soccer, and each republic had its own approach to the sport. Russians and Ukrainians favored one style, while players from the Baltic and Georgia had their own methods. Anatolii Pinchuk, the leading basketball writer of the pre-glasnost era, described the various "schools" with great nuance:

> The followers of the Baltic school are extremely skillful and have a very high level of playing discipline. Knowing the importance of each goal scored they try to avoid any risk by using the maximum of rehearsed combinations and the minimum of improvisation. In short, Baltic basketball is a solid academic game. . . . The Russian school is typified by tremendous physical fitness. . . . This fact, together with rationality and mobility compensated for too much rigidity and flaws in technique. . . . The Georgian school differs quite considerably from both the Russian and Baltic schools. [They have] brilliant ability to play the game at high speed and obvious reluctance to play without the ball; passion for attack and a clearly expressed antipathy for defence. Georgian basketball is colorful but with a hint of anarchism. . . .[58]

These contrasting styles created obvious problems when organizing a national team, but the contrasts also had the advantage of giving the Soviets a versatility that other European teams lacked.

First organized in 1947, the national team quickly came to dominate competition on the Continent, winning all but a few of the biennial European championships. This success bred popularity with Soviet fans. When the European championship was held in Moscow during the late spring of 1953, thirty thousand spectators filled Dinamo Stadium for every session of the eleven-day competition, which was won convincingly by a Soviet team that was more than half non-Russian. This dominance of European basketball would last until the 1970s, when finally the Yugolavs came to present a formidable challenge.[59]

In addition to the European championship, amateur basketball's international body, Fédération Internationale de Basketball Amateur (FIBA), organized a world championship for amateur teams in the mid-1950s. These quadrennial events took place in non-Olympic years and were taken seriously by every nation but the United States. The Soviets would win this competition in 1959, only to have the title taken away. They triumphed again in 1967, under the leadership of Alexander Gomelskii, coach of Central Army, and won again in 1974, when the team was led by Gomelskii's bitter personal and coaching rival, Spartak Leningrad's Vladimir Kondrashin. Their victories did not blind the Soviets to the fact that the United States was still the center of world basketball. The Olympics were the one international event the Americans truly prepared for, and in this competition, the Soviets became the perennial bridesmaids, winning silver every year between 1952 and 1964. The 1967 World Championship gave them cause for optimism going into the Mexico City games of 1968, but that time, they finished only third.[60]

When the Soviets finished third at the 1970 World Championship in Yugoslavia, Gomelskii was arrested for a (set-up) minor customs violation on his return and dismissed from his position. A players' coach, with great psychological sensitivity, Gomelskii was replaced by the hard-driving Kondrashin, whose tactical and organizational brilliance more than compensated for his gruff personality. Kondrashin would lead his team to the Olympic final at Munich in 1972, but few expected anything more than the usual silver.

The 1972 final, nevertheless, took place against the background of the swift growth of basketball's popularity in the Soviet Union. Attendance, while still not tremendous, had increased dramatically. Press coverage had become more extensive and detailed, while the number of televised games increased. Basketball stars began to attain the visibility of soccer and hockey's best-known players, as the growth of the sport attracted more and more talented athletes. As a result, the 1972 Soviet national team was a particularly strong group, whose ability reflected broader trends in the sporting tastes of the Soviet public. The team had the usual multinational make-up, including the swingmen, Modestas Paulauskas of Zhalgiris Kaunas and Mikhail Korkia from Dinamo Tblisi. They were joined by TsSKA's guards, Sergei Belov (later elected to the U.S.-based Basketball Hall of Fame) and Ivan Edeshko. Alexander Belov, Kondrashin's star six-foot eight-inch pupil from Spartak Leningrad, was the center. By contrast, the American team was among the weakest groups ever sent by the United States to an Olympiad. At the height of the Vietnam War, many American college stars, most notably the great center Bill Walton, preferred not to represent a country whose policies they disapproved of.

In the final, the Soviets led comfortably for much of the game, but toward the end the Americans surged back, cutting the Soviet lead to one point (49–48) with thirty-eight seconds to go. The Soviets held the ball as long as they could, but with time running out on the thirty-second shot clock, Alexander Belov was forced to shoot. His shot was blocked, but he grabbed his own rebound with eight seconds to go. Belov, standing next to the baseline, began to lose his balance. Failing to see an unguarded Sergei Belov fifteen feet away, Alexander sent a wild diagonal pass to the perimeter in the direction of his tightly guarded teammate, Zurab Sakandelidze. Doug Collins, the American guard, stole the pass with eight seconds left and set off to the other end. Sakandelidze, however, managed to catch up with Collins and foul him. Three seconds remained.[61]

With Collins going to the line for two foul shots to give the United States the lead, Kondrashin signaled for a time-out. According to the rules then in force, a coach had a choice of taking the time-out before the first or second foul shot but not after both shots had been taken. As a special technical innovation for the Olympics, coaches had been given a button that turned on a red light that alerted officials at the scorers' table that they wanted to take a time-out. Kondrashin intended to take time after the first shot, but the inexperienced German game officials, thinking he had changed his mind when he did not take time immediately, failed to give the Soviets any time-out at all. It is highly unlikely that Kondrashin failed to call the time-out at the proper moment. He was an extremely astute bench coach who, unlike the Americans, played all his games under the prevailing international rules. There is little reason to believe that he would not have called the time-out when it had to be called.

Collins hit both shots, and the Americans went ahead, 50–49. Even before Collins made his second shot, the controversy began. After the first foul shot had been made, the Soviet assistant coach, Sergei Bashkin, was at the scorer's table screaming for a time-out, but he was ignored. The Soviets were required to inbound the ball immediately, which they did. Kondrashin and Bashkin were on the court gesticulating frantically. The referees were forced to stop the game. There was now one second on the clock. The Soviets continued to protest that they should have been given a time-out, and the secretary-general of FIBA, Robert Jones, came down from the stands to intervene. Because the game officials had not granted the time-out the Soviets had originally requested, Jones ruled the situation should return to the moment after Collins' last free throw.[62] He put three seconds back on the clock and gave the Soviets a time-out, over the protests of the Americans. The public address announcer told the audience three seconds were left. The Soviets, who had all but thrown the victory away, were given a reprieve.

Kondrashin looked down his bench and put Ivan Edeshko into the game, as he had intended to do all along. He was to heave the ball the length of the court to Alexander Belov, who was to set up at the center line, fake toward the ball, and take off down court.[63] In games against a touring American team that April, Edeshko had twice made similar passes from the sideline in game-ending situations. Two years earlier, he had performed the same feat in a playoff game for TsSKA against Kondrashin's Spartak team. Kondrashin had not forgotten. The game resumed as one referee handed Edeshko the ball. He threw it the length of the court to Belov, but before the ball could touch Belov, the horn went off. The Americans celebrated, but this time the confused game officials were stopping play because the clock had not been reset. When the referee had handed Edeshko the ball, fifty seconds were showing on the clock instead of the proper three. Finally, the game clock was wound down to show three seconds. Again Edeshko sent the ball just beyond the reach of two leaping Americans and this time found Belov near the basket.[64] Belov faked once (there was no one to be faked since he had knocked down one American and the other had overrun the play) and scored off the glass as time ran out once again. With joyous bedlam breaking out around him, all

Kondrashin could do in his moment of victory was curse Alexander Belov for the earlier mistake that had required the bizarre heroics. "I did not want to need those three seconds," he would later say.[65]

Incensed that the Soviets had been given what seemed like a third chance, the Americans lodged a formal protest, but, given the fact that the decision had been made by Jones, the very head of FIBA, their claim stood little chance and was denied. The United States was no longer undefeated in Olympic play. But no one connected with the Soviet basketball program would ever claim, in the wake of the Munich victory, that the Americans had ceased to be anything but the leaders of world basketball. They knew they had not beaten professionals.

Kondrashin would build on this victory and lead his team to a world championship in 1974, but he was not able to maintain a position at the top of the amateur basketball world. A third-place finish at the 1976 Olympics led to his replacement by Gomelskii, who could do no better in 1980, despite the fact that the United States boycotted the games, which were held in Moscow.[66] For the 1984 games in Los Angeles, Gomelskii felt he had assembled his strongest team ever, led by the astounding young Lithuanian center Arvidas Sabonis. But 1984 was the Soviets' turn to boycott, and Gomelskii's hopes were put on hold. He would have to wait until 1988 to achieve his personal dream of Olympic gold, but in the interim, domestic interest in Soviet basketball declined as a result of the repeated failures at the international level.

The various championships contested by national teams were not the only forms of international competition. Soviet clubs also took part in a variety of European cup competitions, winning their fair share in the 'fifties and 'sixties. Three times, between 1958 and 1960, Gomelskii led his Riga Army team to the European club championship, and he would perform the same feat with Central Army in 1963. The year before, Dinamo Tblisi had won the same European title. By the end of the 'sixties, however, officially amateur European teams, especially in Italy and Spain, began to sign Americans in increasing numbers. Many of these players were former professionals who had ended marginal careers in the U.S. National Basketball Association. Others were rookies who, while talented, were not quite good enough to play professionally in America. Their presence greatly complicated the task of Soviet clubs, whose performances in the various European cups declined. So great was Soviet frustration with this situation that in some years their teams refused to take part.[67] As in soccer and hockey, Soviet success against amateurs in basketball was not repeated when the opponents were professional. American players who appeared for European clubs were officially considered amateurs until 1989, but their official status was one thing; their talent level another. While it would not be fair to say Soviet club teams could no longer compete against the best European teams, wins did become less frequent.

In the Olympic context, it was possible to convince the world of the existence of a powerful, well-supported medal machine, and this success was supposed to be a reflection of the superiority of Communism. By limiting their competition to amateurs, the Soviets were able to mask the weaknesses of their sports system, but when they came to play professionals in commercially successful spectator sports, the problems and contradictions of the Soviet sports world were revealed. The resources simply were not available to achieve victory in every sphere.

"The World's Greatest Sporting Nation"

During the post-war era, athletes from the USSR came to dominate the specific segment of the world sports stage consciously targeted by the state. Successes in space, along with Olympic victories, were loudly trumpeted to give the world the impression of a nation on the march to a glorious and powerful future. I have tried to show that this side of Soviet sport, the one made available to the outside, obscured massive problems and failures. Nevertheless, the system that led others to view the USSR as a sports power cannot be fully ignored.

As it turned out, Soviet elite athletes were not the tip of a vast participant pyramid. Instead, they composed a very thin, narrow layer of talent that rested on long, rotting, and none-too-numerous stilts. The belief that "masters came from mass sport" did not accurately describe reality, but there can be no doubt that the Soviets were able to muster the best of a vast talent pool to surmount the problems of inadequate facilities and produce scores of international victories.

After Stalin's death, the Soviet sports system underwent two structural reforms. In 1959, reflecting Khrushchev's concern for decentralization, government control of sports was diminished, and power devolved to the trade unions and Komsomol. As Riordan has shown, these changes did little to improve conditions at the local level, and in 1966, the Party issued a series of resolutions calling for change. As a result, government control of sports was reasserted in 1968, and the Sport Committee was put back under the authority of the Council of Ministers.[68] Neither the reform nor the counter-reform had much impact on the high-performance system, which had developed its own momentum.

To feed that system, the Spartakiad was revived and reorganized. It was now supposed to reflect the pyramidal structure of the sports system, with local, regional, and republican competitions leading to a quadrennial sports festival among teams from Moscow, Leningrad, and all fifteen republics. The first of the new Spartakiads was held in the summer of 1956 for the dual purposes of celebrating the opening of Moscow's Lenin Stadium and selecting teams for the Melbourne Olympic Games that winter. Thereafter, the national Spartakiad would take place the year before the Olympics and serve as a vehicle for finding and developing new talents.

The Spartakiads of this period were internal Olympics, adorned with the elaborate rituals of opening and closing ceremonies at which each republic's athletes entered Lenin Stadium in national garb. Thousands of gymnasts and other performers took part in these decidedly noncarnivalesque extravanganzas that were reminiscent of the Physical Culture Day parades at their worst.[69] In fact, Physical Culture Day, which was now celebrated in more muted form, always marked the opening day of the Spartakiad in those years it was contested. Like in the Olympics, track and field was the centerpiece of the summer Spartakiad.[70] Soccer and basketball, while on the program, received less attention, given the greater importance attached by fans to the regular season in both sports.

While Lenin Stadium was always filled for the opening and closing ceremonies of the Spartakiad, it is not possible to measure attendance at the events themselves with any accuracy. The press and television, which gave considerable coverage to the Spartakiad, did not report on the number of spectators. Photographs show plenty of empty seats, and until the 'seventies, many sports had to be contested in small venues. By 1973, facilities had improved, and Moscow was the site of the World University Games, an event that the sports authorities used as a springboard for their bid to hold the Olympics.[71]

Multisport competitions (*kompleksnye sorevnovania*) were especially attractive to the state and Party. These festivals of youth and sports, whether they were Olympiads or Spartakiads, embraced what Soviet leaders thought were the humane and timeless values of the classical world in ways that championships in specific sports could not. By bringing together athletes from various nations or various republics, the multisport competition, far more effectively than the single-sport event, evoked a variety of appeals to youth, optimism, and world peace.

At a world championship, the nuances and concerns of the particular sport being played were emphasized. By contrast, at multisport events, the coming together of many peoples dominated the discourse of participants and observers. Messages of shared humanity and purpose became as visible and important in the accounts of these events as the details of the sports themselves. One of the staples of Soviet Olympic press coverage was the happy mingling of sportswomen and men from all over the world in the athletes' village. By contrast, one never read similar stories about soccer's World Cup, during which the teams were sequestered in separate, closed training sites.

Because sport itself took something of a backseat in the multisport competition, non-sporting messages were more easily attached to the Olympiad and Spartakiad than to championships in specific sports. Because of their greater didactic potential, the state preferred these kinds of competitions.

Because multisport events more readily fit the political purposes of the state and Party, the government attached special priority to success in the Olympics. Beginning with 1956, Soviet athletes came to dominate both the summer and winter Games. In press accounts, victories were measured in two ways, the count of medals and the unofficial system adopted by the world press that gave points to the top six finishers in an event. Soviet discussions of the Games put enormous stress on these statistics, even if they were careful to note the unofficial character of the so-called team totals. Only in 1968 was the United States able to overtake the Soviets in the overall point totals. Perhaps surprisingly, that defeat met with only muted criticism at the time, and the USSR came back in 1972 at Munich to score its greatest total of victories before 1980.[72]

The Olympics also produced a galaxy of Soviet sport stars who became world-famous. Women's track and field was one area of great strength, and in the 'fifties the Press sisters, Irina and Tamara, ruled over their events. At Melbourne, the male distance runner Vladimir Kuts emerged as a dominant figure, destroying his opposition in the five and ten thousand meters. In 1960, the record-breaking weightlifter Iurii Vlasov would take center stage. Yet the triumphs at Munich in 1972 produced the greatest number of heroes. Olga Korbut was not the most accomplished of Soviet female gymnasts, but her special blend of personality and showmanship presented the outside world with an athlete who seemed charmingly unorthodox in the Soviet context. By contrast, Valerii Borzov, who ended American dominance of both sprint races, and the massive weightlifter Vasilii Alekseiev, conformed more strictly to the mold of the sober sports hero. The leader of the triumphant basketball team, Sergei Belov, created such an impression that he was actually drafted by an American professional team.

The Olympic triumphs were occasions for quadrennial orgies of cheerleading and self-congratulation. Returning champions were met at the airport by bouquets, bands, and bureaucrats, and medal-winners were received at lavish Kremlin receptions attended by the powerful and famous from all walks of Soviet life.[73] By surrounding their triumphs with so much fanfare, the state and Party did succeed in using the limited arena of the Olympic Games as a stage for demonstrating the triumphs of the Soviet peoples and the superiority of Communism. Athletic success, as the West was all too frequently reminded, was supposed to reflect the superiority of the Soviet system, but ultimately those triumphs hid the weaknesses rather than demonstrated the strengths of that system.

While the Olympics were good for Soviet sports, the Soviets were good for the Olympics. The mimetic and therefore peaceful superpower struggle on the playing fields of the world proved a compelling spectacle for millions who at the height of the Cold War lived in daily fear of possible nuclear annihilation. The visibility and popularity of the Games soared as they became a surrogate for the more deadly United States–Soviet Union military rivalry. In the process, the Olympics attracted ever-higher television and marketing fees. Soviet sports authorities and government leaders then sought to bring the Olympics to Moscow as recognition, indeed a reward, for all they had contributed to the movement. For years their athletes had been required to travel far from home in order to compete, while Soviet citizens, who were denied that luxury of foreign travel, had been forced to watch on television.

The idea of hosting the Olympics was first raised in 1969, but when the 1976 Games were awarded the next year, Montreal won out over Los Angeles and Moscow. The Soviets persisted, and in 1974, after successfully running the 1973 Universiad, they were granted the right to hold the 1980 Games. The entire sports movement now had a clear goal to organize its efforts around, and the anticipation grew with each passing year. The granting of the Games to Moscow was seen as both recognition of the central role the USSR had come to play in world sports and vindication of the practices followed by the official sports system over the years.[74] At the same time, the type of multi-sport competition so favored by the state would now be a spectator activity in the full sense of the word. The public would have a chance to see the Games in person.

By the end of 1979, the stage seemed set for a grand festival of sports that would be a coronation of the USSR as the world's greatest sporting nation, but the Soviet invasion of Afghanistan that December would change everything. In April 1980, the United States confirmed that it would boycott the Games, and fifty-five other nations, including West Germany and Japan, joined them. Whether they had anticipated the boycott or not, Brezhnev and the Soviet political leadership clearly considered controlling the situation in Afghanistan to be more important than the chance of having a fully representative Olympics. Sport was not so important as to let it control crucial geopolitical considerations.

The Soviets, of course, protested mightily, even going as far as to claim that politics should not be allowed to interfere with sports. Great Britain, Italy, France, Spain, and Australia all chose to take part, and the Olympics went on in a holiday atmosphere. While the absence of the United States had the greatest impact on basketball, the sprints and hurdles in track, and the men's events in swimming, enough outstanding performances were recorded to allow the Soviets to claim that the Games were a sporting success. Bryant Gumbel of the National Broadcasting Corporation, in summarizing his company's severely truncated coverage of the Games, noted, "despite the absence of the American athletes, the events of the past sixteen days represent a happening of world importance." NBC also presented a commentary from a BBC announcer who dismissed criticisms of the Games as second-rate, and Gumbel would add, "We missed being there."[75]

For their part, the Soviets tried to go on as if everything were normal. Television coverage noted the boycott only in passing, and instead loudly trumpeted the even more easily achieved dominance of Soviet athletes. The atmosphere in Moscow truly was that of an international festival, and Soviet fans, much like their American counterparts four years later, eagerly attended even the obscurest events. Sports that had rarely attracted more than a few hundred spectators drew tens of thousands when they were presented in the context of the Olympics. Shooting, archery, even canoeing played to more than ninety per cent of capacity. Even field hockey proved to be a hit with Moscow audiences. In all, 5,268,163 tickets were sold, of which 3,944,373 were purchased by Soviet fans. Soccer, despite the second-rate caliber of Olympic competition, predictably drew the largest audience (1,821,624), but track uncharacteristically proved a success at the gate, drawing more than a million spectators and filling Lenin Stadium to 95 per cent of its capacity. Clearly, the chance to witness part of history was sufficiently compelling for Soviet sports fans to buy tickets to events they had always previously ignored. Perhaps this was the final irony of Soviet spectator choice. For decades they had shown only restrained interest in the sports on the Olympic program, but when given a chance to see what they thought was the real thing, they did show up.[76]

The phenomenon of full stands filled with happy fans from all over the world did create a sufficient sense of atmosphere for Soviet press accounts to rhapsodize about the success of the Moscow Games, but there remained lingering doubts among the sports bureuacrats who had put so much effort into obtaining and then organizing the Olympics. Political leaders may have been willing to accept the boycott as a necessary cost of their invasion of Afghanistan, but sports officials were deeply resentful of the Americans, who they thought had rained on their parade. With the next Games to be held in Los Angeles in 1984, these officials were ready for any good excuse to return the favor and spoil the Americans' party. When a number of conservative American groups in Southern California began to announce plans for assisting the defection of Soviet athletes, the leaders of *Goskomsport,* as it was then known, were able to persuade the Party leadership to keep the boys and girls home.[77]

As it turned out, neither Olympics, of 1980 or of 1984, was deemed a failure by those who participated and by those who watched, and neither boycott achieved any clear political purpose outside the realm of sports. As it would turn out, the Soviets' decision to stay home from the Los Angeles

Games proved especially costly for the long-suffering Soviet soccer world. The Soviets announced their boycott two weeks before FIFA was to decide the site of the 1990 soccer World Cup. The USSR had been the leading candidate, but their decision to boycott in Los Anegeles caused the world body to switch their support to Italy. One can only imagine the financial and sports impact on a then-changing Soviet society and sports system had the 1990 World Cup taken place in the cities of the Soviet Union.[78]

The Moscow Games were supposed to be a confirmation of the USSR's position as the world's leading sports nation, but their success, partial as it may have been, did not reflect the deeper problems of Soviet society. By the late 'seventies, the Soviet Union was entering a crisis whose seriousness would only be revealed in the first years of perestroika. After 1985, it became common in the USSR to refer to the last years of Leonid Brezhnev's rule as the "period of stagnation," but, as Moshe Lewin has shown, that stagnation only described the attitudes and activities of an increasingly sclerotic leadership. While Brezhnev and his associates were busy doing little more than boasting about their international sports successes, Soviet society was undergoing profound structural changes.

This incongruence between a rapidly developing social and economic system on the one hand and an unreformed political system on the other would prove a recipe for serious political trouble, which few who attended the closing ceremonies of the Moscow Games could have foreseen. Exclusive attention to Soviet international performances had diverted the attention of the outside world from the many problems of the Soviet sports world. However, an examination of domestic developments during this same period reveals that the crisis which took place during the years of perestroika had been building for several decades.

6

Entertainment in the Age of Soviet Normalcy

Between 1914 and 1953, the citizens of the prerevolutionary Russian Empire and the postrevolutionary Soviet Union lived through the traumas of World War I, the revolution of 1917, the Civil War, forced-draft industrialization, collectivization, the purges, World War II, the difficulties of reconstruction, and the repression of Stalin's last years. In sharp contrast, the period between Stalin's death (1953) and Mikhail Gorbachev's ascension to power (1985) proved to be considerably more tranquil. With Stalin gone, there was hope that the terror could come to an end. The new collective leadership that took over in the wake of Stalin's death quickly arrested Lavrenti Beria and at the end of the year executed him.

As Nikita Khrushchev moved to consolidate his power in the next few years, he strove to turn Soviet high politics into a less deadly game, and in doing so, he also reduced the role of the secret police in society. Stephen Cohen has described the changes: "Millions of prison camp survivors were freed, and many victims who had perished in the terror were legally exonerated.... Many administrative abuses and bureaucratic privileges were curtailed. Educated society began to participate more fully in political, intellectual, and cultural life, and new benefits were made available to workers and peasants."[1] While labor camps and political repression remained a part of Soviet life, the level of fear diminished considerably.

Khrushchev also sought to reorganize the economy and give special priority to the chronically weak agricultural sector. His numerous grand experiments achieved considerable success in the late 'fifties. The Virgin Lands campaign, which planted previously unused territory in the East; the attempt to introduce corn as a fodder crop in order to boost meat production; and the disbanding of the Machine Tractor Stations that controlled agricultural implements in the countryside, all soon caused as many problems as they solved, however. By the early 'sixties, the progress of the postwar period began to stall, and the failures of the agricultural reforms forced the USSR to import grain for the first time in 1963.

Khrushchev's attempt to decentralize the economy by disbanding economic ministries and replacing them with local councils had many benefits, but it soon undermined the remnants of the central planning apparatus. His division of the Party into agricultural and industrial sections, along with the shifting of several ministries outside the capital, forced many bureaucrats to leave the comforts of Moscow for rougher lives in the provinces. Ideologically orthodox elements were similarly threatened by the relatively liberal cultural policies that characterized the so-called thaw of the mid-1950s. By the end of his time in office, Khrushchev had alienated many of the most powerful and privileged elements in Soviet society, and he was removed from office, by Central Committee vote rather than execution, in October of 1964.[2]

The assumption of power by Leonid Brezhnev and Aleksei Kosygin represented the Party's attempt to impose order, calm, and predictability on government policies and personnel. Sometimes termed "re-Stalinization," the Brezhnev years came to be euphemistically called the "period of stagnation." After Khrushchev's unpredictability, the Party and state bureaucracies were particularly concerned with the protection of their positions. Functionaries were granted virtual lifetime tenure, eventually creating a "sclerocracy" by the mid-1980s. Culture, in all forms, also became considerably more conformist.

Not all policies during the Brezhnev era were intended to undo the work of Khrushchev. While the economic system was recentralized, there was a continuing commitment to improving agriculture. Despite chronic shortages, consumer goods also became more plentiful. By the end of the 1970s, though, the pace of economic growth began to slow, as the centrally planned command economy that had been able to speed the pace of industrialization proved incapable of performing the more complex tasks of fulfilling the public's daily needs.[3]

The "stability of cadres" that Brezhnev introduced at the top of the Soviet political system seemed, on the surface, to be an attempt to avoid much-needed reform, but despite those policies, rather than because of them, Soviet society changed dramatically during the three decades following Stalin's death. By 1959, the USSR had become more than half urban, and by the 1970s more than half of the USSR's citizens had been born in cities.[4] Given the universal link between urban life and spectator sports, this demographic shift had important consequences, creating a larger and more diversified audience for sports. At the same time, higher education and technical training continued to expand, creating an ever-higher degree of specialization among Soviet citizens.[5] Society became more complex and articulated, as new social groups of technical specialists, middle-level bureaucrats, and practically engaged intellectuals emerged. The working class itself fissured into a number of subgroups, while the peasantry became less isolated.

Transport and communication improved, bringing the periphery into closer contact with the capital and the USSR into closer contact with the rest of the world. Although the Cold War and the attendant arms race led the government to give an enormous but unmeasurable percentage of gross national product to military spending, many resources were still left over for such activities of secondary importance as sports. Stadiums, training bases, and sports schools were built in record numbers. Aside from more money, there was also more time. By the mid-'sixties, the five-day work week became commonplace.[6] Soviet citizens had more leisure, and both the watching and playing of sports became even more common. It was now easier to go to the stadium. There were more teams and more sports. Larger arenas meant that tickets were no longer so difficult to obtain, and many major cities joined Moscow and Leningrad as centers of sports excitement.

These changes were largely the result of the continued but highly uneven economic growth of the postwar era, which did not begin to slacken until the late 'seventies. Although the USSR was far more involved in world trade than it had been before the war, the economic growth that was achieved was still quite autarkic. Given the priorities of the state, production still was skewed toward heavy industry and military spending. Additionally, the citizens of the USSR continued to be comparatively isolated in their access to information. In the Khrushchev and Brezhnev periods, the Soviet public came to know more about the outside world than ever before, but awareness of that world was still limited and controlled. As a result, the state and Party were able to convince the majority of citizens that their lives had indeed become better, even more joyous. Along with improvements in food, consumer goods, and housing, entertainments also became more numerous and varied. In these years, there were no internally destructive wars and no major upheavals. Millions did not die tragically and needlessly. It became possible for Soviet citizens to live what they thought was a "normal" life.

These changes created great possibilities for the growth of spectator sports. The urban population increased dramatically and became more socially segmented. New sports that previously had found only limited audiences, most notably basketball, could now expand their social base. Television made events available to millions of citizens and propagandized sports into all corners of the Union. Similar changes occurred in the West, where post-war prosperity combined with the power of television to expand the audience for spectator sports even more dramatically than in the Soviet Union.

This last fact must be stressed. It is easy to be misled by the absolute growth of all forms of sports activity in the USSR after 1953, and there can be no doubt that the facilities available for both elite and mass sports did expand rapidly. These successes were loudly, even boastingly, trumpeted at home and abroad, just as the simultaneous emergence of the Olympic system made sports a highly visible component of Soviet foreign policy. None of this expansion, however, should obscure the fact that Soviet society expended fewer resources on both mass and elite sport than did capitalist countries. By no concrete measure—be it percentage of central and local government budgets, percentage of gross national product, the number of large arenas, the amount of television time, or the number of fans attending games—could spectator sports in the USSR compare with the concurrent explosion of activity in the West, especially the United States. Inadequate facilities, equipment, and funding had plagued Soviet sports before 1953, and despite the great growth of amenities after Stalin's death, these problems persisted. Olympic successes only deflected attention from them. Just as the long-term structural flaws of the Soviet economic system became evident only toward the end of this period, so were the weaknesses of the sports system similarly hidden from the outside world.

Expanding the Infrastructure

The expansion of spectator sports in the post-Stalin era was made possible by the construction of hundreds of new stadiums. Big cities built even larger arenas, while tens of provincial centers got their first sizable facilities. Indoor arenas were the most important part of this growth. Before 1956, there were simply no large buildings, except for the circuses, that could house thousands of spectators for sporting events.[7] Given the length and harshness of the Russian winter, this shortage clearly limited the development of sports, both as activity and as entertainment. Between the mid-'fifties and the late 'sixties, this lack of amenities was corrected in the second great wave of Soviet stadium building.

The USSR's most important sports amenity, Moscow's Luzhniki Complex, opened in 1956. Located at the southern bend of the Moscow river, Luzhniki is a huge sports park, filled with soccer fields, running tracks, a swimming stadium, and basketball, volleyball, and tennis courts. At the park's center is Lenin Stadium, which had a capacity of 103,000 at the time of its opening. Built in little more than a year, it was inaugurated in the summer of 1956 with the revived Spartakiad.[8] At the time of its construction, it was one of the largest stadiums in the world, and it replaced Dinamo Stadium as Moscow's main venue for soccer.

As it turned out, Lenin Stadium was actually less convenient for the fans than Dinamo. A fifteen-minute walk from the nearest metro station, the new arena, with its standard running track, placed spectators far away from the action. Dinamo Stadium was still a better and easier place to watch a game, and Dinamo Moscow continued to play its home games there, while Spartak moved to Luzhniki. Central Army (now called TsSKA, *Tsentral'nyi Sportivnyi Klub Armii*) played in both places, while Torpedo appeared at Lenin Stadium, until building its own, comparatively small facility. Ironically, Dinamo Stadium, which had been described in earlier press accounts as a "giant steel and concrete bowl," now came to be called *uiutnyi* ("cozy and comfortable").

In the fall of 1956, the Palace of Sport opened, located just to the west of Lenin Stadium and even farther from the metro. Moscow now had an indoor facility that was comparable to most North American arenas and larger than all but a few indoor venues in Europe. Basketball and hockey could now move inside. The 14,000-seat arena was only the second artifical rink in the Soviet Union, and it would serve as the venue for the most important games of Moscow's several first division teams.[9] With so many teams in Moscow and a wide variety of both sporting and non-sporting demands placed on so few arenas, however, it often became necessary to go back outdoors, and for some time, no Moscow team could consistently train indoors. As late as 1971, some five thousand brave Muscovites would sit through a snowstorm in temperatures of minus-sixteen degrees Centigrade to watch Spartak beat Dinamo. That same year, hockey still was played outdoors in such important provincial centers of the sport as Cheliabinsk, despite the existence of new local arenas.[10]

During the second half of the 1950s, stadiums were built in several other cities. Each town now had to have its own "Luzhniki." Construction of Kirov Stadium in Leningrad was actually completed in 1950, while the city's smaller Lenin Stadium was repaired. Dinamo Stadium in Tblisi was remodeled and enlarged. In Minsk, Dinamo Stadium, a 36,000-seat arena built in the 'thirties, was reconstructed and expanded in 1954 (it had been destroyed in the war). A ten-thousand-seat indoor arena was built in Tblisi, while Kiev constructed its own seven-thousand-seat Palace of Sport.[11] Smaller arenas, largely for hockey, were built in a number of midsize provincial cities.[12] The pace of construction slowed only slightly in the 'sixties. Kiev Republic Stadium, with 100,000 seats, opened in 1965. Baku got the 45,000-capacity Lenin Stadium, while Erevan had to wait until 1971 for the 70,000-seat Razadan Stadium. Leningrad finally replaced its outmoded manège with the 6,500-seat Iubil'einyi Sports Palace. By the end of the decade, the growth had been remarkable. In 1952, the USSR had 1,020 *stadiony* (with more than 1,500 seats). In 1960, there were 2,407 such structures, and by 1968, the number had grown to 3,065.[13]

As a result, it was now possible for spectator sports to expand dramatically outside the capital. As provincial cities grew, their residents desired attractive recreation, and the government willingly provided facilities for watching sports. Yet, for all this expansion, the USSR still lagged far behind the United States. Compared to the scores of massive football stadiums on American college campuses, the Soviets had only a few similar facilities; and as of 1991 there were still only eight stadiums in the entire USSR with capacities above 50,000, compared to nine in the State of California alone.[14] Indoor arenas outside Moscow, in particular, were small by American (but not European) standards, and only the pressure of the Moscow Olympics led to the construction of facilities that were world-class.[15]

The expansion in sports construction was the most striking material sign of the growth of spectator sports in this era. Muscovites now had bigger and warmer places to watch their favorite games, while millions of fans in provincial cities at last had amenities that could accommodate them. The government spared little energy in trumpeting this expansion, but the growth obscured the fact that for a country of its enormous size, the USSR's facilities for spectator sport still were smaller and fewer than those of capitalist countries.

The Boom in Attendance and the Impact of Television

More and bigger venues permitted a dramatic increase in attendance. Throughout the world, the 'fifties and 'sixties witnessed a sharp rise in the number of spectators for big-time sports. Postwar prosperity and the growth of consumer societies supported the expansion of the sports industry. Here the Soviet Union was no exception. Increased leisure and disposable income combined with reasonable ticket prices to make sports truly available to the masses, and those who could not get to the stadium now had a new way of watching sports; namely, television.

Attendance—As before the war, soccer had the largest audience. More stadiums meant that more cities could support teams, and both the first and second divisions were expanded, with the first division oscillating between sixteen and twenty-two teams. The number of games increased and with them the number of spectators. In 1953, 110 first-division games attracted 3,920,000 fans, an average of more than 35,000 per game. By 1967, 342 matches brought in 10,327,000 spectators, an average of 30,200. Soccer reached the height of its popularity in the late 'sixties in the wake of the Soviets' semifinal appearance in the 1966 World Cup. Between 1965 and 1969, almost fifty million fans watched first-division soccer games, an average of more than thirty thousand. By the early 'seventies, those figures had declined dramatically. A lack of international success, boring domestic play, and a diminution of the number of teams in the first division meant that only 17,211,500 spectators attended first-division games between 1970 and 1974, causing a staggering drop in average attendance to little more than thirteen thousand per game.[16]

In the late 'seventies, led by the international success of such club teams as Dinamo Kiev and Dinamo Tblisi and spurred by the revival of Spartak's fortunes, domestic attendance recovered. By the early 'eighties, the first-division roster had stabilized at eighteen teams, playing 306 games per year. Attendance between 1980 and 1984 hovered around six million per year, the average gate was a bit more or less than twenty thousand.[17] These figures disguised enormous fluctuations in attendance. With several huge new stadiums, important games could attract monster crowds. On the other hand, weaker and less popular teams could draw only a few thousand. In the years of Leningrad Zenit's decline, massive Kirov Stadium rarely saw more than four or five thousand forlorn *bolel'shchiki* in the stands, but in the year of their 1984 championship, Zenit averaged 47,000 per game.[18]

Soviet fans followed the universal rule of attendance, good teams draw; poor ones do not. If a new club rose to the top, as Dinamo Kiev did beginning in the 'sixties, its gates at home and on the road rose accordingly. When Arrarat of Erevan had great success under the coaching of Nikita Simonian in the early 1970s, it drew more than 50,000 fans per game to newly built Razdan Stadium.[19] When Dinamo Tblisi, which had always drawn well at home, had its greatest run of success in the early 1980s, they enjoyed similar gates. The only exceptions to this rule have been Spartak and Dinamo Moscow, who, despite changing fortunes and fluctuating home attendance, always drew well on the road.

As the summer season extended into spring and fall, many more games had to be played in bad weather. While March and April attendance could be unaffected by the climate, due to popular excitement about the beginning of the season, many games in November played to crowds in the mere hundreds. Nevertheless, given the right attraction, Soviet fans showed they could brave the elements. In 1980, when Spartak came to Kiev for an October 31 game that would decide the chanpionship, every one of Republic Stadium's 100,000 seats was filled despite below-freezing temperatures and a snowfall. On the other hand, Moscow Lokomotiv versus Krylia Sovetov of Kuibishev in 1966, at the height of soccer's popularity, was watched by only 3,000 on a perfect August day.[20]

International matches, between national teams as well as clubs, were always huge gate attractions. Elimination games for the world and European cups were usually sellouts unless the Soviet *sbornaia* was playing weaker opponents such as Malta, Iceland, or Cyprus. Exhibition games against either national teams or famous foreign clubs were also big draws. Beginning in 1965, Soviet teams came to participate in the three cup tournaments organized by the Union of European Football Associations (UEFA). These games proved to be exceptionally compelling spectacles, particularly when a provincial club won the right to participate and, perhaps, got to welcome some renowned foreign team.

Hockey attendance also grew at a similar pace between 1953 and 1985. Nevertheless, the total number of fans taking in hockey games was considerably smaller than for soccer. Soccer was a truly national phenomenon, played in all republics. Hockey was largely limited to the Slavic heartland. While Moscow lost its dominance in soccer, it continued to occupy the leading position in hockey, with four and sometimes five teams in hockey's first division. Provincial arenas, on the other hand, were extremely small. Until 1980, the largest buildings outside the capital were in Leningrad (6,500 seats) and Kiev (7,000). As a result, total hockey attendance was considerably lower than that for soccer.[21]

The construction of Moscow's Palace of Sport in 1956 did give an enormous boost to hockey in the capital. Before that date, crowds at Dinamo Stadium had continued to be sizable for important domestic matches, and a big international event could attract as many as thirty thousand spectators. Once a closed arena and artificial ice were available, large crowds became even more common. When Central Army played Dinamo or Spartak, all 14,000 seats in the arena would be filled, well into the late 'seventies.[22] But games between provincial teams and Moscow squads were rarely big draws and were usually played in smaller arenas with capacities of three to six thousand.[23] Games in the smaller provincial arenas, on the other hand, drew a large percentage of their limited capacities. Sellouts were guaranteed for the big Moscow teams, and if the local team were having a good season, a game against a strong opponent from another smaller town could also fill the arena. If, however, a team were playing poorly and a weak opponent were scheduled, only a few hundred might show up.

In 1967, roughly 1,200,000 spectators watched domestic hockey games. The next year, attendance rose to 1,346,000. Of the Moscow teams, Spartak, just as in soccer, was the clear favorite of the capital's fans. Despite Central Army's greater success, TsSKA had a smaller following, as did the other Moscow clubs:

Home Attendance of Moscow Hockey Teams, 1967–1968

Team	1967	1968
Spartak	213,000	207,000
TsSKA	110,600	152,500
Dinamo	92,600	124,600
Lokomotiv	51,000	45,000
Krylia Sovetov	37,400	49,400
League total:	1,197,000	1,346,000
League average:	4,494	5,562

Source: *Sovetskii sport,* September 15, 1969

Much has been made of the fact that Leonid Brezhnev particularly liked hockey, and during his ascendancy, Party leaders were expected to attend important games. Resources that might have gone to other sports were supposedly directed to hockey, and television showed many more matches than before 1964. In truth, hockey had already found its place in the affections of Soviet fans, and the progress of these years built on this earlier base. International success, especially the celebrated series with Team Canada in 1972, spurred spectators' interest to even greater heights. Attendance continued to grow through the mid-'seventies, but eventually the practice of loading the Central Army team to serve as the basis of the national team proved destructive for domestic competition, and attendance fell off drastically.[24]

Men's basketball trailed the Big Two spectator sports by a sizable margin, but during this period, it greatly expanded its audience, placing third in the affections of the sports public. In 1953, the European men's championship was held outdoors at Dinamo Stadium, attracting daily crowds of 30,000. Interest in the 1953 national championship, also held outdoors in Tblisi, produced chaotic scenes. *Sovetskii sport* reported that there were so many spectators it was impossible to maintain order, forcing organizers to move preliminary games to a nearby park and play them without any advance notice to the public. In the Baltic hotbeds, thousands gathered outdoors for important, if somewhat more orderly, competitions.[25]

The structure of the domestic basketball competition changed constantly. Some years several teams played a number of round-robin tournaments in different cities. At other times, when public interest was higher, a regular home-and-away league structure was used. In the late 'sixties, basketball's popularity continued to grow, attracting larger audiences and more press and television coverage. Still, the number of fans attending basketball was small compared to soccer and hockey. In the 1967–1968 season, a total of 448,000 spectators showed up for 264 games, an average gate of 1,848. The next season, 602,900 fans attended, raising the average to 2,283. Dinamo Tblisi led the league with an average of more than 8,000, while Lokomotiv of Alm-Ata drew only six hundred spectators per game.[26]

Interest in basketball was spurred by a combination of considerable international success and keen domestic competition. A number of strong teams with contrasting styles and national compositions made for compelling spectacles. Growth in attendance, however, was hampered by the sport's inability to gain consistent access to the largest facilities. The construction of Tblisi's Sports Palace in 1959 provided an enormous boost to the game in Georgia. The arena's 10,000 seats were nearly always filled with the Soviet Union's most intense fans. The 4,500-seat Sporthalle in Kaunas Lithuania similarly became a shrine for the sport as the local team, Zhalgiris, became one of the top Soviet squads. Elsewhere, the situation was more difficult. Kalev's 3,000-seat arena in Tallin was never adequate for the number who wished to attend. In Riga, fans had to be turned away when Alexander Gomelskii's local army team became one of Europe's strongest sides. Leningrad had similar problems until the construction of the Iubil'einyi Arena in the late 'sixties, when Spartak Leningrad enjoyed constant sellouts during its greatest run of success under the coaching of Vladimir Kondrashin.[27]

Moscow, however, proved more difficult. The Palace of Sport was given over to basketball primarily for games against visiting American teams. Between concerts and hockey games, Moscow's largest arena was rarely available. Even European Cup games against teams from Italy, Spain, and other basketball powers were not held there. The city's two strongest teams, Dinamo and Central Army, usually played in small, cramped gymnasiums that held five hundred crushed spectators. In the 'sixties important games were moved to TsSKA's 3,500-seat ice arena. Eventually, both societies built 5,000-seat arenas in the late 'seventies, but until then basketball in Moscow continued to be plagued by the lack of suitable venues. Similar problems occurred in Kiev, where the city's two first-division teams often had difficulty renting the Palace of Sports.[28]

It is significant that this rise in basketball's popularity preceded rather than followed the victory at the 1972 Olympics. The team that won in Munich was riding a wave of fan recognition that contributed to the confidence and sense of mission of both players and coaches. Unfortunately the vogue for basketball soon dissipated. Third-place finishes at Montreal in 1976 and Moscow in 1980 cooled the ardor of the public. Internal squabbling and continued poor organization also hampered basketball's ability to build on the success of the late 'sixties and early 'seventies. Nevertheless, the men's game found a niche. Women's basketball, despite enormous success on the international level, never caught the attention of the largely male sports audience. The attendance figures for men's basketball should make it clear that, when compared to the United States, Soviet attendance levels for the sport were minute. One professional American team could draw more fans than the entire Soviet league. Nevertheless, in the European context, the extent of fan interest was far from insubstantial.

While attendance for basketball was hardly enormous, it still was larger, aside from soccer and hockey, than for any other sport. Of the team sports, only volleyball could claim to compete as an attraction. Individual Olympic sports, which held fewer competitions and rotated the sites of their championships, had even less success. Track and field's chronic problems at the gate persisted. National championship meets usually had to be contested in provincial cities where the public had not been jaded by an abundance of spectacles. Only the highly publicized dual meets with the United States proved successful as gate attractions.

Starting in 1958, the U.S.–USSR meet sold out Lenin Stadium in Moscow on three occasions. Numerous world records were established when the meet was held both in the Soviet Union and in the United States, where attendance was far higher than for other track meets. At these events, the great Soviet high jumper, Valerii Brumel', established his reputation in an intense but friendly rivalry with the American star John Thomas, while the broad jumper Ralph Boston continued his many duels with Igor Ter-Ovanesian. By 1965, however, with fewer top American athletes choosing to compete, the event was moved to Kiev, Minsk, Leningrad, and even such smaller sites as Sochi, the resort town on the Black Sea.[29] Without the special impetus of the politically charged match-up of superpowers, however, no other Soviet track event, including the Znamensky Brothers Memorial Meet, ever had much success in attracting spectators.

Other sports only episodically attracted large crowds. Boxing maintained a respectably sizable following in the early 'fifties, but by 1980, attendance at major competitions was small. Wrestling and weightlifting had only limited success, even in the southern republics.[30] In the early 'seventies, figure skating had a wave of popularity, and such events as the Moscow News Prize filled the Palace of Sports with a largely female audience. In the 1980s, large numbers of women also attended gymnastics competitions, of which one or two important and well-publicized events took place each year in Moscow. Women also watched men's basketball. Fewer women attended hockey, and hardly any could be seen at soccer games.

Soviet attendance figures, if they are compared to the total numbers of those who watched the three most popular team sports in the United States, can only be called paltry. Baseball alone usually drew more spectators in the United States than did all sports in the USSR. Even by more modest European standards, the total number of Soviet sports spectators was not enormous, despite the great size of the country. Nevertheless, while the crowds for soccer, hockey, and basketball may seem far from immense, they were considerably larger than those for the other sports on the Olympic program. Soviet journalists often joked that the spectators at these events were the friends and relatives of the athletes. While these figures do demonstrate that a few sports had won significant, if not enormous, audiences, the interest in sports among the general public was far from universal.

Television: Propaganda or Passivity?—By the mid-'fifties, television began offering a regular diet of sports to the Soviet fans. Initially, nearly all of these events took place in Moscow and were limited to an audience not far from the capital. By 1980, Soviet television had expanded to cover all eleven time zones of the Union, and nearly every home had purchased a set, which was one of the few consumer goods the government made available and affordable. Televised sports were supposed to amplify the long-stated goal of all spectator sports. Instead of thousands, now millions could be inspired to take up physical culture and healthy exercise.[31]

Soccer and hockey were among the earliest events to be shown. The 1956 soccer season was the first to receive extensive coverage, and most matches of the 1957 world hockey championship, held in Moscow, were televised. Major cities and most republics had their own channels, which showed selected home games of local teams.[32] Sports were also accorded a regular five-minute segment on the national nightly news, while discussion and roundup shows supplemented the fare of games. More people and more parts of the country became aware of sports than ever before. What had been a big-city phenomenon now became national. This change had a direct and positive impact on Soviet performance in big-time sports. Youths throughout the nation, not just in a few major centers, were inspired to become athletes; television had helped enlarge the talent pool.

Because of the limited technical capacity of early Soviet television, the majority of games came from Moscow for many years. This practice inspired complaints from provincial fans who felt that Moscow-based announcers were biased in favor of the capital's clubs. Vadim Siniavskii, the pioneer of Soviet sports-announcing on radio, did not make the transition to television, but he was often accused of excess sympathy for Spartak's soccer team. Later commentators would admit in print that they had favorite teams, but all claimed that they struggled to be fair when on the air.[33] This bias was reinforced by the fact that announcers were based in one city and did not travel to the sites of central matches. By the late 'sixties, the power base in soccer had shifted away from Moscow, and television's capacity to show matches outside the capital improved. The problem of objectivity took on an entirely new hue, as Moscow fans now complained that local announcers were biased against the teams from the capital.

The one personality that transcended this localism was Nikolai Ozerov. A former national tennis champion for Moscow Spartak and an actor at the

"I don't let a single sports program pass"
(*Sovetskii sport*, November 11, 1957)

famed Moscow Art Theater, Ozerov did for Soviet sports television what Siniavskii had done for radio.[34] Less intense and florid than Siniavskii, Ozerov still brought a highly emotional approach to his work. While he tried to hide his Spartak loyalties during domestic competitions, Ozerov was an unashamed cheerleader for Soviet athletes performing in international contests. In 1984, toward the end of his run as the USSR's number-one sports voice, Spartak was playing Birmingham's Aston Villa on the return leg of a quarter-final UEFA Cup series. Needing a goal to advance to the next round, Spartak, with time running out, was advancing the ball slowly, when Ozerov, no longer able to control himself, began screaming, "faster, lads, faster!" His performances during Olympic Games, World Cups, and other international events were even more dramatic, and he made no attempt to apologize for his open sympathy for Soviet athletes: "Of course, for a commentator it's always pleasant to report on the victories of Soviet athletes. Your voice seems to take on a major [as opposed to minor] tone and you don't have to search for words. But when there is a defeat, believe me, it's not easy to tell about it."[35] This was not simply a matter of Ozerov's personality. He had been encouraged throughout his career to adopt just such a personal manner. In 1957, the head of Soviet sports television, A. Alekseev, would write: "The television commentator is the viewer's friend. He can tell jokes and laugh together with them, pose questions, teach the game, describe exciting moments with great emotion, and give his opinions about the game. Every commentator must strive for close contact with the viewer."[36] The inculcation of patriotism was, after all, the reason for showing international events, and

Ozerov's emotionality served this purpose well. His career did not survive into the period of glasnost, though, and in reaction to Ozerov's carryings-on, subsequent Soviet announcers took a more subdued tone.

In far more cases, Soviet television's sins were those of ommission rather than commission. A particularly absurd example occurred during the 1984 Canada Cup hockey tournament. One of the members of the Canadian team was Peter Stastny, originally a Czech citizen, who had defected to Canada. Although the international feed showed Stastny several times during the game against the Soviet team and although his name was spelled out on the back of his jersey, Soviet announcers were forbidden to mention his name, even when he scored or assisted.[37]

Beyond such matters of content, the televising of sports events produced many of the same debates it did in the West. Stadium directors protested that showing games cut down home attendance, while television's defenders argued that the medium increased the size of the total audience for sports. Eventually, the pessimists realized what many in the West came to learn. If the attraction were sufficiently compelling, fans preferred the excitement of the stadium. If, however, a game was not that important and the weather was bad, even Nikolai Starostin, who rarely missed one of his team's games, admitted that it was a lot easier "to sit home and drink tea."

By the early 'sixties, the amount of sports programming broadcast on Soviet television's two national and various local channels reached the level it maintained up to 1991. In non-Olympic years, between 500 and 600 events were shown nationally. Of these, between fifty and sixty were soccer games. Under Brezhnev, coverage of hockey expanded to similar levels. Basketball, during its vogue in the late 'sixties and early 'seventies, was also shown frequently, especially locally. In the 1968–1969 season, 66 of 264 league games were shown on national or local television, with Kaunas Zhalgiris the most-watched team. The rest of the television sports diet consisted of national, European, and world championships in the various Olympic sports.[38] These broadcasts were usually edited down to half-hour packages.

Even before the advent of cable television in the West, the menu of televised sports in the USSR was smaller than that which could be found on contemporary American or even British television. Starting in 1968, however, Soviet audiences were finally able to watch the Olympics. In contrast to the regular slim pickings, these telecasts usually occupied one hundred to one hundred and fifty hours of time during their sixteen-day runs. Compared to American television, Soviet Olympic coverage was far more extensive, an emphasis that reflected state goals rather than public desires. After 1985, however, the emphasis of all Soviet sports television would shift. The bulk of televised sports shifted from Olympic sports to more hockey and soccer, although the total number of events stayed roughly the same. Basketball, which had lost mass popularity, began to disappear from the screen, and so-called minor sports were seen even less frequently.

Keeping the Spectacles Interesting—Domestic Competition

Despite the enormous attention given to important international events, it is the daily fare of domestic competition that draws spectators to a sport and maintains their interest. The never-ending cycles of games and seasons give fans a continuous diet of food for thought about their favorite sports, and the discourses generated by internal play constitute the basis of popular thinking about big-time sports. For athletes and coaches, national leagues structure their most basic work routines. For fans and journalists, the core of popular spectator sports is the unfolding of the domestic schedule. International competitions are exceptional moments. Olympics and World Cups come once every four years, but in the meantime, the sporting life goes on. Soviet spectator sports were no exception to these rules. The athletes who appeared in international competition were discovered and trained by individual teams, and they developed their mastery in continuous play against other clubs. As everywhere else in the world, the domestic leagues were the lifeblood of Soviet national teams, and only internal league play could provide the spectator with a continuing diet of entertainment. For these reasons, it was important that high standards be maintained and that the games be interesting and attractive.

In pursuit of these goals, Soviet coaches, administrators, athletes, fans, and journalists took part in rich and continuous discussion of their favorite sports. In comparison to so much else in Soviet life, these conversations were open, forthright, and critical. Methods, approaches, tactics, and personnel were changed in response to this criticism. People aired their disagreements, and in response, officials, players, and coaches had to improve their performances. To be sure, a great deal went on behind the scenes that was never made public, but the same could be said about big-time sports in the West. Significantly, these relatively open debates about sports proved to be an antidote to the stagnation that gripped so much else in Soviet society during the last years of the Brezhnev era. While progress in many areas of Soviet life seemed to grind to a halt, elite sports were able to maintain their standards, and it is reasonable to suggest that the comparatively open discourse about sports had much to do with this success.

Soccer's Hot Samovar League—As soccer became a truly national, rather than simply Russian, pastime, provincial teams came to challenge the clubs from the capital. Throughout the 1950s, Moscow remained the center of Soviet soccer, and in 1954, what had been the city's strongest team—Central

Army—was reestablished. Its players, who had been distributed to other teams, were reunited, but TsDSA, as it came to be called (later TsSKA), did not return to its former glory.[39] Only in 1970 would an entirely new and different Central Army team win the championship, its first title since the "team of lieutenants" and its last until Soviet soccer's final season in 1991.

In 1955, the Starostin brothers returned to Moscow from their twelve-year exile. Andrei came back to begin a career as a sportswriter, while Nikolai resumed his position at the helm of Spartak.[40] In the interim, Spartak had slipped only slightly from its leading position in Soviet soccer. With Netto and Simonian, it had never deteriorated completely. With the return of Starostin, Spartak again assumed a position at the highest level of Soviet soccer, and in 1956, Spartak constituted the base of the national team that won the Olympic title at Melbourne.

Throughout the 'fifties, commentators were continually troubled by the technical inadequacies of Soviet players who could run all day and do so with great speed. But their ability to trap the ball, dribble it with dexterity, pass effectively, use their heads, and shoot with precision remained under-developed compared to the leading teams of Europe and Latin America. The emergence in the late 'fifties of Brazil's great teams, led by Pele, highlighted these inadequacies. The Brazilians' game was distinguished by their superb ability to control the ball, and many Soviet specialists, including *Sovetskii sport*'s leading soccer writer, Lev Filatov, urged Soviet players and coaches to follow the Brazilian example. Others, Andrei Starostin among them, argued that speed and endurance were the basis of the attacking style of Soviet soccer, and they warned that copying the Brazilians would not help.

In truth, the Brazilian style was as much oriented to defense as to attack. They, along with many others, had switched to a new system to replace the old "W," putting four men in defense and leaving only two at midfield and four (not five) in attack. A team with a brilliant tradition of strikers, of whom Pele was only the latest example, could make such a change and still score goals, but others who followed suit found it harder to put the ball in the net. The Brazilians, however, were not the only nation to use such tactics, and the late 'fifties began a long-term, worldwide trend that saw defense eventually come to dominate offense. The Italians, in particular, perfected the art of what was called "negative football," and the Soviets were not immune to the trend.

Many Soviet clubs abandoned the offensive fury of their earlier style, and soccer became less interesting for the fans. In 1955, many had hoped that the emergence of the brilliant Strel'tsov, then just eighteen, would restore offense by serving as an example for other teams, but Strel'tsov's personal demons prevented him from playing consistently, and by 1958, he would be in prison. By the 1960s, as scoring in Soviet league play decreased, commentators throughout the press began to complain of boring and ugly soccer. It became fashionable to hark back to past eras that featured superior and more attractive play. Iakushin, Filatov, Beskov, Andrei Starostin, and many others lamented the decline of the offensive soccer played by the great Moscow teams, most of which had entered periods of decline.[41] It seemed to many that Soviet soccer was not producing the stars and dramatic personalities of previous generations. In fact, they were witnessing a shift in the balance of power in the sport.

As provincial cities grew, their capacity to support big-time soccer teams increased. More and more towns built large stadiums, and more and more local and republican institutions were able to devote resources to the game.[42] Television helped propagandize soccer to all corners of the Union, and citizens throughout the USSR wanted to experience the excitement of sporting "holidays." Soccer in the Soviet Union had always been an urban phenomenon, and a team in the first division was an important status symbol for a city and its leaders. It became fashionable for various powerful "patrons" of the game to attract players and coaches to provincial centers with substantial rewards of apartments, cars, and money. In the past, Moscow's teams had been able to summon virtually any of the nation's best players, but beginning with the 1960s, they faced stiff competition for talent.

One of the first signs of the shift in the balance of power came in 1961 when Dinamo Kiev won the title. This team had perennially played in the first division but had never made a huge impression. Using all the considerable resources of the Ukrainian Communist Party, along with the inventive coaching of Viktor Maslov, Dinamo Kiev was eventually able to assemble not just a strong team but a powerful organization that would remain at the forefront of Soviet soccer thereafter, winning eleven more championships and contending for the title nearly every year. Episodically, other teams from the periphery would follow their example. *Zarya* Voroshilovgrad (1972), *Arrarat* Yerevan (1973), Dinamo Tblisi (1978), Dinamo Minsk (1982), *Dniepr* Dnepropetrovsk (1983 and 1988), and *Zenit* Leningrad (1984) all won championships. During this same period, Spartak took four titles, but in the middle 'seventies its fortunes fell so low that it was briefly relegated to the second division. Of the other Moscow teams, Torpedo and TsSKA won twice, while Dinamo took one title.[43]

By the 'sixties, there were many championship contenders, and the domestic league was nearly always closely contested. Compelling rivalries developed between cities, and the tendency for Soviet clubs to copy each other's styles diminished, as different teams took different approaches. Even scoring increased, although only marginally. The result of this progress was greater attendance and attention, but these advances did not mean that Soviet soccer had surmounted all its difficulties.[44] League games were not seen as ends in themselves. Instead, domestic play was continuously analyzed for signs and implications about international competition. Thus the rise of strong provincial teams complicated the task of the coach of the *sbornaia*. By the late 'fifties, it was no longer possible to sit in Moscow and choose from the talent that came to the capital. In the wake of the 1958 World Cup, Kachalin quickly understood this new situation, and his success in finding younger players from the periphery contributed to the European Cup victory in 1960.

By the late 'sixties and early 'seventies, the clubs were continuously criticized in the press for providing insufficient training for their players who were then not in proper condition to play at the international level. A series of studies was conducted by a variety of institutes of physical culture, which found that Soviet teams trained far fewer hours than the leading teams of Europe. Given the Soviets' historic reliance on speed and endurance, these failures were particularly serious.[45]

League play was most affected by the constant changes in the annual schedule caused by the needs of international play. In most of Europe, regular league games have been played on weekends, while Wednesdays have been reserved for international matches involving both club and national teams. Soviet schedule-makers, however, were never able to resolve the contradictions between the needs of the clubs and the needs of the national teams, precisely because the Soviets' summer season conflicted with the finals of the world and European cups, which took place in June. Initially, clubs with players on the national team lost them for the duration of an extended training period plus the length of the competition. Often the players were gone for more than two months. Since any player good enough to play for the national team was likely to be one of the club's stars, the teams protested this policy. The alternative was to call a halt to league play, leaving all of Soviet soccer with nothing to do while the national team prepared for and contested one of the sport's big prizes.

In 1976, the coach of Moscow Torpedo, Valentin Ivanov, summed up the problem:

> The clubs should consider it an honor to help the national team, but if the national team ignores the interests of the clubs and comes into conflict with them, things will go badly.... Where do these conflicts arise? In the schedule, in the attempts of the national team to tear players away from the clubs for regular games and in the attempts of the clubs to hang on to their players for these games. The schedule must take this situation into account so that any player invited to the national team can always play a regularly scheduled game for his club.[46]

These tensions always existed in capitalist countries, where the needs of the entrepreneurs who owned the teams had to be recognized. Many outsiders long thought that the priority given by the Soviet state to international competition meant that no such conflicts existed in the USSR. They were wrong. An unnamed "observer," writing in *Sovetskii sport,* described the problem in 1967:

> The objective contradiction between the interests of the clubs and the interests of the national team must be studied clearly. Since our leading teams are now participating in the biggest international tournaments [the various club cups sponsored by UEFA], their interests, demands, and desires can no longer be considered "private," a phenomenon of the clubs' interests. We are interested that the clubs representing the sporting honor of the country in the big European tournaments should be able to appear with all their available forces. Not only the domestic, but the international, calendar should be organized to keep the losses that are connected with these contradictions to a minimum.[47]

These complaints about the schedule were but two of literally hundreds voiced by coaches and players once the USSR began to compete in international soccer. When long pauses were introduced into the schedule to allow preparation for international matches, coaches complained loudly that the schedule had no rhythm to it. A team might go twelve days without a game, then be required to play only three days later. Under such conditions, orderly training and preparation were impossible. As a result, the Football Federation was continually fiddling with the schedule, adding or subtracting teams, dividing them into separate divisions, and extending the season further into the winter. The individual clubs continually complained that the lack of a regular and predictable schedule made it impossible for them, not only to run their own affairs, but also to prepare players for the national team.[48]

The most radical attempt to deal with the problem came in 1975. The federation proposed that the normal March to November schedule be broken into two halves, one in the fall and the other in the spring. The fall portion would last from mid-August to mid-November, while the spring season was to begin early in May and continue until mid-July, at which point a champion would be crowned. The purpose of this reform was to put Soviet soccer more or less on the same plane as in the rest of Europe. It was particularly calculated to help Soviet clubs participating in UEFA's cup tournaments. A Soviet champion crowned in November would not begin play in the Champion's Cup until nearly a year later. A lot could happen to a team, not all of it good, during this interval. The proposal to reorganize the season produced an immense debate. The press was filled with arguments and counterarguments, but ultimately the new approach was adopted in 1976. The results, however, proved disastrous. Complaints were loud and angry, and very quickly the old summer schedule was restored. Coaches and players attacked soccer officials for their constant tinkering and experimentation, but the sport's bureuacrats could never seem to let well enough alone.[49]

That same year, another attempt was made to improve the performance of the national team, again at the expense of domestic competition. One of the standard debates, confronted everywhere in composing a national team, concerns the choice of either bringing together a collection of stars or basing the team on one particularly strong club. When Dinamo Kiev won the Cup-Winners' Cup and the Super Cup in 1975, many observers felt that they had witnessed the emergence of the strongest Soviet club of all time, and in the wake of these triumphs, the Sport Committee felt confirmed in its decision, taken earlier that year, to make Dinamo Kiev assume the role of the national team.[50]

In 1973, Valerii Lobanovskii had taken over as coach of what was already a strong Dinamo Kiev team. A former star player for several Ukrainian clubs and an engineer by education, Lobanovskii brought an extremely organized, highly rational approach to his work.[51] Lobanovskii based his style on the play of the contemporary Dutch teams Johann Cruyff starred for. In this approach, called "total football," all players had to be able to perform all necessary offensive and defensive functions. Lobanovskii's variation on this scheme stressed control of the ball at midfield and the elimination of defensive mistakes.

To play in such a style, players had to be in exceptional condition, and Lobanovskii made use of many medical specialists from the Kiev Institute of Physical Culture to help him design an efficient training regimen. Throughout much of his tenure at the helm of the team, Lobanovskii was blessed by the presence of the greatest Soviet goal-scorer of all time, Oleg Blokhin, whose brilliance more than compensated for the otherwise overly defensive character of the coach's system. Lobanovskii's half-backs would control the ball in the middle of the field, eventually forcing even the most disciplined defense to move forward. At this point, they would send long passes to the extremely fast Blokhin who would easily control the ball near the penalty area, outmaneuver off-balance defenders, and put the ball behind the goalkeeper. This style made many of Dinamo Kiev's games exercises in boredom, relieved by one or two moments of Blokhin's lightning. Yet the method was highly successful. Under Lobanovskii, Dinamo Kiev would win eight of its eleven domestic titles, plus another Cup-Winners Cup.

Dinamo Kiev was also able to make use of the resources and power of the Ministry of Interior to collect an extremely talented group of players. One method was familiar. The Ministry of Interior had its own military forces, mainly border guards, for whom they were allowed to draft young men. The army had long made a practice of conscripting young talents and putting them at the disposal of Central Army teams in various sports. The Dinamo societies could do this too, although much less often than the army.[52] Once Dinamo Kiev had been established as the base of the *sbornaia,* it became even easier to recruit players who knew that Lobanovskii's team was their route to international travel, comparative wealth, and considerable fame.

One basis of Lobanovskii's success was his employment of the so-called road or away (*vyezdnyi*) model. When playing away from home, Dinamo Kiev always played for a tie, in order to gain at least one point in the standings, according to universal soccer practice. Only at home did they go for the two points awarded for a win. This approach proved highly effective and helped the team win many a title, but it greatly angered many others in the soccer world. The appearance of a national champion on the road would normally be the cause of a great sporting "holiday" in whatever city welcomed Dinamo Kiev, but fans soon came to know that their chances of seeing an exciting game were minimal when Lobanovskii's team came to their towns.[53]

By 1978, Lobanovskii's methods had provoked sharp criticism in Soviet soccer circles. The complaints had two bases. In the first place, the strategy of making Dinamo Kiev the basis of the national team had produced few results. The burden of playing league, cup, international, and European club tournament games had exhausted even Lobanovskii's well-conditioned players, and they failed to make the 1978 World Cup final round in Argentina. Had they delivered the goods, far fewer aspersions would have been cast their way. In the second place, Lobanovskii's "away model" made for cynical and unattractive soccer that alienated all but the most loyal Kiev fans. Nikita Simonian argued, "it is necessary to play uncompromisingly in every match." He said that when Lobanovskii had used this strategy during the time he coached *Dniepr,* playing for a tie was not all that crucial, but when the leader of Soviet soccer pursued so cynical an approach, the influence on the whole sport could only be negative.[54]

Beskov was even stronger in his criticism of Dinamo Kiev:

The 'away model is rational and economic . . . football, but the approach taken by their coaches in recent years has led the team into a crisis and degraded the abilities of its players. It is regrettable that the conscious refusal to play active football . . . was adopted by several of our coaches as a truly fashionable tactical innovation, then taken up by other teams. This has caused clear damage to our football. Spectators began to lose interest in football when it became weak, lacking in enthusiasm and full-blooded sporting struggle.[55]

To combat Lobanovskii's strategy, the Football Federation adopted a limit on ties. A team could gain a point only for its first eight ties. From the ninth tie on, no points were awarded, making further draws the equivalent of a loss. This rule was only eliminated in 1989, but when it was on the books, it still did not prevent Dinamo Kiev from continuing to use its "away" model and winning several more championships.[56] Other ways of eliminating ties were tried and abandoned in the late 'seventies. Overtime periods were added, and the dreaded and often unjust series of penalty kicks was also used.

There was an even more sinister side to the approach taken by Dinamo Kiev. It was widely rumored (but never proven) that Lobanovskii had already arranged with his opponents' coaches to play for a tie. Many weaker teams, faced with playing the champions on their home turf, were only too glad to settle for a tie, giving them one point. At the same time, Lobanovskii could either rest some of his stars or have his team play with diminished effort. It was never clear if money or other favors changed hands in these "agreed-upon" (*dogovornyi*) matches, but in taking this approach, Lobanovskii was not inventing anything particularly new. "Arranged" matches had long been part of Soviet soccer. Journalists claimed to know of many instances of fixed games, and the practice was often decried in the press and on radio and television. Fans would also claim, especially after a scoreless tie, that a game was "*dogovornyi*," but no one was ever able to offer concrete proof of such transactions, as coaches adopted an oath of silence on the matter when dealing

"Everything is Clear"
(*Sovetskii sport*, August 22,1958)

with the public.[57] The persistent rumors did little for the integrity of the game, creating too many boring matches and driving fans away from the stands.

The other way of rigging a game involved buying off the referee. This was not done, as in the West, by gamblers seeking to make a killing on a fixed game. While wagering was certainly common on soccer games, and some of it was organized by racketeers of various sorts, the practice of sports gambling was less widespread and organized than in the West. Even when the sports lottery system introduced a contest that involved predicting the winners of certain games, there were few rumors and still no proof that a match was fixed by interested "third parties." Instead, the officials of one team, usually the home team, were guilty of "buying" referees. In some cases, this act was not direct. Historically, in Soviet soccer, the home team had the responsibility of transporting, housing, and feeding the referees. Inevitably, they were met at airports by chauffered cars, taken to the best hotels, given beautiful rooms, wined and dined, and a present of some sort was left for their wives. Under these circumstances, many referees felt duty-bound to help the home team in any way they could. Given the considerable latitude exercised by a soccer referee, especially in the awarding of penalty kicks, home teams have usually been able to maximize their advantages without outright bribery. So widespread was the practice that local amateur teams were not exempt from the open hands of referees, who often simply stated the "price" of victory to competing teams.[58]

Other problems persisted in Soviet soccer. Dirty play did not disappear from the game. Virtually every year, several players were disqualified for the usual litany of fighting, kicking injured opponents, and punching referees. Even some coaches were banished for running onto the field in moments of extreme agitation. Perhaps the most egregious offense during this period was committed in 1966 by a player from Dinamo Minsk, named Eduard Zarembo, who kicked and beat Arrarat's team doctor after the doctor had gone onto the field to aid one of his fallen players.[59]

Players' behavior off the field also continued to be a problem. Breaking training and public drunkenness were far from uncommon, but the harshness with which miscreants were treated was diminished. Instead of punishing and criticizing teammates who had transgressed rules, team Komsomol representatives were more likely to defend their colleagues. Coaches would do the same, if a player were sufficiently talented and valuable.[60] As soccer became an increasingly popular phenomenon, especially in smaller cities, local fans refused to see their favorites punished, a situation that bred an even more intense "star syndrome" (*zaznaistvo*), with players now believing they were invulnerable.

These and other difficulties in the sport were caused by the growing influence of "patrons" (*metsenaty*) of the game. These men (they were always men) were usually local Party bosses, plant managers, trade union officials, and KGB or army generals, all of whom were leaders of the various organizations that sponsored teams. Like the meddling owners of capitalist professional teams, the *metsenaty* sought to dismiss coaches at a whim, dictate lineups, determine tactics, buy players, bribe referees, and fix games, regardless of any personal knowledge of the game or training in its intricacies.

In some cases, the interference was less than benign. As Soviet fans came to see soccer as an activity conducted by professionals for the entertainment of the sporting audience, the influence of the "patrons" increased. Their activities were widely and openly discussed in the press, and their growing influence on the game was denounced.[61] Their presence increased the always-full well of fan cynicism and alienated the public.

In 1959, Petr Novikov, an architect and former player during the 'thirties described the role of the "patrons:" "Unfortunately, there are times when the director of a factory or some big firm consider it their duty to tell the coach how to play and whom to play. In general, these people are playing the thoroughly mediocre role of the patron, interfering in all the details of the coach's work."[62] In 1963, *Izvestia* reported that patrons rewarded players in Rostov with radios, watches, and telephones. In 1975, *Sovetskii sport* reported on the Uzbekistan Sport Committee's dealings with the players of *Pakhtator* of Tashkent: "At one meeting the lads were asked what they needed to give a good performance. In reply, it turned out that one needed a better apartment, another needed a telephone installed, and still others wanted hard-to-get (*defitsitnyi*) goods. No one remembered to say anything either about football or about the training process."[63] In 1966, even the players of a third-division team in Cheliabinsk were making the then-princely sum of four hundred rubles a month.[64] Eventually it would be revealed that the 1972 champions of the first division, *Zarya* of Voroshilovgrad, had been a classic case of a team put together by a free-spending patron who bent all the rules.[65]

Given the fact that the profession of "sportsman" did not exist in the Soviet Union, it was necessary that players be registered for some sort of job—at which they rarely appeared. Even players with factory teams did not soil their hands on the assembly line. In 1962, *Sovetskii sport* would report on the "work" of the players of Spartak Tambov: "Even the question of registering the team with the production collective was decided purely formally. The Spartak players are listed as employees of the rubber factory, but their registration has . . . a purely 'juridical' character. The players have no ties whatsoever with the working collective."[66]

The next year, the newspaper received a letter from a worker at a Kurgan machine-tool factory, commenting on an earlier article about "worker-athletes": "Unfortunately, nothing of the sort can be said about the players on our factory team. They are only registered at our workplace, but they 'labor' only on the football field.. . .Do we need these kinds of football teams in our factories?''[67] At the same time, it was revealed that the players of a team from the Kuban were registered at "no-show" jobs at a variety of local factories. The same was the case with the players of *Metallurg,* Lugansk. Reports of this sort became a journalistic staple throughout the 'sixties and early 'seventies.[68] They were significant, but not because of the practices they revealed. Everyone knew these abuses went on. It was certainly no secret that soccer players were professionals. Their importance lies in the fact that the abuses were made public.

It was also common, but only rarely revealed, that players themselves engaged in a variety of dubious practices. Like so many other Soviet athletes, soccer players whose clubs went on foreign tours supplemented their incomes by illegally exporting hard currency, with which they bought "deficit" goods that they sold on the black market when they came home. Unloading these items forced them to deal with the Soviet underworld. The entire process corroded the moral atmosphere of many clubs and left players and many coaches prey to the influence of Soviet society's least-desirable elements. Because of their status, sports figures were usually allowed by customs men to get away with their "import businesses," but every once in a while, an athlete or coach would be caught in a classic case of selective enforcement.[69]

The acquisition of players was the commonest and most serious area of the "patrons' " involvement. Using apartments, cars, money, and gifts to entice players became a big and shady business that was extensively, but only obliquely, discussed in the press. As we have seen, player movement, one of the most salient indicators of professionalism, had been common in Soviet soccer from its earliest days, but in the post-Stalin period, the practice became even more widespread and blatant. The always murky rules on player movement were constantly being rewritten to control the process, but no sooner were new regulations in force than the *metsenaty* found ways to circumvent them.[70]

Formally, players had to submit applications to the Sporting-Technical Committee of the Football Federation, which could approve or disapprove a transfer. The Presidium of the Federation did have the right to overrule any decision of the committee. The authorities claimed to be guided by strictly sporting considerations. How would the move affect competitive balance? Could the team losing the player afford to let him go? Was this a case of a young player moving up to a higher level of competition or of a veteran seeking a better deal from another team? What were the implications of any transfer for the international goals of Soviet soccer? Unlike in the West, the team losing a player received neither money nor other players in compensation. Since a player could not be the property of a team and no contracts

"If you thought this was a good excursion, the
next one will be to the factory where we're
registered as workers. That one's really
interesting."
(*Sovetskii sport*, September 18, 1963)

"The one on the right must be the 'student.'
Right?"
(*Sovetskii sport*, February 4, 1966)

were signed, Soviet athletes actually had more freedom within the Soviet
market than did contemporary Western players in theirs.

What really went on only rarely reached the press, and every transfer
produced its share of rumors. The Federation had its rules, but, as *Sovetskii
sport* would note in 1968, not even they could enforce them: ''[the rules] are
violated and often by the federation itself, which acts against its own instruc-

tions under the influence of the patrons.''[71] Up-and-coming second-division clubs who aspired to a place at the top ranks of the sport complained that they could not keep the young stars that they produced. At the same time, Moscow teams were losing many of their most promising products to aggressive provincial clubs, whose agents "operated in the shadows, avoiding responsibility."[72]

In 1970, the situation reached absurd heights when a young star from Khazan, Viktor Kolotov, who had played for the national team, signed three different applications to play with three different teams—Dinamo Kiev, TsSKA, and Torpedo. It seemed that whenever a team met with Kolotov, they made a new offer to him and his parents. Kolotov, with the ante now raised, would change his mind.[73] For his actions, Kolotov was banned from the game for a year. Eventually he came to play for Dinamo Kiev and enjoyed a long career at the international and national levels, but by this time it was clear to the Federation that reform was necessary.

In 1972, new rules were introduced to restrict the number of players a club could invite and the number of times a player could move in his career. In principle, the only tranfers that were looked on favorably were those from a lower division to a higher one. Yet the new rules provided only temporary relief. Soon thereafter, coaches were complaining about rivals who spirited their best players off to other cities, and players were complaining about harassment from agents of clubs who were seeking to attract them.[74] Until the rules were clarified during perestroika and a contract system was instituted, the situation remained unclear and, no doubt, quite corrupt.

Rigged games, bribed referees, bought players, cynical tactics, and all the tricks of the "patrons" meant that soccer came to reflect the ways the broader economy and much else in Soviet society actually operated during the age of "normalcy." Formal structures were supplemented by a wide range of informal practices. Among many possible examples: enterprises were forced by circumstances to adopt the use of a variety of middlemen called "pushers," or *tolkachi,* to obtain the raw materials and other favors required to fulfill centrally mandated plans. These people had no formal title, but industry could not have operated without them. Formally, the economy was highly controlled, but, in fact, it could not function without a wide variety of supposedly informal mechanisms. Similarly, the shady agiotage around soccer conflicted with the officially stated noble aims of Soviet sports. The fans, however, wanted winning teams, and the *metsenaty* were willing to do whatever was necessary to please them. In this way, soccer reflected the many real contradictions of Soviet life in ways other sports did not. It became a true phenomenon of popular culture of the type described by Hall, Bourdieu, and de Certeau. Its actual practices were not simply imposed from above but were the result of interaction between those who produced and those who consumed the game.

Keeping Control on Ice—Hockey's domestic situation differed sharply from that of soccer. Instead of disorder and chaos, there was predictability and stability. Tensions between the needs of the national team and those of the clubs were minimal, and the internal league season was organized around the demands of the international schedule. Beyond this, the Soviet style of play contrasted sharply with the brawling physicality of the Canadian game. As a result, there was much less public violence by players. Fans were more easily controlled within the confines of indoor arenas than could be accomplished in larger stadiums. The result was a spectacle far better suited than soccer to official needs and concerns. Finally, the fact that the entire enterprise enjoyed considerable international success made hockey especially attractive to Party leaders.

The most salient fact about Soviet hockey, from its earliest days, was the extraordinary dominance of the team representing the Central Army Sports Club. We have already seen how the army was able to capitalize on its postwar popularity to build strong teams in a number of sports, most notably soccer. The dissolution of the "team of lieutennats" in 1952 prevented the army from winning another soccer championship until 1970, but the hockey team carried on as if nothing had happened. If anything, the team was strengthened in the wake of Stalin's death, when Vasilii Stalin's Air Force team was disbanded before the 1953–1954 season and its players combined with the army into a new team representing the entire Ministry of Defense. Bobrov and others who had left TsDKA came back to their old club. This change created some confusion in the initial season for the new team, and that year Dinamo managed to sneak away with the title. Soon, however, order was restored, and Central Army, this time renamed TsSKA, was back on top.[75]

It would be easy enough to attribute the success of Central Army to the power of the military and the privileged position it enjoyed in Soviet society. The army was able to construct excellent facilities and organize youth hockey more quickly and effectively than less endowed institutions. It was also able to draft promising young stars and force them to play for TsSKA. Yet the army was not the only powerful organization in Soviet society, nor was it the only Soviet entity that could draft young men. As has been noted, the Ministry of Interior, whose relationship with the KGB oscillated, was also wealthy and extremely interested in sports. On a much smaller scale, it, too, drafted soldiers for its internal control forces, and it supported strong teams in many sports, including hockey. Outside the state security sector, Spartak had long ago demonstrated that civilian groups could also sponsor strong teams in a number of sports. Therefore, the mere power of the army is not a sufficient explanation for its success in ice hockey.

In the particular case of army hockey, it is difficult to overemphasize the central role played by Anatolii Tarasov. The Soviets had developed a tradition of great coaches. Most of these men and women were expected to have received higher education in the powerful institutes of physical culture. This necessity for obtaining a level of qualification fostered a scientific, even intellectual approach to sports and placed, therefore, a special emphasis on originality and innovation as opposed to practical knowledge and repetition. Over the course of Soviet history, there were many brilliant coaches in many sports, but Tarasov must be seen as one of the most outstanding products of this tradition. On the international level, he worked closely with Arkadii Chernyshev, whose cool temperament complemented Tarasov's volatility, but in domestic play, Tarasov consistently got the better of his rival.[76]

TsSKA maintained its grip on the championship throughout this period. Other teams might occasionally interrupt the reign but no one could consistently replace them at the top. In the 'fifties Dinamo was their chief rival. In the 'sixties, Spartak emerged with Starshinov and the brothers Maiorov to win in 1962 and again in 1967 and 1969. After Tarasov stepped down in 1972, other teams enjoyed a brief window of opportunity. Boris Kulagin would lead Krylia Sovetov to the crown in 1974, but in 1977, Viktor Tikhonov came from a successful run with Dinamo Riga to take over both TsSKA and the national team. A former defenseman with both the Air Force and Dinamo, Tikhonov proved a worthy successor to Tarasov, and despite difficulties after 1985, he brought Central Army back to the top.[77]

There was one fundamental difference between the reigns of Tarasov and Tikhonov. In the 'fifties and 'sixties, TsSKA usually won the championship, but it nearly always received spirited competition from its Moscow rivals. The title was not usually decided until relatively late in the season, and in a few cases the title was won at dramatic, season-ending games. Since Dinamo and Spartak had larger followings than TsSKA, fans could still maintain interest in domestic competition, knowing their favorite team retained some chance of victory. By the 'eighties, Tikhonov had made Central Army so much better than anyone else there was never any question of who would win, either the title or any single game.

Tikhonov was far more ruthless than Tarasov in using all the army's advantages to gather the very best of all Soviet hockey talent onto his team. In doing this, he was able to count on the support of sports officials and the toleration of an increasingly senile Brezhnev.[78] The result was the complete destruction of domestic competition. In some years, TsSKA lost as few as two out of forty-four games. The weaker provincial teams were merely cannon fodder for the champions. When these teams came to Moscow to play

TsSKA, a few early goals were enough to get them to quit, leading to lop-sided scores. The schedule soon become filled with what were called *prokhodnoi* (''walkover'') games of little interest to anyone outside the TsSKA coaching staff.[79]

Tikhonov pursued the obsessive stocking of his team because he wanted it to serve as the base of the national team.[80] The strategy that would fail in soccer proved successful in hockey. As a result, TsSKA was always able to attract the best Soviet players because a place on this team meant international travel, wealth, fame, and a secure military career after retirement. The importance of this last reward should not be overlooked. Since the legal job description of ''professional athlete'' did not exist, players had no pensions and few avenues after their playing careers. Many of them would slip into lives of organized crime. By contrast, the army seemed to offer more security.

The hockey federation, which was supposed to control player movement in order to maintain competitive balance, consistently permitted the stocking of the army team. Not only were the best young players in lower divisions channeled to TsSKA, but when stars emerged with provincial first-division clubs, they soon were called or invited either to Central Army or to another Moscow team, where their progress could be monitored by the coaches of the national team. When Tikhonov came to TsSKA from Dinamo Riga, he would bring his slick-skating, high-scoring star, Helmut Balderis, with him. *Khimik* of Voskresensk, founded and coached by Nikolai Epstein, consistently developed new talents and maintained a solid position in the middle of the league standings, but no sooner did Epstein find a new star than he lost him to TsSKA.[81] Torpedo Gorky and Traktor Cheliabinsk suffered many similar losses.

The league calendar was organized with the needs of the national team first in mind. While there were constant changes in the size of hockey's first division and in the structure of league play, the season itself had become a September-to-May marathon, numbering between forty and fifty domestic matches. In order to allow the sport's stars to prepare for important international competitions, long intermissions became a standard part of the schedule. December came to be an off-month as the national team prepared for what became the annual Izvestia Prize tournament in Moscow. Starting in 1975, several top club teams would make the annual trek to North America to take on NHL clubs. A month was usually taken off around the time of the annual world championship in the spring, and even more time was used before each Olympic Games.[82]

This approach allowed the national team to reach a level of cohesion that it would not otherwise have attained, but it did cause severe problems for the rest of hockey. Coaches whose teams did not go abroad were stuck with the task of keeping their players in condition. Many clubs were able to organize relatively lucrative foreign tours to Europe and Japan, while others played in meaningless, poorly attended tournaments with each other in provincial cities. When play would resume, these teams were forced to play against TsSKA and Dinamo, whose players had not lost a beat. As a result, coaches and players from the weaker teams complained that the schedule was designed to perpetuate their inferior position, and it cannot be said they were wrong.[83]

Most public arguments about hockey concerned playing style. Analytical and hortatory articles by Tarasov became a journalistic staple during the 'fifties and 'sixties. Even after stopping coaching, he continued to report on hockey for the Soviet wire service, Tass, and his words were always noted and feared. Like Tikhonov, Tarasov was most concerned to use the domestic league as a laboratory for international play. Such innovations as substituting all five skaters at a time or dropping the center farther back in order to play more like a halfback in soccer, were first tried by TsSKA in league play. Throughout this period, Tarasov urged players to use their bodies more on defense, and he continually searched for an answer to chronic Soviet weaknesses in goal.[84]

He and others harped on the inability of Soviet players to shoot from all but the closest of positions. Nikolai Epstein went as far as to attribute this failing to the chronic shortage of sticks at all but the highest levels of the sport. Young players were afraid to take hard shots for fear of breaking their hard-to-obtain sticks. For this reason, they never practiced this technique. Tarasov wrote as late as 1979 that he witnessed many youth games, even in Moscow, in which an entire team had seven or eight sticks that they exchanged as they came on and off the ice.[85]

Soviet observers were fond of stressing that their version of ice hockey was orderly and disciplined compared to the brawling, fighting, and stick-swinging that characterized the North American game; and fights in Soviet hockey were indeed rare. Yet players were capable of using their sticks to injure opponents, and many were fond of returning pucks to referees with just a bit too much force when they were dissatisfied with a call. Soviet hockey players did prove as capable of breaking training as soccer players, and when drunk, they acted as badly as any other athletes. Perhaps the most celebrated case of such misbehavior took place in 1977, when TsSKA's Boris Alexandrov, in a state of extreme inebriation, beat up a fifty-five-year-old woman waiting at a bus stop. Press reports did not mention whether or not she was a fan utilizing the relative autonomy of sporting discourse to criticize his performance.[86]

Despite the progress of the 'fifties and 'sixties, the facilities available to Soviet hockey teams continued to be limited. Provincial arenas below the first-division level were small, often run down, and few in number. As of 1985, the entire Soviet Union had only 102 indoor rinks, compared to more than 9,000 in Canada. Fans were far less orderly in the periphery than in more easily controlled Moscow, and players took their cues from this atmosphere, comporting themselves in a far less gentlemanly manner. Players on many lower-division provincial teams were not only young stars on the way up. Many were aged mercenaries looking for a last payday as well.[87]

Yet the greatest single domestic problem facing Soviet hockey was the absurd domination TsSKA achieved. All suspense and intrigue evaporated from the league schedule, with Tikhonov's team clinching the title sometimes as early as six weeks before the end of the season. The vast majority of games were one-sided walkovers, played with little intensity. As a result, the fans, especially in Moscow, stopped coming. By the beginning of perestroika, Soviet hockey would face a serious attendance crisis that threatened its ability to continue producing players and teams at the sport's highest possible level.

The City Game for the New Cities—During the Soviet era of "normalcy," men's basketball evolved from its limited status to join soccer and hockey as a significant spectator attraction. Both soccer and hockey were first played in Soviet cities, but elsewhere in the world they were also rural, played either in the villages of Britain or on the prairies of Canada. By contrast, basketball (Indiana excepted) has been the most agressively urban of all sports everywhere it has been played. Accordingly, it is not surprising that, as Soviet cities grew in both size and number, basketball should become more popular. The construction of larger indoor venues in many towns, in turn, allowed basketball to become a winter sport, competing for fans with hockey rather than with the much more popular soccer.

At the same time, women's basketball began to be widely played throughout the entire USSR, and Soviet teams achieved enormous international success. Given the overarching patriarchalism of Soviet society, though, especially in the sphere of sports, the victories achieved by Soviet women did not translate into fans in the stands for their contests. Yet the fact that so many women played basketball gave the sport a potentially wider social base than either soccer or hockey, which were watched almost entirely by men. Of the three sports I have chosen to emphasize, only men's basketball had many women in the audience.

The comparative smallness of the basketball audience did create problems when structuring domestic competition. For teams to travel the country, playing in each other's arenas, enough tickets had to be sold to cover the costs of transportation and lodging. The organizational form of a national league, which had contributed so much to the growth of soccer and hockey, was possible for basketball only after the mid-'sixties, when organizers felt the game's popularity had sufficiently increased. Before that time, various tournaments had been held at the republican and national levels. Even when a first division was finally formed, several teams were often brought together in one city to play several games against each other over the course of a week. The creation of a full-scale league greatly enhanced the popularity of the sport, but when attendance began to fall again in the mid-'seventies, it was necessary to go back to the old tournament system, in which some teams never got to play a single home game during the entire season.[88] Both the league and tournament approaches had their supporters, and the merits of each were constantly debated.[89] The league system raised interest in basketball and created more events for fans to attend. On the other hand, the tournament structure, with its many stretches of inactivity, allowed the national team greater flexibility in preparing for important events.

Coaches and officials also constantly debated techniques, strategies, and approaches. Basketball's "cursed question" was the proper choice of defense. Given the implications of domestic play for international competition, it was not enough simply to let each coach pick what worked best for him. Instead, the merits of the zone defense versus what was called "personal" (man-to-man) was the subject of ongoing controversy. In the 'fifties, intense pressing man-to-man predominated, but by the 'sixties, zone defenses were more common. In the late 'sixties, Vladimir Kondrashin rendered the whole debate fairly meaningless. When he took over Spartak Leningrad, Kondrashin claimed that no Soviet team played good defense, regardless of the system. Unlike other Soviet coaches, he devoted the majority of his practice time to defense, and soon his team was regularly at the top of the league standings.[90]

The dominant team of this period was Central Army, which began its run of success in the early 'sixties when Alexander Gomelskii left the Riga Army Club to come to Moscow. Using all the advantages of the army, Gomelskii was able to recruit from throughout all the republics and, at times, literally draft his rivals' stars to play for TsSKA. Unlike the situation in hockey, Central Army was not without rivals. Dinamo Tblisi was a consistently strong opponent, as was *Stroitel* of Kiev, but it was Kondrashin's team that became TsSKA's most intense rival in the 'seventies. The competition between these two teams was fanned by the traditional rivalry between the two cities and the deep mutual personal dislike of the two coaches.[91]

During the early 'eighties, Zhalgiris Kaunas became TsSKA's most powerful opponent with the emergence of the superbly coordinated seventeen-year-old center Arvidas Sabonis in 1982. Until then, Zhalgiris had been a strong presence in the league throughout its existence, but it had not been dramatically superior to the other Baltic teams, especially the Estonian team, *Kalev*. With the arrival of the young basketball genius, Zhalgiris was transformed from a very good team into one of the strongest sides in Europe. Its rivalry with TsSKA became intense and often bitter, as Zhalgiris became a surrogate for Lithuanian nationalist sentiment, which, before glasnost, had to find indirect forms of expression.[92]

While basketball was widely played by men and women throughout the Soviet Union, it never attained the status it achieved elsewhere, becoming the second-most-popular team sport in the world after soccer. It found an audience with Soviet fans, but only in certain cities, especially those in the Baltic and the Caucasus. Of the so-called student sports, it became the most popular, achieving a position on the Soviet sports menu, but despite its successes, it did not attain the profound popularity of soccer and hockey. Its roots in the working class were always limited, and compared to the Big Two, its social base was considerably more elite. Its growth, however limited, may be seen as a reflection of the increasing numbers of educated and technically trained citizens who had composed its public before the war.

Soviet Sports Fans

There is nothing monolithic about the reasons various people are drawn to sports. Each person brings his or her experiences to the process of watching and making sense of sports. Here Soviet fans were no exceptions. There have been as many explanations for fanship in the Soviet Union as there have been Soviet fans. Accordingly, the discourse about the attractions of spectator sports has been rich and varied, a continuing topic of discussion in both the press and in popular literature. Some of the ideas that have been advanced are clearly bogus, justifications for offical attitudes, while others drip with sincere emotion.

For the sports journalist A. Patrikeev, the hockey of the mid-'seventies was attractive because of its role as a social leveler: "The academic, the hero, and the carpenter, are all now under the power of hockey. In our educated age, people need spectacles no less (indeed even more) than many centuries ago, and hockey has become this all-conquering spectacle."[93] For Evgenii Rubin, one of the most acute of all sports journalists during the sixties, hockey combined intensity of feeling with visual beauty: "This spectacle is able to satisfy the most unquenchable thirst for strong feelings. Hockey is a beautiful spectacle. It is played on a milk-white stage of ice, cut across by red and blue stripes. The ice and the multi-colored uniforms of the players seem brighter, more sharply contrasting when seen under the lights of the arena from the darkness of the stands."[94]

Many other observers talked of sports as an arena of male socialization. The comedian Iurii Nikulin was interviewed in 1974 and described being taken to soccer games by his father, who "had a big collection of information guides and books on soccer dating back to the 'thirties." Another journalistic staple was the account of soccer-mad families passing down love of the game from generation to generation.[95] The renewal of the soccer season each spring always evoked thoughts about the fan's love of sports. In 1962, the writer

Iurii Trifonov was asked by *Sovetskii sport* to describe his feelings on opening day: "To write about the start of the football season is about as difficult as describing spring. What new can you say about spring? What words can give off but a part of the freshness that a young green leaf gives off? And what words can give a sense of even part of the tension experienced by the fan when he sees the first attack on that lustrously green field?"[96] Lev Filatov waxed similarly rhapsodic. "Our hearts begin to beat with healthy, sporting tension as soon as the referee's whistle blows, sounding like the first bird of spring, as soon as the first moves are made on the green field."[97] Even the regular description of an opening day game was cause for excitement for Viktor Ponedel'nik, who became a sportswriter after his retirement: "What a truly surprising spectacle opening day is! Everywhere there are smiles, flowers, songs, and posters. It seemed that all the citizens of ancient Erevan were hurrying toward their beautiful stadium, Razdan."[98] Others, perhaps fancifully, claimed that spectator sports could actually have an impact on industrial production. In 1959, an engineer from Kuznetsk wrote in *Sovetskii sport:* "I'm not discovering America if I note that after a victory by our favorite team, we fans are in a much better mood. You feel as hardy and healthy as if you had taken part in the game yourself. Our work goes well. . . . But if you see a game in which your team plays a weak opponent and does poorly. . . all the time at work, you are thinking about why they played so badly."[99] A worker from Voroshilovgrad struck a similar note in 1971. "The victory of our favorite team pleases us and creates a good working atmosphere. Things go swimmingly. But, let's be open. We don't like defeats although we know they are inescapable in sport."[100]

Coal miners all over the USSR followed the fortunes of Shakhter Donetsk: "All miners below ground can see the football field, even here in Moscow[?]. We have an excellent telephone line at the mine. All the dispatchers, engineers, and bosses of the mine are used to the fact that when Shakhter plays, they will hear confused voices coming up from the depths of the earth, and they all ask one and the same question. How are things going?"[101]

Despite the dangers of partisanship, this version of fanship—of rooting for favorites rather than simply watching objectively—was accepted as part of the appeal of spectator sports. Other observers were less approving. Supporting a particular team intensified the experience of spectator sports and made it more compelling than participation. By the late 'seventies, women increasingly began to complain about husbands who were glued to the television for every sporting event. The small amount of sports available on Soviet television did not create a Soviet correlate of the "football widow," but the trend toward passive consumption, as opposed to participation, caused by the growth of television was troubling to many.[102]

During the 1950s, Soviet cities continued to grow at a swift pace, welcoming many new emigrants from the countryside. The rude and brusque style of the peasantry became a signal feature of urban life in the USSR, and new arrivals who found their way to the stadium did not always view the proceedings in ways that longtime city residents considered to be "cultured." In 1959, *Sovetskii sport* began a campaign against ill-mannered spectators. Fans who whistled (the equivalent of booing) and shouted (*krikuny*) were singled out. Many of them were said to curse visiting teams in the crudest terms. "Break them" and "beat them" were among the milder epithets. "Empty their blood" was one of the stronger curses that made it into the press at this time. Soviet journalists have also mentioned "tear their cocks off" as another fan favorite.[103]

In other instances, fans so harassed goalkeepers that the targets of their curses simply walked off the field in the middle of games. A newspaper staple throughout the 'sixties and early 'seventies was the letter to the editor that complained that a few ill-mannered *krikuny* could spoil the atmosphere for all other, well-mannered, fans. Even actions that by Western standards would not be considered improper were criticized in the press. Fans of Zhalgiris Kaunas' basketball team were taken to task for having the temerity to whistle and shout when the visiting team took a foul shot. When supporters of Dniepr's soccer team shouted at the referee to "get off the field," this too, was seen as being beyond the bounds of good taste. Fans' dissatisfaction with referees was seen as a sign that many new spectators did not know or understand the rules of the game, and the press urged television to use half-time breaks to explain those rules to the uneducated.[104]

The importance of teaching respect for the referee was not only a question of culture and knowledge, it was also a matter of public order. Referees had to control games, just as police and volunteers (*druzhiny*) had to control fans in the stands. When play on the field degenerated, spectators, too, could lose control, as occurred during a 1960 game in Moscow between TsSKA and Dinamo Kiev when angry fans invaded the field. The entire question of the relationship of the spectator to the player was raised by the issue of behavior. If players acted crudely and violently, this influenced the fans. Players were urged to remember their responsibilities, and rough play was often explained by the fact that teams had lost touch with "society." On the other hand, a team could get too close to "society," as was the case when fans of Chernomorets Odessa were accused of continually inviting players out to restaurants for evenings of dance and drink.[105]

During the late 'sixties and 'seventies, players began to grow their hair long and fail to tuck in their shirts, duplicating the youth culture fashions of Western players. This trend was also criticized as setting a bad example for Soviet youth and, in the process, undermining respect for order.[106] Nor did the atmosphere in the stadiums contribute to order. Not all directors of these arenas sought to make a sports event a true "holiday." In the 'fifties, these structures were put on a *khozraschet* (self-supporting) basis, and often little was expended on making the spectator's experience more pleasant. Ushers and ticket-takers were kept to a minimum to keep down expenses. Scoreboards were often not used. Despite gloomy weather or approaching sunset, lights were not turned on. Ticket distribution was handled in such a way as to let many tickets fall into the hands of scalpers.[107] Starting times were changed arbitrarily, and in 1955 one fan reported a bizarre incident in a letter to *Sovetskii sport:*

> I was able to get tickets for the football match between Dinamo Moscow and Dinamo Kiev on July 2. We set out for Dinamo Stadium [in Moscow]. As we got out of the subway train and stood on the platform we heard a voice on the public address system announcing that the game would not take place. Thousands of spectators turned around and went back home. Imagine our surprise when we returned home, put on the radio and heard the beginning of the match that "was not taking place."[108]

All of these practices made it difficult to accomplish what *Sovetskii sport* sought, "to raise much higher the culture of the sport spectacle." Of course, all this behavior was fueled by alchohol. While intoxicating beverages were not sold in the stadiums, there was no shortage of beer bars in the parks surrounding the arenas, and vodka-selling stores along routes to the stadiums were the scenes of long, disorderly lines hours before game time.[109] Beskov described the behavior of these fans in 1960: "I've often had to observe, either as individuals or as groups, how these people warm themselves with spirits. Look at them and you will see that with each minute, they lose control over themselves. They begin to whistle, shout, and curse. Sometimes, they make bets with each other, and then any violation of the rules by 'their own' and any success of 'the opponent' calls forth abuse."[110]

By 1970, the situation had become so serious that *Sovetskii sport* began an anti-alchohol campaign. The editors asked, "Why has it become impossible to imagine any soccer game without some drunk, disturbed people who push you on the shoulders at the entrances and who, in the stands, harass their neighbors for an hour and a half?"[111] Police were interviewed, and stories of mass confiscations of bottles and other contraband became a regular feature.[112] The problem, of course, did not go away with stricter control, but it is worth noting that it seems to have been largely restricted to the relatively all-male experience of watching soccer. Hockey crowds were smaller, and indoor arenas were more easily controlled. Basketball disorders, when they happened, were more likely to be caused by events on the court than by chemicals in the fans' brains.

No sooner had the furor over drunkenness died down than a new phenomenon arose that was even more disturbing to older fans and officials. Beginning in 1973, the teen-age fans of Spartak regularly began to sit together in the cheap seats during games at Lenin Stadium. By the late 'seventies, they had developed a group identity and accompanying rituals, creating their own cheers and wearing homemade red-and-white caps and scarves (the team colors), much like English fans. Unfortunately, the desire to emulate English "lovers of football" extended to many of the more antisocial practices of British soccer hooligans. Not content simply to observe and root, these Spartak *fanaty,* as they were called, consciously and very specifically took to heart the actions of the Scottish fans who had invaded the field during the 1970 Cup-Winners Cup final between Glasgow Rangers and Dinamo Moscow.[113] While the actions they admired were obviously pathological, the *fanaty* were trying to go beyond passive spectating in order to put their own stamp on the game. More so than other forms of entertainment, spectator sports do allow for the influence of the audience in both negative and positive ways, and Spartak's supporters were simultaneously seeking to influence the outcome of action on the field and draw attention to themselves.

By the late 'seventies, these youths came to form semi-organized gangs of teen-age and young fans, drawn from a broad range of social groups. In response, Dinamo and TsSKA supporters organized smaller but equally militant gangs, and the rivals soon found themselves clashing in the city over territory and team loyalties. One particularly interesting aspect of these gangs was their use of graffiti, whose meanings have been subtly studied by John Bushnell. It was particularly revealing that changes in the fortunes of the various Moscow teams had no impact on the messages the young gang members were writing on walls. Bushnell has estimated that when the gangs were at their height in the early 'eighties, there were some 30,000 youths involved in one way or another.

Less violent than their British counterparts, Soviet *fanaty* did terrorize metro riders after games and often clashed with each other. Many of them traveled to Spartak road games and wreaked havoc on the local populations, who had their own, somewhat less violent, *fanaty.*[114] While nothing was ever proven in the matter, it is possible their roughhousing may have played a role in the tragic exit panic that killed as many as 340 people, many of them teen-age boys, after a 1982 UEFA cup game at Luzhniki between Spartak and a Dutch team.

While soccer was the subject of the graffiti produced by the gangs, the phenomenon was more a youth problem than a sports problem. Not all *fanaty* were gang members, and not all gang members were close students of the game. The activities of semi-organized soccer gangs peaked around 1983, as angry youths would pass on to other ways, mainly rock and roll, to express their alienation. At their height, the soccer gangs were profoundly disturbing to the Komsomol and to sports offiicals. Clearly, a segment of the young population had resisted accepting the larger lessons the state wished to ascribe to spectator sports. Yet the gangs never presented any clear political alternative, nor did they offer a profoundly different approach to the consumption of spectator sports. Bushnell has described the limited political consciousness of the gang members with great precision:

> . . . the gangs were not politically self-conscious. Gang members understood that they were defying explicit and official social norms and that the regime considered their actions anti-social, but they did not equate social deviance with political dissent. Moscow's fan gangs were no more political entities than are American street gangs, or British football hooligans, similarly engaged in establishing an identity and realm of activity for themselves.[115]

Soccer gangs and all the other phenomena mentioned here demonstrate the many similarities between Western and Soviet sports fans. The attractions of sports, espcially the need to intensify the experience by picking favorite teams and players, seem much the same. Even the manifestations of antisocial behavior are roughly similar. The fundamental difference between the West and the USSR was the didacticism of the offical Soviet approach to spectator sports. Nonconformity in the Soviet Union was a more serious choice, precisely because of the use the state sought to make of sports. In that sense, gang violence and other forms of fan misbehavior do have a political dimension, although, as Bushnell makes clear elsewhere, it is a politics of a decidedly unconventional sort.[116]

By the beginning of the 1980s, the era of Soviet normalcy was coming to an end. During these thirty-two years of relative calm, spectator sports had grown as a leisure pursuit of the urban masses. Millions had come to watch games in person and even more regularly observe them on television. Spectator sports attained this visibility and importance not because the state and Party wished it, but because the Soviet public desired it. The state system that produced so much Olympic success had grown massively during these years, but as we have seen, this expansion did not signify acceptance of its activities by the sporting audience. Between 1953 and 1985, spectator sports continued to be a highly problematic tool of government control, and they would still be an arena of both conscious and unconscious contestation as, after 1985, Soviet society came to enter a new era of reform and struggle.

7

Perestroika and
Professionalism (1985–1991)

When Mikhail Gorbachev came to power in 1985, he initiated a long overdue but ultimately unsuccessful attempt to overhaul and reform the Soviet Union. While Soviet society had changed significantly during the post-Stalin era, the structures of the state and economy had failed to do so, and Gorbachev quickly came to realize that the USSR had entered a crisis. The bureaucratically controlled command economy, with its emphases on heavy industry and military needs, had long outlived its usefulness. Rapid industrialization had been achieved at enormous human cost, but further progress was blocked.

The hypercentralized planning apparatus, so effective in achieving certain gross goals, had proven incapable of handling the more complex task of satisfying human needs in a technologically sophisticated world. The historic aim had been to overtake and surpass the West, and in the late 'fifties, with Sputniks in space and Soviet worldwide popularity high, that hope had seemed realizable. But the growth that was achieved had been relatively self-sufficient. Even after the Second World War, the USSR was not an active participant in the global economy, and eventually the Soviets would pay for their comparative isolation. By the end of the 1970s, the time had come to satisfy the long-suffering consumer sector, but the old structures could not respond to this new need.

Even before the 1980s any nation wishing to maintain a standard of living comparable to that of other industrial nations had to participate in an increasingly global economy. It was no longer possible for countries to continue to grow and prosper outside the world market, but the USSR, its currency not convertible, was only a partial and certainly not a very successful player in that market. Soviet living standards, which had never been particularly high, began to decline. Average life-expectancy dropped during the 1980s. For all the construction of the post-war period, housing was still insufficient, and so was diet.

It also became increasingly difficult to hide these facts from the people. Soviet citizens had long been told that they lived in the greatest of nations, and more than a few of them, in their isolation from the rest of the world, had come to believe this. But as the world economy changed, so did global mechanisms of communication. After Gorbachev came to power, it became increasingly difficult to cut the Soviet Union off from the rest of the world, and as they learned more about conditions beyond their borders, many Soviet citizens came to realize they did not live in the greatest of all countries.

Before 1985, the Soviet citizens who were already aware of the depth of the crisis were forced to confront a state engaged in painting ever-brighter pictures of an ever-grimmer situation. By the beginning of perestroika, the divergence between a steadily deteriorating reality and its increasingly false descriptions had finally become untenable. The result was acute demoralization in both society and the Party. The need to make the state's assertions bear at least some relationship to reality led to the campaign for glasnost or openness. A newly honest and critical press was to play a central role in Gorbachev's reform campaign. It became possible to expose abuses and problems, and the regular media adopted the critical approach that the sports press had long practiced.

As we have seen, very similar divergences between the hopes of the state and the realities of society had also developed over the years in the sports world—divergences between the state's presentation and the public's consumption of spectator sports. In order to achieve Olympic dominance, the government had long chosen to emphasize success in the full range of international sports. It had also attempted to give the appearance of equality between male and female sports. The majority of sports fans, however, were always far more interested in the popular team sports played by, and for the most part watched by, men. Few males ever attended women's events. Women, who were always less interested in sports than men, rarely attended women's events, with the exception of the occasional gymnastic or figure skating competition.

The Moscow public's limited support for the teams of the Dinamo Society and the Central Army Club represented another such divergence. To be sure, these teams had enjoyed moments of enormous popularity during their long histories, and both continued to have sizable followings. Great heroes like Iashin and Bobrov had drawn many supporters to these powerful clubs. But Spartak, the team of Moscow's "hooligans and intellectuals," was always the fans' favorite. Spartak had its own powerful political patrons, but these supporters were in the civilian sector and were not part of the state's institutions of repression. Had the official messages of the sports authorities been accepted uncritically by the public, one might have expected guardians of order—soldiers and policemen—to have been the greatest heroes of the Moscow sports fan, but this was not the case. Instead, the nonmilitary Spartak Society always enjoyed the broadest base of support in the capital.[1] The fans chose their own heroes.

Soviet sports spectators, even at the height of Stalinism, had always been able to make choices in the way they patronized sports events, and these "consumer options" took on added significance with the beginning of perestroika. The ultimately unsuccessful attempt to graft some form of capitalism onto the economic practices of what was called the "command-administrative system" gave those choices a special importance. Heavily subsidized institutions and enterprises were left to their own devices after 1985, as the state could no longer afford to do everything. The many pressing needs of the perestroika process, not to mention the crisis it eventually provoked, once again pushed state support for sports to the background. With the economy grinding to a halt by 1990, the government was unable to divert new resources to any leisure practice, and the sports world increasingly found itself thrown back on its own devices, forced to generate its own support.

Many firms and institutions had to become self-financing as the USSR lurched toward the establishment of market relations. Goskomsport and the various sports federations lost much of their government funding, and eventually the Sports Committee would disappear with the breakup of the USSR. The various clubs, however, would continue to exist even after the end of the Union, and they had long been required to make their own money even before perestroika began. Nevertheless, after 1985, self-financing required teams to reexamine the once-scorned practices of commercialism, but this change would prove to be less dramatic and unprecedented in the sphere of spectator sports than it seemed at first glance.

For years, the state's sports authorities had earned hard currency with foreign tours of athletes in a wide variety of sports. By the mid-'eighties, Goskomsport was actually paying more in taxes to the Ministry of Finance than it was receiving from the state. Over the years, the Sports Committee had become an especially bountiful source of hard currency.[2] After 1987, though, virtually no commercial opportunity was passed up, regardless of how deleterious it may have been either for the health of the athletes or for the larger needs of sports. The new emphasis on making money, in turn, led to a search for an updated version of the partial professionalism of the prewar period. The possibility of organizing spectator sports on what was called an openly professional basis challenged the bureaucratic approach followed for decades by the various versions of the state sports committee. Between 1985 and 1991, a variety of independent forces sought new ways to organize the production of spectator sports, as athletes, coaches, and club officials attempted to wrest power from state functionaries.

Yet the debates on this subject were not, in fact, about professionalization. As we have seen, the paying of athletes had always been one of the realities of the Soviet sports world. Instead, a struggle took place during perestroika between state-appointed bureaucrats and professional specialists for the control of big-time sports. The issue was, not professionalization, but rather commercialization. Would big-time sports now become a money-making enterprise? and who would control the profits it generated?

This contest for power over the production of sports did not entirely change the ways Soviet citizens consumed their sports events. Sport spectators had never doubted that the clubs and players they rooted for were professionals. Few fans ever believed that the teams representing particular institutions had any real contact with those institutions.[3] While many welcomed the removal of some of the more obvious hypocrisies, most fans continued to seek pleasure and entertainment from their sports viewing, regardless of who was in charge. Nevertheless, changes in the process of production had the potential to change the attitudes of the public. Openly commercial, rather than didactic, sports spectacles projected different values and produced different kinds of heroes. Yet the spectators, who had long ignored the state's attempts to control the meaning of sports, were always well ahead of the authorities, and many saw the struggle for control of sports simply as a contest between two warring elites, neither of which had much in common with the average fan.

The debates about sports, in turn, mirrored the struggles, most of them indecisive, that took place in other spheres of life during the period of perestroika. In distinction from the past, the many battles of this period took place under the glare of the increased media scrutiny that characterized the era of glasnost. In the sports world, the Soviet fan, often kept in the dark, was now given a front-row seat at the contest for control of the production of sports spectacles. What had in the past been only rumor was now reported publicly. While the public still saw spectator sports as an arena for diversion and pleasure, the newly critical approach of the media did create the possibility of changing the ways society made sense of the sports spectacles it watched during this final period of Soviet history.[4]

Changing Modes of Consumption

Nowhere in the world has the experience of spectator sports been limited simply to attendance at games. Sports fans read about games and competitions in newspapers and magazines. They watch events on television, and always they discuss developments among themselves. These discourses about sport also turn out to be the sources by which both the public and the outside observer acquire information about spectator sport. Accordingly, these practices should not be seen simply as "sources" in the narrow scholarly sense. As was the case everywhere else in the world, the sporting press, game attendance, televised events, and discussion with both friends and strangers were all ways the Soviet fan consumed sports, and the character of all these experiences shaped the attitudes of the public.

The Sporting Press—Before 1991, the central sports organ in the USSR was the national sports daily, *Sovetskii sport.* The state's sports agencies published a number of periodicals throughout Soviet history, but *Sovetskii Sport* was the most successful and widely circulated of all. By contrast, the rest of the press provided only limited coverage of sports. *Pravda* and *Izvestia* regularly published a few results each day, along with the occasional analytical article. The youth newspaper, *Komsomolskaia Pravda,* the labor daily, *Trud,* and the conservative *Sovetskaia Rossiia,* also gave considerable attention to sports, but following the common European practice, the main source of sports news was the national daily.

First published in 1924, and known as *Krasnyi sport* until 1946, *Sovetskii sport* was one of the most popular newspapers in the Soviet Union. It regularly sold out its daily run of more than five million copies, which its editors claimed made it the most popular, certainly the most widely read, sports periodical in the world. Without doubt, it was the one Soviet newspaper whose journalistic practices closely resembled those of its counterparts in the West. The reporters of *Sovetskii sport* attended events, recorded what happened, and then straightforwardly described it to their readers. They did this with comparative accuracy and honesty; often, but far from always, without regard to questions of immediate politics.

Before the changes brought on by glasnost, this approach made *Sovetskii sport* something of an exception among Soviet newspapers. It had maintained a critical tradition long before 1985. Over the years, coaches, athletes, fans, and sports bureaucrats came under severe scrutiny, even condemnation. One could even speculate that these critical practices played a role in the Soviet Union's sports success. Coaches who stayed on past their usefulness, players who misbehaved, authorities who could not organize were forced to improve or depart. It is difficult to imagine that these necessary changes would have been made without such criticism. In this sense one could argue (but certainly not prove) that Soviet sports journalism provided a model for the role the press assumed under glasnost.

After 1985, however, *Sovetskii sport* expanded its criticism and embarked on a variety of muckraking campaigns that led some sports figures to call it a "scandal sheet." The relative protection enjoyed by athletes ended. In the past, the press, under orders to preserve the heroic image of sacrosanct role models, had not always exposed the foibles of sport stars. Under glasnost, everyone became fair game. One might have expected this new approach to increase fans cynicism about their favorites, but serious followers of the scene had always maintained a well-developed rumor mill that, correctly or incorrectly, identified alchoholics, shirkers, and game-fixers. Indeed, the trading of unreported rumors was itself part of the fun of fan discourse, just as it has always been everywhere else in the world.

Perhaps *Sovetskii sport*'s biggest exposé of the perestroika period concerned the tragic events at Lenin Stadium on October 20, 1982. An exit panic at the end of a UEFA Cup game between Spartak and Haarlem of the Netherlands had caused numerous deaths. Press accounts at the time gave the impression that the toll was little more than a dozen, but in 1989, *Sovetskii sport* would reveal that as many as 340 people, many of them teen-age boys, had died.[5] A late Spartak goal had caused those who were leaving the stadium early to reverse their exit, whereupon they ran head-on into thousands of others still on their way out. In the ensuing carnage, hundreds were trampled to death, and, according to *Sovetskii sport*'s 1989 account of the events, ambulances did not appear until half an hour later.

Yet, for all its virtues, *Sovetskii sport* was still a state newspaper under the ultimate control of whatever version of the Sports Committee happened to exist at a particular time. Although its sins were more often those of omission rather than commission, the newspaper's journalists still had to walk a fine line. As a vehicle for the dissemination of information on the most popular spectator sports, *Sovetskii sport* was further limited by the fact that its state patrons always insisted that equal if not greater time be given to physical culture and items of general political interest. If the General Secretary of the Communist Party gave an important speech, that speech was invariably on *Sovetskii sport*'s front page, even if no mention was made of sports in the speech. If new methods of production gymnastics were developed, these, too, would be prominently featured.

For all the prestige of working for *Sovetskii sport* and for all the (limited) protection one got from writing in a field that enjoyed some freedom from state control, many of its writers found that they still could not work there. In the summer of 1991, a sizable group of *Sovetskii sport*'s top writers, nearly all specialists on big-time sports, broke away to form the first independent sports daily in Soviet history. This newspaper, called *Sportexpress,* was to concentrate on the games Soviet fans actually liked to watch. Its core was to be soccer, hockey, and basketball, with a strongly international perspective.[6] It was financed by the state bank and the government of the Russian Republic, both of which loaned, rather than gave, the new newspaper its necessary working capital.

Television—As became true throughout the world, the Soviet public increasingly watched most of its sports on television. Even after 1985, however, this most visible mode of consumption differed from the sports press. The tradition of criticism found in the print media was far more muted on television, even under glasnost. Yet sports on Soviet television, especially after 1988, were virtually free of ideological reference and overt political meaning. Not especially critical, Soviet sports television did eschew egregious cheerleading, even when covering international events. There can be no doubt, of course, that Soviet commentators, even under the conditions of glasnost, continued to take pride in the frequent successes of their countrymen. Yet even before perestroika, one rarely heard specific claims that a particular victory constituted proof of the superiority of Communism. Patriotic pride was acceptable, but such televised didacticism usually went no further. Given the propagandistic opportunities created by the combination of television and sports, it is surprising that shameless self-congratulation occurred more rarely than one might have expected, but this was very much the case.

Any examination of sports on Soviet television must note one simple, telling, and long-standing fact. Soviet viewers were never able to see as much of sports as their counterparts in the United States or Western Europe, a contrast that became even starker with the explosion of cable television in capitalist countries. For many years, there were four channels in Moscow. Of these, the first and second national programs, plus the local station, showed a variety of sports events, exercise shows, documentaries, and round-ups. In 1986, an average of twelve sports programs were shown per week. By 1988, this number declined to nine, as the temporary success of political discussion shows and rock music diminished the amount of time given to sports.

According to surveys conducted by Ellen Mickiewicz, only two per cent of air time during the week and seven per cent on weekends was devoted to sports viewing.[7] This highly limited menu contrasts with the roughly fifty events on cable and regular television available to an American viewer during an average week. Outside the United States, the difference was also enormous, even before perestroika. In the United Kingdom, the BBC alone showed 1,500 hours of sports in 1982. Its main competition, ITV, devoted a roughly similar percentage of its air time (12 per cent) to sports. By contrast, a total of 920 hours of sports television were planned on all channels for Soviet sports fans in 1989.[8]

While a wide variety of sports was televised in the USSR, the emphasis during perestroika shifted to soccer and ice hockey. During four separate two-week periods in late 1987 and early 1988 (one period for each season of the year), seventy sports events were shown on Soviet television. Of these, twenty-three were devoted to soccer, fourteen to ice hockey, and only four to men's basketball. While a wide variety of other sports was shown, they received only occasional exposure. Thus the bulk of sports television came to be devoted to the major team sports preferred by Soviet fans, and those in charge of sports programming expected this percentage to increase as market forces played a larger role in state television's offerings.[9]

The Olympic Games were always exceptions to the normal slim pickings. At these times, the Soviet viewer was subjected to quadrennial winter and summer two-week floods. Both national channels alternated coverage. During the summer of 1988, 190 hours of the Seoul Games were shown by Soviet television in contrast to what was an unprecedented 179 hours telecast in the United States. Soviet announcers, for the first time other than in Moscow, were able to provide on-site interviews of their own athletes, but unlike the U.S. Soviet television took its images from the host country and then provided its own commentary.[10] Events were covered continuously for considerable chunks of time. There was little, if any, hopping from one venue to the next. Entire soccer and basketball games were shown without interruption, and important events that did not involve Soviet athletes were also given extended coverage.

Until 1988, there had been no commercials during Soviet sports events. Coverage of the Seoul Games was, however, occasionally interrupted for brief, highly visual commericals for Pepsi-Cola, the American soft drink sold widely in the USSR. These segments were Western-produced with Russian-language voice-overs. The commercials appeared unannounced in the middle of previously taped segments. No attempt was made to warn the audience, and no notice was paid when the program returned.

Because they used images provided by the host country, Soviet broadcasters were not able to focus on their own athletes with the single-mindedness of their American counterparts. Less overt nationalism was therefore manifested, and the viewer got a greater sense of the internationalism of the Games. Because events were covered for longer periods of time, one saw not only victors but also-rans as well. As a result a greater emphasis was unconsciously placed on participation than on winning. Having said that, it should be noted that Soviet coverage rarely ommitted victory ceremonies involving Soviet athletes, and interviews with losers were few and far between.

Thus, the bulk of sports on Soviet television, especially after 1985, consisted of domestic games of the major leagues of the two most popular team sports. The commentary was usually flat, descriptive, and nearly always done by one announcer. There were few interviews. One rarely got more than a second's glimpse of the announcer's face. There were no pre- or postgame shows. Instead, the always well-prepared commentators established the context, gave lineups, and provided background during the early moments of a game. The absence of commentary before and after games meant less setting of the scene than in Western telecasts. Soviet viewers were actually freer to react to an event as they wished. When a competition ended, the transmission also ended, leaving it up to the viewer to decide the meaning of what had transpired. Ironically, television, one of the Soviet government's ultimate methods of control, proved to be less controlling than its Western counterpart in this particular way.[11]

If most sports on Soviet television had few, if any, commercials, it also must be said that they contained no hidden commercials for the state and Party. While viewers may have drawn a variety of possible political conclusions from what they viewed, overt politics and ideology were almost entirely absent after 1985 and rare before that date. There were also few attempts to create false drama to attract viewers. The irrational aspects of sport were downplayed, with commentators taking a detached, straightforward, even scientific tone. As a result, watching sports on Soviet televsion was less exciting than in America, Europe, or Latin America.

This lack of bombast also extended to the visual aspects of telecasts. Soviet television was considerably less technically sophisticated than its Western, especially American, counterparts. Slow-motion replays were used from the early 'seventies, but camera angles were minimal and on-screen graphics quite primitive. Directors did not switch quickly from one camera to another, and spectators were shown only during lulls in the action. By 1989, however, these practices began to change. Attractive computer graphics were introduced, and a few Soviet directors began to show audience reaction far more often.[12] The comparatively primitive technical quality of Soviet coverage also began to improve as a result of external commercial pressures and opportunities. In January 1989, Soviet television started showing games of the U.S. National Basketball Association and the North American National Hockey League. These programs were financed by the sale of commercial time to foreign firms interested in the Soviet market. Six minutes of commercials were shown during a one-hour program of taped highlights. Soviet announcers provided the commentary but did not participate themselves in any commercial activity.

While television was always less critical than the newspapers, it was not immune to glasnost's impact. Before a temporary clampdown in the fall of 1990, it became common to hear commentators talk of the need to "restructure" the particular sport they were covering. The extremely dour Evgenii Maiorov, former Spartak star and a leading hockey announcer, continually criticized the organizers of the hockey league for contributing in various ways to the attendance crisis the sport suffered between 1985 and 1991.[13] On the other hand, Maiorov did not publicly join the storm of print criticism that centered on Viktor Tikhonov before the 1988 Olympics.

As is universal, Soviet announcers always felt free to challenge the tactical decisions of coaches or to chastise players for poor performances. Yet this, too, was usually done indirectly and tactfully.[14] More startling, and utterly out of keeping with previous practices, was a tendency for sport commentators to speak critically on matters with direct political import. In July 1988, one of the best announcers, Vladimir Pereturin, covered a regular-season soccer game between Spartak and Zhalgiris of Vilnius. He spoke about the recently completed European championship, in which the Soviet national team had made the final only to lose to an excellent Dutch team. Everyone throughout the Soviet sports world had been enormously pleased by the team's performance. Pereturin, however, noted the lack of Soviet fan support at the final, played in Munich. He said that forty thousand Dutch supporters attended, in stark contrast to no more than four hundred Soviets. Without saying the result would have been different, Pereturin did remark on the relationship between fan support and team performance. He complained about the absence of Soviet fans at the final match: "We think this is incorrect. Our life is changing—in football, travel, and professionalism. People should be able to go to various countries. The process of filling out forms should be made faster. It is necessary that our fans should go abroad to support our teams."[15] He then suggested that the fans judged to be the most orderly in support of their favorite team should be given the right to purchase trips to Italy for the World Cup in 1990.

In the last months of perestroika, much of this sort of candor was reduced. Beginning with the fall of 1990, Gorbachev increasingly began to ally himself with more traditional bureaucratic elements. He named a new, more conservative head of *Gosteleradio,* Leonid Kravchenko. Many of the more critical shows were taken off the air, and more progressive commentators were silenced. It is perhaps not insignificant that Kravchenko, who had previously led the Tass News Agency, was also president of the hockey federation. After the failure of the August coup, he was dismissed, and many of those who had lost their jobs were reinstated. This political tug-of-war did not affect either the amount of sports shown on Soviet television or the mix of different kinds of sports presented. Commentators were more careful during these few months, but the differences were fairly subtle.

Given the important historic propaganda function played in Soviet society by television, it would be reasonable to expect that sports programming would have been equally, if not more, didactic, but this was not the case. Repeated viewing of Soviet sports programs over a period of years, both before and after perestroika, usually removed whatever exoticism they may have held. Westerners who expected to see events interpreted through an ideological grid were disappointed. In some sense, the most striking feature of sports on Soviet television was their utter ordinariness. Few attempts were made to enhance drama that may have been lacking in the event itself, and this very pedestrianness made it different from its Western counterparts, for whom even the dullest game between the weakest rivals always had to be promoted as a "key matchup" in order to generate an audience.

It must also be repeated that in comparison to the flood of televised sports in the United States, the Soviet audience experienced merely a trickle. When all is said and done, perhaps the most salient aspect of televised sports in the USSR was the fact that there was always so little of it. This emphasis, or lack of it, reflects the limited importance of sports in Soviet society. While sports were popular, they were far from a national obsession. In this sense, the programming decisions of state television reflected not only the government's limited concern for sports, but also the audience's relatively quenchable appetite.

Game Attendance—As we have seen, most of the arenas and stadiums of the Soviet Union were comparatively small, and beginning with the early 'eighties they were far from full. An attendance crisis developed in Soviet spectator sports, particularly in hockey, and primarily in Moscow. The problem arose despite the relative affordability of tickets and persisted beyond the end of Soviet power in December 1991. One of the clichés of Soviet sportswriting was the simple truth that spectator sports could not exist without spectators, and journalists frequently quoted coaches and players who stressed that the "games are for the spectators." Thus there was always a firm understanding that spectator sports should provide the public with compelling entertainment. Soviet scholars of sports had similarly argued that the consumption of spectator sports had to be a pleasurable and exciting act, different from the everyday work world of the average fan.[16]

The organizers of these competitions did not always understand this to be their task. As a result, the sold-out arena, especially in Moscow, became the exception. Throughout the 1980s, the Soviet sporting public grew even more indifferent to the official messages and "products" presented to them. The rush to the stadiums and arenas died down, and fans came to refer to the late 1960s and early 1970s as a lost "golden age" of sport. The fans' lack of response was not an organized resistance to the authorities who presented sports events, nor did it signify the lack of desire for sports. Instead, Soviet citizens were doing what they always had done—voting with their feet. By making choices about attending some events and not attending others, fans were, in Pierre Bourdieu's words, "contesting," more aggressively than ever before, the meanings and practices surrounding the sports spectacles presented to them.

Soccer, the best-attended game, drew an average first-division crowd of 20,000 during the early 'eighties, an entirely respectable figure that placed the USSR fourth among European nations. In the wake of the national team's surprisingly attractive play in the 1986 World Cup, attendance rose in the 1987 season to 27,000 a game, but by 1988, despite a closely contested season, the average first-division crowd declined to 23,000. In 1989, the average dipped well below 20,000, and in 1990, under the impact of the economic crisis and that year's unexpected World Cup failure, only 16,000 showed up per game. The next year, as the crisis worsened, only twelve thousand could find the time away from food queues to show up at each game. Even such a fixture as Spartak versus Dinamo Kiev could only attract 30,000 to Luzhniki.[17]

International matches, involving both clubs and the national team, were still popular. If the game was sufficiently attractive, fans, despite all the obstacles, were able to find their way back to the stadium. In the spring of 1991, Spartak reached the semifinal of the European Champions Cup. On the way they played such European powers as Napoli (with Diego Maradonna), Real Madrid, and Olympique Marseille. Each time Lenin Stadium was filled to capacity, despite bad weather, local television, and higher ticket prices. Similarly, when Dinamo Kiev played the great Spanish power, Barcelona, in the 1991 Cup-Winner's Cup, Republic Stadium was also sold out.

In the case of hockey, the attendance crisis was largely a Moscow problem. Aside from Kiev and Leningrad, most of the other first-division teams were in such relatively smaller provincial cities as Sverdlovsk, Cheliabinsk, Voskresensk, and Nizhnii Novgorod. In these places, there was little else to do, and teams played to ninety per cent of capacity in small local arenas. Of the four teams in Moscow (TsSKA, Dinamo, Spartak, and Krylia Sovetov), only one, Krylia Sovetov, had its own home rink, built in 1980. As attendance steadily declined, games were moved from the Palace of Sport to the 9,000-seat Small Sports Arena.

In the late 'eighties, only games between Spartak and either TsSKA or Dinamo sold out, but when Spartak's fortunes fell during these years, even their games filled barely half the seats. Under the right circumstances, however, TsSKA versus Dinamo could also fill the Sports Palace even during this period. The situation eventually bottomed out during 1990. Spartak, coached by its former star Alexander Iakushev, returned to contention, and the once-mighty Central Army, having lost its best players to the West, no longer could dominate. The drop-off in quality of play was not that marked, but with the return of uncertainty and intrigue to the domestic season, many fans, despite the difficulties of surviving the winter, began to reappear at the arena. Dinamo Moscow would win the 1990 and 1991 championships, seriously challenged both years by Spartak. Several games were moved back to the Palace of Sports, and, when Spartak faced Dinamo at the end of the 1990–1991 season, with the title on the line, the old building was filled again. Notwithstanding this pleasant counter-trend, hockey attendance was far below the levels of the 1960s and 1970s. Despite the revival of interest in 1990, crowds still averaged only 3,200 per game.[18]

There were many explanations for the collapse of sports attendance in Moscow. Compared to the provinces, there was simply much more competition for the entertainment ruble in a capital city of ten million. The days when "football was our only spectacle" had long disappeared. This fact made the demand for soccer and hockey tickets in Moscow highly elastic. With so many teams in the city, loyalties were divided. There was a surfeit of games; many of them were meaningless. Events were poorly advertised and promoted.[19] The days when buses and trams carried announcements of upcoming contests had long disappeared. Teams did not distribute schedules; nor did newspapers, even *Sovetskii sport,* regularly carry advertisements for games.

Once they got to the stadium, fans confronted conditions that seemed a throwback to the prewar era. Food at stadium buffets became minimal and unappealing, when it was available at all. As the economic crisis deepened, this last fact became a very serious problem. After waiting in lines all day to feed their families, many fans were too tired to take in a contest. Since games usually started as early as six-thirty, there was little or no time to return from work, grab a bite, and then go out to the stadium. In the midst of society's gloom, journalists and fans complained that one did not have a feeling of "holiday" (*prazdnik*) at a game.[20]

Yet sports did not entirely lose their capacity to help people forget their troubles. When an attractive game drew a big crowd, the press rarely failed to remark on the moment. In the spring of 1990, after a thrilling 5–4 soccer game between Spartak and TsSKA had filled the indoor Olympic stadium, the most eloquent of Soviet sportswriters, Leonid Trakhtenberg, wrote:

Is there really anything to hide? Our life is hard these days. There are so few joyous faces around us, so many sullen and anxious ones. Is there anything to be particularly joyful about, as goods disappear from the shelves of stores and the press of our daily problems becomes greater? But the day before yesterday the sun shone from behind the clouds, and so many positive emotions flowed. That evening, not everything the players tried succeeded, but the game satisfied us all. No one could be indifferent to it. We can stand the suffering of no meat or flour, but, without this kind of football, we cannot live.[21]

I have already noted the fundamental reason for the collapse of attendance in the sport of hockey. The massive competitive imbalance that had
emerged in domestic competition became even worse. After 1985, TsSKA
came to dominate the league even more thoroughly than it had done before.
During this period, there were years when TsSKA would lose no more than
two games in a forty-four game season. Yet the head of the Administration
for Hockey and Soccer, Viacheslav Koloskov, speaking in 1987, defended
the right of TsSKA and Dinamo to collect the best available hockey talent.
The state, he argued, had spent large sums on developing these players, and
it was proper that teams supported directly by the state should make use of
their talents.[22]

Valerii Sysoev, head of the Dinamo Society, supported this view. In
1989, he was interviewed on television by the always-critical Pereturin, who
approvingly noted the large number of teams in the National Hockey League
of roughly comparable levels. Sysoev replied, "All of our structures are organized not around the needs of the clubs but of the national team. The
National Hockey League is a purely commercial organization. It seeks the
maximum number of fans. They balance the teams in various ways in order
to get an artificial equality." Pereturin, in turn, asked if perhaps, the Soviet
authorities had created an "artificial inequality."[23]

While televising a January 1989 game between Spartak and Dinamo, Pereturin commented on the problem, "Once we thought the main thing was the international level, the world championships, the Olympics, but why should this
ruin our internal competition, not only in hockey but in other sports?"[24] Evgenii
Maiorov, never very vocal, joined in the criticism of the hockey federation for allowing far too many transfers to TsSKA.[25] *Sovetskii sport* and its weekly supple-
ment, *Futbol-khokkei,* began to complain repeatedly about the long-range
impact of the stocking of TsSKA. These critics argued that the policy was short-
sighted, as the creation of "super clubs" always had the potential to kill interest
in domestic competition. Since the league was the lifeblood of the sport, initially
attracting most young athletes to hockey, there were fears that boring internal
competition would influence the most talented to choose careers in other sports.
Many observers were afraid that the deep talent pool could dwindle.[26] In 1989,
the long-time observer of hockey Dmitrii Ryzhkov would write, "The conclusion is clear. The policy of 'everything for the national team' has been turned upside down—a mass of minuses for the organism of our club hockey and for its
future."[27]

By the late 'eighties, the public came to complain loudly that there were
no longer any stars. The great players of the 1970s had all had individual
styles and staggeringly high levels of skill. By the end of the 'eighties, the
methods employed by Tikhonov had so influenced other coaches that all
teams came to play a roughly similar style. The individual expressiveness of

the young hockey player was discouraged, and some of the intricate passing and spectacular skating was reduced in favor of a more physical, defense-minded style that sought to reduce mistakes.[28]

Spectators also lost interest in hockey when conflicts and disputes, rather than results, came to dominate news of the sport. During 1988, charges of excessive control and dictatorial methods were leveled at Tikohonov in the pro-perestroika weekly *Ogonek* by one of his stars, Igor Larionov. Larionov also publicly denounced Tikhonov at a meeting of the hockey federation for treating the players like "chess pieces rather than personalities." In January 1989, the outstanding defenseman Viacheslav Fetisov, captain of TsSKA, claimed Tikhonov was hampering his efforts to play in the National Hockey League, and Fetisov went as far as to quit the team after requesting to resign his army commission. After sitting out the second stage of the 1988–1989 domestic season, Fetisov agreed to play for Tikhonov on the national team, and somewhat reluctantly, Tikhonov bowed to the wishes of the players, who wanted their captain back.[29] In the spirit of glasnost, Soviet media did not ignore this conflict. Television showed Fetisov in the stands at TsSKA games, and newspapers gave ample space to both sides of the argument. While most fans supported Fetisov, they all knew that one of the sport's most attractive performers was not playing, giving them yet another reason not to attend.

As we have seen, tensions between the demands of national teams and the needs of clubs were a part of big-time team sports throughout the world, but in no sport did the emphasis on external success prove as destructive as in Soviet hockey. In the interests of international glory, the sport's organizers succeeded in alienating the game from its base of support. The Moscow public chose not to buy the product offered by the state, just as it had long refused to purchase so many of the other shoddy consumer goods made available. Domestic hockey games became the sporting equivalent of the hideous and poorly made shoes that sat forlornly on Soviet shelves for so many years.

Soviet hockey was a case of the professionalized, elitist, state-oriented approach to big-time sports carried to its most absurd extreme. Under Tikhonov, international goals obscured the domestic role played by spectator sports. As a result, ice hockey lost much of its entertainment value. In response, many in the hockey world called for a fundamental reorganization that would put the sport on an openly professional basis, a step that was certain to diminish many of the advantages previously enjoyed by TsSKA.

Ways of Watching: Old and New

The combination of small facilities and half-empty stands clearly indicated one absolutely central fact about spectator sports in the Soviet Union. Neither the Party nor the public could be described as "sports-crazy." While there was always considerable interest in sports, even passion for them, it would hardly be correct to argue that either state or society was obsessed with watching sports. The resources available for these activities and the time devoted to them were always limited compared to the other needs of society. Sport played a decidedly secondary role in Soviet life. Loyalties may have run deep, but few fans ever defined their own happiness in terms of the success or failure of their favorite teams.

Nevertheless, we have seen that there was always the potential for passion-driven disorder when large numbers of people gathered at any spectacle, especially in the Soviet Union, and the problem grew even more acute during perestroika. There were numerous outbreaks of fan violence in the various republics, fueled by local nationalisms. The most acute situation appeared in the course of the fighting between the Armenians and the Azerbaidzhanis over Nagorno-Karabakh. Games between the Erevan and Baku teams had to be moved to neutral sites. Other incidents assumed the hallowed and familiar form of fans invading the field to protest referees' decisions. One such disturbance took place May 21, 1989, in Tblisi, just a month after twenty nationalist protesters had been killed by troops in the city's main square. The game was held up for several minutes, as a few spectators tried to attack the referee. Order was quickly restored, and most spectators remained in their places. Those who were arrested later denied their actions had anything to do with the recent disorders. A similar riot took place in Erevan in July 1991, right after Ararat's 1–0 defeat at the hands of TsSKA. Not only did Armenian spectators attack the referees and TsSKA's players, but so did Ararat's coach and team president. While police investigations did not reveal any overtly nationalist component to these events, it is difficult to imagine such sentiments did not contribute to the rage of the Erevan fans.[30]

This was not the first disorder involving the army team during the last season of Soviet soccer. In the spring of 1991, with coalminers on strike in the city of Donetsk, TsSKA, then leading the league, came to town to play the local team, Shakhter. Suprisingly, Shakhter was in second place at the time, and despite the events in the city, a large crowd of thirty thousand showed up. With one minute to go and Shakhter ahead 1–0, the referee awarded TsSKA a penalty kick, which they converted to tie the game. Hundreds of angry fans invaded the field, and a full-scale battle ensued with the police. There were numerous injuries on both sides. To striking miners, the symbolism of a game stolen from them and given to the army, the powerful representatives of the center, must have been especially galling. Over the years, Donetsk fans had acquired a reputation as fair-minded, orderly, and knowledgeable spectators. They had often won the annual award for best-behaved crowd.[31] Thus their actions were truly exceptional and demonstrated the depth of their rage.

Those involved in much of the other soccer violence during this period were of a different order than the fans in the republics. The *fanaty*, the Russian equivalent of the soccer hooligan were still a prominent part of the scene. The press described these rioters as young, disaffected teen-agers and workers. Their social profile was roughly similar to that of soccer hooligans elsewhere, and in many cases, they displayed similar levels of informal organization.[32] Starting with the emergence of the Spartak *fanaty* in the 'seventies, soccer had been an arena in which adolescents could express their alienation. Sports was one of the few cultural spaces in which hooliganism and non-conformist behavior were even mildly tolerated. But as popular music became more interesting under the impact of glasnost, Soviet teen-agers drifted away from sports to rock culture as an expression of their anarchic rage and disaffection.

During perestroika, the most serious incident of fan violence involving youths occurred on September 19, 1987, in Kiev. Spartak and Dinamo Kiev met in a late-season game that would determine first place. The atmosphere had been charged days before the game, with window-shopping players from Spartak being attacked on the street by Kiev fans. After the game, there were fights outside the stadium involving visiting Spartak supporters. By the time they arrived at the train station, rocks and bottles were flying. Windows were broken. People were brawling all over the station. Blood was spilled, and the startled and outmanned police only made thirteen arrests, despite the hundreds involved in these events.[33] It would be easy to speculate that some of this violence was the result of national tensions between Ukrainian fans of Dinamo Kiev and Russian supporters of Spartak. Yet the players and coaches of Dinamo were never exclusively Ukrainian, and it was far more likely for a Russian living in Kiev to support Dinamo than to root for Spartak on grounds of national loyalty.

The incident after this game was so violent and visible that it set off a series of investigations and articles in the press.[34] The next year, when Spartak visited Kiev, the fans from Moscow were met at the train station by members of Dinamo's newly created supporters' club. The Spartak *fanaty* were put in buses, seated in a special section, presented with gifts from the local Komsomol, put back in buses after the game, and taken immediately to the railway station. Later, when Dinamo Kiev came to Moscow, things were quiet in the stadium. A number of fights broke out in the metro after the game, however. During the 1989 season, serious security measures were taken before, during, and after Spartak's April visit to Kiev. A few disorders erupted and a large number of bottles, knives, and other weapons were confiscated from fans.[35]

On November 10, 1988, during a European Champions Cup match against a Romanian team, young Spartak fans invaded the field after a game-long display of bottle throwing and drinking. According to the police, they had been chanting the following song throughout the first half:

> One fan, two fans will be an army
> One murder, two murders that's democracy
> We are the Moscow fans (*fanaty*)
> We are the punishers (*karateli*).

The crowd attempted to storm the field, leading to a bloody clash with police. Some made it onto the stadium floor. After the game, street battles continued outside the stadium and in the metro.[36] So feared had the Spartak *fanaty* become that their appearance at road games provoked special police measures in every town they visited. This, in turn, led local fans to take on the red-and-white-clad *fanaty*. In 1988, the supporters of Zhaligiris Vilnius went as far as to attack Spartak supporters after the game. The next year, several Vilnius toughs went one step further and beat up several players from Dniepr who were shopping in the town market before the game.[37]

These kinds of events were not limited to soccer. The championship basketball finals in 1988 between Zhalgiris Kaunas and TsSKA witnessed numerous postgame brawls when the series switched to Moscow. Even volleyball matches in Moscow were not immune to this phenomenon. Press accounts described those involved in the disorders as the young and the restless. Bored teenagers and disaffected, relatively nihilistic young workers dominated the newspaper accounts of fan violence. Much of the discussion revealed a generational split. Older commentators, not without some piety, denounced youths for acts that the elders claimed they could never possibly have committed.[38]

One theme in these discussions was the belief that the young "hooligans" were not especially interested in sports, soccer in particular. Unlike rioters in the national republics, the average Soviet soccer hooligan showed no special emotion if his team won or lost, nor did victories prevent outbreaks of violence. Instead, these *fanaty* were primarily interested in fighting, drinking, and other forms of disorderly conduct. As in England, sizable groups of young supporters traveled to away games despite the greater distances in the USSR, and wreaked havoc on trains and hotels along the way. In Tblisi, a small group of supporters of TsSKA, of ages between sixteen and twenty-three, journeyed from Moscow to support their soccer team. They drank, accosted old people, and demanded money. When they were refused, they beat up several pensioners.[39]

A *Sovetskii sport* reporter questioned several teen-agers after the brawls at the previously mentioned basketball finals. Their replies reflected a combination of the adolescent smart aleck and the alienated and cynical youth:

SS: Why do you root for TsSKA?
Fans: Because Spartak isn't playing. (*laughter*)
SS: Do you like basketball?
Fans: Yah. Until soccer begins. (*laughter*)
SS: What do you like most about being a "fan"?
Fans: That there's lot of us, that people fear us, and that it gives us a chance to fight.
SS: Do your parents know that you are "fans?"
Fans: What do we do? Report to them?
SS: Will there be fights today?
Fans: What do you think we're here for? [40]

Shortly after the riots in Kiev, *Sovetskii sport* published an interview with an Aleksei Osipov, who was described as a twenty-three-year-old worker at a Moscow watch factory. Osipov, a "fan" of TsSKA's soccer team, explained a distinction between "left" and "right" supporters. "Lefts" only attended home games, while the "rights," of which he was a member, traveled to away matches as well. He considered it an important matter of honor never to pay for a train ticket and claimed he had been riding free to games for over two years. Usually, Osipov said, "there is nothing to do in the towns we go to. Museums? Yeah, I saw the Hermitage in Leningrad, but usually we search out the places to drink. Before the game we get drunk. I do it just a little bit, but others get smashed. Why do we drink? It improves our mood and we root all the harder.... For me the main thing is the journey. I love the adventure."[41] The scope and violence of these disorders paled beside comparable events in Europe and Latin America. Nevertheless, the growth of conscious soccer hooliganism, as opposed to the occasional spontaneous riot, was further proof of the dangers and pathologies that so often accompanied spectator sports.

It must be noted that neither form of violence was specific to the period of perestroika, and there is some evidence to suggest that the *fanaty* became less antisocial when other forms of youth culture became more attractive than sports. It would not be possible to describe events of this type as any sort of organized or politically coherent form of resistance. No alternatives were offered, in the realm either of politics or of sports activity. Even the neo-Fascist and racist tone of much Western soccer hooliganism was largely absent. Rather, spectator sports became a vehicle through which broader forms of youthful alienation were expressed. Instead of operating as a spectacle for instilling certain desirable values, the sports event became a place for expressing anger and boredom—an arena for seizing a sense of strength and power that otherwise many young people did not feel.

The authorities did not seek to control these outbreaks simply by the application of greater force. In fact, police often watched helplessly as fans brawled, and very few arrests were made. Those failures prompted the usual calls for increased police presence and more forceful punishment of youthful offenders. The sports authorities took a different, more prophylactic approach to the rise in soccer hooliganism. In the wake of the 1987 Kiev events, the Administration for Soccer and Hockey called for the formation of team fan clubs (*kluby liubitetl'ei futbola*). Groups of this sort had long been a fixture in Europe and Latin America and had done little to stem the tide of violence associated with the sport. Nevertheless, in 1988, clubs were organized by several teams. Working with the Komsomol, these groups were supposed to educate young fans in proper behavior, and to offer meetings with coaches and players, videotapes of games, discotheques, and trips to away matches. The clubs did have some success in signing up members, but, predictably, they failed to attract the very *fanaty* whose behavior they were supposed to modify.[42]

In April 1989, Goskomsport invited several hundred of the *fanaty* to a Moscow meeting in order to discuss the problem and learn their desires. The meeting hall was filled with teen-agers wearing leather jackets and torn jeans. They dismissed the supporters' clubs as useless, and the organizer of one club was forced to agree. L. Makharinskii, secretary of the Central Army fan club, complained: "In my opinion this has occurred because the majority of the clubs were created, not by initiative from 'below,' but on orders from above, after the famous riots in the Kiev railroad station two years ago. As a result, our work suffers from a lack of organization. There is no real democracy. The *fanaty* don't come to us."[43]

Fan violence was always an implicit danger of any spectator sport, and even in the Soviet Union this wave of hooliganism was not unprecedented.[44] Some conservative observers sought to explain these disorders as a product of the relaxation of social controls during perestroika. Yet the phenomenon of soccer violence predated the reform period. What was new were the attitudes of the young fans. Spectator sports, with their partisanship and rooting, may inflame the emotions of the public, but the very cynicism of those interviewed by the press during perestroika would seem to indicate that such matters as team loyalty and game results were irrelevant to Soviet soccer hooligans. Earlier riots may have been the result of the excessive zeal of spectators, but the later wave of disorderly conduct was different.

Soccer violence by the *fanaty* was less a sports problem than a youth problem. As teen-agers and young workers shifted their interests from sports to rock and roll, disorders at Soviet stadiums began to take on their more traditional character. The 1991 field invasions at Donetsk and Erevan marked a return to the old-fashioned "kill-the-umpire" riot. The persistence of fan violence throughout Soviet history highlights the inherent difficulties involved in using spectator sports as a tool of social control. The spontaneity of the contests, the emotions of the players, and the often-tribal irrationality of many fans all undermined the orderliness with which spectator sport should have proceeded, if it were to have played its official function.

Public Attitudes: The Sociological View

Aside from these more impressionistic journalistic accounts, a limited number of sociological surveys of sports spectators were conducted by Soviet scholars both before and after 1985. One of the contributions of Western sports sociology has been a precise delineation of differing responses to sports by different social classes. This specificity, however, has not been possible when analyzing the Soviet sports fan. There was a long and rich tradition of time-budget studies dating back to the 1920s, but this research, when it even mentioned sports, only rarely made distinctions between participating and watching. There were very few surveys solely about sports spectating, and the subjects of these studies were always simply called "workers." It is, therefore, difficult to determine if low-level white-collar workers, factory managers, the technical-cultural intelligentsia, or Party officials responded to spectator sports in different ways from those who labored in factories.[45]

While the revival of the sociological profession in the USSR witnessed several serious examinations of both participant and spectator sports, many of the most detailed surveys on this topic were done ten or twenty years ago. I have, however, chosen to discuss all of them in this chapter, since the contrasts between the earlier and later surveys reveal the extent to which spectator sports can reflect broader changes in society. The more recent surveys reveal a sharp drop in public interest in all sports, and they particularly emphasize the erosion of the link between elite and mass sports. While these differences do raise the question of the accuracy of the earlier surveys, there is nevertheless abundant anecdotal evidence to confirm these trends.

A 1969 time-budget study of 407 industrial workers revealed what was called a "high level of interest in sports spectacles." Three-fourths of all male and female respondents said they read the sports press. Eighty-eight per cent watched sports on television, and sixty-four per cent attended events. A 1973 survey of metal workers in Magnitogorsk produced similar results.[46] This high level of involvement came during a period of rapid increase in leisure time and international success in the Olympics and elsewhere. The late 1960s and early 1970s were an era of excitement and newness with a gallery of attractive stars. By the late 1980s sports spectacles had become repetitive and less compelling, and attendance dropped.

Nevertheless, if public interest in spectator sports waned, they still proved to be far more popular than participant sports.[47] A 1986 study, as well as research from 1980, both by the dean of Soviet sports sociologists, Oleg Mil'shtein, revealed that the link between high-performance and participant sports had eroded extensively even before the years of perestroika.[48] A study by V. N. Sokolov and L. P. Polkova done at the same time, also showed that fans had become indifferent to the moral qualities big-time sports were supposed to instill.[49] A 1986 survey of Moscow workers by Ponomarchuk and Molchanov challenged the notion of vast public interest in sports. In contrast to earlier research, these authors concluded that less than thirty per cent of workers could be said to have a deep and serious interest in spectator sports and far fewer were involved in any form of participant sports.[50]

This research contrasted with a study from the late 'seventies done by L. P. Matveev and his collaborators who surveyed 243 industrial workers in an unnamed large industrial city.[51] They found that eighty per cent of the men and women they interviewed considered themselves "sports fans," but this large number encompassed a wide range of involvement. Fifty-eight per cent of those interviewed spent more than ten hours a week watching sports both on television and at the stadium, while only seven per cent did nothing. Matveev noted that women attended sports events 3.7 times *less* frequently than men did. Among men, the consumption of sports spectacles through television, the press, and game attendance was the third most popular leisure activity. Among women, sports spectating in all its forms rated the tenth most popular leisure activity.[52]

The survey revealed a considerable drop in game attendance among workers over the age of thirty, as males between twenty-six and thirty composed the largest group of those who regularly went to the stadium. The two commonest reasons given for attending sports events were interest in a local or national team and the excitement of seeing "fine-looking, physically developed people" perform great feats. Perhaps surprisingly, most age groups said they were more concerned with the fate of their local teams than that of national teams.

Equally surprisingly, a deep, expert knowledge of a particular sport was the least frequent reason workers gave for attending games. Previous participation in sports was equally rarely given as an explanation for workers' interest. In their research, Ponomarchuk and Molchanov actually found that the men most involved in watching sports were far less likely to engage in physical activity than were the fans with a casual interest in big-time sports.[53] This last finding is unusual since a number of studies in capitalist countries have asserted a link between participation and spectating.[54] This last point is extremely important. We have seen repeatedly that the historic function of the Soviet sports spectacle was the encouragement of exercise.[55] While the evidence here is limited, it does confirm the larger impressionistic finding that spectator sports did not play their assigned role. The link between *massovost'* and *masterstvo,* always tenuous, had been broken well before the coming of perestroika.

Along much these same lines, one of the historic staples of Soviet sports journalism was the "raid" on facilities for mass participation. There was no moment in Soviet history when such exposés did not reveal highly inadequate amenities and insufficient participation. Those interviewed in these articles always complained that they simply did not have the time to exercise regularly. After 1985, the press and television were still filled with such stories.[56] Viktor Artemov's 1981 study confirmed this picture. Only twenty-eight percent of urban residents replied that they regularly participated in sports, and John Bushnell has drawn similar conclusions from leisure-time studies conducted as early as the 1960s.[57]

Changing Modes of Production

The sports world was not untouched by the government's search for a new way of organizing the economy. A state that for decades had boasted of its generous support for sports could no longer afford to fund such matters of secondary importance. The institutions of the sports world had to scramble to generate whatever money they could. Yet this shift turned out to have a greater impact on the many sports that were part of the Olympic program. The team sports emphasized in this study were always less dependent on the government. The resources the state actually devoted to sports were not as lavish it claimed and outsiders believed. The various voluntary sports societies had long practiced a wide variety of ways of raising money on their own. State funding had been only one of the ways athletics were supported. While the changes begun under perestroika were certainly wrenching, it would be an exaggeration to say that the impact of the state's new priorities was immediately catastrophic in the sphere of spectator sports.

Funding—The crisis provoked by perestroika did not involve the sudden closing of what had been a freely flowing spigot. The Soviet government's limited emphasis on sports was always reflected in historically constrained budget support. Despite the elaborate lip-service paid to sports, there were always more important political, social, economic, and even cultural concerns. The pressing needs of *perestroika* further decreased what had already been limited support. As James Riordan has shown, sports historically had a low budget priority. While the total amount spent on sports rose between 1946 and 1958, they did not increase their share of the total state budget. By 1970, 0.03 per cent of the budget went to sports, the same percentage as in

1924.[58] This amount, however, was never the entire picture. Other state institutions, notably the Ministry of the Defense and the Ministry of Interior, devoted a considerable portion of their monies to sports. So did the trade unions, which, before perestroika, had little to do with their members' dues. Much of the money to support the teams in the major Soviet leagues had come from sources outside the state budget. Trade unions and factories devoted a considerable portion of their means (10–15 per cent) to both participant and spectator sports.[59] For the sports societies, ticket sales for games involving their teams was always an important source of funds.[60] Modest membership dues also provided some revenue, as did the rental of facilities and the organization of social events. Lotteries, long a feature of the West European sports scene, were first organized by the sports committee in the 1960s. By 1987, some lotteries were actually tied to the correct prediction of game results in the major sports.[61] Such practices clearly opened up possibilities for corruption and game-fixing. No such scandal linked to the lottery was reported publicly, no doubt because the prizes were not grand enough to compensate for what would be the considerable cost of rigging a game.

The sports committee was also able to generate monies on its own, long before perestroika. The sale of *Sovetskii sport* was a constant source of rubles, and for many years the appearances of Soviet athletes abroad generated a great deal of hard currency. The 1987 United States tour of the Soviet national basketball team, one of many examples, netted $300,000. The appearance of the soccer team in the finals of the 1988 European Championship was worth two million dollars. Tours of gymnasts, figure skaters, hockey teams, and many others were a long-standing source of the hard currency needed to continue supplying elite athletes with the best-quality equipment, little of which could ever be purchased domestically.[62]

If one were to include the nongovernment sources of revenue, the total percentage of the Soviet gross national product spent on sports and physical culture was estimated by Soviet economists to be no more the 0.46 per cent in 1988.[63] This figure compares to two or three per cent in most West European countries. The contrast is even more staggering with the United States, where sports, in all forms, were a fifty-five-billion-dollar business in 1988.[64] If the USSR was, as it claimed, the greatest sporting nation on earth, then it managed to achieve this status with a minimal expenditure of what must be seen as scarce resources. By comparison, Western societies during this same period gave much more of their wealth to sports.

Professionalism and Khozraschet—Faced with the need to generate their own revenues, Goskomsport, the various federations, and the sports societies responded to the demands of perestroika by exploring the possibilities of commercialization and open professionalization. They did this, however, with a confusing mix of ambivalence and inexperience that make it difficult to characterize the embrace of professionalism and all its consequences as a new and consistent policy. Instead, there was tremendous uncertainty about how far to go in imitating Western practices. The embrace of open professionalism did, on one level, represent a break from what had been recent practice, but it was not entirely unprecedented in Soviet history.

As I have noted, official amateurism had been the by-product of the government's decision to join the Olympic movement after the Second World War.[65] Soon, however, it became clear to outsiders that the ''soldiers'' and ''students'' who were producing so many victories were engaged in something far more time-consuming than a mere hobby. As a result, Western representatives demanded changes in Olympic standards of eligibility in order to allow the best capitalist athletes to compete. Professionals were then permitted to take part in a number of Olympic sports. At the same time, some previously amateur sports, most notably basketball and track and field, reorganized on an open basis. The Soviets found that the professionalization of amateurism they had fostered as part of their state sports system had become standard practice throughout the rest of the world. By the 1988 Olympics they realized that the time had come to drop the veil and eliminate the hypocrisies of official amateurism.

During perestroika, the state came to insist that most institutions and enterprises had to become self-sustaining to survive. This shift was caused by the revival of the long-familiar but poorly understood concept of *khozraschet*. The Russian term always had a number of meanings, ranging from something as seemingly minor as ''cost-accounting'' to a far more problematic notion of ''profitability.'' *Khoraschet* had been part of the mixed economy of the New Economic Policy, but it did not entirely disappear, even with the early Five-Year Plans. Thus, no one was certain just what the term signified in the context of perestroika. As a result, the movement toward the open professionalization of sports was inconsistent.

If sports entertainments were to stand on their own, the process had to start with the most-watched sports; but given the attendance problems, this change was not a simple process. Accordingly, the first experiments were in soccer, and the first team to declare itself to be fully professional was Dniepr of Dniepropetrovsk, the champion in 1983 and after that a leading contender for the title. Led by its dynamic chief executive, Gennadii Zhizdik, Dniepr reorganized its practices, severing its historic ties to mass soccer in the city. In order to survive financially, the team proposed to make the bulk of its money from the sale of tickets, optimistically projecting an average attendance of thirty thousand (in a 35,000-seat stadium). Funds also were to come from memberships in the Dniepr supporters' club, along with the sale of souvenirs, programs, and other paraphernalia. While the team was to be formally independent from its long-time patron, the huge Southern Machine Tool Factory, it continued to look to this enterprise for financial support, which now was to be given in the form of commercial sponsorship. Additionally, the soccer team became part of an ensemble of other enterprises, some of them private (called "cooperatives" at the time). The effect of this last step was to have a body that could absorb some of the team's possible losses.

Players and coaches signed three-year contracts, and a larger portion of their pay was to come from performance bonuses. Dniepr also proposed to take the unprecedented step of officially rewarding players differentially, based on individual performance. The players were consulted and publicly approved of the step, but they did not have an actual vote in making the change.[66] They may not have been enamored of the new approach, since the new structure created more insecurity for the players, who were now under pressure to perform at a high level so the team might win, draw fans, and make money.[67]

At the end of the 1987 season, in which Dniepr finished second, it lost two of its stars, Oleg Protasov and Gennadii Litovchenko, to Dinamo Kiev. The new professional structure was not cited as a reason for these departures. The players instead claimed that moving to Dinamo Kiev enhanced their chances of being named by Lobanovskii to the national team. Dniepr complained that both players had been trained in their schools and had spent seven years with the team. Having trained them, Dniepr was now to lose them without any compensation; but such was the power of Dinamo Kiev that Dniepr's complaints were ignored.

As it turned out, the 1988 season was extremely successful for Dniepr on the field. They led the first division for most of the season and won the championship. Their leading rivals, Spartak and Dinamo Kiev, were weakened by selling outstanding players in the middle of the season to foreign clubs. Dniepr's success on the field, however, did not lead to an increase in attendance. Team officials cited local transportation problems and difficulties in distributing tickets throughout the city. Fans complained that the concerts and lotteries, organized to make the games more festive, required the team to charge more for tickets, making what had been a reasonable expense now a costly one.[68] Ultimately, the machine-works had to supply financial assistance to the team, and those monies, plus considerable profit from the sale of advertising to Soviet firms, permitted Dniepr to break even.

After the 1989 season, Zhizdik would leave the team, further weakening its financial picture. By 1990, the Dniepr experiment had proven a failure. Attendance, as it did everywhere during the economic crisis, continued to plummet, and the team had to be reorganized as part of a new ensemble of private enterprises. Zhizdik, who would die in 1992, had moved on to second-division Metallurg of Zaparozh'e, which he reorganized as part of a complex of cooperatives, and the next season his new team had won promotion to the first division.[69]

In 1988, however, the experiment of Dniepr would be deemed sufficiently successful for other clubs to follow suit. Spartak, Ararat, Dinamo Tblisi, Shakhter, and Zenit all took the plunge.[70] Dinamo Kiev expressed similar intentions, but their plans raised problems. The Kiev club's massive popular support (a league-leading average of 40,000 per game in 1988) made it particularly well suited to the opportunities created by *khozraschet*. Yet, as a member of the national Dinamo Society, subject to the demands and disciplines of the state security agencies, the team's intentions raised a number of contradictions, and the step was delayed for a season.

Enthusiasm for self-financing was not universally shared. The responsibilities of the sports societies had always gone beyond the fielding of teams in the big-time team sports. They also trained younger players and made their facilities available for mass sports. As they relinquished financial responsibility for participant sports, the societies further distanced their teams from the rest of their work. Ticket sales for their teams had been a principal source of society revenues, which were then used to support mass participation. Accordingly, the heads of not only the Dinamo societies but Spartak as well expressed fears that without the money from big-time sports, mass participation would wither even further.[71]

There were also potential political and ideological ramifications to the process of professionalization. The requirement of self-financing posed a threat to the dominance of big-time sports by the army and the Dinamo societies. As state organizations of special importance to the government, the Ministry of Defense and the Ministry of the Interior had been generously funded, and they, in turn, had generously funded their teams. But if clubs supported by other entities could generate their own funds, new groups could begin to compete on a more even basis with the army and Dinamo teams. Since one of the instrumental roles of Soviet spectator sports had been the creation of the healthy role-model, it was always especially desirable for the state that sports heroes be guardians of order, either soldiers or policemen. It was feared that professionalization might diminish the success of these teams, allowing new, independent civilian heros to emerge, a process that would undermine big-time spectator sports' ability to teach official values.[72]

The concerns of more traditional sports administrators, therefore, gave rise to much public doubt about the trend toward open professionalization. During 1989, several Dinamo athletes, in an open letter to *Sovetskii sport,* reminded the public about the great tradition of military athletes and rejected charges of elitism from those outside the world of military sports. Early in 1989, the 1988 Olympic pole-vault champion, Sergei Bubka (then in an army sports club), published a lengthy front-page letter in *Sovetskii sport,* along with several other army athletes. He and his collaborators defended the long-standing practices of Soviet sports. The thrust of the article, however, was an attack on the world chess champion, Gary Kasparov, who a few weeks earlier had called for open professionalism in a controversial and bitter interview that appeared in the pro-perestroika weekly *Ogonek.*[73]

The flamboyant Kasparov created an immense stir with his remarks, going beyond the demand for professionalization to attack Goskomsport. He decried the deterioration of mass sports, which, he claimed, had been neglected in the name of producing an elite of Olympic medal-winners, and he criticized Goskomsport and its commercial agents for the arbitrariness and inefficiency with which they had negotiated contracts for Soviet athletes competing in the West. Bubka and his colleagues accused *Ogonek* of sensationalism and personally attacked Kasparov, who was then defended in an open letter to *Sovetskii sport* signed by former basketball great Sergei Belov and eleven other notables. Belov and his allies described the Bubka letter as a document reminiscent of the ''era of stagnation.'' They said it was necessary to differentiate between the abrasiveness of Kasparov's personality and the substantial correctness of his remarks.[74]

The Brawn Drain—Faced with mounting financial difficulties, Goskomsport and many clubs sought to raise hard currency through a variety of sponsorship deals with foreign firms. A separate body, called *Sovintersport,* was set up in 1987 to handle all sports contacts with foreign entities, and Soviet national teams began to carry advertising for Western companies on their uniforms. Soccer clubs taking part in the European cup competitions had already been wearing the names of foreign firms, and an Italian company put its logo on the jerseys of several teams during domestic league games as well. Following this example, several Soviet enterprises purchased space on the uniforms of both the Spartak and Dinamo Moscow hockey uniforms, and *Sovetskii sport* urged Soviet companies to establish sponsor relationships with certain teams. The newspaper even went as far as to suggest using prominent athletes as spokespersons for the products of those firms.[75]

By far the largest source of hard currency, however, was earned by the selling of Soviet athletes to foreign teams. Beginning in 1987, both Goskomsport and the clubs managed to keep afloat by allowing their players to compete for teams in Western Europe and North America. The first attempts along these lines were halting and poorly negotiated. Initially, several soccer stars over thirty were signed to less-than-lucrative contracts in Finland and Austria. These included Dinamo Kiev's Oleg Blokhin, who played in 1987 and 1988 for a team in the Austrian second division.[76] These contracts were severely criticized in the Soviet press for being way below the proper international market value even for such older players.

By the summer of 1988, the situation would change dramatically. The Soviet soccer team finished second in the European Cup and Sovintersport had learned important lessons. The 1986 Soviet player of the year, Dinamo Kiev's Alexander Zavarov, was sold to the Italian team Juventus for five million dollars, while Spartak's national-team defender Vagiz Khidiatulin was transferred to the French club Toulouse for less money. Soon thereafter, Spartak's Rinat Dasaev, voted the best goalkeeper in the world for 1988, was dealt to Seville of Spain for more than two million dollars.[77] In the years after those first deals, dozens of Soviet players went to England, Spain, France, Germany, Greece, and Sweden, as well as Spain and Italy. Initially, only those who had passed their twenty-eighth birthday were allowed to leave, but as the nation's financial crisis deepened, this barrier was dropped. Players still at the peak of their careers, like Protasov and Litovchenko of Dinamo Kiev, signed with European teams for sums that were not disclosed but that must be considered substantial.

It was long common for the leading soccer stars of Europe and Latin America to play for teams outside their homelands. In most cases, this practice did not prevent them from performing for their national teams. In European soccer, the Soviets had come to engage in a practice that was long considered a normal part of the world soccer scene. Nevertheless, the novelty of the step inspired great public interest, and *Sovetskii sport* provided extensive and continuing coverage of the performances of the first "foreign legion." The fact that the leading teams of Europe were interested in Soviet players was a reason for pride, and the Soviet fan was intensely curious about their chances for success.

There was, however, fear that the exodus of the country's best players would erode interest in domestic competition, and in the 1989 season, attendance declined considerably despite a closely contested race. It was good that Soviet players were wanted by the sport's powers, but it was not desirable that the domestic league become a farm system for Western Europe. Many team officials, though, argued that the sale of veterans to foreign clubs actually prevented stagnation and gave opportunities for younger players to advance. They were not altogether wrong, as the 1990 season revealed a galaxy of new stars, including Sergei Iuran of Dinamo Kiev, Igor Shalimov of Spartak, Andrei Kanchel'skis of Shakhter, and Igor Dobrovolskii of Dinamo Moscow. Yet no sooner had this new galaxy emerged than they, too, were offered contracts in Western Europe, and none of them finished the 1991 season playing in the Soviet first division.

Their emergence also did not bring fans back to the stands. The Soviets' disastrous performance in the 1990 World Cup and the worsening economic crisis combined to reduce attendance to 14,000 per game. The first of the "foreigners" (Zavarov, Dasaev, and Khidiatulin) had performed poorly at the World Cup, confirming fears about the impact of a "football diaspora."[78] The loss of such stars clearly did hurt the short-term interests of both the clubs and the national team, but their presence in Europe was seen as part of a process of normalization Soviet sports had to pass through. As the nation's crisis deepened, the hard currency earned by these deals became even more desperately needed. With attendance dwindling and no near prospect of increased television revenues, many clubs came to survive entirely by the sale of players and by foreign tours. Even Spartak found itself in this situation, with often-disastrous results for its on-the-field performance.[79]

Valerii Lobanovskii, in response to criticism about the sale of Zavarov, replied that with five million dollars he could develop another five Zavarovs. In fact, Dinamo Kiev saw only two million dollars of this money. The rest was split between Goskomsport, the Football Federation, and the state budget. Even this kind of distribution was disputed by the various interested Soviet parties, and set rules and procedures were not established as each participating group sought its piece of the action. The case of Dinamo Kiev's player sales proved even more embarrassing in 1991, when it became known that much of the money raised by the sale of players to foreign clubs was not even going back into the club's soccer operation. Instead, the hard currency was used to fund a number of dubious business ventures, few of which had anything to do with sports. Nor was the team's reputation enhanced when it was revealed that they had cooperated in a tax-evasion scam with the Greek team whom they had sold Protasov and Litovchenko to, both of whom had come over from Dniepr just two years earlier.[80] For that player transfer, Dniepr did not receive a kopeck.

In basketball, a few older players were allowed in 1987 to play for what were then officially "amateur" teams in Finland and Spain. After April 1989, however, the FIBA declared basketball an open sport, and two young Soviet stars were given permission to play in the National Basketball Association. Sarunas Marciulionis, a Lithuanian guard who had played for the gold-medal-winning 1988 Soviet Olympic team, signed a contract with the Golden State Warriors of the NBA and Alexander Volkov, also an Olympic champion, agreed to play with the Atlanta Hawks. At the same time, the great Lithuanian center Arvidas Sabonis rejected the Portland Trail Blazers' longstanding offer and reached an agreement with a Spanish professional team, as did his Zhalgiris teammate Waldemaras Khomichus. Other basketball players signed to play in West Germany and Finland, and a sizable number of female players joined teams in Western Europe. These actions were viewed by Soviet basketball specialists with much the same ambivalence as their soccer counterparts. While all were intrigued by the possibilities of the situation, some experts feared a similar "basketball diaspora" would kill domestic interest in the sport.[81] Others suggested that with the coming of competition against American professionals, it was necessary to send players to America to learn how the game is played at the highest level.[82] Sadly, it would turn out that both sides in this debate were correct.

The situation in ice hockey proved to be more confused than in any other sport. For many years, North American teams had drafted Soviet players, and when professionals were allowed to take part in the 1988 Olympics, the last barrier to Soviet stars' signing with the National Hockey League was removed. It was widely expected in the West that after the Calgary Games the veteran captain of TsSKA and the national team, Viacheslav Fetisov, would be allowed to play for the New Jersey Devils. Fetisov wanted to play in the NHL, but he did not wish to defect. He resigned his officer's commission and obtained the signature of his coach, Tikhonov, on the necessary documents. Yet, several months later, Fetisov still had not been allowed to leave. He claimed that, while Tikhonov had given formal permission, the coach was dragging his feet behind the scenes, causing the Ministry of Defense to delay acceptance of Fetisov's resignation from the army.[83]

Ultimately, the first Soviet player to sign with a National Hockey League team came instead from *Krylia sovetov,* a trade-union team that the more conservative Ministry of Defense had no control over. Sergei Priakhin signed to play for the Calgary Flames in March 1989 at the close of the regular Soviet hockey season. The relatively young Priakhin, who on occasion had played for the national team, was considered expendable for the world championships, held in April 1989. Ultimately, it proved easier for a less visible and controversial figure to be the first to make this historic step; but no sooner had Priakhin joined the Flames than the situation was further confused by the defection of Alexander Mogilnyi, a young forward from TsSKA, who did not return to Moscow with the national team after their victory in the 1989 World Championship in Sweden. Instead, Mogilnyi went to the United States, where he joined the Buffalo Sabres of the National Hockey League, the first time a Soviet hockey player had ever defected.[84]

Earlier that year, Mogilnyi had been involved in the most violent on-ice fight in recent memory, severely injuring a Spartak player. Mogilnyi was suspended for ten games, docked a month's pay, and stripped of his title of "honored master of sport."[85] Mogilnyi's defection, in turn, distressed representatives of the National Hockey League, who had been working for years to improve relations with the Soviet hockey federation and Goskomsport. At the heart of both the defection and the complaints of Fetisov and Igor Larionov was the estrangement between the players of TsSKA and their coach, Tikhonov.

By the middle of May 1989, the Ministry of Defense had not yet acted on the requests of TsSKA's stars, who were still asking to be relieved of their army commissions. This foot-dragging persisted despite the publicly expressed willingness of Goskomsport to allow the players to sign with the NHL teams holding their rights. The situation changed soon after a May 18 meeting of the ice hockey federation at which Larionov spoke, repeating his complaints against Tikhonov and accusing the coach of striking Mogilnyi during the Calgary Olympics. Larionov also argued that thousands of Soviet specialists were working abroad where "they labor honestly and gain hard currency for the nation," and he claimed that hockey players should be treated no differently.

Tikhonov then rose to defend himself. Since he had punched Mogilnyi in full public view during the last, inconsequential game of the Olympics, Tikhonov was in no position to deny the accusation. Instead he claimed that he had documents concerning Fetisov and Larionov, which, if he were to operate "according to the principles of glasnost," would send the two away for six to eight years. The accusations concerning Tikhonov's treatment of Mogilnyi, however, may have had an effect on the Ministry of Defense. Larionov, who had elsewhere criticized Mogilnyi for defecting, nevertheless had provided a plausible explanation for Mogilnyi's act. Perhaps fearing further defections, the army freed the players from their commissions a week after the meeting of the hockey federation.

As a parting shot, Fetisov and Larionov published an open letter in *Sovetskii sport* challenging Tikhonov to release the so-called incriminating documents in his possession. They said such acts were typical of Tikhonov's treatment of players, and they accused him of blackmail. "We consider such an attitude toward people to be inconsistent with democratic government. It is an anachronism from the times of Stalin."[86] Soon thereafter, both players, plus TsSKA defenseman Sergei Starikov, and Larionov's linemates Sergei Makarov and Vladimir Krutov, signed contracts with the NHL.[87]

Very few of the first wave of Soviet athletes distinguished themselves. In soccer, Zavarov came under heavy criticism for his play with Juventus, where he was not given a translator and was forced to play out of position. Dasaev had similar difficulties when, after his first season, he was dropped from Seville's starting lineup in favor of a Spanish goalkeeper. Of the hockey players, only Sergei Makarov performed well in his first year, winning the NHL "Rookie of the Year" Award. As for the basketball players, neither Volkov nor Marciulionis received much playing time in his first season. By 1991, however, Marciulionis had established himself as a first-rate player. Volkov, however, had been forced to sit out his second year with an injury and continued to struggle with the difficulties of adapting to the American style of play until a teammate's injury at last gave him adequate playing time. Afforded an opportunity, Volkov was able to demonstrate that he, too, was a solid professional.

Many of the older athletes, who dominated the first wave, found it difficult to adjust to living on their own in the West. Throughout their playing careers they had lived in dormitories where they were fed and watched. Having to feed and transport themselves proved disorienting and difficult. Many were not up to the task. When Soviet athletes, who had long been considered professionals by those outside the USSR, came to play in the West, it turned out that they were less, not more, disciplined than Western professionals, who were subject to fines for all manner of infractions and who knew their livelihood depended on their performance. Soviet coaches, as it turned out, actually had less control over their players than Western coaches, and the Soviet athletes who came to play in the West had difficulty adapting to the new situation. Many of them learned that the tyranny of their coaches and the lack of democracy they had experienced as elite athletes were intensified rather than diminished in the West.

By 1990, with younger, more adaptable players going abroad, the situation improved. While Protasov, Litovchenko, and Iurii Savichev of Torpedo played well for Olympiakos of Piraeus, Aleksei Mikhailichenko of Dinamo Kiev was forced to play out of position at Sampadoria Genoa, after which he was purchased for more than three million dollars by Glasgow Rangers, the same team that earlier had signed Mikhailichenko's Dinamo Kiev teammate, Oleg Kuznetsov. Once in Scotland, Mikhailichenko would play well and lead Rangers to the title. Shakhter's young national-team attacker, Andrei Kanchel'skis, found a regular place in the lineup of Manchester United in the fall of 1991.

During the 1990–1991 season, several younger hockey players showed promise in the NHL, although the best Soviet newcomer was the Detroit Red Wings' twenty-year-old Sergei Feodorov, who, like Mogilnyi, had defected from TsSKA. By the next season, the situation had improved even further. Eighteen Soviets were playing in the NHL. Dmitrii Khristych of the Washington Capitals, Andre Lomakin of the Philadelphia Flyers, and Sergei Nemchinov of the New York Rangers were among their team's leading scorers. Fetisov, who had been joined in 1990 by his fellow TsSKA defenseman and personal enemy Aleksei Kasatonov, began to play better after initial difficulties. With the addition of TsSKA's twenty-year-old Pavel Bure to the Vancouver Canucks, Larionov's play finally reached the level that had been expected of him for two seasons. Feodorov, who had made his peace with the Soviet hockey authorities, and Mogilnyi, who had not, were invited to play in the 1992 All-Star Game.[88]

By the end of 1991, the process of adaptation appeared to be complete and successful. It had taken three years for former Soviet athletes to find their way in the West, longer than most had anticipated. Once younger athletes were allowed to leave, they proved far more flexible in adjusting to life in the world of capitalist, high-performance spectator sports. Eventually, many Soviet hockey and basketball players found that the leagues of Western Europe made for an easier transition than the NBA and the NHL. Europe offered less taxing and less frequent competition. There were fewer games, and the caliber of opposition was weaker than in North America. Also, many financially successful European clubs could make economically competitive offers, in some cases outbidding American teams. Especially in basketball, only those truly dedicated to performing at the highest level chose to play in North America, where they were offered less money and even less playing time. Older and less ambitious players soon found working in Europe to be a preferable alternative to the rigors of North American schedules.

New Attitudes Toward an Old Professionalism—At a May 1989 symposium, K. Romenskii, an assistant to the director of Goskomsport's economic administration, remarked on the changes in the world of Soviet sports: "Once we covered professionalism with the figleaf of amateurism and considered the question to have been resolved. Now, we have learned to look truth in the eye. We are doing much to bring sport into harmony with the realities of our economic and social life."[89] As we have seen, this new situation was created by the opportunities that came with commercialization and open professionalization, but these new practices also created their own problems. The attitudes of players, coaches, fans, journalists, and team administrators began to change under the pressures created by the new practices of organizing and presenting Soviet spectator sports.

At no moment in Soviet history had the rights and obligations of coaches, players, and teams ever been clearly delineated by any set of rules or laws.[90] Certain customs and norms did develop, but they were continually violated when it proved convenient for powerful parties to do so. Under the impact of perestroika, however, it was necessary to elaborate new rules and procedures consistent with the demands and opportunities of the new order. This process proved highly contentious, and, while some progress was made, it had only begun to be elaborated when the failed coup of August 1991 further complicated the task of reorganizing spectator sports on a fully professional basis.

Open professionalism put special burdens on athletes. While outsiders had long felt that Soviet state professionals worked harder than Western amateurs, Soviet coaches and officials had for some time feared that their high-performance athletes worked with less seriousness and discipline than did Western professionals. The experience of those Soviet athletes who went to play in foreign leagues confirmed those fears. Soviet coaches did not fine players for training infractions, and suspensions for violating discipline, while not uncommon, required serious transgressions. Even as tradition-minded a figure as Tretiak suggested that the lack of insecurity facing the elite Soviet athlete made him or her less motivated than the Western pro.[91] In Tretiak's sense of the term, "professional" implied a serious and disciplined approach to one's work regardless of the formal label applied by particular rules of eligibility.

For others like Mikhailichenko, the term signified an honest approach to the work one actually did. When asked in 1988 if Soviet soccer should be organized on a professional basis, Mikhailichenko had replied, "Football in these times, at its highest level, is a profession like any other."[92] The same sentiments were echoed by Nikita Simonian, who was serving as chief organizer of the Soviet national soccer team: "Football is a profession, a means of earning an income. We must have legalisation of the professional status of football players. It is, for them, work."[93]

Other sports authorities came to accept the fact that open professionalism would change the social role of big-time sports and force changes in decades-old practices. During the same 1989 symposium at which Romenskii spoke, A. Kolesov, a vice-president of Goskomsport, remarked on the changed climate:

> How should we define big-time sport today? As a show, as a highly profitable vehicle for advertising, or as a form of human self-expression?. . .It is clear that such sport is developing its own structures. It is less and less tied directly to mass sport. To develop an athlete at the highest level, it is no longer necessary to have millions engaging in participant sport. . . .The task of the day is to reduce the numbers of those professionally involved in sport. . . .We are ready to give more to each athlete and his coach, but to do this we must narrow the circle of those involved in big-time sport.[94]

Throughout Soviet history, the link between elite sports and mass participation may have always been more apparent than real. Yet, at the very least, this particular relationship had been one of the distinguishing elements of Communist sports theory. Under the impact of professionalization, that relationship, already highly attenuated, was even more severely threatened.

Under conditions of open professionalism, relationships between coaches and players also began to evolve, and a number of conflicts arose quite quickly. Yet it was not clear if the limited authority of coaches was weakened or strengthened by the process of professionalization. Soviet athletes who played abroad regularly emphasized the system of fines used by Western teams to assure discipline. On the other hand, the traditional Soviet practice of having players live at training bases during their seasons had always exposed athletes to arbitrary actions and closer supervision by coaches.[95]

Like their counterparts in the West, Soviet coaches were completely insecure in their relationship with the administration of the sports society that employed them. Midseason dismissals were as common as, if not more common than, in the West.[96] One highly celebrated case of just such an unexpected dismissal occurred the winter before the 1989 soccer season. Konstantin Beskov, who had coached Spartak's soccer team for twelve highly successful years, found himself removed from his position after a dispute over player selection with Nikolai Starostin, who, at the age of ninety, was still the team's president. It was announced that Beskov, then sixty-five years old, had retired.[97] Given the stature of both men as major figures in the development of Soviet soccer, and in light of Beskov's run of success with Spartak, his dismissal was seen as a particularly telling example of the insecurity of the Soviet coach. In the wake of Beskov's dismissal, Spartak team members were asked to choose, by secret ballot, their next coach. By all accounts, this was a genuinely democratic and honest process, the kind that would never occur in a capitalist league. The players chose a former Spartak mid-fielder and assistant coach, Oleg Rumiantsev, and under his guidance, Spartak started the season successfully, playing in much the same style as Beskov's teams and ultimately winning the 1989 championship.[98]

Player Movement—Because player movement had historically been one of the shadier aspects of Soviet sport, it was hoped that new rules could clarify the situation. The problem, as always, was most acute in soccer. Lawyers for the Football Federation suggested in 1990 that players sign contracts, usually for three years. When that term was finished, the player was free to sign with anyone else he wished.[99] While some of the trends involved in professionalization may have given athletes greater power, the creation of a contract system binding players to a particular team actually weakened their positions. Until then it had been relatively easy for a dissatisfied player to quit his team and find work elsewhere the next season.

In the past, there had been neither player trades nor sales of contracts that forced athletes to go to cities they did not want to live in. Published sources rarely revealed the real reasons for a player's desire to move. Those who applied to the federation for permission to transfer had usually given a variety of blatantly fictitious reasons for their desire to change teams.[100] Until 1989, the team losing a player in a transfer received no compensation, but it took one highly controversial case, in the new environment of perestroika, to change all that.

On the eve of the 1989 soccer season, Oleg Salenko, a young forward for Leningrad Zenit and a star of the national junior team, applied to transfer to Dinamo Kiev.[101] Zenit had played well in the 1988 season but had undergone much internal turmoil. They objected to losing one of their few first-rate talents. In particular, they were outraged by the fact that Lobanovskii, having sold several mature players to European teams, was now attempting to restock Dinamo at the expense of weaker Soviet teams.[102] It seemed to many that Lobanovskii was using all of Soviet soccer as a farm system for Dinamo Kiev, which would then continue to make profits by selling those players abroad. The original clubs received nothing. Protasov and Litovchenko, for example, had spent the best years of their careers with Dniepr. They had been trained in the team's schools, but Dinamo Kiev, not Dniepr, pocketed the massive fees for their transfers.

After considerable discussion, the Football Federation's technical committee gave permission for Salenko's transfer on the grounds that his desire to move to one of the nation's leading teams was "completely understandable." A few days later, however, the presidium of the federation, as was its right, annulled Salenko's transfer. Their decision overlooked one crucial detail. Salenko, along with his entire family, had already moved to Kiev, where the team had installed them in a large apartment.[103] Salenko's reasons for seeking the transfer could have been given by any promising star in any country: "It sounds childish, but ever since I was a kid, I have rooted for Dinamo Kiev.... The main thing, of course, is the unlimited perspectives for growth. The Kiev team is a window on European soccer.... I have done this all openly and honestly. People in Leningrad have no reason to be angry with me."[104] Officials of Dinamo protested the presidium's decision and threatened to go to court. They claimed the federation had violated the Soviet Constitution, which guaranteed both the right to work and freedom in choosing one's place of residence. To any Soviet citizen who had longed and waited for permission to live in Moscow, Leningrad, or any other large city, this particular legal claim, even in the context of perestroika, seemed absurd.

Fearing a decline in attendance and demanding compensation for their years of training Salenko, officials of Zenit demanded half a million rubles from Dinamo. Ultimately, the Adminstration for Football and Hockey intervened and set the sum at 37,000 rubles. This amount was established according to published instructions on transfers that the administration had presented during the winter at a special seminar in Leningrad on the economics of the new professional structures. The standard compensation fee for any first-division player was to be 25,000 rubles. If he were a member of the national team, that amount would be doubled; and if, like Salenko, he were on the junior team, the fee would be increased by fifty per cent. Salenko played for Dinamo in 1989 with mixed success, but for Zenit the results were disastrous, as they wound up finishing next to last and were relegated to the second division for 1990.

The Salenko affair led to the payment of the first legal and above-board transfer fee in the history of Soviet sports, and it seemed that one of the iron laws of capitalist sports had been established. Rich teams succeeded and poor ones failed. Weaker teams in smaller cities could be expected to find such payments burdensome, although the presence of some local "patron" still could create possibilities even for those on the periphery. By 1991, though, the contract system seemed to have taken effect, and many stransfers were blocked because the contracts of the players in question had not expired. The most visible such case involved Sergei Iuran, who had been prepared to move to Spartak but was required to stay with Dinamo Kiev.[105] Soon thereafter, however, he would be sold to the famous Portuguese team, Benfica, with Dinamo getting the fee.

All the changes that came with open professionalization forced teams to raise ticket prices, but the sluggish market for spectator sports was not able to support such developments. Professional sports in the West had historically been fanned by the public's enormous appetite for this form of entertainment. While there remained a latent desire for sports among Soviet citizens, it was far from clear such a desire was sufficiently extensive to support a freestanding professional sports system, especially in the context of the economic crisis, which robbed spectators of the leisure time they needed to get out to the stadiums.[106]

The Life and Death of the Soccer Union—The debate concerning the restructuring of big-time soccer in the USSR proved highly controversial. On August 2, 1987, the Council of Ministers, the trade unions, and the Komsomol issued a joint resolution calling for the creation of a "Soccer Union." This new organization was to replace many of the functions of the existing Football Federation and put the sport on the openly professional basis so many had been calling for. Late in 1988, the Administration for Soccer and Hockey, headed by Viacheslav Koloskov, published a draft charter for the new union.[107] These steps were taken in conjunction with representatives of the trade unions, the Komsomol, the Ministry of Defense, and the Dinamo societies. Thus, these first documents to frame the debate over professionalization expressed the views of established sports bureuacrats rather than the opinions of coaches, players, journalists, and fans.

Consistent with the demands of *khozraschet,* the new organization was to divorce big-time soccer from its responsibilities in the field of mass participation. The Union was to conduct the annual league season, support clubs taking part in European cup tournaments, and organize national teams for various international competitions. The old federation was to continue to organize participant and youth soccer. Koloskov's group envisioned a league in which self-financing teams would co-exist with the traditionally state-supported clubs. Distinctions (soon to be meaningless) were drawn between full professionals and those formally in the armed forces.[108]

As soon as these proposals were published, they provoked a hail of criticism. The loudest outcry came from those who earned their livings from the sport—players, coaches, team officials, referees, and journalists. The critics of the draft charter focused their attention on what had been omitted or neglected. *Sovetskii sport* published a wide variety of letters, most of them from professional insiders. Many, including Lev Iashin, complained that the new group did not differ much from the old federation. Others argued that insufficient attention had been paid to the legal consequences of the planned reform, while the presidents of teams complained of the virtual omission of any concern for financial matters.[109] When the founding conference of the union was held in Moscow on December 13, 1988, the players, coaches, and administrators who attended were still extremely dissatisfied with the proposed shape of the new body.

Lobanovskii and other Dinamo Kiev officials advanced an alternative charter for what they called a "Union of Football Leagues." This group was to unite the clubs of all three divisions of Soviet soccer in a "self-administered organ" of Goskomsport that would be a separate juridical entity and have complete financial independence. Lobanovskii sought to create an autonomous organization of soccer professionals that would be free of bureaucratic tutelage and able to raise revenues on its own. Lobanovskii said his new group was to be based on a rigorous concept of legality in which the rights and obligations of players, coaches, and teams would be clarified and protected. To put it most simply, Lobanovskii and his allies were asking to be left alone in order that they, not the state, might run a soccer enterprise.[110]

The debate produced by the conflicting proposals was, to borrow a phrase, stormy and prolonged. A fundamental issue had been raised. Would control of the Soviet Union's most popular sport remain in the hands of the state and Party figures who had tried to shape it for official ends, or would soccer pass into the control of an elite of trained experts who sought to protect their own positions, while producing entertainment for the public? After much wrangling, the conference ultimately decided to form a new editing commission to rework the charter. A second meeting was scheduled for later in the spring of 1989.[111]

The new editing commission met in Moscow on January 5, 1989. According to the later testimony of one of its members, a new document was worked out that incorporated most of the concerns raised by Lobanovskii's proposal. On March 12, 1989, the head of the editing committee, V. S. Artemev, appeared on the weekly television show *Football Roundup,* and announced that his group had finished its work. He said that the new charter differed sharply from the old document, in which "there was no autonomy." Artemev promised that the planned association was to be an "independent *khozraschet* organization."[112]

These statements raised expectations. As a result, there was shock and outrage when Goskomsport published a new draft charter on April 6 that differed little from the original unsatisfactory document. It quickly became clear that the functionaries of Goskomsport had largely ignored the work of the editing committee and produced a document that satisfied no one's interests but their own. Journalists and professionals were outraged. Viktor Ponedel'nik, who had become editor of the popular weekly *Futbol-khokkei,* bitterly attacked the sports bureaucrats. He quoted one Vladimir Ivanov, a member of the Adminstration for Soccer and Hockey, who said, "You know. I don't know anything about football but . . . I can put together documents and letters." In citing this case, Ponedel'nik was criticizing the fact that people trained in administration and not sports ran Soviet soccer. He condemned these people as incompetent and said their presence in positions of power was "accidental." Lobanovskii was equally quick to express his dissatisfaction. "In comparison to the old document that was rejected," he objected, "there is nothing new in this one." He emphasized the need for an independent organization run by professionals, not functionaries who happened to find themselves in charge of soccer.[113]

The intensity of the debate, however, seemed to have cooled on the eve of the June 1 meeting at which the matter was to be decided. Koloskov and Lobanovskii gave simultaneous interviews to *Izvestia*. Both men were mutually respectful, and both indicated their willingness to compromise. When the delegates finally assembled in Moscow on June 1, a compromise did in fact occur, and press accounts reported that Lobanovskii's "Association of Football Leagues" had won the support of the gathering. Of 295 delegates present, 174 voted for the Kiev variant that called for full and open professionalization.[114] Ponedel'nik, the opponent of the *chinovniki,* was elected president of the new body. On the surface, it appeared that Lobanovskii's soccer specialists had won the battle. In return for professionalization, however, they granted Goskomsport a considerable measure of continuing control. According to the final agreement, "the union of leagues is a self-administering professional organ working together with Goskomsport and the Football Federation on the basis of parity."[115] Soviet soccer had abandoned its false amateurism, but it was still far from genuine independence.

The new Union of Leagues took few steps in its first months, disappointing many who had voted for its creation. By the fall, Koloskov seized on the Union's lack of initiative and counterattacked. Using the thinnest of semantic pretexts, Koloskov claimed that the resolution of August 2, 1987, had called for a "Soccer Union," not a "Union of Soccer Leagues," and on November 21, 1989, he announced the creation of a new, reformed, and independent Football Federation. The new federation asserted its control over all of Soviet soccer, with the exception of the top two divisions of the domestic league. In response, the Union unilaterally announced that for the 1990 season the first division would expand to eighteen teams from the present sixteen and that the second division would have thirty-eight teams, divided into two geographical zones. The logic behind the Union's move was obvious. If they were to control only a limited part of Soviet soccer, they at least wanted that part to be as large as possible.[116]

This move, taken without any consultation, proved to be a costly tactical blunder, which alienated most of the Union's earlier supporters in the lower reaches of the soccer system.[117] Seizing the initiative, Koloskov decried the Union's unilateral action and stated that the 1990 season would be contested on the same principles as that of the previous year. The two groups traded charges throughout January 1990. By the end of the month it became clear that the initiative had swung back to Koloskov's camp. Many of the coaches and officials who had supported the creation of the Union had switched sides in light of the Union's inaction. Early in February, Koloskov and Ponedel'nik announced that a "compromise" had been reached, and the 1990 season would be conducted on the same basis as the previous one. In fact, what had occurred was a complete triumph for Koloskov and his many allies. He had been able to mobilize support in the highest ranks of the Party to block the legal registration of the Union, and he used his position as one of the vice-presidents of FIFA to get the general secretary of the organization to write a letter expressing the international governing body's support for the Federation.[118] The Union of Leagues had been completely routed and soon disappeared, leaving soccer in the hands of a newly independent federation that still retained many personal, political, and financial ties to previously existing structures.

In defending his stewardship of the sport against the attacks from the partisans of the Union, Koloksov took pains to note that whatever the faults of the old system, it had achieved certain international successes, chiefly a gold medal at the 1988 Olympics and the runner-up position in the European Cup that same year. Therefore, the performance of the national team at the 1990 World Cup in Italy would be another "examination" of the state of the sport in the wake of this new and divisive controversy. Lobanovskii, as he had so often done, selected a team based largely on Dinamo Kiev, but he faced a problem no Soviet national coach had ever faced before. How best to integrate the so-called foreign legion that had been playing in Western Europe? His task was made more difficult when his team was placed in what turned out to be an especially strong preliminary group including Romania, defending champion and eventual finalist Argentina, and the surprise of the tournament, Cameroon, under the tutelage of a little-known Soviet coach, Valerii Nepomniashchii.

When the Soviets surprisingly lost their first game, 2–0, to Romania, they were in deep trouble. Their next contest was to be against Argentina in Naples, the city in which Argentina's star, Diego Maradonna, played his club soccer. Another 2–0 loss in that game, in part the result of dubious officiating that ignored a hand ball by Maradonna in the penalty area, combined with Cameroon wins over Romania and Argentina to require a nearly impossible five-goal margin over Cameroon to advance. The Soviet team would win 4–0, but this would not be enough. For the first time in all their appearances in World Cup final competition, the Soviets had failed to get past the first round. Lobanovskii, who had announced that this World Cup would be his last, came under severe criticism, as did nearly everyone else associated with the sport.[119]

Critics attacked Lobanovskii for staying too long with players who had aged considerably since the 1988 European Cup. They noted that the Soviet team was the oldest of all the teams in the tournament. Others criticized Lobanovskii's training methods and tactical choices. All of these complaints were predictable and standard. There were, however, other problems that demonstrated the difficulties faced by Soviet soccer as it dealt with the new commercial and organizational realities. The players who had gone abroad had played poorly. Reintegrating them into the routines of the national side proved difficult. At the same time, there were disputes over payment of the players, particularly concerning monies earned by sponsorship and advertising. The team had appeared in commercials and promotions for several Italian companies, and the players demanded the bulk of the money.[120]

Finally, the team was riven by factionalism and cliques. Simonian, who was head of the delegation, later remarked that there were three groups—those who had played in Europe, the Dinamo Kiev group, and the rest.[121] The players, others argued, had lost their patriotism and with it their desire to represent their nation. Those who had spent the year in Europe were accused by Lobanovskii of thinking of money rather than national pride. Whether these charges were true or not, the new world of open professionalism clearly required profound adjustments in a wide variety of practices, ranging from physical preparation to the thorny issue of compensation for the players.

To be sure, the problems confronting Soviet soccer in the 1990 World Cup were neither unprecedented nor especially unusual in the larger history of the sport. National teams had always faced difficulties in getting foreign clubs to release players, and athletes had always been motivated as much by greed as by patriotism. For the Soviets, however, all this was new. Perestroika had necessitated the abandonment of bureaucratic structures in sports and in many other spheres of life, and the results were far from encouraging. The global marketplace for athletes and sports spectacles required adjustments from all those involved with the production of sports, and the failure to respond to the changes contributed to the disaster in the World Cup.

The battle over the Soccer Union turned out to be a struggle between two competing elites for control of the production of the sport. Would bureaucrats or specialists call the shots and reap the benefits? Calls for democracy, legality, constitutionality, and autonomy hid the fact that neither of the groups contending for power over Soviet soccer was particularly concerned about such niceties. Lobanovskii certainly was no democrat, nor were the subsequent actions of the Union based on a firm respect for legality and procedure. While the life and death of the Soccer Union can be seen a microcosm of the failures of perestroika, the peculiarities of the sports world also do much to explain why this reform did not work. The criticisms of Ponedel'nik, Lobanovskii, and their allies were well founded, but these men had only a dim sense of what was needed to replace the old structures. People in the world of Soviet sports tended to be far more comfortable with giving and taking orders than people in other fields of professional endeavor. Acceptance of the authority of coaches, referees, and officials is a requirement for the smooth functioning of any sport, and the soccer insurgents were neither dissidents nor radical reformers.

The millions of Soviet citizens who had come, by 1991, to oppose the state and Party may have been sports fans. Yet it is highly unlikely that many of these partisans of change would have accepted the restraints on expression and individuality that have always been demanded by high-performance sports, regardless of where they have been practiced. In this sense, the world of sports lagged behind the changes that took place during the period of perestroika. Sports were not on the cutting edge of reform, but neither could they escape the impact of the swift changes. Commercialization, self-financing, and market relations all had an effect, ambiguous as it might have been, on Soviet spectator sports. When perestroika ended in December 1991, the problems posed by professionalization were still unresolved, and soccer's short-term prospects were dubious. The continuous attendance crisis and television's steadfast refusal to pay rights fees made it altogether unclear how professional sports could survive under the new order.

The Last Olympic Gasp

The open professionalism that came with perestroika was no doubt welcomed by athletes and coaches whose true status and social role were now recognized. By the time of the 1988 Olympics, the state's sports authorities had ceased to show much concern for the niceties of official amateurism. The publicly acknowledged ruble and hard currency bonuses for medal winners clearly created incentives that were responsible for the Soviets' excellent showing at the 1988 Games. This new system of bonuses represented an adjustment to the demands of perestroika, although special rewards for Olympic success were not in themselves unprecedented. In the past, though, they had been kept secret.

Otherwise, the Olympic sports system was still little affected by the larger societal crisis that would later envelop it. The Seoul Games were a huge sporting and diplomatic success for the USSR. The athletes who had been training for many years remained in place, and the resources available to the sports system were still sufficient to assure victory in 1988.[122] Sergei Bubka's triumph in the pole vault led an unexpectedly good performance in track and field. Men's and women's gymnastics remained powerful. Soviet fans were even more pleased by victories in team sports. The Olympic soccer team surprisingly defeated Brazil in the final, while the upset victories in basketball over the United States and Yugoslavia proved one of the highlights of the Games.

The Seoul Olympics were a diplomatic victory as well. Perestroika was still in its early stages, and the world had warmed to Gorbachev's openness and statesmanship. Although the USSR had no diplomatic relations with South Korea, the Soviets ignored North Korean appeals for a boycott in Seoul. In gratitude, the South Korean hosts showered the Soviets with hospitality and cheered their every triumph. When American athletes were involved in a series of embarrassing incidents, the South Korean hosts, to assert their independence from their American masters, were quick to emphasize the contrast with the well-mannered sportsmen and sportswomen of the USSR. In 1988, it appeared all was still well in the world of Soviet sports and that little had changed.[123]

To the Soviet fans who witnessed the introduction of new practices in the production of domestic spectator sports, it also seemed that little had changed. For them, open professionalism was not especially significant. They had regarded their own sporting heroes in much the same way Western fans had regarded theirs. Soviet spectators had always known that the high-performance athletes they watched were paid. Those who watched were concerned, first and foremost, that the spectacles they chose to view were compelling. Yet it was by no means clear that the organizational practices engendered by perestroika made spectator sports inside the USSR any more interesting, joyful, or entertaining.

The Soviet public's love of sports remained undiminished, but in the context of the economic crisis, it was by no means clear that the will or resources existed for Soviet sports to make the transition to open professionalism and overt commercialism without major hardships. The modes of consumption of spectator sports did change during perestroika, but it would be an exaggeration to claim that these new approaches led to a revolution in the attitudes of the fans. Spectators still wanted to have a good time and see an entertaining spectacle, and it was far from clear that perestroika and open professionalism provided them with the fun and pleasure they sought from sports.

In embarking on his reform program, Gorbachev succeeded in weakening the old structures and methods, but he never was able to replace them with a coherent and functioning new system. The result was economic free-fall. On the other hand, political reform proved to be much more successful. Authentic elections were held. Insurgent groups controlled the governments of the largest cities, and society was mobilized to take its fate into its own hands. It appeared to many that a healthy process had been initiated, but two crucial turning points came in 1990. On the political front, reformers, led by the former Communist Boris Yeltsin, left the Party that summer when it became clear they could not take it over. On the economic front, Gorbachev rejected the 500-day transition to a market economy advocated by his adviser, the economist and ardent soccer fan Stanislav Shatalin. To many of his earliest allies, it seemed Gorbachev had lost his nerve and made his peace with more orthodox elements in the Party. Change within the Party no longer seemed possible.

In the wake of the coup of August 1991, Gorbachev would, therefore, be unmourned when his new allies among the opponents of reform betrayed him, only to have their poorly planned conspiracy blow up in their faces. The breakup of the Soviet Union came some months later, leaving fifteen newly independent nations with uncertain futures. Change would come, but it would not be in the context of perestroika. The Communist Party would play no formal role. In these processes, sports, spectator sports in particular, played the role of a "mirror of life." They followed rather than led developments. Ultimately, the attempt to reorganize sports during the years of perestroika would only be a partial success. It would be generous to say the same thing about perestroika itself.

8

Bread or Circuses?
Choose One!

In this discussion of Soviet spectator sports, I have not given primary attention to specific institutions.[1] Instead of with parties, resolutions, ministries, and committees, my concerns have been with more amorphous messages, images, signs, and responses. The political goals of Soviet sports authorities were always obvious—to generate support for the Party and government by fostering attitudes and practices that enhanced discipline, order, productivity, preparedness, and ultimately the physical health of the nation. In contrast to the clarity of the state's aims, the responses of Soviet citizens were diffuse and disorganized. Failure to attend events, hooliganism, critical letters to various editors, and rooting for the "wrong" heroes may not have constituted coherent or concrete political alternatives to the government. Nevertheless, these were non-conformist varieties of behavior the state disapproved of. Given the government's historic concern with obedience, it is not insignificant that spectator sports proved to be one part of life in which it was possible to swim safely against the current, an arena in which one could trangress the boundaries of acceptable behavior and often get away with it.

Throughout this work, I have attempted to accord attention not only to the state but to society as well. The state may have wanted to use spectator sports for certain obvious political ends, but this particular form of popular culture proved to be ill-suited as a tool of domination and control. A narrow focus on the government's aims led many observers to view Soviet sports as Orwellian and totalitarian, and, seen from the outside, the sports system always seemed one of the most Stalinist elements of Soviet life. For a state to have been truly totalitarian, though, it must have been capable of enforcing both its aims and its presence, not to mention its will, in virtually *all* of

239

society's institutions. At least as far as spectator sports were concerned, the Soviet state never succeeded in doing this.

As we have seen, there was always far less of spectator sports in the USSR than in the West—fewer games, fewer teams, fewer stadiums, fewer sports, fewer newspapers, less television coverage, and much less advertising. Spectator sports in the USSR did not occupy as extensive a portion of the available cultural space as they did in the West. Ultimately, this great difference in quantity became one of quality as well. The metaphors of sport did not dominate Soviet culture. The vocabulary of sport was rarely adopted by other spheres of life. Aside from those who were professionally involved with sports, few Soviet citizens devoted all their free time to the consumption of spectator sports. There were no twenty-four-hour cable channels; no home satellite dishes to inundate the lover of sports with a continuous flood of events. Eventually, even the most fanatic devotee had to find something else to do with his or her time.

Sports and "Real Politics"

While society resisted the state's sports goals, many sports officials—those who produced the spectacles—were resistant to the changes that came with perestroika. While it would not be fair to characterize all Soviet sports bureaucrats as Stalinists, it is safe to say that large numbers of them proved to be less than comfortable with the course of reform. The elections to the Congress of People's Deputies that took place in March 1989 revealed with great clarity that Soviet sports officialdom was very far from the cutting edge of political change.

The Congress was to number 2,250 members. About half of the deputies were to be chosen in open elections, while the other half were allotted to the various institutions of Soviet society. The sports world was accorded three deputies, who were to be chosen on March 17, 1989, at a gathering of representatives of sports organizations. Before this conference, the various groups concerned with sports—the trade unions, the Ministry of Defense, the Dinamo societies, and others—nominated six figures, none of whom was associated with any of the most popular spectator sports. The candidates included three highly experienced sports officials: the previously mentioned Valerii Sysoev, president of the Dinamo society; Boris Rogatin, from the trade unions; and Anatolii Akentiev, from the sports organization of the Armed Forces. The other candidates were three recently retired athletes: the swimmer Vladimir Sal'nikov, the sprinter Vladimir Muraviev, and the figure skater Natalia Linchuk.[2]

While all of the candidates remarked on the grave problems confronting the sports world and all spoke positively about the reform process, only

Akentiev presented something that resembled a program. Sal'nikov said his program would take shape as he spoke with representatives of society, and Sysoev was even more empty-handed. When asked about his program in a televised interview with Vladimir Pereturin, Sysoev replied, "I am a Communist and so my program is the program of the Communist Party." Reflecting a traditional but self-serving distance from politics, all the candidates expressed surprise that they had been nominated and all lamented the severe problems in the area of mass sports. The link between participant and big-time sports, they all admitted, had been broken. The Olympic successes of 1988 had done nothing to solve the problems of inadequate facilities, insufficient equipment, and growing public indifference.

The candidates offered no sharp criticism of sports officialdom, nor did the Party or government become their explicit targets. There were also no sharp differences of policy. Indeed, the only distinction among the nominees was age. There were three middle-aged sports bureaucrats and three young, recently retired athletes. It was a measure of the delegates' lack of appetite for change that they chose the three bureaucrats.[3] This is not to say that the younger nominees constituted any sort of insurgent group, but this episode does make clear that there were few ardent advocates of perestroika among those who had long controlled the presentation and organization of Soviet sports.

Within their own sphere, sports officials may have been uncomfortable with change, but once the Congress itself met, they could no longer protect themselves from broader currents. Iurii Vlasov, the former Olympic weight-lifting champion, was elected as an at-large deputy from Moscow. During his athletic career, Vlasov, who later became a talented fiction writer, had championed the official goals of Soviet sports, but after his retirement, he became a vocal critic of Soviet sports practices. At the Congress, he gave an impassioned speech attacking the KGB. Another former sports star, the hockey player Anatolii Firsov, was also elected as a delegate from Moscow. By contrast, his views, while not uncritical, were considerably less confrontational than those of Vlasov. The Congress, in turn, elected a newly empowered Supreme Soviet to serve as the nation's legislative body. In reviewing the nominations of seventy-one ministers put forward by the government, the new parliament's committees rejected six men. Included in this group was the long-time head of Goskomsport, Marat Gramov, a Brezhnev holdover, who was attacked for incompetence, political insensitivity, and excessive bureaucratism.[4] He was replaced by an assistant, Nikolai Rusak.

Spectator sports were also severely affected by the tide of nationalist sentiment that began to rise once limits on expression were lifted. Both Lithuania and Georgia withdrew their teams from most "All-Union" sports leagues in 1990. These decisions had the greatest impact on soccer. While

Dinamo Tblisi had not played well in recent years, the historic Georgian contribution to Soviet soccer had been enormous. As for the Lithuanians, Zhalgiris of Vilnius had become one of the USSR's most interesting and successful teams, eventually competing in the UEFA cup. Georgia formed its own league. Dinamo Tblisi was renamed ''Iveria'' and was joined by several teams in smaller towns. The opening games of the 1990 season filled stadiums throughout the republic. Fans soon realized that the level of play had declined, however, and audiences plummeted to the hundreds. In Lithuania, Zhalgiris tried to find competition, but the team soon collapsed. Several players signed with European teams, while others joined clubs in the Russian Republic. A number of Georgians did the same. By the summer of 1991, a new Lithuanian soccer league was organized, with a reconstituted Zhalgiris winning the championship. While Zhalgiris was able to attract average crowds of six thousand, none of the other fourteen teams had much success at the gate.[5]

While the overall impact on Soviet soccer of the Georgian and Lithuanian moves was far from insignificant, the Lithuanians' and Georgians' decisions had a negative impact on sports in both republics, especially for the athletes themselves. Lack of continuous high-level competition makes it impossible for the elite athlete to maintain form, and a year away from the ''big time'' can lead to more than a year of subsequent substandard play. Yet there are times in the history of nations when politics becomes more important than sports. Given the fact that these teams had long been among the few legally acceptable vehicles of national expression in both Georgia and Lithuania, it can hardly be surprising that the republics' leaders should have taken these steps and used sports as a political vehicle. Nevertheless, playing standards did suffer with so little domestic competition.[6]

The possibility of a separate Ukrainian league was, however, far more threatening to Soviet soccer than the exit of the Georgians and Lithuanians. There had been extensive public discussion about the formation of a separate Ukrainian league more than a year before the August coup. During the summer of 1990, Koloskov, at a public meeting in Kiev, had been shouted down by partisans of a Ukrainian soccer championship, and after the debacle at the World Cup, calls for a separate Ukrainian league became even louder. Aside from Dinamo Kiev, many other Ukraine-based teams, notably Dniepr, Shakhter, and Chernomorets, had long been fixtures in the first division. Their absence would have dramatically lowered the level of league play. Unlike the Georgians and Lithuanians, though, the Ukrainians did not decide to form their own league until after the collapse of the Soviet Union. There were forces working in the opposite direction as well. Nationalist sentiment had always been strongest in the western part of the republic, but all five first division teams during 1991 were located in cities in the eastern and central parts of the republic, where the urban population, even before the 1917 rev-olution, had been as much Russian as Ukrainian.[7] The players and coaches of these teams were also far from exclusively Ukrainian, and the majority of clubs in the Ukraine had always recruited talent from outside as well as inside the republic.

While harming Soviet soccer, nationalism threatened to destroy Soviet basketball, the most multinational of all spectator sports. The independence of the Baltic states was expected to hamper Soviet efforts to retain a place in the elite ranks of the sport. When Lithuania withdrew from league play in 1990, its players also refused to compete for the national team. Latvia and Estonia did not immediately take such a course in sports matters, although they, too, declared their independence along with Lithuania. Half the twelve-man gold-medal team at Seoul in 1988 had been from the Baltic; four were from Lithuania. Yet the significance of this fact can be overstated. In 1989, the Soviet team with all four Lithuanian stars only managed a third-place finish in the European championship behind Yugoslavia and Greece, while the next year, without the Lithuanians, the Soviet team actually finished sec-ond to the Yugoslavs, beating out the usual collection of American college players who won the bronze. Considering the fact that the 1990 Yugoslav team was one of the strongest squads in the history of European basketball, the Soviets were well pleased with their result.

This kind of success, however, would prove episodic. Unable to muster their best players for the preliminary rounds, the Soviets failed, for the first time in history, to make the final stage of the 1991 European championship.[8] Things were not much better inside Lithuania. The great stars, Sabonis, Mar-ciulionis, Kurtinaitis, Khomichus, and Iovasha, all chose to play abroad, and one younger talent, Arturas Kornishovas, actually enrolled at an American college. Those who remained in Lithuania, especially younger players, had little serious competition. This exodus effected all of Lithuanian sports, and beginning with 1990, as many as 160 athletes and coaches left the republic to work in a variety of foreign countries.[9]

Good Clean Fun, But Not That Much

The Western understanding of Soviet sports was so dominated by the image of a state-sponsored, medal-producing assembly line that it is difficult some-times to remember that Soviet citizens did not follow sports events with the intensity outsiders thought they did. The discourses of sports did not come to dominate the daily language of Soviet citizens.[10] Olympic victories, with their attendant claims of national greatness and political superiority, were only part of the Soviet sports scene. We have seen that the Soviet audience for sports picked and chose what the state placed before it, and those choices did not always please the authorities. During the perestroika period, society, through a variety of nongovernment groups and entrepreneurs, was able to generate its own entertainments and leisure practices, all of which had meanings quite different from those historically presented by the state. Private promoters put on professional boxing and wrestling shows. Moscow also saw its first dog races, body-building competitions, and beach volleyball, as well as a not-inconsiderable number of "Erotic Ice Revues."

Given the resistance of its leaders to the changes begun with perestroika, the sports world continued to play a so-called Stalinist role, well after the rest of society had ceased to resemble anything that might be called totalitarian. Nevertheless, the specific phenomenon of spectator sports was never an element of direct control or totalitarian rule. It proved to be a highly imperfect weapon in the hands of the authorities, and, in limited ways, it fostered counter-hegemonic forms of behavior.[11] Sports spectacles in the USSR may have provided the same safety valve function that they did in the West, affording pleasurable entertainment while compensating for the disappointments of people's work lives; but we have also seen that Soviet spectator sports provided ways for workers and other groups to evade and subvert social and political controls by misbehaving at some games, boycotting others, rooting for anti-heroes, and complaining to the media when sporting spectacles failed to provide pleasure.[12]

We also now know that Olympic success, especially during the 1950s, was achieved on a shoestring. Despite significant investment, training facilities were only rarely comparable to top world standards, but for decades the Soviets claimed and the West believed that Olympic victories were the product of a nation massively involved with sports. What we saw in the international arena was supposed to be the tip of the iceberg, but the reality was far more limited. The Soviet Union was always a poorer country than either the United States, Japan, or most of the nations of Western Europe. Through industrialization, war, reconstruction, perestroika, and finally terminal crisis, the USSR always faced more pressing priorities than sports. While the best Soviet facilities may have seemed impressive, we now know that, in many cases, they were the only facilities of their type.

Again, this difference of quantity becomes one of quality. The Soviet public was always interested in sports, but it was never truly obsessed. Both the character of that interest and the enjoyment fans derived from sports were much the same as in the West, but the experience of being a sports fan was always considerably less intense in the USSR than elsewhere. In all my years of watching sports in the Soviet Union, I never met anyone who would "die for dear old Spartak" or "bleed Dinamo blue." One of the great psychic dangers of fanship is vicarious identification either with a team or with individual stars. When the boundary between the self and the other is obscured and the fan sees a team's victories and defeats as his or her own, there can be no doubt that this phenomenon is unhealthy.

Yet I know of no record of a suicide being caused by the defeat either of a club team or of the Soviet national soccer team. This type of psychological confusion would seem to have occurred only rarely in the Soviet Union, and then primarily in the various national republics, where a single team may have embodied the aspirations of an entire ethnic group. Victories were always loudly trumpeted for maximum political effect, while defeats produced much hand-wringing and criticism. Players and coaches lost positions, titles, and privileges, but as far as we know, no one was executed or exiled to Siberia simply for losing a championship. Even the "team of lieutenants" did not suffer such a fate. In fact, the athletes and coaches who were arrested under Stalin were more likely to have been winners than losers.

If we recall the possible public responses to popular culture suggested by Stuart Hall, it is clear that the Soviet audience's relationship to the events and attendant messages put before it can best be described as "negotiated" rather than "dominated." Fans attended only the games and watched only the sports they wanted to watch. They were not compelled to attend. In some cases, the choices made by spectators reflected limited popular interest in a particular sport. In others, a strong latent interest in a particular game may have been overridden when the competition was not sufficiently compelling to attract those seeking exciting entertainment.

At the same time, it would be pushing the evidence too far in the opposite direction to claim that fan violence, poor attendance, public wisecracking, and open complaining constituted a movement that could be called "oppositional." Some of society's responses to spectator sports may have been counter-hegemonic, but primarily in the limited sense that many members of the audience were not accepting the values of order and discipline. Disenchantment with the official production of sports spectacles did not represent an organized alternative to the official sports spectacle. Rather, it demonstrates that spectator sports in particular, and popular culture in general, were less-than-powerful instruments of direct state domination in the Soviet Union. They did little to produce control and even less to generate consent to the power of the authorities.

In a limited sense, Soviet sports fans were like the subtly rebellious consumers described by Michel de Certeau. While their resistance was disorganized and episodic, there was, nevertheless, a political dimension to their actions, even if those actions were not the politics of parties, platforms, and formal organizations. The long-term impact of the eternally frustrating processes of consumption was, without doubt, one of the causes of Stalinism's collapse. The state's failure to satisfy the public and give it pleasure pushed millions of citizens into "black and gray markets" in search of comfort and fun. This subtle and often private alienation undermined the government's quest to obtain the consent of the governed and put much of the population outside a poorly defined concept of legality.

If Soviet spectator sports were not as "serious" as their organizers would have wished, can we then choose the other offered alternative, that of "fun"? In one sense, the answer must be yes. If these activities did not give people pleasure, then there would not have been the numbers of teams, games, stadiums, publications, and television transmissions that did exist. Just as in the West, there was a Soviet sports industry that, while smaller, provided spectacles for mass audiences.

During perestroika, self-financing was supposed to diminish state control of spectator sports and reorganize them on a self-sustaining basis. But the arguments over professionalization, fostered by the campaign for autonomy, were not about paying athletes nor were they about making sports events more "fun" for the fans. Rather, the battle over professionalization was a struggle for the control of the production of sports spectacles. Specialists who earned their livings from sports sought to take control away from bureaucrats. These attempts to change the nature of Soviet sports were only partially successful during perestroika. But for the fan, concerned with the entertainment value of his or her favorite sport, little changed. Soviet spectators had always regarded big-time soccer in particular as a "professional" sport. Thus fans were indifferent to the question of which group would control the game. The reorganization of soccer did nothing to halt the decline in attendance, and by the final season, the average crowd had fallen to 12,000.

Soviet entry into the global economy after 1988 also had a deleterious effect on domestic sports. In the world market for top-flight athletes, a poorer USSR had difficulty retaining its best talents, and an "athletic diaspora" soon developed. The top stars of Soviet soccer, hockey, basketball, volleyball, team handball, track, tennis, and cycling came to work in North America and Europe; not at home. They became part of a global monoculture of high-performance sports tied to increasingly sophisticated international networks of advertising and promotion that were themselves arms of a wide variety of multinational enterprises.

Historically, the Soviet Union had spread its talent across the whole range of Olympic sports. Early in their teen years, talented youngsters were required to pick a specialty, and coaches from various sports competed with each other for the best athletes. The comparative material rewards of soccer, hockey, and basketball, on one hand, and wrestling, swimming, and rowing, on the other (to cite just a few examples), were not that great. Since the chance for foreign travel was always the greatest privilege a Soviet citizen could aspire to, it made sense for some to specialize in the sports in which competition for places on national teams may have been less intense. As foreign travel became easier, many Soviet observers came to expect young athletes to pursue sports in which the chances for money and fame were the greatest. It was thought that the talent pool for the big-time spectator sports would actually expand, while the minor or non-revenue sports would wither.

The possibility of big-time sports inside the USSR being organized as an enterprise threatened the teams that had historically received the highest level of state support—the army clubs and the Dinamo societies. These most traditional elements feared that civilian teams supported by trade unions, cooperatives, and enterprises would have enhanced opportunities for generating wealth and for using that money to increase their success on the field. This trend also had the potential of changing the political and ideological role of the Soviet sports heroes. They would no longer be soldiers or policemen. Instead, the new stars would be civilians who were far less likely to be models for official values.

The growth of open professionalization under perestroika also threatened to cut ties between spectator and participant sports. The link between *masterstvo* and *massovost'*, imagined or real, was one of the distinctive elements of Soviet sports, and the institutions that gave meaning to this relationship were the voluntary sports societies. The teams supported by these organizations were supposed to inspire large numbers of citizens to participate in healthy physical activities that were organized by the sports societies. For many years, the societies had been neglecting their responsibilities in the area of mass sports, and there was no reason to believe that the introduction of capitalist business practices would make them more likely to pay attention to the recreational needs of the public.

The new reliance on the market was viewed by many Soviet journalists and scholars, as well as numerous outsiders, as yet another failure of the grand Soviet experiment to change a human nature best suited to capitalism. In this light, the adoption of Western professional sports practices could be seen as yet another indicator of this phenomenon. Instead of being tied to labor and defense, sports could have become an arena of pure play or entertainment. Huizinga's beloved fundamental drive of human nature would seem to have at last triumphed.[13] If Soviet sports organizers chose to emulate Western entrepreneurs, it would seem to confirm the autonomy of spectator sports and support the words of the American culture critic Cyndi Lauper that, in consuming mass culture, "girls [and boys] just want to have fun."[14]

Sports, as we have seen, had never effectively performed the function of direct political control, and one could argue that the Soviets, after decades of politicized sports, were forced to recognize this fact. But Huizinga did not extend his concept of culture-creating play to the world of modern, professional spectator sports. He reacted to the organized leagues of the late nineteenth century as negatively as did Victorian aristocrats who revived the concept of amateurism in order to keep the working classes out of sports.[15] There was nothing pure or autonomous about the entrepreneurs and others who produced the spectacles, nor was there anything particularly noble, in Huizinga's eyes, about those who watched them. Huizinga realized full well that capitalist spectator sports were not an arena of unfettered play.

Therefore, the growth of commercialization in Soviet spectator sports cannot be seen as the acceptance of an eternal truth about the relationship of sports to an unchanging human nature. From well before antiquity, people have received pleasure from watching the feats of highly skilled athletes, but they did this in very different ways during different epochs.[16] The apparent timelessness of that impulse turns out to be less important than the changing ways the practices of sport were organized in various cultures and historical periods.

Spectator sports emerged in the USSR during the 1930s. At that time, Soviet philosophers and administrators of sports were still concerned with the dangers of commercialization, exploitation, and public passivity. The embrace of high-performance sports in the USSR did not lead to the abandonment of a Marxist critique of professional sports under capitalism. The rational organization of a bureaucratic sports apparatus, with highly instrumental goals, was intended to avoid the problems experienced in the West, but in the process these structures developed distortions of their own.

By 1988, official amateurism had been abandoned. Curiously, jettisoning the myth of the amateur was itself an adjustment to Western complaints about the original Communist invention of the state professional. Soviet sports authorities, in turn, accepted the necessity of competing with outsiders under conditions dictated by the international market for sports spectacles. Soviet sports authorities recognized that the successes of their athletes contributed to the appeal of these events, and they were eager to enjoy the commercial advantages generated by these competitions.

We may recall Trotsky's expectation that the popular desire for various, possibly shady, forms of public entertainment would not disappear soon after the revolution. More than seventy years later, those desires persist. Trotsky hoped that socialist forms of amusement, fun, and laughter would emerge with the development of the revolutionary process. Many more experimental Soviet thinkers devoted considerable time, thought, and energy to just such a project during the 1920s.[17] Communists, after all, wanted to have fun, too. By the 1970s, the state had recognized that the satisfaction of individual desires was sufficient justification for a wide variety of pleasurable activities. Ben Eklof has noted, ''Recreation is an excellent example of privatization. Despite feeble attempts to convince the population to devote time to self-improvement and to participate in civic happenings and organized outings,

the state has now tacitly accepted the right of one to be alone, to seek frivolous entertainment, and to waste one's time.''[18] Of course, as John Bushnell
has argued, wasting time is something Russians did exceedingly well during
the many centuries most of them lived in the countryside.[19] The modern,
urban practice of watching professional sports may differ in important ways
from the traditional and customary leisure practices that are still a part of
Russian daily life. Nevertheless, for some members of the sports audience,
watching games ultimately proved to be little more than a pleasurable way
of wasting time.

With the breakup of the Soviet Union and the demise of orthodox Communism, it is no longer possible to regard the history of the USSR as a
chronicle that describes the elaboration and fine-tuning of a powerful and
effective state machine. Had Communism functioned as seamlessly as some
claimed, the collapse would never have come. Accordingly, histories that
demonstrate the limitations of state power and the weaknesses of ideology
can provide a better explanation for the end of the Soviet period of history
in what once was the Russian Empire. The collapse of Communism in the
USSR was the result of many long-term and powerful processes. It was not
the unintended consequence of a single enlightened leader's failed dreams.
In embarking on his course, Gorbachev was responding to problems that had
existed long before he became the General Secretary of the Party. With the
Soviet period now closed, historians can finally embark on the task of ex-
plaining how this supposedly immutable system ultimately changed so
dramatically.

In 1970, American and Soviet students could sit on the steps of Moscow
State University, strum their guitars, and think rock and roll would change
the world. Behind this naïve wish was an intuitive understanding of the in-
compatability of modern popular culture with orthodox Soviet Marxism. Re-
gressed pleasure and fun for its own sake were never comfortable parts of a
system of thought that saw production as the central concern of humanity.
The Party's long-standing attempt to harness the various forms of mass
(rather than popular) culture faced enormous obstacles. Even in the West,
popular culture in all its forms may have been mind-numbing and far from
ennobling, but it was never the mighty weapon of mind control that its critics
claimed. As often as not, popular (rather than mass) culture fostered anarchy
and rebellion rather than domination and consent.

It would be difficult but not impossible to make a similar argument for
spectator sports. Baseball may not be the Beatles, and soccer is most defi-
nitely not the Stones. Ping-pong may have re-opened China, but no one (with
one or two individual exceptions) thinks basketball, or any other game, can
change the world. Nevertheless, spectator sports throughout much of Soviet

history provided people with an escape, reminded them of their humanity, and reinforced a healthy and authentic utopianism that the rest of life often denied. At its best moments, when they have not been an arena of rampant hucksterism, greed, egoism, jingoism, and violence, spectator sports in the West have done many of the same things. This is why it is fun, but of a very serious kind.

Notes

List of Abbreviations

KS	*Krasnyi sport*
SS	*Sovetskii sport*
I	*Izvestia*
P	*Pravda*
FS	*fizkultura i sport*
KP	*Komsomolskaia pravda*
FK	*Futbol-khokkei*

The system of dating used in the footnotes is that employed in the United States, with the month followed by the day and the last two digits of the year; e.g., 9/27.59.

Notes to Preface

1. Christine Brennan, "That Mighty Red Star," Washington Post Service, re-printed in *International Herald Tribune,* June 18, 1991. This article then went on to describe in some detail the impact of the present economic crisis on Soviet sports, but it fully accepts that until recently there was a "Soviet Olympic Machine."

2. *Los Angeles Times,* July 25, 1991.

3. Victoria de Grazia, *The Culture of Consent: Mass Organization of Leisure in Fascist Italy* (New York, 1981), p. 21.

4. Two English-language works that are based on the physical and psychological aspects of Soviet sports training are Grigori Raiport, *Red Gold: Peak Performance Techniques of the Russian and East German Olympic Victors* (New York, 1987); and Michael Yessis, *Secrets of Soviet Sports Fitness and Training* (New York, 1988). For a thorough description of the highlights of Soviet research on physical culture and sports before 1974, see Oleg Milshtein, "Main Trends, Ways, and Prospects of the

Development of Sociology of Physical Culture in the USSR,'' *International Review of Sport Sociology,* vol. 2, no. 9, pp. 137–146.

Notes to Chapter 1

1. *SS,* 6/4/46.

2. Wray Vamplew, *Pay Up and Play the Game: Professional Sport in Britain, 1875–1914* (Cambridge, England, 1988), pp. 1–76.

3. A. B. Serebriakov and N. I. Ponomarev, *Sotsiologia sporta SShA na sluzhbe kapitalizma* (Moscow, 1987), p. 139. O. A. Mil'shtein and V.S. Stoliarov, ''Sport v sovremennom obshchestve,'' *Sotsiologicheskie issledovania,* no. 2 (1981), p. 209. S. P. Shpilko, ''Vzaimosviaz' 'bol'shogo sporta' s massovym fizkul'turnym dvizheniem,'' *Sotsiologicheskie issledovania,* no. 3 (1986), pp. 33–42. S. I. Guskov, ed., *Rol' pravitel'stv vedushchikh kapitalisticheskikh stran v razvitii fizicheskoi kul'tury i sporta* (Moscow, 1987). V. M. Zitsorskii, ed., *SShA: Sport i pravitel'stvo* (Moscow, 1988).

4. No author, *A Pageant of Youth* (Moscow, 1939), n.p.

5. Cited in Tony Mason, *Association Football and English Society, 1863–1915* (Sussex, 1980), p. 237. This attitude toward sport was widespread on the British left, but it was not held equally on the Continent. The German Social Democratic Party, in particular, was successful in organizing its own workers' sport clubs, organized around the idea of healthy participation. See Chris Waters, *British Socialists and the Politics of Popular Culture* (Palo Alto, 1990), p. 2.

6. Cited in Waters, *British Socialists,* p. 35.

7. John Hoberman, *Sport and Political Ideology* (Austin, 1984), p. 147.

8. Eugen Weber, *France: Fin de siècle* (Cambridge, Mass. 1986), p. 225.

9. Hoberman, *Political Ideology,* p. 217.

10. Theodor Adorno, *Introduction to the Sociology of Music* (New York, 1976), pp. 49–50, cited in Hoberman, *Political Ideology,* p. 246. Max Horkheimer and Theodor Adorno, *The Dialectic of Enlightenment,* (New York, 1969).

11. Hoberman, *Political Ideology,* p. 14.

12. Johan Huizinga, *Homo Ludens: A Study of the Play Element in Culture* (London, 1949), p. 3.

13. *Ibid.* pp. 196–198.

14. Hoberman, *Political Ideology,* pp. 133–134. John J. MacAloon, *This Great Symbol: Pierre de Coubertin and the Origins of the Modern Olympic Games* (Chicago, 1981).

15. Ortega y Gasset, *The Revolt of the Masses* (New York, 1932), p. 12.

16. Max Scheler, *Ressentiment* (Glencoe, 1961), p. 13.

17. Leon Trotsky, ''Vodka, the Church, and the Cinema,'' in *Problems of Everyday Life* (New York, 1973), p. 32.

18. Lynn Mally, ''Egalitarian and Elitist Visions of Cultural Transformation, The Debate in the Proletkult Movement,'' in M. Ferro and S. Fitzpatrick, eds., *Culture et revolution* (Paris, 1989), pp. 137–146.

19. James Riordan, ''Sport and Social Change in the U.S.S.R.,'' *Journal of Sport and Social Issues,* vol. 6, no. 1 (Spring/Summer 1982), p. 14.

20. James Riordan, *Sport in Soviet Society* (Cambridge, England, 1977), pp. 127–132. On the 1930s campaign against equality, see Richard Stites, *Revolutionary Dreams: Utopian Vision and Experimental Life in the Russian Revolution* (Oxford, 1989), pp. 231–235. Vera S. Dunham, *In Stalin's Time: Middle-Class Values in Soviet Fiction* (Cambridge, England, 1976), p. 14. A. Lunacharskii, the first Soviet Minister of Culture and a representative of pre-Stalinist views on sports, also advocated a more egalitarian approach to sport. See *Mysli o sporte* (Moscow, 1930), p. 25.

21. Lewis H. Siegelbaum, *Stakhanovism and the Politics of Productivity in the USSR, 1935–1941* (Cambridge, England, 1988), p. 213.

22. Hart Cantelon, "The Rationality and Logic of Soviet Sport," in Cantelon and Richard Gruneau, eds., *Sport, Culture, and the Modern State* (Toronto, 1982), p. 247.

23. Hoberman, *Political Ideology*, p. 162.

24. Richard D. Mandell, *The Nazi Olympics* (New York, 1971).

25. Hoberman, *Political Ideology*, pp. 19 and 84.

26. The best-known of Lenin's texts that cast doubt on spontaneity is, of course, *What Is to Be Done*. In other works, however, Lenin was far less fearful of popular spontaneity, especially that of the peasantry, and in his concrete political practice he was scarcely in control of the processes that brought him to power.

27. John Hargreaves, *Sport, Culture, and Power* (Cambridge, England, 1986), p. 118.

28. *Istoria fizicheskoi kultury i sporta, uchebnik dlia tekhnikumov fizicheskoi kultury* (Moscow, 1984), pp. 47–49. S. V. Briankin, *Strutura i funktsiia sovremennogo sporta* (Moscow, 1983), po. 58. N. I. Ponomarev, *Sport and Soviety* (Moscow, 1981).

29. *I*, 9/11/63.

30. See Barry D. McPherson, "Sport Consumption and the Economics of Consumerism," in Donald W. Ball and John W. Loy, eds., *Sport and Social Order* (Reading, Mass., 1975), p. 252.

31. Hargreaves, *Sport, Culture, and Power*, p. 2.

32. Janet Lever, *Soccer Madness* (Chicago, 1983), pp. 4–6.

33. Ponomarev, *Sport and Society*, 1981, p. 230.

34. Ponomarev, *Sport and Society*, 1981, p. 74.

35. Norbert Elias and Eric Dunning, *The Quest for Excitement: Sport and Leisure in the Civilizing Process* (Oxford, 1986), p. 43.

36. *Ibid.* p. 61.

37. Moshe Lewin, *The Gorbachev Phenomenon: An Historical Interpretation* (Berkeley, 1988), p. 80.

38. Henry Morton, *Soviet Sport: Mirror of Soviet Society* (New York, 1963), p. 62. Riordan, *Sport in Soviet Society*, pp. 120–152. Hoberman, *Political Ideology*, p. 191.

39. A. Starostin, *Sport in the USSR* (Moscow, 1939), p. 7.

40. Ponomarev, "Sport as Show," *International Review of Sport Sociology*, vol. 15, nos. 3–4 (1980), p. 73. A. A. Korobkov, "Predislovie," in A. A. Frenkin, ed., *Kritika burzhuaznoi sotsiologii sporta',* (Moscow, 1965). Soviet televison, second program, October 5, 1987.

41. Cantelon, *Rationality*, p. 247. *New York Times*, September 22 and October 2, 1988.

42. Siegelbaum, *Stakhanovism*, p. 218. Riordan, *Sport in Soviet Society*, pp. 183–206.

43. Lewin, *Gorbachev*, p. 43.

44. Ponomarev, *Sport and Society*, p. 77.

45. Michel de Certeau, *The Practices of Everyday Life* (Berkeley, 1984), pp. xii–xiii, xv, and xvii.

46. *SS*, 6/1/87, 9/17/87.

47. *SS*, 10/4/87, 11/26/87.

48. Riordan, *Sport in Soviet Society*, pp. 235–243.

49. Peter Stallybrass and Allon White, *The Politics and Poetics of Transgression* (Ithaca, 1986), p. 18. Mikhail Bakhtin, *Rabelais and His World* (Cambridge, Mass., 1968), pp. 11–12.

50. Allen Guttman, *From Ritual to Record: The Nature of Modern Sport* (New York, 1978), p. 65. Guttman, *Sports Spectators* (New York, 1986), p. 153.

51. Hoberman, *Political Ideology*, p. 240.

52. Jean-Marie Brohm, *Critiques du sport* (Paris, 1976). Gerhard Vinnai, *Fussballsport als Ideologie* (Frankfurt, 1970).

53. Martin Jay, *The Dialectical Imagination*,(Boston, 1977), p. 187.

54. *Ibid.* p. 216.

55. Rob Beamish, "Sport and the Logic of Capitalism," in Cantelon and Gruneau, *Sport and State*, p. 169.

56. John Hargeaves, "Sport and Hegemony: Some Theoretical Problems," in Cantelon and Gruneau, *Sport and State*, p. 132.

57. Eric Hobsbawm, "Mass-Producing Traditions: Europe, 1870–1914," in Hobsbawm and Terence Ranger, eds., *The Invention of Tradition* (Cambridge, 1983), p. 283. Robert F. Wheeler, "Organized Sport and Organized Labor: The Workers' Sports Movements," *Journal of Contemporary History,* vol. 13, no. 8 (April 1978), p. 191.

58. T. J. Clark, *The Painting of Modern Life: Paris in the Age of Manet and His Followers* (Princeton, 1984), p. 204.

59. Waters, *British Socialists*, p. 4.

60. Steven J. Ross, "Struggles for the Screen: Workers, Radicals, and the Political Uses of Silent Film," *American Historical Review,* vol. 96, no. 2 (April 1991), pp. 333–367.

61. Stuart Hall, "Notes on Deconstructing the Popular," in Raphael Samuel, ed., *People's History and Socialist Theory* (London, 1981), p. 232.

62. *Ibid.*, p. 229.

63. Hall's views are given this precise summation by Tana Modleski, "Introduction," in Modleski, ed., *Studies in Entertainment* (Bloomington, 1986), p. xi.

64. This approach, derived from the thought of Antonio Gramsci, supports the view that sports promote social integration in capitalist societies. Hargreaves, *Sport, Culture, and Power*, pp. 204–223. John Hoffman, *The Gramscian Challenge: Coercion and Consent in Marxist Political Theory* (Oxford, 1984), p. 57. Antonio Gramsci, *Selections from the Prison Notebooks* (New York, 1971), p. 417.

65. Raymond Williams, *Marxism and Literature* (Oxford, 1977), p. 110.

66. Pierre Bourdieu, "Sport and Social Class," *Social Science Information*, vol. 17, no. 6 (1978), p. 830.

67. Hargreaves, *Sport, Culture, and Power*, 1986, p. 222.

68. Raymond Williams, "There's Always the Sport," in Alan O'Conner, ed., *Raymond Williams on Television: Selected Writings* (New York, 1989), p. 95.

69. Basile Kerblay, *Gorbachev's Russia* (New York, 1989), p. 107.

70. Dunham, *Stalin's Time*, p. 4.

71. Martin McCauley, *The Soviet Union Since 1917* (London, 1983), p. 260.

72. Christel Lane, *The Rites of Rulers: Ritual in Industrial Societies—The Soviet Case* (Cambridge, England, 1981), p. 3. Clifford Geertz, "Deep Play: Notes on the Balinese Cockfight," in *Interpretation of Cultures* (New York, 1973), pp. 412–453.

73. John Bushnell, "Urban Leisure Culture in Post-Stalin Russia: Stability as a Social Problem?" in Terry L. Thompson and Richard Sheldon, *Soviet Society and Culture: Essays in Honor of Vera S. Dunham* (Boulder, 1988), p. 60. The most complete account of Soviet time-budget studies can be found in Jiri Zuzanek, *Work and Leisure in the Soviet Union: A Time-Budget Analysis* (New York, 1980), pp. 113–144.

74. Raymond Williams has noted that silence does not mean acceptance by the masses: "Inertia and apathy have always been employed by the governed as a comparatively safe weapon against their governors. Some governing bodies will accept this, as at least being quiet." Cited in Alan O'Conner, *Raymond Williams: Writing, Culture, and Politics* (New York, 1989), p. 67.

75. Stephen F. Cohen, *Rethinking the Soviet Experience: Politics and History Since 1917* (New York, 1985), p. 7.

Notes to Chapter 2

1. Jeffrey Brooks, *When Russia Learned to Read: Literacy and Popular Literature, 1861–1917* (Princeton, 1985), pp. 269–294.

2. Jay Leyda, *Kino* (New York, 1960), pp. 17–90.

3. F. P. Pavlov, *Za desiat' let praktiki (otryvki iz vospominanii, vpechatlenii i nabliudenii iz fabrichnoi zhizni)* (Moscow, 1901), in Victoria Bonnell, ed., *The Russian Worker: Life and Labor under the Tsarist Regime* (Berkeley, 1983), p. 150.

4. Victor Peppard, "The Beginnings of Russian Soccer," *Stadion*, nos. VIII–IX (1982–1983), p. 153.

5. Riordan, *Sport in Soviet Society*, p. 15.

6. *SS*, 4/5/47, 5/17/58.

7. *KS*, 2/21/36; *I*, 10/14/40; *SS*, 8/30/58. Alexander Starostin, *Bol'shoi futbol* (Moscow, 1964), p. 12. M. Martynov, *Liubimaia igra* (Moscow, 1955), p. 3. V. V. Frolov, *Futbol v SSSR, Spravochnik* (Moscow, 1951). p. 5. K. Esenin, *Moskovskii futbol* (Moscow, 1974).

8. Nikolai Tarasov and Sergei Tikhonov, *Futbol-istoriko-sportivnyi ocherk* (Tblisi, 1948), p. 4.

9. Frolov, *Futbol*, p. 5.

10. *Ibid.*, p. 6. Nikolai Starostin, interview with author, Moscow, September 25, 1990.

11. A. Starostin, *Bolshoi Futbol*, p. 243. *SS*, 4/25/73. Frolov, *Futbol*, p. 17.

12. Frolov, *Futbol*, p. 7. Riordan, *Sport in Soviet Society*, p. 22. *SS*, 8/25/57. Nikolai Starostin, *Futbol skvoz' gody* (Moscow, 1989), p. 75. A. Starostin, *Bolshoi Futbol*, p. 11. Pavel Batyrev, "Pobeda novoi taktiki," in N. A. Panin-Kolomenkin, ed., *Stranitsy iz proshlogo* (Moscow, 1951), p. 87. *Russkii sport*, 3/3/11, 11/11/11, 1/15/12.

13. Riordan, "British Influence on the Development of Russian Football," *Proceedings of the Sixth International Congress of the International Association for the History of Physical Education and Sport* (April, 1977), p. 529.

14. Riordan, *Sport in Soviet Society*, p. 29. I. Korshak, *Staryi, staryi futbol* (Moscow, 1975), p. 39. Peppard, "A Comparison of Soviet Soccer and Hockey with the Major American Sports," in March Krotee and Eloise Jaeger, eds., *Comparative Physical Education and Sport*, vol. 3 (Champaign, Ill, 1986), pp. 227–237. N. Kiselev, *70 futbol'nykh let* (Leningrad, 1970). *Russkii sport*, 12/25/11. *SS*, 10/12/48.

15. *SS*, 10/25/1957. Mikhail Iakushin, *Vechnaia taina futbola* (Moscow, 1988), p. 11. Martynov, *Liubimaia igra*, p. 4. A. Starostin, *Bolshoi Futbol*, p. 24.

16. Batyrev, *Pobeda*, p. 94. Panin-Kolonenkin, *Stranitsy*, pp. 163–165.

17. Iakushin, *Taina*, p. 46.

18. *KS*, 1/3/37. Panin-Kolonenkin, *Stranitsy*, p. 163. S. A. Savin, ed., *Khokkei s shaiboi* (Moscow, 1953), p. 3.

19. *Russkii sport*, 3/6/11, 9/23/11. *SS*, 1/4/58.

20. Riordan, *Sport in Soviet Society*, p. 69.

21. *SS*, 8/3/48. V. I. Vinokurov, ed., *Dinamo Moskva, '67* (Moscow, 1968), p. 8.

22. Riordan, *Sport in Soviet Society*, pp. 95–101.

23. Mally, *The Culture of the Future*, p. 10.

24. Peppard, *Beginnings*, p. 231.

25. Stites, *Dreams*, p. 230. Riordan, *Sport in Soviet Society*, p. 106. *SS*, 12/21/49, 11/6/57. Frolov, *Futbol*, p. 10.

26. *KS*, 6/12/27, 11/6/27. *FS*, 6/16/28, 7/14/28, 8/18/28. *P*, 6/7/28.

27. *KS*, 6/12/27.

28. *KS*, 11/6/27. *FS*, 6/16/28, 6/23/28. Anatolii Lunacharskii, *Mysli o sporte* (Moscow, 1930).

29. *KS*, 3/30/35.

30. *I*, 6/12/39, 8/12/39, 9/23/39.

31. *KS*, 11/19/38.

32. *KS*, 2/17/34. *I*, 10/17/65

33. *I*, 6/24/35.

34. *KS*, 11/15/36.

35. *I*, 1/16/36. *KS*, 3/1/36, 8/29/38.

36. *P*, 7/25/28.

37. *KS*, 7/25/25, 9/18/27. V. Mikkel's, "Orgkomitet spartakiada," *Fotoal'bom spartakiada* (Moscow, 1929), n.p.

38. V. Mikhailov, "Massovaia fizkultura," *ibid.*, n.p.

39. A. Enukidze, "Proletarskii sport," *ibid.*, n.p.

40. *P*, 7/28/28. Iu. A. Dmitriev, *Gul'ian'e i drugie formy massovykh zrelishch* (Moscow, 1968).

41. *P*, 7/27/28, 8/23/28. *SS*, 8/7/

42. V. Riabokan', "Futbol," *Fotoal'bom spartakiada,* n.p.

43. *P*, 7/28/28, 8/17/28, 8/22/28, 8/24/28. *FS*, 8/25/28, 9/1/28.

44. *FS*, 8/4/28, 8/18/28. *P*, 7/18/28, 7/29/28.

45. *P*, 8/14/28. *FS*, 8/25/28. Riabokan', n.p.

46. *FS*, 8/18/28.

47. Ia. Ianel', "Massovaia khudozhestvennaia samodeiatel'nost' i puti sotsialis-ticheskogo razvitiia isskustva," *Literatura i isskustvo,* no. 3/4 (1930). *P*, 2/18/32. *KS*, 8/29/36, 8/5/38. *I*, 7/22/35, 7/26/35, 7/28/35, 7/30/35, 8/6/35, 6/8/36, 7/26/36, 7/29/36, 9/8/36, 9/9/36, 9/14/36, 7/11/37, 7/18/37, 2/15/38, 2/20/38, 7/21/38, 8/2/38, 8/9/38, 8/13/38, 11/16/39.

48. Frolov, *Futbol,* p. 24. *SS*, 12/14/48. *KS*, 9/7/24, 9/14/24, 7/7/36. *P*, 1/4/28, 2/4/28, 5/23/29, 7/24/29.

49. Rosalinde Sartori, "Stalinism and Carnival: Organization and Aesthetics of Political Holidays," in Hans Gunther, ed., *The Culture of the Stalin Period* (London, 1990), pp. 41–77.

50. *I*, 7/24/38.

51. *I*, 5/12/37, 5/29/37, 7/4/37, 7/6/37, 7/9/37, 7/12/37, 7/20/37, 7/23/38, 7/5/39. 7/17/39.

52. *I*, 7/8/37. Nikolai Starostin, *Zvezdy bol'shogo futbola* (Moscow, 1969), p. 164.

53. N. Starostin, *Futbol skvoz,* pp. 29–32.

54. *I*, 7/20/39.

55. *I*, 7/26/38.

56. *I*, 7/12/37, 7/23/40.

57. *I*, 7/24/38.

58. *I*, 7/24/38.

59. *I*, 7/26/38.

60. *SS*, 11/22/59.

61. G. Akopov, *Dinamo Tblisi* (Moscow, 1975), p. 5. Frolov, *Futbol,* p. 17. A. Starostin, *Bolshoi Futbol,* p. 243. Iakushin, *Taina,* p. 12. Vinokurov, *Dinamo Moskva,* p. 8. *SS*, 5/1/57, 4/25/73.

62. N. Starostin, interview, Moscow, 9/25/90; N. Starostin, *Futbol skvoz,* p. 22. A. Starostin, *Bolshoi Futbol,* p. 167. *SS*, 11/14/50. *I*, 7/12/37.

63. *SS*, 5/28/46. *P*, 5/14/29, 5/21/29, 5/30/29, 6/9/29. *I*, 6/21/35.

64. Iakushin, *Taina,* p. 17.

65. *KS*, 9/28/24.

66. *Futbol,* February 3, 1991.

67. These ticket prices compared to a ruble to a ruble and a half for a good seat at a first-run Moscow movie theater. See Denise Youngblood, "The Fate of Russian Popular Cinema During the Stalin Period," *Russian Review,* vol. 50 (April 1991),p. 150.

68. A. Starostin, *Bolshoi Futbol,* p. 44. *P*, 5/1/28, 5/22/28, 6/19/28, 7/20/28. *KS*, 8/23/25, 11/17/25, 6/23/28, 6/30/28.

69. *P*, 6/2/29, 7/14/29. *I*, 5/19/32, 9/30/35. *KS*, 8/24/24, 9/14/24, 8/23/28, 9/28/25, 10/10/25, 5/23/26, 10/30/27, 11/6/27. *FS*, 5/12/28, 6/7/28.

70. Iakushin, *Taina*, p. 17. *KS*, 1/1/37. *SS*, 3/26/46. *I*, 11/3/40.

71. N. E. Shmidt and A. C. Poleev, *Sportivnye sooruzhenia v SSSR* (Moscow, 1970), p. 11. N. Starostin, *Futbol Skvoz*, p. 23. N. Starostin, *Zvezdy*, p. 329. N. Starostin, interview, Moscow, 9/25/90; *FS*, 6/7/28, 6/30/28, 7/28/28. *KS*, 5/30/35, 11/3/35, 2/25/36, 5/19/36, 5/31/37, 9/11/38. *P*, 5/28/29. *SS*, 4/16/46, 7/16/46, 3/20/51, 11/22/59. *I*, 8/30/35, 11/3/35, 5/23/36, 11/5/36, 12/22/38, 4/24/39, 11/16/40, 6/24/41.

72. *I*, 9/28/35. *KS*, 11/6/27.

73. Iakushin, *Taina*, p. 20. *FS*, 7/14/28, 7/21/28,7/28/28, 8/4/28. *KS*, 7/11/25, 8/15/25, 9/12/25, 7/31/27. *SS*, 7/6/57. N. Starostin *Futbol Skvoz*, p. 23.

74. *KS*, 10/16/27.

75. *KS*, 8/7/34, 8/27/34.

76. Iakushin, *Taina*, p. 29. *SS*, 5/17/58, 11/28/76.

77. *KS*, 8/31/35.

78. This team did not include players from the strongest Prague teams, *Sparta* and *Slavia*, who had not been allowed to play the Moscow team the year before. Iakushin, *Taina*, pp. 32–33.

79. *KS*, 9/9/35.

80. *I*, 12/23/35.

81. *I*, 1/3/36. Martynov, *Liubimaia*, p. 31. Iakushin, *Taina*, pp. 48–53. Arkadii Galinskii, interview with author, Moscow, 10/16/90. Richard Henshaw, *The Encyclopedia of World Soccer* (Washington, D.C., 1979), pp. 676–678.

82. Moshe Lewin, "Society, State, and Ideology during the First Five-Year Plan," in Sheila Fitzpatrick, ed., *Cultural Revolution in Russia* (Bloomington, 1978), p. 50.

83. *KS*, 5/2/26.

84. *FS*, 5/5/28.

85. *Ibid.*

86. *KS*, 10/23/35, 12/13/35.

87. Iakushin, *Taina*, p. 40. N. Starostin, *Futbol Skvoz*, p. 188. *KS*, 4/12/35.

88. *KS*, 11/14,26, 2/20/27, 6/15/27.

89. *KS*, 5/31/34, 6/12/34, 4/25/35.

90. *KS*, 3/30/35.

91. *KS*, 9/25/27.

92. *KS*, 4/3/27.

93. *I*, 6/21/35, 3/22/37. *KS*, 5/15/27, 7/23/34, 5/23/36.

Notes to Chapter 3

1. J. Arch Getty, *The Origins of the Great Purges: The Soviet Communist Party Reconsidered, 1933–1938* (Cambridge, England, 1985). pp. 196–206.

2. Sartori, *Stalin and Carnival*, pp. 41–77.

3. Lewin,*Society, State*, p. 56. See also Sheila Fitzpatrick, "Stalin and the Making of a New Elite, 1928–1939," *Slavic Review*, vol. 39 (1979), pp. 377–402. Kendall Bailes, *Technology and Society Under Lenin and Stalin: Origins of the Soviet Tech-*

nical Intelligentsia, 1917–1941 (Princeton, 1978). Nicholas Timasheff, *The Great Retreat: The Growth and Decline of Communism in Russia* (New York, 1946).

4. Dunham, *Stalin's Time*, pp. 13–17. Sheila Fitzpatrick, "Stalin," p. 21.

5. *I*, 6/27/36. *KS*, 1/1/37. Riordan, *Sport in Soviet Society*, p. 126.

6. N. Starostin, interview, Moscow, 9/25/90.

7. *KS*, 2/17/36, 11/5/36.

8. *KS*, 5/23/36.

9. *SS*, 10/5/46. *I*, 7/28/36, 6/21/38, 8/27/38. *KS*, 8/7/38.

10. *KS*, 5/29/37, 9/3/38, 11/ 23/38. *I*, 11/19/40. *FK*, 3/4/90.

11. *KS*, 8/21/38.

12. *SS*, 5/14/46, 5/18/46. *KS*, 1/9/36, 5/1/36, 5/7/36, 6/1/36, 6/5/37, 11/17/38. *I*, 5/10/38, 5/30/38, 9/15/38, 5/18/40, 8/27/40, 9/21/40, 3/21/41, 5/18/41, 6/13/41.

13. *KS*, 9/13/38, 8/25/38, 9/17/38. *I*, 3/21/40.

14. Youngblood, *Fate*, pp. 148–162. Youngblood *Soviet Cinema in the Silent Era, 1918–1935* (Ann Arbor, 1986). Richard Taylor, *The Politics of the Soviet Cinema, 1917–1929* (Cambridge, England, 1979).

15. Frederick Starr *Red and Hot: The Fate of Jazz in the Soviet Union* (New York, 1983), pp. 3–180.

16. Katerina Clark, *The Soviet Novel: History as Ritual* (Chicago, 1985).

17. N. Starostin, *Futbol Skvoz*, 1989, p. 83.

18. *I*, 8/20/36, 9/22/36, 9/26/36, 6/11/37. *KS*, 5/5/36, 9/13/36. Iakushin, *Taina*, p. 56.

19. After the defeat of the Republican side in the Spanish Civil War, the entire Basque team moved as a group to Mexico, where they played as a team in the Mexican league. They were so strong that they dominated the league and eventually had to be broken up. Some then went to play in Argentina. Others remained in Mexico, and a few returned to Spain. Carlos Blanco, interview with author, La Jolla, California, March 7, 1991.

20. *I*, 6/17/37, 6/26/37.

21. N. Starostin, *Futbol Skvoz*, p. 39. Iakushin, *Taina*, pp. 63–71. *KS*, 6/11/37, 6/29/37. *I*, 6/11/37, 6/15/37, 6/17/37, 6/22/37, 6/26/37, 6/28/37, 7/15/37, 7/16/37.

22. Boris Lavrentievich Nazarov, interview with author, Moscow, October 6, 1990.

23. N. Starostin, *Futbol Skvoz*, p. 40.

24. N. Starostin, interview, Moscow, 9/25/90.

25. *I*, 11/14/38.

26. N. Starostin, *Futbol Skvoz*, p. 48. *KS*, 9/13/39. *I*, 9/14/39, 10/28/39, 11/5/39.

27. Riordan, *Sport in Soviet Society*, p. 124.

28. N. Starostin, interview, Moscow, 9/25/90. N. Starostin, *Futbol Skvoz*, p. 42.

29. *SS*, 5/8/90.

30. *I*, 3/20/40. *KS*, 6/14/37.

31. Evgenii Ivanovich Eliseev, "Futbolom spressovannye gody," *Sportivnye igry* (July, 1990), p. 7.

32. Riordan, *Sport in Soviet Society*, p. 134.

33. *I*, 8/5/35.

34. *I*, 9/18/37.

35. A. Galinskii, interview, Moscow,10/14/90. While I have found no published confirmation of Galinskii's allegation, no one who recalls this period ever suggested to me this particular practice did not take place. When Soviet teams became more heavily involved in international competitions after the war, it became more difficult to organize such exhibitions, and other means had to be found for subsidizing the players.

36. *KS*, 9/29/36.

37. *KS*, 3/25/40. *I*, 3/21/40.

38. *KS*, 4/7/36, 4/11/37. *I*, 3/23/40, 3/12/41.

39. *KS*, 6/27/36, 7/1/36, 2/17/37.

40. *KS*, 8/27/36, 4/17/37, 12/17/38. Starostin, p. 186.

41. N. Starostin, interview, Moscow, 9/25/25. N. Starostin, *Futbol Skvoz*, p. 41. *SS*, 5/8/90. *I*, 1/30/38, 12/1/38. *KS*, 4/7/36, 5/1/36.

42. *I*, 9/30/39.

43. *KS*, 10/1/40.

44. *I*, 6/24/36, 9/27/36.

45. *I*, 8/5/37, 12/23/38, 9/24/39.

46. *KS*, 11/23/38, 2/17/38, 9/13/39.

47. *KS*, 11/23/38.

48. *I*, 5/6/40.

49. *I*, 6/12/39. *KS*, 4/25/36, 9/5/36, 9/15/40.

50. Ilya I'lf and Evgenii Petrov, "Chestnoe slovo bolel'shchika," in N. Elinson, ed., *Eto futbol* (Moscow, 1967), p. 154.

51. *KS*, 4/15/37.

52. Riordan, *Sport in Soviet Society*, p. 133. *KS*, 9/15/38, 11/23/38, 7/2/40, 5/8/45.

53. *I*, 7/18/39.

54. *I*, 5/21/32, 6/11/35, 5/14/37, 12/23/37, 6/16/38, 6/18/38, 6/24/38, 12/21/38, 12/26/38, 12/27/39.

55. *I*, 6/17/40. *KS*, 12/3/38, 7/28/39, 8/25/39.

56. *KS*, 9/28/24, 6/16/28, 3/29/34, 4/12/35, 5/19/37, 5/25/37, 8/19/38. *I*, 4/8/35, 8/18/35, 8/20/37.

57. *KS*, 7/27/40. See also Alfred Senn, "American Lithuanians and the Politics of Basketball in Lithuania, 1935–1939," *Journal of Baltic Studies*, vol. XIX, no. 2 (Summer 1988), pp 101–110.

58. *FS*, 6/2/28.

59. *KS*, 4/1/34, 6/12/34, 3/21/35, 5/30/35.

60. *I*, 1/13/37; 2/28/38, 3/3/38; 1/15/41.

61. *KS*, 2/20/27, 1/21/34, 2/17/36, 5/9/36, 1/17/37, 1/19/37. *P*, 12/20/28.

62. *P*, 2/7/28. *I*, 3/11/35, 1/13/38. *KS*, 12/12/25, 1/30/27, 2/27/36, 12/13/36, 1/15/37, 3/1/37, 3/3/37, 3/7/37, 1/25/39, 2/1/40, 12/10/40.

63. *KS*, 11/21/34, 3/31/34, 2/5/36, 1/7/40.

64. *KS*, 2/7/40.

65. *KS*, 10/21/36.

66. *Khokkei v SSSR, Spravochnik* (Moscow, 1955), p. 88. Hart Cantelon, Jr., ''The Organization of Hockey in the USSR,'' *Journal of the Canadian Association for Health, Physical Education, and Recreation*, vol. 42, no. 2 (December 1975), p. 31.

67. *KS*, 12/17/35, 10/21/36.

68. Iakushin, *Taina*, p. 117.

69. *KS*, 10/21/36.

70. *KS*, 1/13/39. *I*, 11/21/38, 1/27/38.

71. *I*, 8/28/40.

72. *KS*, 6/7/28, 9/15/35, 6/19/37. *I*, 2/4/35, 5/24/35, 9/10/35, 9/12/35, 2/3/37, 2/11/37, 2/17/37, 8/23/40. *SS*, 1/4/47, 7/8/58.

73. *KS*, 8/21/36.

74. *KS*, 6/20/26.

75. *I*, 6/24/35, 9/20/36, 6/11/40, 6/30/40.

76. *I*, 1/15/37. Vladimir Geskin, interview with author, Moscow, October 2, 1990. *KS*, 5/15/27, 5/13/37, 10/13/38.

77. *KS*, 9/23/38.

78. N. Starostin, *Futbol Skvoz*, p. 72.

Notes to Chapter 4

1. I. D. Chudinov, *Osnovnye postanovleniya prikazy i instruktsii po voprosam fizicheskoi kultury i sporta, 1917–1957* (Moscow, 1959), p. 189. Cited in Jim Riordan, ''To Be or Not to Be: Soviet Entry into the Olympic Movement'' (unpublished paper), p. 3.

2. Frolov, *Futbol*, p. 11. A. Galinskii, interview, Moscow, 10/16/90 . N.N. Romanov, *Trudnye dorogi k Olimpu* (Moscow, 1987), p. 87.

3. *SS*, 9/14/46.

4. *FK*, 4/8/90. Iu. Arutiuniu, *Vsegda molodoi futbol* (Moscow, 1989), p. 119.

5. *Dinamo'67*, p. 27.

6. *I*, 5/1/74, 11/28/80.

7. Galinskii, interview, Moscow, 10/16/90. N. Starostin, *Zvezdy*, p. 80. Arutiuniu, *Vsegda*, p. 120. *FK*, 4/8/90.

8. P. Sobolev, L. Borodina, and G. Korobkov, *Sport in the USSR* (Moscow, 1958), p. 56.

9. *KS*, 1/12/43, 2/19/43, 3/9/43, 3/16/43, 3/30/43, 5/11/43, 6/27/43, 8/10/43, 9/28/43, 12/21/43, 1/18/44, 4/11/44, 4/25/44, 5/9/44, 5/10/44, 5/22/44, 5/30/44, 7/11/44, 8/1/44, 8/15/44, 8/24/44, 8/29/44, 8/29/44, 10/3/44.

10. *KS*, 4/11/44.

11. N. Starostin, *Futbol Skvoz*, pp. 61–65. *FK*, 7/23/89.

12. N. Starostin, *Futbol Skvoz*, pp. 85–90. *FK*, 5/13/90. *SS*, 5/11/90.

13. *KS*, 9/28/43.

14. A. Starostin, *Bolshoi Futbol*, p. 7.

15. N. Starostin, *Futbol Skvoz*, pp. 113–127.

16. For a detailed discussion of these struggles inside the Party and their impact

on science, philosophy, and culture, see Werner G. Hahn, *Post-War Soviet Politics: The Fall of Zhdanov and the Defeat of Moderation* (Ithaca, 1982), pp. 182–185.

17. *KS*, 10/4/45.

18. *SS*, 1/1/49.

19. *SS*, 5/4/52.

20. *KS*, 6/12/45, 5/22/45, 10/16/45.

21. *KP*, 7/20/79. *FK*, 3/4/90.

22. *London Times*, November 13, 1945.

23. *Manchester Guardian*, November 11, 1945.

24. Iakushin, *Taina*, p. 71.

25. *Manchester Guardian*, November 14, 1945.

26. *London Times*, November 14, 1945.

27. *KS*, 11/20/45.

28. *Manchester Guardian*, November 19, 1945. *London Times*, November 19, 1945. Iakushin, *Taina*, p. 77.

29. *London Times*, November 21, 1945. *Manchester Guardian*, November 21, 1945.

30. *London Times*, November 22, 1945.

31. *Manchester Guardian*, November 22, 1945. *KS*, 11/27/45.

32. *London Times*, November 29, 1945.

33. *SS*, 5/4/46, 5/25/46, 6/1/46, 6/4/46, 8/5/46.

34. *SS*, 10/11/47, 10/14/47.

35. *SS*, 5/11/46, 6/15/46, 9/25/46.

36. *SS*, 11/11/50.

37. *SS*, 4/16/49.

38. Vladimir Kuchmi, interview with the author, Moscow, October 12, 1990.

39. *SS*, 7/9/46, 8/24/46, 6/21/47.

40. *I*, 3/26/74.

41. *SS*, 7/27/46, 7/30/46, 8/3/46, 8/6/46, 8/10/46, 8/13/46, 9/14/46.

42. *SS*, 8/23/47, 8/26/47, 10/25/47, 10/28/47, 11/4/47, 11/11/47.

43. *SS*, 11/13/51, 5/15/52, 6/12/52, 7/1/52, 7/8/52.

44. Frolov, *Futbol*, p. 12.

45. *SS*, 6/29/46, 7/13/46, 8/12/47, 10/2/48, 6/2/49.

46. *SS*, 11/11/50, 4/24/51, 7/31/51, 10/4/51, 8/16/52, 10/18/52.

47. Hahn, *Moderation*, p. 136.

48. *SS*, 2/17/48, 5/15/48, 6/19/48, 6/26/48.

49. *SS*, 12/27/48.

50. *SS*, 3/1/49.

51. *SS*, 9/25/48.

52. *SS*, 10/28/48.

53. Hahn, *Moderation*, p. 142,

54. *SS*, 6/18/49, 4/15/50, 6/17/50, 6/22/50, 12/31/50, 5/26/51, 6/30/51, 2/21/53.

55. *SS*, 1/1/49.

56. *SS*, 5/4/52.

57. *KS*, 10/14/45.

58. A. Galinskii, interview with author, Moscow, 10/16/90.

59. *SS*, 5/4/52.

60. See Ilf and Petrov, *Eto Futbol*, chap. 1, p. 47.

61. *SS*, 7/23/49.

62. *SS*, 4/26/47, 4/26/49.

63. *SS*, 6/4/46.

64. *SS*, 6/1047.

65. *SS*, 6/1/46, 6/8/46, 4/16/49, 11/11/49, 6/8/50, 3/31/51.

66. *SS*, 9/25/48, 9/28/48.

67. Iakushin, *Taina*, pp. 150–152.

68. *SS*, 7/22/52.

69. Martynov, *Liubimaia igra*, p. 39. Frolov, *Futbol*, p. 22. *SS*, 8/5/52.

70. *SS*, 7/26/52, 8/7/52, 8/12/52, 9/20/52, 10/23/52.

71. Iakushin, *Taina*, p. 156. *SS*, 9/9/52.

72. S. Tokarev and A. Gorbunov, "Tochka razryva," *Sportivnye igry* no. 6 (June 1988), pp. 8–10; no. 7 (July 1988), pp. 25–27, 33; no. 8 (August 1988), pp. 24–29; no. 9 (September 1988), pp. 23–26; no. 10 (October 1988), pp. 25–27.

73. Gorbunov and Tokarev, *Tochka*, no. 10 (October, 1988), p. 26.

74. Gorbunov and Tokarev, *Tochka* (June, 1988), p. 8.

75. Iakushin, *Taina*, pp. 150–156.

76. *SS*, 3/31/51, 10/16/51, 10/18/51, 5/4/52.

77. *SS*, 4/20/90.

78. *SS*, 4/21/90.

79. *SS*, 4/24/90.

80. *SS*, 4/25/90.

81. One exception to this consensus is Lawrence Martin's journalistic history of Soviet hockey, in which he makes clear the centrality of Russian hockey as the basis for the transition. Lawrence Martin, *The Red Machine: The Soviet Quest to Dominate Canada's Game* (Toronto, 1990), p. 26.

82. *Khokkei s shaiboi* (Moscow, 1953), p. 4. *SS*, 12/31/46.

83. *SS*, 1/14/47.

84. *SS*, 12/21/46. Frolov, *Futbol*, p. 6.

85. *SS*, 12/10/46.

86. *SS*, 12/24/46.

87. *SS*, 2/4/47.

88. *I*, 2/20/79. *SS*, 1/28/47.

89. *KP*, 1/11/48.

90. *SS*, 12/2/47, 2/2/48.

91. *SS*, 12/2/47, 11/18/48, 12/25/47, 2/2/48. *I*, 9/10/70.

92. *SS*, 3/6/48, 3/20/48, 3/8/49. Anatolii Tarasov, *Road to Olympus* (Toronto, 1969), p. 89.

93. *SS*, 3/12/49, 1/26/50.

94. *SS*, 4/3/51.

95. *SS*, 12/18/51.

96. *KP*, 12/10/78.

97. *SS*, 10/6/49.

98. *SS*, 1/14/47, 12/20/47, 1/27/48, 2/10/48.

99. *SS*, 12/12/48, 1/8/49, 2/9/50, 3/10/51, 3/13/51.

100. *SS*, 3/12/49.

101. *SS*, 6/25/47, 1/5/52.

102. *SS*, 1/8/49, 1/25/51.

103. *SS*, 3/23/50.

104. *KP*, 12/10/78.

105. *SS*, 4/9/46, 9/3/46, 1/29/49, 2/5/49, 10/18/49, 6/20/50, 8/1/50, 11/25/50.

106. *KS*, 5/8/45. *SS*, 4/16/46, 4/23/46, 4/31/46, 5/11/46, 5/28/46, 3/16/47, 10/11/47, 9/7/48.

107. *SS*, 5/6/47, 9/27/47, 4/18/48, 9/18/48, 3/5/49, 1/7/50, 9/12/50, 10/3/50.

108. *SS*, 5/1 9/51.

109. Vladimir Titorenko, interview with the author, Moscow, October 15, 1990.

110. *SS*, 8/24/46, 8/27/46, 9/18/50. Nineteen athletes were sent. They won six gold, fourteen silver, and two bronze medals.

111. *SS*, 11/19/46, 5/31/47, 9/6/47, 9/13/47, 9/7/48, 8/19/50.

112. *SS*, 6/12/48.

113. *SS*, 8/2/47.

114. *SS*, 3/11/47, 7/13/48, 10/5/48, 9/13/49, 9/22/49.

115. *SS*, 11/23/49, 12/4/48.

116. *SS*, 3/17/49, 10/27/49, 2/14/50.

117. *SS*, 8/12/45, 7/22/47, 7/24/47.

118. *SS*, 8/20/47.

119. *SS*, 8/8/50, 7/21/51, 7/19/52.

120. Riordan, "To be or Not to Be," p. 6.

121. *SS*, 1/8/52.

122. *SS*, 8/5/52, 8/7/52.

123. *SS*, 8/5/52.

Notes to Chapter 5

1. Baruch Hazan, *Olympic Sports and Propaganda Games, Moscow, 1980,* (New Brunswick, 1982), pp. 19–49.

2. *SS*, 2/3/59, 2/10/59, 2/11/59, 2/13/59.

3. *SS*, 2/18/60, 5/28/60.

4. Morris Kurtz, "A History of the 1972 Canada-USSR Ice Hockey Series," Ph.D. diss., Penn. State, 1981, p. 22. *I*, 2/24/62.

5. *SS*, 1/5/74, 1/22/74. *I*, 12/17/73.

6. *SS*, 7/23/53, 7/28/53, 8/23/53, 8/25/53, 8/27/53, 9/3/53, 10/1/53, 10/24/53, 10/27/53, 11/11/53, 11/24/53, 10/15/53, 10/17/53, 10/20/53, 10/24/53, 10/27/53.

7. *SS*, 10/7/54, 11/11/54, 10/30/54, 6/12/54, 6/19/54, 10/23/54, 10/28/54, 10/30/54, 11/11/54,

8. Micheal Healy, *The Pictorial History of Soccer* (New York, 1990), p. 50.

9. Lev Iashin, *Schast'e trudnykh pobed* (Moscow, 1985), p. 89.

10. *SS*, 8/9/55, 11/12/55, 7/9/55, 7/12/55, 8/15/55, 8/23/55, 9/6/55, 9/10/55.

11. *SS*, 7/12/56, 9/18/56, 9/25/56, 10/23/56.

12. *I*, 12/28/83.

13. *SS*, 6/25/57, 11/28/57, 6/4/58, 6/10/58, 6/12/58, 6/18/58, 6/29/58. Brian Glanville, *A History of the Soccer World Cup* (New York, 1973), p. 110. Jack Rollins, *Complete World Cup Guide* (London, 1982), p. 72.

14. *SS*, 4/18/57.

15. *Futbol*, March 10 and May 19, 1991. Iashin, p. 112. Aleksandr Nilin, ''Velkii Strel'tsov,'' *FS*, no. 4 (April, 1991), p. 8. See also Yuri Brokhin, *The Big Red Machine: The Rise and Fall of Soviet Olympic Champions* (New York, 1978), p. 82.

16. Richard Henshaw, *The Encyclopedia of World Soccer* (Washington, D.C. 1979), p. 755.

17. *SS*, 7/12/60, 6/6/61, 3/13/90. *Futbol*, April 28, 1991.

18. *SS*, 8/24/62.

19. *I*, 6/26/62.

20. Glanville, *History*, p. 163. Healy, *Pictorial*, p. 61. Henshaw, *Encyclopedia*, p. 755. Walt Chyzowych, *The World Cup* (South Bend, 1982), p. 36.

21. Cited in Glanville, *History*, p. 160.

22. Iashin, *Schast'e*, p. 139. *SS*, 3/13/90.

23. *Futbol*, March 3, 1991.

24. *SS*, 12/2/89. *Futbol*, 3/3/91.

25. *I*, 7/27/66. *SS*, 7/27/66, 8/14/66.

26. Glanville, *History*, p. 200.

27. Henshaw, *Encyclopedia*, p. 755.

28. *SS*, 6/9/68, 6/12/68.

29. *I*, 6/2/70, 6/9/70, 6/18/70. *SS*, 6/9/70, 6/16/70. Donald Ford, *Official FIFA Report World Championship Jules Rimet Cup* (Sussex, 1972), pp. 95–98. Glanville, *History*, p. 234. Chyzowich, *Cup*, p. 53.

30. *SS*, 6/19/70, 7/2/70, 7/17/70.

31. *SS*, 6/1/71, 5/14/72, 6/20/72, 6/20/75, 4/25/76, 9/1/76, 11/1//76. *I*, 7/11/72, 5/20/75, 9/26/76. *KP*, 5/26/77, 4/8/78. Arkadii Galinskii, *Ne sotvori sebe kumira* (Moscow, 1971), p. 202.

32. Filip Bondy, *The World Cup, The Players, Coaches, History and Excitement* (New York, 1991), p. 41.

33. *SS*, 1/27/66, 9/22/67, 10/5/67, 5/26/72, 6/9/72, 5/16/75, 10/8/75, 3/19/76.

34. *I*, 4/19/58. *SS*, 7/29/76, 8/3/76, 12/4/76, 7/30/80, 8/3/80.

35. *SS*, 3/12/75.

36. *SS*, 3/12/75.

37. *SS*, 4/8/76.

38. Kurtz, p. 27.

39. *SS*, 8/25/76. *I*, 2/26/72.

40. Tarasov, *Olympus*, p. 11. *SS*, 3/24/53, 11/2/53, 2/14/53, 1/5/54, 2/16/54.

41. Harry Sinden, *Hockey Showdown: The Canada-Russia Hockey Series* (Toronto, 1972), p. 3. *SS*, 2/25/54, 3/9/54. Frank Cosentino, ''Hail the Conquering He-

roes: The Team Canada–Soviet Series of 1972,'' *Proceedings of the Fifth Canadian Symposium on the History of Sport and Physical Education* (Toronto, 1982), p. 485.

42. Ken Dryden with Mark Mulvoy, *Meeting at the Hockey Summit* (Boston, 1973), p. 14.; Sinden, *Showdown*, p. 42. *SS*, 3/8/55, 2/7/56.

43. *SS*, 2/19/57, 3/7/57.

44. *I*, 3/22/59. *SS*, 2/19/57, 3/7/57, 3/11/58, 3/13/59, 3/17/59, 2/27/60, 2/29/60, 3/1/60, 4/29/60, 10/16/60, 3/9/61, 3/14/61.

45. *SS*, 3/19/63, 3/11/66, 3/29/67, 2/17/68, 2/20/68, 4/1/69, 3/31/70, 4/3/71, 4/6/71, 2/15/72, 4/21/72, 4/14/73, 4/5/74, 4/21/74, 4/18/75, 4/10/76, 4/23/76, 2/16/80, 2/24/80. *KP*, 5/16/78. *I*, 3/3/66, 3/25/67, 3/24/69, 2/17/76.

46. Dryden, *Summit*, p. 138. Vladislav Tretiak, *Tretiak, the Legend* (Edmonton, 1987), p. 11. Tarasov, *Olympus*, p. 63.

47. Dryden, *Summit*, p. 17. Tretiak, *Legend*, p. 48. John Macfarlane, *Twenty-Seven Days in September* (Toronto, 1973), p. 7. Gilles Terroux, *Le Match du siècle* (Montreal, 1972). Kurtz, p. 32. Tarasov, *Olympus*, p. 169. *SS*, 10/27/57, 11/30/57, 12/10/57, 1/26/58, 1/11/69, 1/6/70, 9/4/71. *I*, 1/18/69, 11/16/71. Martin, *Red Machine*, p. 58.

48. Tretiak, *Legend*, p. 50. Dryden, *Summit*, pp. 4, 18, and 31. Kurtz, p. 98. Sinden, *Showdown*, p. 33. Brokhin, *Big Red*, p. 188. Henk W. Hoppener, ed., *Death of a Legend* (Toronto, 1972), p. 18.

49. Brokhin, *Big Red*, p. 171. Martin, *Red Machine*, pp. 112.–113.

50. Sinden, *Showdown*, p. 20. Dryden, *Summit*, p. 50.

51. *SS*, 9/5/72, 9/6/72.

52. *I*, 9/26/72. *SS*, 9/8/72, 9/10/72, 9/14/72, 9/14/72, 9/25/72, 9/26/72, 9/27/72, 9/28/72, 9/29/72, 9/30/72. Tretiak, *Legend*, p. 55. Martin, *Red Machine*, p. 122.

53. Brokhin, *Big Red*, p. 170.

54. Tretiak, *Legend*, p. 56.

55. *SS*, 10/8/72. *I*, 12/17/73. Tretiak, *Legend*, p. 57.

56. Martin, *Red Machine*, p. 149.

57. *SS*, 9/7/76, 9/14/76. *I*, 7/25/75, 11/25/75, 9/8/76. Martin, *Red Machine*, p. 159.

58. Anatolii Pinchuk, ''From Helsinki to Munich,'' in V. Kuznetsov and Lukashev, eds., *U.S.–USSR Sports Encounters*, pp. 105–106, translated by John Williams.

59. Pinchuk, *Helsinki*, p. 105. *SS*, 5/26/53, 5/28/53, 6/2/53, 6/4/53, 6/21/55, 6/2/57, 5/10/61, 10/15/63, 6/10/75, 6/17/75. *I*, 5/26/53, 6/5/53.

60. *SS*, 9/5/60, 4/11/69. *I*, 1/19/68.

61. V. Zhemaitis, *Modestas Paulauskas* (Moscow, 1985), p. 70. Pinchuk, *Helsinki*, p. 112.

62. *New York Times*, 9/10/72, 9/11/72. *Los Angeles Times*, 9/10/72, 9/11/72, 9/12/72. *Washington Post*, 9/10/72, 9/11/72.

63. *SS*, 10/7/72.

64. *SS*, 9/12/72.

65. Zhemaitis, *Paulauskas*, p. 77. Pinchuk, *Helsinki*, p. 119.

66. *SS*, 7/7/76, 7/28/76, 7/31/80, 9/9/80.

67. Soviet television, Second Program, March 6, 1987. *SS,* 5/17/60, 7/1/62, 8/2/63, 8/11/74, 12/30/74, 12/5/75, 12/13/80. *I,* 12/7/76, 3/17/81.

68. Riordan, *Sport in Soviet Society,* pp. 213–217. *SS,* 2/27/59, 4/19/59, 4/21/59, 4/28/59.

69. Stallybrass and White, *Transgression,* pp. 14–15.

70. *SS,* 7/3/56.

71. *I,* 8/8/59, 7/30/67, 8/11/73. In 1957, Moscow hosted the World Youth Festival, one part of which was a huge sports competition. *SS,* 7/23/57, 7/28/57, 7/19/57, 7/30/57, 8/3/57, 7/2/58, 8/6/59, 8/9/59, 8/10/63, 7/29/67, 7/14/71.

72. *I,* 12/9/56, 10/29/68, 9/4/72, 2/25/80. *SS,* 4/16/55, 11/24/56, 12/8/56, 1/10/57, 8/14/60, 8/26/60, 9/3/60, 9/13/60, 9/16/60, 10/20/68, 10/30/68, 11/14/68, 2/15/72, 2/18/72, 9/6/72, 9/7/72, 2/20/76, 7/18/76, 8/3/76.

73. *I,* 8/3/76, 2/21/84. *SS,* 8/5/76.

74. *I,* 11/22/69, 5/21/70, 1/11/79. *SS,* 11/22/69, 3/6/70, 9/15/71, 8/15/73, 10/24/74.

75. National Broadcasting Corporation, "Moscow Olympics," August 2, 1980. *I,* 8/5/80. *SS,* 3/6/80, 4/2/80, 7/20/80, 7/27/80, 8/1/80, 8/4/80, 8/9/80.

76. I. T. Novikov, ed., *Games of the XXII Olympiad,* official report of the Organizing Committee of the Games of the XXII Olympiad, vol. 2 (Moscow, 1981), p. 530.

77. *I,* 4/17/84, 5/13/84, 5/14/84, 5/14/84, 8/17/84.

78. *SS,* 6/16/90.

Notes to Chapter 6

1. Cohen, *Rethinking,* p. 135.

2. Alec Nove, *An Economic History of the U.S.S.R.* (Hammondsworth, England, 1986), pp. 324–370. Roy and Zhores Medvedev, *Khrushchev: The Years in Power* (New York, 1978), pp. 24–37, 117–128, 143–158.

3. Nove, *Economic History,* p. 370.

4. Boris Kagarlitsky, *The Dialectic of Change* (New York, 1989), p. 285.

5. Nove, *Economic History,* p. 352. R. and Z. Medvedev, *Khrushchev,* pp. 143–145.

6. Riordan, *Sport in Soviet Society,* p. 232.

7. *SS,* 11/22/55. The term "stadium" has a much less grand connotation than in English. *Stadion* can signify simply a playing field without stands. In other accounts, a *stadion* has 1,500 or more places. N. E. Shmid and A. S. Poleev, *Sportivnye sooruzhenia SSSR* (Moscow, 1970), p. 18.

8. *SS,* 5/26/55, 8/2/56, 8/7/56, 8/8/56, 8/16/56, 10/31/71.

9. *SS,* 4/17/56, 4/24/56, 5/10/56, 10/11/56, 11/7/56. An outdoor artificial rink with four thousand seats opened in Sokolniki Park that spring.

10. *SS,* 1/19/71.

11. *SS,* 7/21/56, 1/20/59, 9/30/59.

12. These buildings held between 3,000 and 5,000 spectators. *SS,* 1/3/58, 9/1/66, 8/19/71.

13. *SS,* 8/8/60, 8/13/60. Shmid and Poleev, *Sooruzhenia,* pp. 18–20.

14. Those eight stadiums were in Moscow (two), Leningrad, Tblisi, Erevan, Tashkent, Kiev, and Minsk. There are, however, fifty-one stadiums with a capacity of 25,000 to 50,000.

15. *SS*, 4/24/80. For the Moscow Olympics, a 35,000-seat indoor arena was built on Prospekt Mira, the Sokolniki arena was covered and expanded to 11,000, a similar size building was constructed at Izmailogo, and the 9,000-seat Small Sport Arena was covered. A 25,000-seat indoor theatrical and sports complex was built that same year in Leningrad.

16. *SS*, 9/19/53, 6/9/68, 11/18/75.

17. *I*, 3/24/81, 11/17/81; 11/30/82; 2/22/83; 12/27/84.

18. *I*, 3/24/81, 11/17/81, 11/30/82, 2/22/83, 12/27/84.

19. *SS*, 11/12/59, 11/12/69, 8/18/70, 8/27/70, 10/11/70, 11/16/73, 6/20/80, 7/1/80, 7/27/80. *I*, 11/28/65, 12/4/66, 6/7/77, 11/25/80. Spartak was the usual leader in attendance with the exception of the times when Dinamo Kiev and Dinamo Tblisi were at the height of their success.

20. *SS*, 8/25/66, 11/1/80.

21. In most cases, attendance was noted in game accounts, but not always. For just two seasons were figures given for the entire league (1967 and 1968).

22. *SS*, 3/14/53, 1/4/55, 2/5/55, 8/27/66, 10/9/67.

23. *SS*, 10/26/61, 10/26/61, 10/27/61, 10/29/61.

24. *SS*, 4/24/69, 5/13/69, 1/18/70, 4/23/70, 3/21/76, 11/4/80.

25. *SS*, 8/24/54, 8/25/55, 7/11/56, 7/8/68.

26. *SS*, 5/16/68, 7/9/69.

27. *SS*, 4/30/61, 6/6/68, 2/22/69, 12/13/69, 1/30/70, 2/1/70, 2/25/72, 1/16/73, 11/14/76.

28. *I*, 7/10/71, 11/23/71. *SS*, 2/18/66, 12/10/69, 2/7/70, 11/27/70, 12/2/76, 12/10/76, 3/3/80.

29. *I*, 3/24/76, 7/5/77. *SS*, 8/22/58, 11/158, 5/24/60, 5/25/80. Rostislav Orlov, ''Twenty-four Rounds of the 'Match of Giants,' '' in Kuznetsov and Lukashev, eds., *USSR-USA Sports Encounters* pp. 33–52.

30. *SS*, 4/6/54, 4/10/54, 6/30/59, 10/29/66.

31. *SS*, 6/9/56.

32. *SS*, 9/6/56, 2/28/57, 4/25/57, 4/27/57.

33. *SS*, 7/3/57, 12/17/69, 1/30/72.

34. *SS*, 5/19/90.

35. *SS*, 8/30/70.

36. *SS*, 8/28/57.

37. Personal communication with author, Viktor Bortnevskii, St. Petersburg, February 23, 1992.

38. *SS*, 5/10/61, 11/3/68, 2/23/69, 7/8/69, 8/6/75, 2/8/80, 6/15/80.

39. *SS*, 8/29/53, 2/27/54.

40. Soviet fans around the nation became aware of Nikolai Starostin's return when he covered a Dinamo-Torpedo game for *SS:* 6/11/55.

41. *SS*, 12/8/55, 12/22/55, 3/30/57, 7/7/57, 8/20/57, 8/17/58, 2/1/59, 5/19/59. *I*, 11/20/55, 11/15/59.

42. *SS*, 11/5/69. *I*, 12/10/75.

43. *FK*, 3/11/90.

44. *I*, 2/19/74, 9/26/77, 3/24/81. *SS*, 12/26/61, 12/10/66, 10/31/68, 10/30/73, 9/476, 12/17/76, 2/9/80, 6/3/80, 12/6/80.

45. *KP*, 12/9/79. *I*, 4/4/67, 11/14/78. *SS*, 5/22/69, 4/4/72, 12/20/74, 4/17/75.

46. *SS*, 12/18/76.

47. *SS*, 4/2/67.

48. *I*, 9/2/59, 3/22/64, 4/4/66, 11/11/70, 4/4/77, 10/23/84. *SS*, 4/9/53, 1/19/58, 9/4/59, 1/5/60, 4/27/60, 8/21/60, 6/12/62, 11/3/62, 11/16/62, 11/11/63, 11/30/63, 4/10/66, 4/7/66, 2/22/67, 8/11/68, 8/25/68, 3/11/69.

49. *I*, 10/2/75, 10/12/76, 11/16/76. *SS*, 9/30/75, 10/5/75, 10/17/75, 11/15/75, 8/20/76.

50. *SS*, 1/10/75.

51. *SS*, 11/11/75.

52. Anatolii Demianenko, *Garmonii igry* (Kiev, 1989), p. 9. Demianenko reveals that when he was contemplating moving from Dniepr to Dinamo Kiev, he wavered. At one point, an officer of the Ministry of Interior appeared at his house to inform him he had been drafted and would be serving his duties in Dinamo Kiev's defense.

53. *KP*, 5/15/78.

54. *KP*, 11/28/78. *Televedenie i radioveshchanie*, no. 3 (1985), p. 32.

55. *KP*, 11/21/78.

56. *FK*, 3/11/90.

57. Interviews with author, Moscow, Leonid Trakhtenberg, October 11, 1990; Vladimir Titorenko, October 15, 1990; Arkadii Galinskii, October 16, 1990; Vladimir Geskin, October 2, 1990. All of these men are journalists who have worked for *Sovetskii sport*. All claim the practice of the "arranged" game is common and of long standing, but all admit that they have no way of proving such practices have gone on. *I*, 1/16/73. *SS*, 10/26/69, 8/22/58.

58. *KP*, 5/17/77. *I*, 11/11/71.

59. *SS*, 7/14/53, 7/8/54, 4/13/57, 10/2/57, 1/25/58, 11/5/58, 7/30/60, 4/17/66, 4/30/75, 6/25/75, 9/4/75, 6/12/80.

60. *SS*, 7/12/57, 7/19/58, 9/7/63, 10/11/63, 10/22/71.

61. *I*, 8/16/67, 8/26/67, 2/5/74, 3/24/79. *SS*, 9/21/58, 7/16/63, 8/1/70, 4/12/75.

62. *SS*, 2/8/59.

63. *SS*, 10/25/75.

64. *I*, 1/21/66.

65. *SS*, 1/14/73. *I*, 1/21/66.

66. *SS*, 7/8/62.

67. *SS*, 9/18/63.

68. *SS*, 11/18/61, 10/17/63, 3/19/69.

69. Galinskii, interview with author, Moscow, 10/16/90.

70. *KP*, 2/15/77, 8/1/78, 9/12/78. *I*, 4/6/61, 3/31/63, 6/9/66, 1/23/79. *SS*, 1/25/61, 1/9/63, 1/17/63, 2/16/63, 3/15/68, 7/26/68, 9/6/68, 11/16/68, 11/15/69, 2/7/71, 2/12/72, 9/11/71, 9/12/71, 1/28/72, 2/23/73, 3/13/75.

71. *SS*, 8/31/68.

72. *SS*, 6/22/68, 12/16/70.

73. *SS*, 12/16/70.

74. *KP*, 1/18/77, 7/5/77. *SS*, 3/29/73, 3/3/76. Riordan, *Sport in Soviet Society*, p. 239.

75. *SS*, 12/1/53, 2/10/55, 5/26/56, 9/26/56.

76. *SS*, 4/19/60, 9/9/66, 4/14/70.

77. *KP*, 10/4/77. *I*, 5/13/69, 5/1/71, 10/31/73. *SS*, 4/17/62, 5/5/67, 3/1/74, 5/24/74, 6/4/80.

78. Martin, *Red Machine*, p. 174.

79. *SS*, 9/21/80.

80. *KP*, 11/15/78. *SS*, 5/15/68, 2/12/80.

81. *SS*, 7/26/69, 6/4/72. *I*, 3/20/79.

82. *SS*, 11/30/54, 10/1/59, 5/27/60, 2/26/69, 6/13/71.

83. *SS*, 4/25/64.

84. *KP*, 4/5/77. *SS*, 4/15/54, 10/17/57, 10/4/58, 8/6/59, 10/29/60, 1/17/62.

85. *KP*, 4/10/79. *SS*, 3/28/68.

86. *KP*, 1/7/59, 3/16/78, 12/26/78. *I*, 3/26/63, 10/25/60, 3/11/63, 7/26/76, 10/3/69, 10/28/69, 4/7/76, 7/15/76.

87. *I*, 12/15/63, 1/4/67.

88. *SS*, 6/6/68, 10/23/80.

89. *I*, 4/13/66. *SS*, 1/29/57, 10/29/74, 4/27/76.

90. *SS*, 10/11/55, 5/23/74. *I*, 3/23/62.

91. *SS*, 9/22/55, 4/26/68, 4/18/75, 11/12/76. *KP*, 5/12/77. *I*, 11/15/66.

92. *I*, 3/20/84. *SS*, 2/23/68, 4/23/71, 5/18/73.

93. *SS*, 4/5/75.

94. *SS*, 11/1/67.

95. *SS*, 3/31/63, 3/10/74.

96. *SS*, 4/26/62.

97. *SS*, 3/30/57.

98. *SS*, 4/13/72.

99. *SS*, 6/24/59.

100. *SS*, 4/4/71.

101. *SS*, 8/31/58.

102. *KP*, 9/11/79, 10/17/79.

103. Vladimir Titorenko, interview with author, Los Angeles, February 10, 1991. *SS*, 9/11/59, 9/27/59.

104. *SS*, 7/4/57, 11/12/59, 12/12/69, 11/19/70, 5/13/71, 1/26/72. *I*, 4/20/63, 5/18/68.

105. *SS*, 2/11/56, 10/6/59, 7/24/60, 8/2/60, 8/17/60, 10/1/60, 3/30/61.

106. *SS*, 5/12/74, 8/22/75.

107. *I*, 10/24/60. *SS*, 8/7/54, 10/10/57, 1/25/67, 7/30/68.

108. *SS*, 7/4/55.

109. *SS*, 11/17/59, 8/9/75.

110. *I*, 8/7/60.

111. *SS,* 8/5/70.

112. *SS,* 8/4/70, 8/27/70.

113. Klub bolel'shchikov Spartaka, "Poka v narode khodiat legendy," unofficial program for Spartak-Rotor, September 24, 1990. The authors of this description of the history of the *fanaty* specifically cite the 1970 game as their inspiration. D. V. Ol'shanskii, *Neformaly, gruppovoi portret v inter'ere* (Moscow, 1990), p. 13. I am grateful to John Bushnell for this reference.

114. *KP,* 11/7/77. John Bushnell, *Moscow Graffiti: Language and Subculture* (London, 1990), p. 30.

115. Bushnell, *Moscow Graffiti,* p. 40.

116. *Ibid,* p. 59.

Notes to Chapter 7

1. Anatolii Pinchuk, "Igra v kotoruiu igraet Litva," *Sport i lichnost'* (1986), pp. 72–82. The Moscow situation is not usually replicated in other cities because it is very rare for there to be more than one top team in any sport in one city. Gennadii Larchikov, interview with the author, Moscow, September 24, 1990. *SS,* 11/25/59, 2/23/59, 2/23/89, 3/25/89.

2. *SS,* 8/28/88, 8/29/89. After the fall of 1990, Goskomsport was renamed "Gossport." Shortly after the disbanding of the USSR, it was dissolved.

3. *SS,* 11/26/87, 1/20/90.

4. *Moskovskie novosti,* April 30, 1989.

5. *SS,* 7/8/89.

6. Telephone interviews with author, from Moscow, June 13, 1991, with Leonid Trakhtenberg, and July 10, 1991, with Vladimir Titorenko. Interview with author, Lev Rossoshchik, Costa Mesa, Calif., July 17, 1991.

7. Ellen Mickiewicz, *Split Signals: Television and Politics in the Soviet Union* (Oxford, 1988), pp. 153–154. A similar survey, conducted by P. Vinogradov and G. Nikitin of the All-Union Scientific-Research Institute of Physical Culture, found that 8.5% of programming was devoted to sports for the two-week period from October 1 to 14, 1988. *SS,* 2/22/89.

8. *SS,* 1/1/89. Hargreaves, *Sport, Culture, and Power,* p. 7.

9. Mickiewicz, *Split Signals,* pp. 190–196. Lewin, *Gorbachev,* p. 70. V. A. Ivanitskii, interview with author, Moscow, October 10, 1990.

10. Soviet televsion, Second Program, February 18 and 20, 1988.

11. Soviet television, Second Program, April 24, 1987.

12. The practice is more common during hockey games because so few women attend soccer. A hockey game on the Second Program, March 8, 1988, was the first telecast I saw to use this technique repeatedly.

13. Soviet television, Second Program, December 17, 1987.

14. Soviet television, Second Program, December 18, 1986, April 24, 1987; December 18, 1987.

15. Soviet television, Second Program, July 14, 1988.

16. *SS,* 7/9/87, 9/24/87.

17. *FK,* 4/30/89. *SS,* 12/24/88, 4/29/89. *FS,* no. 5 (1990), p. 8.

18. *SS,* 10/19/90, 11/23/90, 12/14/90.

19. *SS,* 10/11/87, 11/25/87, 11/29/87, 5/7/88. Soviet television, Second Program, October 6, 1987, and March 8, 1988.

20. *SS,* 5/23/87, 12/23/87, 3/19/88. Soviet television, First Program, January 24, 1989.

21. *SS,* 3/18/90.

22. *SS,* 12/27/87.

23. Soviet television, First Program, February 13, 1989.

24. Soviet television, First Program, January 24, 1989.

25. Soviet television, First Program, November 29, 1987.

26. *FK,* 9/9/88.

27. *Nedelia,* July 10, 1989.

28. *SS,* 1/18/89.

29. *SS,* 1/18/89, 3/21/89, 5/20/89. *Ogonek,* no. 42 (1988). *FK,* 10/30/88, 1/22/89.

30. *SS,* 4/10/88, 5/23/89, 7/30/91.

31. *SS,* 3/23/89.

32. Basile Kerblay, *Gorbachev's Russia* (New York, 1989), pp. 58–59.

33. *Los Angeles Times,* 11/14/87.

34. *SS,* 9/27/87.

35. *SS,* 4/22/89.

36. *SS,* 11/1/89.

37. *SS,* 4/2/89, 10/15/89.

38. *SS,* 12/30/87, 4/27/88, 10/10/88.

39. *SS,* 9/5/87.

40. *SS,* 4/27/88.

41. *SS,* 10/10/87.

42. *SS,* 9/9/87, 10/14/87, 2/2/88, 2/16/88, 3/3/88, 3/11/88, 3/29/88, 4/19/88, 5/5/88, 10/30/88, 11/11/88. Soviet television, First Program, October 24, 1989.

43. *SS,* 4/29/89.

44. Riordan, *Sport in Soviet Society,* pp. 235–243. Guttmann, *Sport Spectators,* pp. 159–172.

45. Jiri Zuzanek, *Work and Leisure in the Soviet Union: a Time-Budget Analysis* (New York, 1980).

46. Ponomarev, *Sport and Society,* p. 86. Iu. S. Tarabiukin, "Fizicheskaia kul't-ura i sport v strukture svobodnogo vremeni proizvodstvennoi molodezhi," in G. I. Kukushkin, ed., *Sotsial'nye problemy fizicheskoi kul'tury i sporta* (Moscow, 1973), p. 82.

47. James Riordan, "Playing to New Rules: Sport and Perestroika," *Soviet Studies,* vol. 42, no. 1, January 1990, pp. 133–145.

48. O. Mil'shtein and S. Molchanov, "Vlianie zrelischnoi aktivnostina priob-chchenie k zaniatiem fizkul'tury," *Sotsiologicheskie issledovania,* no. 2, 1982, p. 173.

49. V. M. Sokolov and L. P. Polkova, "Nravstvennye kachestva fizkul'turnikov i sporstmenov," *Sotsiologicheskie issledovania,* no. 1, 1982, p. 118.

50. V. A. Ponomarchuk and S. V. Molchanov, "Chelovek na stadione," *Sotsiologicheskie issledovania,* no. 2 (1986), p. 91.

51. L. P. Matveev, O. A. Millshtein, and S. W. Moltchanov (*sic*) "Spectator Activity of Workers in Sports," *International Review of Sport Sociology,* vol. 15, no. 2 (1980), p. 5. The city in question was Minsk.

52. *Ibid,* p. 13. See also M. A. Arvisto, "Sport as Value Aspects of Sport Activities," *International Review of Sport Sociology,* vol. 2, no. 10 (1975), pp. 79–81. Y. G. Kriukov and V. Y. Matash, "Mass Sport, Personal Contacts and Integration," *International Review of Sport Sociology,* vol. 3, no., 13 (1978), pp. 65–73.

53. Ponomarchuk and Molchanov, *Chelovek na stadion,* p. 92.

54. Lever, *Soccer Madness,* p. 111. Guttmann, *Sport Spectators,* p. 152. McPherson, *Sport Consumption,* p. 252.

55. Sokolov and Polkova, *Nras'tvennye,* p. 116.

56. François Huot, "Les Loisirs en URSS: La TV d'Abord," *Loisir Plus* (February 1978), pp. 12–13. Huot, "Les Loisirs en URSS comme chez Nous," *Loisir Plus* (March, 1978), pp. 12–14. These articles summarize the findings of one of the most important Soviet studies of leisure time, by L. A. Gordon and E. V. Klopov, *Chelovek posle raboty: sotsial'nye problemi byta i vnerabochego vremeni* (Moscow, 1972). *SS,* 5/20/88. Soviet television, Second Program, June 22, 1987.

57. Viktor Artemov, "Athletic Activity in the Lifestyle of Urban and Rural Residents Based on Time-Budget Data," *International Review of Sport Sociology,* vol. 16, no. 1 (1981), pp. 53–57. Bushnell, *Leisure,* pp. 60–61. Soviet television, Second Program, November 5, 1986; and June 22, 1987. See also Riordan, "Sport Made to Measure: The Formal Organization of Sport in the Soviet Union," *Arena Review,* vol. 12, no. 2 (November 1988), p. 114.

58. Riordan, *Sport in Soviet Society,* p. 254.

59. *Ibid.,* p. 255.

60. N. Starostin, interview with author, Moscow, 9/25/90.

61. *SS,* 1/9/88.

62. *SS,* 5/28/88, 8/29/89. *FS,* August, 1989, p. 1.

63. *SS,* 10/25/89.

64. Dale Hoffman and Martin J. Greenberg, *Sport$biz: An Irreverent Look at the Big Business in Pro Sports* (Champaign, 1989), p. 3.

65. Riordan, *Sport in Soviet Society,* p. 163.

66. Soviet television, Second Program, September 29, 1987.

67. *SS,* 11/29/87.

68. *SS,* 10/18/88.

69. *Futbol,* 8/12/90. *P,* 5/15/90. *FK,* 2/12/89. *SS,* 3/28/91.

70. *SS,* 1/6/89, 1/10/89, 2/11/89, 2/22/89. *FK,* 2/11/89, 2/19/89, 2/28/89.

71. *SS,* 1/16/89.

72. Soviet televison, First Program, February 13, 1989.

73. *Ogonek,* no. 3 (1989). *SS,* 1/26/89, 2/11/89, 3/25/89.

74. *SS,* 4/11/89.

75. *SS,* 9/17/87, 3/29/88, 4/20/80, 5/6/88, 5/8/88, 1/11/89.

76. *Ogonek,* no. 38 (1988). *SS,* 8/1/87, 9/11/88.

77. *SS,* 8/28/88, 9/11/88, 11/3/88. *FK,* 11/6/88.

78. Sergei Aleinikov from Dinamo Minsk had joined Zavarov at Juventus for the 1989–1990 season. Unlike Zavarov, who had dropped out of Juventus' starting lineup, Aleinikov had a good World Cup. The next season, however (1990–1991), neither he nor Zavarov was retained by Juventus. Zavarov went to France to play for Nancy, a team near the bottom of the first division. Aleinikov stayed in Italy, playing for Lecce. Despite his own good play, Aleinikov could not prevent Lecce's relegation.

79. *SS,* 7/19/89. Perhaps the most egregious case of the desperate need for hard currency came in April 1991. Spartak took a quick tour of Japan on the eve of the first leg of their European Champions Cup semifinal against Olympique of Marseilles. Travelling back and forth through nine time zones cannot have helped their performance. They lost at home by a score of 3–1. Worse yet, they had skipped two domestic games (one against Dinamo Kiev at Kiev) to go to Japan. Initially, the Football Federation sought (quite rightly) to count the no-shows as forfeits, but events of this type have occurred often in the past, although rarely so flagrantly. Usually games are rescheduled to let teams take advantage of such opportunities. Spartak's fault was in not giving sufficient lead time. Eventually they were fined 200,000 rubles, which, given what they must have made in Japan, was not a huge sum.

80. *SS,* 9/7/88, 6/2/91, 6/13/91.

81. Soviet journalist and television commentator from Kaunas, Lithuania, Arunas Pakula, personal letter to author, November 21, 1988.

82. *SS,* 1/21/88.

83. *SS,* 1/28/88.

84. *New York Times,* 5/6/89. *SS,* 5/6/89.

85. *SS,* 5/7/89, 5/9/89. *FK,* 5/14/89.

86. *SS,* 5/11/89, 5/20/89, 5/25/89, 5/27/89, 5/31/89. Martin, *Red Machine,* p. 241.

87. *New York Times,* 6/27/89, 7/2/89, 7/8/89. *SS* 6/27/89, 7/2/89. Tod Hartje with Lawrence Martin, *From Behind the Red Line: An American Hockey Player in Russia* (New York, 1992), pp. 199–209.

88. *New York Times,* January 18, 1992.

89. *SS,* 5/20/89.

90. *SS,* 2/3/89.

91. *SS,* 12/3/88.

92. *SS,* 5/20/88.

93. *World Soccer,* February 1989, p. 25.

94. *SS,* 5/20/89.

95. *SS,* 7/22/87, 5/29/88, 4/7/88.

96. *SS,* 1/19/89, 2/24/89, 4/1/89.

97. *SS,* 12/27/88. *FK,* 1/1/89.

98. *SS,* 3/3/89. *FK,* 3/26/89. Spartak team members and many Soviet journalists

contend that this election was genuine. It is difficult to imagine the owners of any Western professional team asking their players to perform a similar task.

99. Boris Nazarov, interview with author, Moscow, October 6, 1990.

100. *SS*, 10/10/87, 1/18/89.

101. *SS*, 1/18/89, 2/12/89.

102. *FK*, 2/19/89.

103. *FK*, 3/19/89. Soviet television, First Program, 3/12/89.

104. *Ibid.*

105. *Futbol*, January 6, 1991. *SS*, 3/30/89, 4/2/89, 4/5/89.

106. Alexander Ivanitskii, interview with author, Moscow, October 10, 1990; *FK*, 2/12/89.

107. *FK*, 12/4/88. *SS*, 8/20/88.

108. *SS*, 8/20/88.

109. *FK*, 12/12/88. *SS*, 11/29/88, 12/1/88, 1/10/88.

110. *FK*, 12/12/88. *SS*, 12/15/88.

111. *World Soccer*, February 1989, p. 22. Soviet television, First Program, 3/12/89.

112. *FK*, 5/21/89, 6/1/89. Soviet television, First Program, 3/12/89. At the June 1, 1989, gathering that voted for the Lobanovskii proposal, Artemev spoke and affirmed that the document originally worked out by the editing committee did, indeed, more closely approximate the so-called Kiev variant.

113. *SS*, 4/13/89, 4/25/89, 5/4/89, 5/19/89. *FK*, 4/16/89.

114. *FK*, 6/4/89. *Sotsialisticheskaia industria*, 6/2/89. *Leningradskaia pravda*, 6/2/89. *KP*,6/3/89. 5/23/89.

115. *SS*, 6/3/89.

116. *FK*, 12/10/90. *SS*, 11/11/89, 11/21/89.

117. Leonid Trakhtenberg, interview with author, Moscow, October 11, 1990. Galinskii, interview with author, Moscow, 10/16/90.

118. *FK*, 11/7/90, 1/14/90, 2/11/90, 2/18/90, 3/18/90. *SS*, 12/7/89, 1/10/90, 1/30/90, 2/8/90, 2/13/90, 3/16/90.

119. *SS*, 6/15/90, 6/16/90, 6/20/90.

120. *Futbol*, 6/22/90, 7/1/90. *SS*, 7/1/90.

121. *Futbol*, 7/8/90. *SS*, 7/1/90, 7/14/90, 7/19/90.

122. Sergei Guskov, *Igry XXIV olimpiady 1988 goda: itogi i razmyshlenia (dlia sportivnikh rabotnikov, lektorov i propagandistov* (Moscow, 1989), pp. 36–41.

123. Vsesoiuznii nauchno-issledovatel'skii institut fizicheskoi kul'tury, *Novoe myshlenie i olimpiskoe dvizhenie,* materialy Vsesoiuznogo nauchnogo simpoziuma 'mezhdunarodnoe olimpiskoe dvizhenie: problemy i tendentsii razvitia na sovremennom etape, Riga, May 11–13, 1989, pp. 110–121.

Notes to Chapter 8

1. For an extremely lucid discussion of those institutions, as well as recent changes see Riordan, ''Sport Made to Measure,'' pp. 105–115.

2. *SS*, 2/17/89, 2/19/89, 2/22/89, 2/24/89, 2/26/89, 3/2/89. Salnikov was ap-

pointed head of the swimming federation. Muraviev was earning an advanced degree in biomechanics, and Linchuk was a coach.

3. *SS*, 3/18/89, 4/8/89.

4. *SS*, 6/28/89. *New York Times*, 7/2/89.

5. *SS*, 3/30/90, 4/13/90, 7/15/91, 7/27/91. Soviet television, First Program, 3/4/90, 3/11/90, 5/13/90.

6. *SS*, 3/15/90, 3/16/90, 3/27/90, 4/18/90, 4/21/90, 5/24/90, 6/10/90, 6/15/90, 6/16/90.

7. *SS*, 8/25/90. *Futbol*, 11/18/90.

8. The team that was eliminated did not include many of the players who were working abroad. The failure to muster the best available talent showed the difficulties facing the basketball federation in the new era of internationalization.

9. *SS*, 5/18/91.

10. R. N. Artiomov, "Socio-Linguistic Research in Sociology of Sport," *International Review of Sport Sociology*, vol. 2, no. 3 (1978), pp. 95–105.

11. On cultural hegemony as an alternative to direct rule in early Soviet history, see Ronald Suny, "Class and State in the Early Soviet Period: A Reply to Sheila Fitzpatrick," *Slavic Review*, vol. 47, no. 4. (Winter 1988), pp. 614–619.

12. Hargreaves, *Sport, Culture, and Power*, p. 2.

13. Huizinga, *Homo Ludens*, p. 22.

14. Serebriakov and Ponomarev, *Sotsiologia sporta*, p. 121.

15. Huizinga, *Homo Ludens*, p. 190. Hargreaves, *Sport, Culture, and Power*, p. 137.

16. Guttman, *Sport Spectators*, p. 10.

17. Stites, *Dreams*, pp. 79–100. See also Lunacharskii, *Mysli o sporte*, p. 25.

18. Ben Eklof, *Soviet Briefing: Gorbachev and the Reform Period* (Boulder, 1989), p. 174.

19. Bushnell, *Leisure*, p. 59.

Index